NORTH CAROLINA
STATE BOARD OF COMMUNITY COLLEGES
LIBRARIES
CAPE FEAR COMMUNITY COLLEGE

D1212893

SURVEYING
SMALL CRAFT

Other titles of interest

Surveying and Restoring Classic Boats: J C Winters
ISBN 0-7136-3611-4

This book is intended to guide potential buyers through the traps and pitfalls of embarking on a restoration project. It will help readers assess: What condition is the boat in? Can she be moved? What are the likely weak points? How much will it cost to put these right? What unexpected expenses might there be?

The Boat Data Book: 3rd edition: Ian Nicolson
ISBN 0-7136-3953-9

This essential technical handbook is full of details and specifications for boat construction, repair and equipment, given in a series of easy-to-read tables and diagrams. This new edition contains data about such things as the latest high-tech rigging and anchors.

The Complete Book of Yacht Care: 2nd edition: Michael Verney
ISBN 0-7136-3773-0

Essential reference for all boatowners, this highly illustrated volume contains practical guidance on maintaining and repairing every item of gear found on a yacht. It is the most comprehensive manual available on the subject and includes price comparisons that will help the reader save money.

Metal Corrosion in Boats: Nigel Calder
ISBN 0-7136-3479-0

The only book available on a subject of vital importance to owners of all types of vessel: covers both traditional and modern practices in prevention and cure.

Boatowner's Mechanical and Electrical Manual: Nigel Calder
ISBN 0-7136-3251-8

The yachtsman's complete do-it-yourself manual. Extensively illustrated and very broad in scope, it takes novice and experienced boatowners through minor to major repairs of electrical systems, engines, electronic equipment, plumbing, pumps, stoves, spars and rigging.

Cold Moulded and Strip-Planked Wood Boatbuilding: Ian Nicolson
ISBN 0-7136-3524-X

A complete guide to these methods, starting with design requirements, necessary tools, working conditions and choice of timber, through to step-by-step construction and repair.

Designer's Notebook: Ideas for Yachtsmen: 2nd edition: Ian Nicolson
ISBN 0-229-11801-1

Revised paperback edition of a classic manual; it incorporates many new ideas for yacht owners to improve their boats.

SURVEYING
SMALL CRAFT

Third Edition

Ian Nicolson

ILLUSTRATIONS BY THE AUTHOR

ADLARD COLES NAUTICAL

LONDON

Property of Library
Cape Fea
Wil

To Martin, Kate, Amanda, young Martin,
and Mary Ann Barnes.

Third edition
Published 1994 by Adlard Coles Nautical
an imprint of A & C Black (Publishers) Ltd
35 Bedford Row, London WC1R 4JH

Copyright© Ian Nicolson 1974, 1978, 1983, 1994

First edition published by Adlard Coles Ltd 1974
Reprinted with amendments 1978
Second edition 1983
Third edition published by Adlard Coles Nautical 1994

ISBN 0-7136-3949-0

All rights reserved. No part of this publication may be
reproduced in any material form (including photocopying or
storage in any medium by electronic means and whether or not
transiently or incidentally to some other use of this
publication) without the prior written permission of the
copyright owner.

A CIP catalogue record for this book is available from the
British Library.

Typeset in Monophoto Palatino 11/12pt by August Filmsetting, St Helens
Printed and bound in Great Britain by
Butler and Tanner Ltd, Frome and London

CONTENTS

PREFACE TO THE THIRD EDITION

This book is full of practical information, but a competent surveyor also needs know-how, experience in boats offshore, a broad knowledge of engineering and shipbuilding – and much more besides. Just as important, a surveyor should have 'oblique' skills: the ability to work outside in foul weather, a store of hearsay, and a memory for technical disasters. It is important to listen to foremen and bosuns, yard managers and riggers, painters and plumbers. The chat in the cockpit, yarning with charge hands in the bilge of a boat being repaired, and technical articles in magazines all add to a surveyor's education.

Anyone starting out in the industry, whether amateur or professional, starts at a disadvantage, which this book will help to minimise. It is not easy when setting out in any field to hold one's own in conversation – it helps to know some of the mythology. Here is part of the surveyor's standard repertoire:

A surveyor was on his way to inspect a boat lying in the harbour alongside a village. Just before he got there, his car broke down. There was a garage nearby, so he walked to it, and handed the manager his car keys, saying, 'Get my car repaired, and I'll collect it this evening, after I've examined a boat down in the harbour.'

He picked up his survey equipment and strode off down the road to the harbour, a couple of miles away. In the evening, when he had completed his work and was tired, he dropped into the pub for a dram before collecting his car. He was amused to hear the locals discussing a 'ghost' car that had been seen in the nearby lanes. The surveyor, being a practical man, listened for a short time, then scoffed at the whole story. He then had another quick drink before hitching his kit-bag on his shoulder and setting off to collect his car.

It was a stormy night, with a gale blasting in off the sea. The country road quickly left the houses behind. It was narrow and the trees on each side met overhead. They clashed together and cast wild dancing shadows. An owl flew low, giving out an eerie hoot as it passed the surveyor, who pulled his collar higher and shuddered.

He was well out into the country with no light in sight when he heard behind him the soft crunch – such as is made by a car tyre on gravel. At that moment the clouds thinned and the moon shone down, bright and clear. The surveyor could not stop himself from turning to see what had made the noise … and there behind him was the 'ghost' car.

He knew at once what he was looking at because he could see through the windscreen – and though the car came towards him, there was no one inside. Not daring to breathe, he stood on the verge and let the car come right up to him. As it did so, he saw that the driver's door was swinging slightly open. In a moment of madness he pulled the door fully open and slid into the driver's seat.

He sat absolutely still, except to stretch out his hand to see if there was anything – anyone – on the seat beside him, or to discover if an unseen hand grasped the steering wheel. There was nothing. The car continued to move forward at a snail's pace.

Minutes went past. Suddenly the driver's door was wrenched open and a furious voice from the outside yelled, 'Hell and Damnation! How long have you been lounging there while I've been pushing this car?'

There are lots of lessons to be learned here, not least being the danger of listening to locals and the importance of reliable transport.

In the twenty years since the First Edition of this book was published, a whole new generation of people have come into the industry. I have talked to many of them as well as to old-timers, and take this opportunity of thanking them for ideas they have passed on to me for inclusion in this new edition.

I would like to thank individuals like Bob Wallstrom and firms like International Paints, Blakes Paints, Proctor Masts, Kemp Masts, Scott Bader and the Wolfson Institute. These, and all the other individuals and organisations that have helped me, are owed a debt of gratitude by everyone connected with small craft.

I have almost completely rewritten this book, but have retained some paragraphs because they contain unchanging truths. The wind and the sea do not change, except that the waters we sail on are more polluted, and therefore there is a greater chance of hitting something hard that is floating but submerged. The incidence of damage when on passage has risen substantially in the last few years. This means that surveyors have to be even more careful, sharp-eyed and thorough. Only surveyors themselves realise that, between them, they may be responsible for saving more lives than the lifeboatmen and the coastguards.

Ian Nicolson
1994

GENERAL CONSIDERATIONS

....

THE SURVEYOR'S LOT

A surveyor has to be a detective. He spends his working life looking for clues that are often hard to see, and ones that are sometimes deliberately hidden by the owner, crew or repairer of the boat. The police detective looks for bruises on the victim, and the small craft surveyor looks for similar marks on the boat. The police detective looks for the way the criminal has broken into the building; the surveyor tries to find out how water has seeped into the cabin.

The surveyor has to be an artist, using appropriate talents like imagination, foresight and a knowledge of human nature. He has to be a scientist, with all that that implies. It means he has to observe accurately and continuously, in spite of adverse conditions like cold, wet weather. He has to be dispassionate even when this may mean the loss of income or friends. He has to be able to note what he sees in an understandable language that is not littered with an excess of technical terms. He has to behave in a professional manner even if he is an amateur and a beginner. Nowadays, he also needs a good knowledge of the law and accounting procedures. He has to keep track of advances in technology as well as changes in the legal requirements and the demands of the taxation system.

It is important that he keeps fit and lean – or he will not be able to squeeze into small lockers. He needs a good supply of old clothes, some of which will be completely destroyed in the course of a day's grubby investigation. He needs a lot of common sense and sharp perception. He has to get on with everyone from buyers to brokers, from yard foremen to boat sellers, from designers to mast-makers, from apprentices to sailmakers – and all the while he is turning out reports that by their nature are bound to irritate or anger a great many people. It helps if he remembers that the only person who matters is the person who is paying for the current survey – and his professional indemnity underwriter.

It helps to be a sympathetic listener. Apart from anything else, listening often provides useful information about the vessel's earlier life, the troubles she has been through, the people who mended or mis-mended her, accidents she has had, and the lack of maintenance she has suffered. One of the problems when surveying is that successive owners of a boat may cherish or neglect her. It takes a sharp eye to see neglect that is shielded by subsequent years of good maintenance.

A surveyor must always be sceptical. If the owner says a yacht is perfect, he is simply expressing his love for the boat. If the broker says she is perfect, he is just coaxing up her price. If the boatyard manager says she is perfect, he is keeping his fingers crossed and spreading a little verbal insurance. If the crew says she is perfect, it's relevant to ask how long they have been with the boat and how much experience they have. If another surveyor says she is perfect – but NO! No surveyor ever says any boat is perfect, certainly not a new one, and certainly not one he has surveyed.

At the back of the surveyor's mind there should always be the thought that if he misses a defect or makes a mistake, then the boat may sink, or the mast fall down, or the engine seize. Surveying is not easy, and as craft become more complex the job gets more difficult.

This book is for amateur surveyors

With practice and experience, it is possible for anyone to become a competent judge of a boat's condition. It also helps to read a lot of technical books and articles in magazines, and it is important to go to sea in mixed weather.

Anyone intending to buy a boat usually views a selection and then decides that two or three approximately meet the requirements. (A buyer who expects a boat to be exactly right is going to be disappointed.

All craft are compromises, and none will suit every circumstance at sea and in harbour. It has to be remembered that speed is gained at the price of comfort, just as lots of accommodation and furniture seldom make for easy maintenance – to give two common examples.

Having found a small batch of boats that seem just about right, it will be expensive to have them all professionally surveyed. Some professional surveyors will make a preliminary inspection of each and pick out those that seem to be the best, but this initial work still has to be paid for. A competent amateur can make a good partial survey of each boat under consideration and decide which is the soundest before calling in a professional. It is easy even for a beginner to detect signs of poor workmanship such as electric cables unclipped and loose in the bilge, or water pipes that cannot be drained fully because they sag between bulkheads.

It is still important when buying a new boat to make an inspection that is so thorough that it amounts to a survey. Just because a manufacturer has turned out a thousand identical craft, it does not follow that he has eliminated all the faults. He may genuinely not know about the defects, or he may reckon that it's cheaper to leave the production line unaltered than introduce changes to iron out building mistakes. One of the advantages of calling in a professional surveyor is that he can often tell you the 'standard' built-in faults of a particular production line.

A first inspection by an amateur of a new or secondhand boat can save money and future problems. In fact, should save twenty times the cost of this book! It may well reduce the price that has to be paid for the vessel, or result in some of the faults being corrected before the professional surveyor arrives.

A firm that exhibits at a boat show presumably offers craft that have been specially and carefully prepared. However, anyone who has looked round a show will remember seeing important faults – engines that are extremely awkward to lift out, engine filters that are hard to see (let alone replace), settee bases that collect condensation, sink drains with no trap beneath, stemhead fittings with sharp edges that will chafe warps, and so on.

When buying a boat, the more troubles that can be eliminated early by an amateur surveyor, the better the relationship will be between owner and craft – and the more money saved.

This book is for owners

It takes many years to learn how to do a *deep* survey, but this book is a useful guide for the owner who wants to maintain his boat better and forestall accidents – as well as keep his insurance costs down. Preventive maintenance reduces the off-season work, and this book is packed with information that will help to reduce this annual workload. There is a trend away from doing the necessary annual refitting on all types of boats – from yachts to commercial craft, from work launches to fishing vessels. The owner who ensures that his craft gets enough loving attention will be keeping up her value. He will also enjoy increased pride of ownership.

There are many books about fitting out and laying up, all of which aim to reduce the labour and expense of looking after a boat on the principle that prevention is better than cure; and of course when the time comes to change to a different boat, the owner who is also an amateur surveyor has a host of advantages. He can look for a new boat using his enhanced knowledge, and when he finds the right one he can bargain effectively with the seller, the brokers and with boatyard managers.

This book is for professional surveyors

Becoming a good surveyor means absorbing a vast amount of knowledge about every type of craft. In theory, surveying should have become easier over the last few years because most boats are now built in a limited number of factories. Once a surveyor has examined three or four of a class, he should in theory be able to predict much of the trouble he is likely to find in any boat of the same make. Even if the boat is not of exactly the same *class* as the one he is familiar with, he will know what to expect if the vessel comes from the same designer and the same factory. The firm that puts inadequate washerplates under the eyebolts for the backstays in their 33 footer will probably do the same for both their larger and smaller craft.

In practice, things are not quite so simple: designers and builders make improvements and learn from past mistakes; modifications are made in production lines; and there are annual changes (in the best factories) to lift the quality of the boat – and hopefully to tempt owners of early models of that craft to trade up to the newly modified version. Thus a fault that we expect to find (something we note in our report as we do the preliminary preparation the night before the inspection) is not always there when we examine the boat the next day. This causes all sorts of head scratching, grovelling in awkward lockers, and double rechecking. We cannot believe our eyes. For the past eight years we have been noting this defect every time we look at a 'Wavegobbler 33', and here is one that does not have it. Has the owner got rid of it, and how? Or has the whole class taken a turn for the better? Therefore professional surveyors need not only a fund of knowledge, but a constantly updated store of facts.

There is another aspect to this matter of changing specifications. Sometimes alterations are made to reduce the cost of building. If the factory is not making a profit but the boat is popular, the price has to be raised. There is a limit to how much this can be done, depending on the competition in the boat market. Professional surveyors soon learn that a change does not always mean an improvement. The Sigma 33 class was given an opening and a sealed window each side of the cabin, in place of the original long fixed window that graced the class for the first nine years of its successful existence. The idea was to give better ventilation and improve the appearance. What a pity, though, that the new opening windows were prone to leak.

When a production line is losing money, builders will resort to much more radical changes than alterations to the windows. On the Sigmas the change raised the specification and made the boat more attractive to people sailing in hot conditions. But what the surveyor has to watch out for are reductions in hull thickness, fewer keel bolts, flimsier spars and low-quality plywood that has no resistance to rot. This book is a contribution to the fund of knowledge that a surveyor needs.

A good surveyor concentrates intensely throughout the job and will not want anyone else present, except perhaps a co-operative notetaker. Such an assistant has to be intelligent, know when to be quiet, and when to remind the surveyor that he has found trouble at the port aft chain plate, but has forgotten to look at the starboard one. A good helper supplies the surveyor with coffee at frequent intervals, but keeps the whisky till after the job has been completed. A helpful assistant does not complain that rain is trickling on to the note-book, but remembers to bring a plastic bag to keep the notes (or dictating machine) dry. Being a notetaker is an excellent way of becoming a professional surveyor. It is certainly not a supine job, and anyone good at it will be tired by the end of the day.

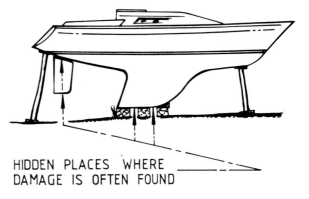

HIDDEN PLACES WHERE DAMAGE IS OFTEN FOUND

Fig 1

A surveyor has to lie on his back and look upwards at some of the inaccessible areas under the hull and rudder. Why is it that there are always such large puddles under boats, just where the surveyor has to lie? He also looks down on the top edge of a fibreglass rudder for cracks at the join line.

The majority of surveyors do not want the owner or buyer or their representatives present during a survey. If the boat is of wood, such people will get distressed when a steel spike is eased into the planking and frames. If the hull is steel, it will jangle the nerves when the surveyor bashes away noisily with his hammer — and even a *surveyor* sometimes feels considerable tension if the hammer goes right through the plating. I once did this three times in a minute. It would not have mattered so much if the third bash had not been rather near the waterline. I got a nasty surprise when I rowed ashore to the nearby boatyard and was told that the yacht was too large for the only local slipway. Did I detect a certain amount of glee when the yard manager told me that the boat could not be hauled out of the water without making an open sea passage to an island 300 miles away? With age and experience, one learns not to give way to urgent requests to begin a survey afloat immediately while the buyer arranges for the hauling up of the yacht.

Professional surveyors need tact (and sometimes bluntness) to get rid of spectators, especially those who are biased one way or the other. A good technique is to work out when the survey will be finished and then invite the buyer, or whoever it is who wants to know about the boat, to come aboard about an hour before the end. By then, most of the information should be gathered. The surveyor will be tidying up, and he can point to the corrosion on the keel bolts before he replaces the sole boards; he can invite the visitor to try to spot the peeling glassfibre bulkhead edging deep down in the dank locker up forward; he can suggest that the other fellow might like to squeeze into the chain locker to see the condition of the bolts that are holding the stemhead fitting. And if this exploration results in a sensational rip across the trousers, so much the better – the visitor will realise how expensive in clothes (and how difficult and physically demanding) the job of surveying is.

Surveyors have to be thick skinned yet tactful, for they often bring bad tidings. To survive without being assaulted, they have to learn how to tell the horrible facts without upsetting the owner who loves the boat more than his girlfriend. I only know of two surveyors who have been physically attacked. The owner of a commercial craft lunged at a friend of mine with a heavy spade because a rather serious defect had been discovered deep down in the bilges, and repairs were going to use up a vast amount of money. This particular surveyor has an international reputation for being blunt, so maybe there is a moral here. The other assault was by a broker on a surveyor. The latter kept discovering that the professional boat seller was not being sufficiently selective in the standard of craft he was offering to the public. Then a succession of surveys resulted in buyers rejecting the boats and going to different brokers.

Everyone tends to assume that unless a boat appears to be falling to pieces she is in good order. It does not help that some brokers will not tell enough of the truth all of the time. They tell potential buyers how skilled the designer is, but omit to mention that the owner is a penniless rogue who has neglected the vessel for the past ten years; they describe the delights of the drinks locker in the saloon without checking under it to see if its glass bonding is peeling, or has been forgotten entirely.

Professional surveyors appreciate that the only successful way to carry out their job is by being ruthless. They know horror stories about boats that have been lost due to unsoundness. There was the case of the cruiser that was wrecked in Wemyss Bay against the sea wall. The crew were drowned and their bodies, encased in lifejackets, were recovered the next day. The flesh of the hands of each victim was torn away right down to the bone where these drowning men had tried to scale the vertical sea wall. If only they had had a surveyor's warning, they would never have gone to sea in that particular boat.

Time afloat – the essential ingredient

Surveyors need to know all about small craft construction. They have to know about fibreglass and steel, spar-making and keel-casting, about resins and upholstery, about erosion and corrosion. It's a long list. Above all, though, they need experience afloat. It's on the water that boats get into trouble and this is where the surveyor learns much of his job.

He should get afloat in different craft and in a variety of situations. It might seem that crewing on a racing yacht is not necessarily the best way to pick up knowledge, but racing boats are often overstressed. Some go through more crises in a day than many cruisers do in a month. Racing crews are sometimes callous, and impose outrageous demands on the hull and equipment – and certainly a succession of wild broaches does give a good idea of what loadings come on to spars, rigging and chain plates. However, it is better for a surveyor to be a crew than a helmsman on a racing boat, as there is time to observe and absorb the right knowledge.

It is best to go afloat in a variety of craft, from dinghies to fishing vessels, from pilot boats to survey launches. Doing deliveries of new boats is good experience because unexpected faults show up on untried craft. Owning a boat can mean ample time afloat, but this is partly offset by a more narrow view that is confined to one boat. Finally, bad weather afloat is when experience is gained fast: anyone who has been through a big gale in a small boat is unlikely to become a slovenly surveyor.

PROFESSIONAL SURVEYORS

A large meeting of professional surveyors seldom takes place because these people are scattered thinly around the world. A busy coastal area may have five or ten surveyors if the population is large enough to support them, but it must not be supposed that all the local practitioners get together at frequent intervals. They are too fully employed during the busy season, and in the quiet times many are occupied with other jobs, or away sailing or mountaineering – or whatever takes their fancy.

Professional surveyors normally work alone, or with a junior to assist in opening the boat up and help record the findings. A few survey offices have two professionals: sometimes one will specialise in yachts and the other in fishing boats. Or one may stick to commercial craft and the other to pleasure craft. Obviously the idea of two people working in one office is to keep the overheads down to a minimum. If two or more surveyors share a single building, a single phone, one computer, and so on, then the cost per earning person is more or less halved. As so much of a surveyor's time is spent working in boatyards, two can just as easily operate from the same office space as one. However, this scheme is only viable if there is enough work in the locality for both of them. There used to be a theory that it needs local population of 500 000 people, plenty of them high earners, to support one surveyor.

Some readers will have noted that I have so far referred to surveyors using the masculine gender. Of course, there are female surveyors, but the percentage is very small. One reason may be that this is often a dirty job (and thus unappealing), and another may be that the training is hard to obtain – especially, perhaps, for a woman.

Surveyors are not often found in groups, and all over the world they tend to be loners. Surveying is as much an art as a science, and each person has his own techniques, his own specialities and, above all, his own way of working. As there is no central training scheme, and no agreed syllabus for learning the job, there are dozens of different ways of doing it.

Various attempts have been made to group surveyors into organisations. Some of these have flourished for many decades, but others have faded away after a few years. In Britain, the leading organisation for ship and boat professionals is the Royal Institution of Naval Architects at 10 Upper Belgrave Street, London SW1X 8BQ. However, this body is biased towards large ships, though recently it has made a strong attempt to capture the interest of people concerned with small craft. Undoubtedly, it remains principally a designer's institution. In the United States, the National Association of Marine Surveyors has had a long and successful life. In Britain there is the Yacht Brokers, Designers and Surveyors Association, and it will be noted that the surveyors come third on the list. (Perhaps brokers have more time to attend the meetings.) The addresses of professional organisations can be obtained from the advertisements in the yachting magazines of the relevant country.

Any professional person, in any industry, finds that an organisation that aims to look after his interests is only as good as the people at the top. To make life more complex, if the chairman, president, or whoever the senior person is, has a highly successful business, he will usually be too active looking after his own office to put in ample time as chairman or president – and if his own office is not busy, then what sort of practitioner is he? The same applies to the vice-chairman, and so on down the scale. It is different in major companies where there are lots of executives and they can share the burden of non-productive work in the knowledge that while they are away the factory will still be turning out 'widgets' to make a profit. When a surveyor is not surveying, he is obviously not earning.

This situation has resulted in the inevitable rise and fall, sometimes followed by the rise again, of various societies and associations for surveyors. Anyone who talks to ten successful surveyors will find that some are too busy to join a society or association. Some have tried joining and found they do not have the relevant qualifications, even though they run a successful business. Some dislike the annual fees that are either too low (and therefore the association is ham-strung for lack of funds) or too high (and therefore hard to pay when times are bad).

Just because someone is not a member of one of the societies that claim to represent the interests of surveyors does not mean that he is no good. He may simply be astute and cautious as to where he places his loyalty. Conversely, if a surveyor is a member of five such organisations, it does not necessarily mean that he excels at his job. On the contrary, if he is thoroughly supporting so many institutions, how does he have time to earn a living, keep up with the necessary monthly technical reading, run the office efficiently, and spend the necessary time on each inspection?

A small proportion of surveyors have university degrees, but the degrees are not always in naval architecture. In any case, naval architecture faculties do not teach the techniques of surveying and are seldom interested in the special problems of small craft. It can be argued that a general engineering degree is as good as one in naval architecture, and in some universities such courses share lecturers in subjects like mathematics, metallurgy, and so on. A practical degree is certainly a good basis for learning the job. It teaches the ability to work long and hard; it should impart skills for getting on with all sorts of people; it gives a 'feel' for technology, and a familiarity with oily hands and subtle practical problems.

Another good way to learn the job is to go on a practical boatbuilding course that has a theoretical content. These are run in Britain at Southampton, Lowestoft and Falmouth. Information about them is available from the British Marine Industries Federation at Meadlake Place, Thorpe Lea Road, Egham, Surrey TW20 8HE. The best of all options might be a degree followed or preceded by one of these courses. The boat design and management courses at Southampton University also have a lot to offer, though here, as elsewhere, the interests of surveyors are largely ignored because there are so few of them.

Undoubtedly the best way to learn the job is to work alongside a good surveyor. Some will pass on information in a steady torrent of useful facts, opinions, surmises and anecdotes. Others will disappear into the bilge, and nothing emerges other than a grunt. Whichever type you are with, it is essential to keep your eyes and ears open. The surveyor is not superhuman and will appreciate the occasional suggestion – especially if he has missed out a locker, or forgotten to check a piece of equipment.

What all professional surveyors need is a range of experience. They want chances to learn about structure and gear, fabrication and assembly, about accidents and designs. Boatyards are the best places to get this knowledge, especially ones with a variety of craft. A specialised yard or a boat factory is good for learning about part of the job. After a time in such a place, though, it will be important to move somewhere different, unless the surveyor wants to work in a specialised area of expertise. It may not be possible to earn enough by only concentrating on dinghies, or fishing boats, or inland waterways craft. On the other hand, a specialist may find that his expertise is so much in demand that he is better to keep clear of anything except his chosen field. I rather doubt it though, until the industry has become much bigger.

The one thing too few surveyors do is repair and build boats with their own hands. Cutting and fitting, contriving and securing in and around a hull gives a 'feel' that no amount of reading or listening to lectures imparts. As a surveyor often has to give orders in a boatyard, it is a great help if he is known to have 'every finger a screwdriver'. If he speaks with authority and certainty about a repair or alteration because he has done the job himself, then he has an enormous advantage.

The learning by doing need not be expensive or difficult. It is usually best to start by building or mending a dinghy – and then another and another. After this, something more ambitious, ideally with an engine, should be tackled. If the builder or repairer has a financial stake in the job, then this helps. A few surveyors do boat repairs in between inspections, but it is hard to make a financial success of both because the two activities peak in the spring. On the other hand, restoration work fits in with surveying. It can be done in the slack periods, and the cost of buying materials can be spread over many months.

There are longshoremen, retired seamen and others who set up as fringe surveyors. Their characteristics are a tendency to undercut the normal scale of charges, and to produce skimpy reports that are suspiciously unsigned. A man who takes five hours to survey a 20 m (66 ft) motor-cruiser and charges a third of the normal price is swindling the buyer in two ways. First, he is only partly doing the job, and second, he is overcharging for the number of hours put into the job. Also, he will probably be uninsured, so neither he nor his client has protection if something goes wrong.

Established surveyors have professional indemnity insurance. This covers them if they make a mistake and miss a defect, then get sued by the client. The policy typically pays for a lawyer to defend the case and, if he loses, it then pays the aggrieved party. This insurance may protect the policy-holder against few or many arrows of misfortune, depending on the wording of the document. Wise surveyors get an insurance broker to shop around for the best deal. The cost of the policy varies wildly, according to how the insurance industry is fairing. The underwriters who cover surveyors also look after a variety of different professionals – from engineers to architects. If, as happened a few years ago, a bridge designer invents a clever new way of making bridges but gets the mathematics wrong, there can be a series of gigantic claims. To recoup, the insurance industry has to raise premiums. So a professional surveyor may find he is paying twice as much next year, but, if he is lucky and the pendulum swings the other way, the cost may drop even more dramatically.

To save some of the annual cost of insuring, it is sometimes possible to join an insurance 'club'. The members all pay into a central organisation that insures them, but no one else. They meet the costs of each other's claims. There are no shareholders or outside people who are trying to make a profit on the operation, so that constitutes a saving. Another reason why a club should be cheaper than conventional insurance is that every member has a strong financial interest in keeping down costs, claims and expenses. If there are too many claims, the members may have a 'call'. This is a demand for a further payment on top of the premium. In a very bad year this could double the annual premium. Well-run clubs save their members lots of money, but bad ones do the opposite.

Behind every good surveyor there is usually a brilliant secretary. This person has to know about boats, surveying, keeping accounts and running an office. One famous surveyor attributes his success to marrying the right wife and finding a brilliant secretary, then ensuring that the two remain good friends.

There is no doubt that the 'back-up' team have to be dedicated, knowledgeable and prepared to work long hours. My own contribution to the surveyor's art consisted of discovering just how good at surveying children are. Many are the tiny lockers that my children have climbed into, and they have a very good track record of discovering troubles that previous surveyors have not noticed. One year I took my three children to the London Boat Show and turned them loose to explore. Two hours later I boarded a cruiser to find the salesman, a friend of mine, purple in the face, while a prospective buyer walked away. My friend explained that he was just getting to the point where he was clinching a sale when three children asked very politely if they could look round the yacht. He said 'Yes' in a distracted way, watching the cheque book being drawn out of the buyer's pocket. Just before the cheque could be written, the children, none of them aged over 11, hauled up a floorboard and peered into the bilge. One said: 'Look! No transverse floors. This boat's no good. That's *just* what Dad warned us against. Come on, let's go and look at a good boat.'

Anyone who starts a new survey office has the problem of how to generate enough income from the first month. Some surveyors are also designers, just as some designers turn to surveying to augment their income and increase the available services they can offer. The person who has designed a boat should be the best person to survey it in later life, since he should know all about her. However, if he is not experienced, he may have made a design error and not yet realised it. He may genuinely believe that a 40 mm ($1\frac{9}{16}$ in) rudder shock is strong enough for a 11 m (36 ft) cruiser when making the design. So when he surveys her, he may not mention the probability of rudder failure, unless time has opened his eyes.

Many designers stick to a narrow range of craft. They should obviously be competent when surveying in this field, but what about smaller or larger craft? A survey office is seldom so busy that it can turn down work outside a designer's limited knowledge. At least there will seldom be a conflict of interests between the design side and the survey department of the same office. Where problems do arise is in those triple offices that offer surveying, design work and brokerage. There are rules laid down by professional organisations against 'running with the hare and the hounds'. No one should sell a boat and also do the survey on her, unless the buyer specifically asks for this.

It is not unusual for a design office to have a favourite client who returns every five years for a new boat. Such a man or woman knows and likes the work from this office, and trusts the craftsmen working there. Naturally when the current boat is to be sold and replaced by a new one, both the brokerage of the earlier boat and the design of the new one are handled in the same office, with cost reductions being made for both services. If the buyer appreciates the advantages of having the same office do the survey, he may overcome worries he has about a conflict of interests. Everyone has to agree beforehand, and it is only good sense for the surveyor to get the request for his services in writing, with a clause inserted that confirms that the buyer is aware of the situation.

From all this it can be seen that professional surveying is difficult. No figures are available for the success rate, but my guess is that for every three or even five people who try to break into the industry, only one succeeds. The figure may be as high as one in ten, especially if we exclude people who continue as surveyors even when they are not making a proper living out of it, but are relying on a pension or some other means to survive financially.

There is a saying that to be a success as a surveyor one needs three average-sized commissions a week: the first one pays the office expenses, the second pays the surveyor his wages, and the third covers major expenses like a new car or computer. This 'three-every-week' standard is fine in theory, but few people buy boats in the middle of December when the snow is deep on the roads and transport is at a standstill. Hardly anyone buys in the middle of July –

they are away sailing or on holiday. So it is hard to earn an income all the year round – although the office expenses and the deep-freeze at home demand money week after week. It is no wonder, then, that many surveyors drop out of the industry in the first five years. They cannot manage to live on a very small income. In addition, some find it lonely – working for hours on end in the silence of a deserted hull, sometimes down in the deep, dark, smelly bilge of a big motor-cruiser with only the occasional rat for company.

The qualities of a professional surveyor are varied, but he does have to be slightly fanatical. He has to like both the job and small craft enough to put up with the bitter cold of a February night and the driv-ing rain across an exposed deck. He needs to appreciate when the money is coming in fast in the spring that this is not the time to dash out and buy a new car, because the income may dry to a trickle within three months or so. Even when beset by money worries, he has to remain detached enough to concentrate totally on the survey in hand. He has to be able to work on his own, make decisions without help, balance probabilities and possibilities, and all the time remain alert so that he notices the tiniest of clues. When he goes afloat, which he should do frequently, he has to recharge his mental and physical facilities; at the same time, he must appreciate the dangers of the sea, and take action to defend his clients against them.

· ·

THE MONEY SIDE

Many surveys are 'self-financing' because the defects they report reduce the price of the vessel by more than the cost of the inspection. The majority of those selling boats honestly do not know about the troubles in their craft, apart from the obvious ones that everyone can see. A surveyor may discover a dozen or even fifty places where repairs are needed, and the boat sale goes through at a reduced price that reflects the need to rectify these faults. It can be argued that the cost of repairs pushes the cost of the boat back up, but this is not always so, especially if the buyer can do some of the renewal work himself.

There are many occasions when the survey throws up problems that alarm the seller. He may panic, or decide to cut his losses, and so bring down the asking price with a big jump. So before asking how much a survey costs, it is worth noting that sometimes the answer is, for all practical purposes, 'Nothing'.

There is more to it than this, though. Some insurance companies insist on a survey before they will underwrite a risk. If the boat is over ten years old, most insurance firms now require at least a partial report. In this instance, the survey may be described as part of the insurance cost. Where there is need for boatyard work before the vessel can be commissioned, the report may form the basis of a contract between the yard and the owner. This may reduce the cost of the yard work, and it will certainly speed up these repairs.

The price of a survey varies from area to area, but is normally based on the size of yacht. The Yacht Brokers, Designers and Surveyors Association, based in the south of England, has invented a formula for working out the survey costs. It goes like this:

Overall length of boat × beam = the cost in pounds sterling. The dimensions are in feet. To this must be added travelling and other expenses, and VAT applies to the whole sum. The length overall is traditionally taken as the distance from the fore side of the stem to the aft side of the transom and does not include bowsprit, bumpkin, pulpit, and so on. The beam is to outside of the topsides and does not include rub rails, etc. When the formula was invented, the length × beam part of the formula had a divisor, and this figure was reduced almost annually as inflation drove up costs. By the time this page is being read, there may be a multiplier, giving a formula of: (length × beam) × 1.1. As inflation rises the 1.1 will become 1.2, then 1.3, and so on.

Sometimes the cost is just a factor of the overall length of the boat, and sometimes it depends on how much work the surveyor has. If he is short of work, he may quote below his normal standard fee scale.

Another approximate guide is the 'average weekly wage of a blue-collar worker'. This is roughly the cost of a survey of a boat about 26 ft (8 m) long overall. The fee for a survey of a 38 ft (11.5 m) boat is twice this 'average weekly wage', and for a 52 ft (16 m) craft it is four times this wage. And so on, pro rata. However, it has to be said that this guide varies a great deal from country to country, and even within a particular country.

Some people charge according to the selling price of the boat or according to the number of hours spent on the job. These are the methods favoured in Canada and the United States. Europeans working on a damage survey charge by the hour or by the day. Some American surveyors say they charge extra for research or writing, but I've noticed they tend to be quick when it comes to doing reports, using more computer technology and standard forms and phrases than their European rivals. On the other hand, they tend to spend less time on each job, both during the inspection and afterwards. Of those I have spoken to, few seem prepared to spend an hour or two going over the written report line by line with the client, as I myself always do. One interesting difference between American and European surveyors is that the former charge their clients not only for the air fare when making a long journey to a job, but also for flight insurance.

A day's work surveying is typically charged out at a rate below that of a lawyer of the same seniority, though no one can explain why. A surveyor's fees for a day or hour are typically the same or a little less than those of a professional engineer. Fees may not rise in the spring, but they certainly never fall. This is when surveyors are busiest, and sometimes rushed off their feet. A good surveyor can get all the work he wants between February and the middle of June. At other times he may be under-employed, even if he is at the top of his profession. Not many people buy boats or damage them in the week before Christmas, which is why surveyors have plenty of time to spend with their children during the festive season.

A surveyor charges the client all the relative travelling and hotel expenses, as well as for a midday meal during the day of the survey. If the survey goes on late, or extends over more than one day, the cost of evening meals is included. By tradition, he travels first class on trains, but not when flying. Anyone who stints his surveyor is practising false economy, because a tired operator makes mistakes. In some localities it is necessary to sleep on the boat being surveyed because there is no choice. Living on board can either be tough or surprisingly comfortable: I recall one ship's chef who fed me so well for five days that I wondered if I would ever again get into the small lockers. In contrast, I did one survey on an uncivilised island where there was nowhere to sleep except on the yacht, and each night I had to barricade the cabin doors to keep out the local thieves.

Because travelling is so costly, surveying very small boats seems expensive when compared with the purchase price of the craft. This is especially true of dinghies and open motor boats. One way to minimise the cost is to get the buyer to club together with one or two people buying in the same area. The surveyor then checks all the boats together, and has only one lot of travelling charges to split between the clients. In this situation, the surveyor may be retained by the day.

Once or twice a year a surveyor may be asked to do a survey 'as and when convenient'. For instance, this applies to some insurance inspections. The job may not be urgent, so the surveyor fits it in when he is in the vicinity looking at another craft. This saves travelling twice to one region, and pleases the surveyor who does not want to spend more time on the road than is essential.

Where the buyer commissions the surveyor to give a quick initial look at a batch of craft, in order to pick out the best, the charge is normally made on a 'per day' or 'per hour' basis. There may be extra costs here if the surveyor uses his own car. Sometimes the buyer takes time off to accompany the surveyor, and may even take notes to get the best out of the opportunity. On such an occasion it can make sense to travel in the buyer's car – and this is *not* just because some surveyors who are starting up in business have such dreadful vehicles. Surveying properly is hard work, and if the job is to extend over 12 or 15 hours it makes sense for the surveyor to relax between inspections.

It is the buyer who pays for a 'Purchase Survey', never the seller. However, occasionally someone selling a vessel wants to know that it is in perfect condition and will commission a survey. He may display this report along with the description and photos of the craft, and arrange for it to be circulated to potential buyers. This technique is used by people trying to sell large and prestigious yachts. Even so, the buyer usually employs his own surveyor to check over the boat – the risk in trusting a seller is too much for most people. Damage surveys are normally paid for by the insurance underwriter, but sometimes the owner has to pay first and then be reimbursed by the insurer.

If the person who commissions the survey does not go ahead with the purchase, the report may be sold by the surveyor to another potential buyer. It is usual but not universal for the surveyor to ask the first person interested if he has finished with the report, and if he will permit a second copy to be sold to someone else. This is as much as anything a courtesy. After all, if the first buyer refuses permission, the surveyor just revisits the boat, checks that there have been no changes in the few days since the first inspection, and writes out a virtually identical report. The cost of a second copy of the report for a new client will vary a lot. It may be one-quarter of the original cost, or one-half, or perhaps even two-thirds or more. Much depends on circumstances, such as the type and location of the vessel, her future use, and so on. The fee goes in part to pay for a small proportion of the surveyor's professional indemnity insurance. It also covers the consultation after the second copy has been read. This discussion with the second buyer may go on all day; or, if the craft is large, it can extend even longer and may need enhancing with drawings, phone calls to boat repair yards, and so on.

Most surveyors ask for a proportion of their fee before work is started. It may be one-third or a half. Once the money has been received, the work is carried out and the report posted off, together with an invoice for the remainder of the fee. Another approach is for the surveyor to inspect the craft, dictate the report, then let the buyer know it is ready and will be posted when the full fee has been paid.

When a boat is being sold it is common practice for the broker to take a deposit from the buyer, as a sign of good faith, and to clinch the contract. This is usually (but not always) 10% of the agreed purchase price. It is returned to the buyer if the boat is found to be so unsound that a sale cannot take place. Once in a while a surveyor does damage during his work, however careful he is. This damage has to be paid for by the buyer. If he refuses to pay, money is taken from the 10% deposit held by the broker. This 10% is sometimes also used to pay the surveyor, if the buyer decides he does not want to go ahead with the pur-

chase. This is just the sort of situation where a dishonest buyer is inclined to renague on his payment to the surveyor, so the 10% may be used to pay the inspection fee.

One reason why surveyors do not like lifting seized floorboards and suchlike is that the edges may get chipped or crushed. This is why the job is done by shipwrights who are (or should be) trained to do the job; also, they should have a good selection of tools to accomplish the task. However, even a specialist can cause damage and any repairs have to be paid for by the person who commissions the survey.

Experienced surveyors take a lot of trouble to ensure that a report only goes to the person who orders it, and no one else. These reports can affect the value of a vessel by a substantial amount, perhaps showing that she is in fact worth much less (or, very occasionally, more) than she is being sold for. Brokers, rival buyers and owners of similar craft are among the people interested in getting hold of survey reports for their own gain.

There was a period during one of the economic slumps when quite a few craft were bought without surveys. The thinking behind this rashness was that prices were so low that they would not be further depressed by reports listing lots of faults. Buyers were working on the basis that they could find troubles in the bilge, tucked away at the end of the counter, and under the engine without professional help. They reckoned they were being clever by saving the cost of survey fees. What happened was that insurance companies realised these boats were being bought very cheaply, and guessed their condition was doubtful or worse. Some craft became uninsurable, others turned out to have far worse troubles than the buyers expected, and a few were just used and used until they became so dangerous that no one would go aboard.

To summarise, a survey is well worth its cost because it buys so much peace of mind. It protects the investment and it often saves money. It also makes it possible to get insurance. When the cost of quite a small accident afloat is considered, the double defence of a good survey and an insurance policy are not just worth having – it is complete madness to try to do without them.

THE BASIS OF SURVEYING

A survey is carried out by examining every part of the ship concerned. This involves crawling and climbing all over the hull and superstructure, going into every locker, under the sole and sometimes slithering under the engine. A surveyor has to burrow and peer into all the dark corners and inaccessible crannies. He goes under, over, round and through wherever he can, so this is no job for anyone who is overweight or unfit. If the masts are standing, the surveyor goes up them provided the vessel is afloat. All the time he makes notes or talks to his dictating machine about everything he sees. It is a time-consuming job and there is no way it can be rushed.

Notes are made of future, present and past troubles. If the ground tackle is less than excellent, this is noted because it is likely that the vessel will drag ashore in windy weather. Prevention is far better than cure, and vastly cheaper. Predicting crises is often the most effective way a surveyor earns his fee. I once told a buyer that unless a certain flexible fuel pipe was properly secured, it would swing against the engine fly-wheel when the boat rolled in rough seas. The warning was taken, and an engineer was told to clip up the pipe carefully. Just to be safe, the purchaser put some spare flexible fuel piping in his sea-going engine spares kit. However, the mechanic was unsupervised and did a rotten job. The next week the boat was out in partial gale-force conditions, in a narrow fiord between rocky shores. The fuel pipe chafed through, just as the survey notes predicted, and the engine stopped. The owner guessed at once what the trouble might be. He hurriedly fitted his reserve piping and got home safely.

Troubles that are already present are more quickly detected than those that are going to arise in a month or a year. It is easy to see that a chain plate has shifted slightly as a result of inadequate fastenings. It is more difficult, though, to appreciate from the unstressed condition of the sails that a yacht has probably never been out in severe weather and to realise that when she is in a gale her chain plates are liable to start easing upwards because of undersized bolts. A surveyor has to use his knowledge of boatbuilding, engineering and seamanship to see and predict

Damage on the front of the stem is common, and is often caused by anchors being hauled aboard. Normally it is 'skin-deep' and not important, but it should be noted in a survey report and repaired. This yacht has had untreated damage for so long that mildew growth has started. A sign of long neglect like this is a useful indicator, warning a surveyor to look for other comparable defects.

troubles. Year after year, he must read and use his imagination as well as draw upon his experience.

Past troubles on a boat have to be scrutinised critically. Just as a boat may have a building deficiency, so she can have inadequate repairs. It is not enough to double over a fractured stiffener or beam if the strength of the new reinforcement is no greater than the part that has been *proved* inadequate. At the same time, the cause of the failure has to be discovered and preventative measures recommended. If a beam breaks, it may have done so when the whole crew gathered on the foredeck to haul in a fouled anchor. This event can occur again, so maybe extra beams should be glassed in at the gaps between the existing ones, or stringers glassed on under the deck, or pillars or beam knees fitted. Sometimes, the best surveyors suggest more than one way of curing a trouble.

In one way I was lucky to start sailing at a time when my father had been ill for a lengthy period. This meant that I got very little advice from him, so I remembered what he did tell me. I also started boat-owning with too little money, and thus got involved in assorted crises afloat. Before I was 20 I had been aground in various boats and weather conditions, been dismasted in fog, pumped to save myself from drowning, got washed off the foredeck, and owned dinghies that could only be kept afloat by non-stop bailing. Since then, on two occasions I've been aloft when the mast-winch holding me has broken, I've discovered a lifeline was rusted through by leaning on it and falling overboard, had to re-secure chain plates coming adrift in the middle of the Pacific, and twice brought rudderless boats back to harbour without help. Surveyors need first- and second-hand experiences and must learn to use them in their work.

A surveyor's first duty is to his client, who is paying the bill. However, he also has a duty to the underwriter who will insure the craft, and to the crews of other ships that may pass by. They do not want to be rammed because of defective steering gear. Nor do they want to have to put themselves in danger to rescue a boat in trouble as a result of poor construction and maintenance. All this means that a surveyor has to be fearless when drafting his reports, and he will inevitably make enemies. Some people fail to see that it is not the surveyor who puts the defect in a boat, but that he is only the person who detects the trouble. There are also some who are foolish enough to try to shoot the messenger bringing bad news.

One of the hardest parts of the job is being dispassionate when writing out reports. Builders who think their craft are perfect are vociferous, sometimes in the face of clear evidence. Some owners insist there is nothing wrong with their boats, even though they are spending a tenth of the proper annual maintenance costs. Brokers are certain the boats on their lists are in excellent order, even though they have not been up the mast, or hauled all the sails out of their bags, or even looked under the floorboards. Surveyors are constantly abused by such people. Under these circumstances it is not easy to remain thoughtful and imaginative when predicting problems, nor is it always straightforward to detail existing and past troubles. Therefore an important part of the job is maintaining integrity – sometimes in adversity.

· ·

LIMITATIONS OF A SURVEY

An effective way of examining a small craft would be to slice up every component into thin slivers so that each part could be seen in section at close intervals – this would give a very good idea of the condition of the boat prior to her being reduced to a pile of granulated waste! Thus the surveyor has to steer a course between doing serious damage in order to discover what is hidden in the structure, and being so cautious that no proper research is carried out.

What makes life so difficult are the many areas, some of them large, that cannot even be seen – let alone tested; and even where the surveyor can look over the structure, he may not be able to reach it. The aft end of a thin counter, under an engine, beneath and inside tanks are all typical, inaccessible regions. With decks and topsides there are often large areas that can only be seen on one side, with the other being sealed over with glued-on lining or hidden behind panelling. In the old days, when the majority of boats were made of wood, a lot could be learned by taking careful selective borings, though this technique seems to have been rarely used in the United States.

With fibreglass it is very rare to bore through structure, though one does hear of it on special occasions. For instance, if there is doubt about the quality of the fibreglass lay-up, a hole cutter may be used below the waterline so that a circular sample of the hull shell is obtained. The same sample may be resined back in place, or the hole filled with fresh material. When a new skin fitting is being put in this is an ideal opportunity to see the quality of the glass lay-up. This sort of rather radical testing may be used when a boat is setting off on a long arduous world-circling voyage.

If there is no staging, the surveyor cannot work his way round the topsides, though he will stare hard at each area and get the best view he can. On large yachts and fishing boats, even with staging it may not be possible to look closely at more than half or even a third of the total area. Some of the modern types of adjustable wheeled platforms are a great help here, but they are not found in many yards – and even they have limitations since they cannot reach in under all overhanging areas, or work between slipway cradle supports, or move over rough terrain. Looking down from the deck is no substitute for complete all-round staging, especially where there is flare in the hull. When other means of access have failed, I have perched on a bobstay trying to inspect the fore side of a stem, but this is unsatisfactory. It is almost impossible to use tools or write notes while emulating a bird on a telephone wire.

At the beginning or end of the survey report there is a list of the areas that have not been inspected, but this is not always fully detailed. For instance, it may say that the mast is standing, but not mention that the mast was not seen above eye level. The surveyor may assume that everybody knows that if the boat is ashore the mast cannot be climbed. If an area is not mentioned in a written report, the inference must be that it is sound, or cannot be seen or reached properly. If the surveyor gives a detailed list of everything *not* inspected, the report becomes extremely long with a high percentage of useless information.

A whole set of problems arise when the matter of the annual refit is considered. Is a surveyor to list all the work needed for this refit, or is he to assume that the person who commissions the survey knows about winter maintenance, or will get the boatyard to do all that is necessary? Besides, where is the line to be drawn between repairs and normal annual refitting? Probably the best guide is to say that all work that is normally done annually is regular maintenance work, and need not be mentioned in a survey. For instance, applying anti-fouling paint, revarnishing bright-work, cleaning the bilge, and changing the engine filters and oil should hardly need to be noted in a report. It is more difficult to be so certain about maintenance work that is done at larger intervals, like the removal and testing of the seacocks every three or four years, and the replacement of the guardrail wires every five years. To err on the safe side, it is probably best to recommend this work.

Plenty of surveyors do not mention the need to replace the wires through the stanchions, but they would agree that a bent rigging screw on one of these wires should be noted. There are riggers who will ignore a mild bend in the stem of a tensioning screw in the misguided belief that if it survived the previous year it might well last another season. Equipment, or the absence of it, also raises problems. Is a surveyor to draw attention to the lack of lee cloths or lee-boards on the berths? Generally speaking, I would have thought not, unless the vessel is intended for offshore cruising and the buyer has specifically asked for the fullest information about such items. However, no cruiser but the very smallest should go to sea with one anchor. If the surveyor finds there is no second anchor, and on larger vessels no third one, it is an idea to mention this.

Surveying is more difficult than usual when the boat is new or nearly so. Both buyer and seller have what amounts to a reverent attitude towards the pristine finish, seldom remembering that what matters in a gale is strength and integrity not fancy furniture. Both sides of the deal get upset if the surveyor wants to see behind well-secured lining; but once a few notable defects have been found, the buyer swings to the surveyor's viewpoint and may become more enthusiastic than anyone to open up hidden areas. As surveying becomes more sophisticated with the introduction of electronic test gear, the need to open up panelled-over and padded areas will not decrease, because meters cannot normally work properly through linings and ceilings.

When it comes to engines, machinery like charging sets, electronic equipment, fridges and freezers, self-steering gear and so on, the average boat surveyor has to pass the work on to the specialists. They in turn may have to do quite a lot of dismantling before they can be sure that everything is in good working order. Sometimes their final opinions cannot be given until the boat is afloat and taken out on trials.

When it comes to the limitations of surveying, few people outside the field can appreciate just how numerous and extensive are the areas that cannot be examined on the majority of small craft.

PREPARING CRAFT FOR A SURVEY

All sorts of advantages accrue if the surveyor can visit the boat a few days before carrying out the inspection. He can see what staging is available, how much rubbish there is in the bilge, whether the boat needs pumping out, and he can even mark the fastenings and seacocks that he wants taken out. He can check that the boat key is available and give the necessary instructions for the preparation to the boatyard, owner or buyer.

Ideally, of course, all the preparation, organisation and work should be done by the person commissioning the survey, so that the surveyor does not waste time and can concentrate on his true job. If a surveyor arrives to start his survey and finds that no preparation has been done, the sharp edge may be taken off his concentration. This is especially true if he has to empty lots of lockers. It can be gruelling work humping boat gear like outboard engines and heavy sails up through a narrow companionway and down a rickety ladder secured to the boat's side.

In some yards the management do not allow certain work to be done by anybody except yard employees. Elsewhere there are trade union restrictions stating that only certain men employed by the yard are allowed to do jobs such as removing fastenings, lifting out ballast, and even emptying the boat of loose gear. Some work simply cannot be done by a surveyor without help. If the spars are packed in among lots of others, possibly on racks high above the ground, then one person cannot lift them down on his own. Sometimes dinghies are packed away inaccessibly, and often only a yard foreman can identify the correct spars and other equipment.

Ideally the boat should be exactly upright and on a level keel, if for no other reason than for sighting along the sheer and keel for fairness. In practice, very few craft are exactly level or upright. Relatively few owners are interested in the expenditure needed to achieve this desirable state of affairs, and on most occasions the surveyor has to accept the boat as she is. However, sometimes there may be a need for additional chocks or supports if the boat appears to be tilted too much and is dangerous to board. In this connection it is important to remember that a glossy fibreglass shell does not allow props and wedges to grip easily. These supports should therefore be well under the turn of the bilge and should be angled as near as possible normal to the shell to prevent a wedging action forcing props away. One reason for employing only a professional surveyor is that his professional indemnity insurance policy should cover the cost of repairing damage if his movements on board a boat cause her to tip over. It's worth remembering that a boat that tips over in a yard may well be close to others and start a chain reaction, knocking over all the adjacent vessels also.

The majority of boats laid up ashore no longer have covers over them. This is good for surveyors, because it makes for easier access. It is advantageous for boatyards because it ensures a rapid rate of depreciation and therefore more work in future years. However, it is bad for owners because boats go downhill if they have no protection from winter winds and rain. Where there is a tarpaulin or other cover spread over a boat, it should be turned right back before the surveyor arrives. When he leaves, the boatyard should resecure the cover, particularly as the job requires some skill and knowledge. A canvas cover not properly tied down may cause the boat to blow over in a gale. The lashings should never be made fast to the props, nor to the props of the boat alongside. Wind under a cover causes the lashings to jolt and pluck props out, with swift efficiency. If the cover is not tightly tied down, the wind may get under it and blow the whole boat over, even when the lashings are secured under the keel and round the counter.

Before the surveyor arrives, the hatches should be unlocked and it is a good idea to open them all slightly so that the boat is aired. However, on a wooden boat some surveyors prefer the hatches to be left closed, so that they can smell rot as soon as they climb down the cabin steps. In theory, the boatyard should lift up all the trap doors and other portable or semi-portable access panels.

All loose gear should be taken off the boat with the exception of the fire extinguishers. It is just as important to remove the warps and fenders from the aft lazarette as it is to take out the cushions. Anchor chains should be fed out over the stemhead roller and ranged neatly in 2 m (6 ft) zigzags on the ground. Good owners do this when the boat is laid up and this is often a clue as to whether the boat has been well looked after each winter. Skylight and winch covers should be taken off, cockpit lockers should have their padlocks removed, and steering gear be unlocked. In short, every part of the boat and every component should be made easy to view. In practice, every surveyor knows that each year he will waste a great deal of time because two or three boat keys have been lost and the boatyard has no duplicate.

Tank access panels should also be taken off, but this is seldom done. Obviously the contents have to be removed first, especially if the door is on the side of the tank! Nominally, every vessel hauled up, particularly if she is in a shed, should have all fuel tanks empty. It is a requirement of insurance companies that boats laid up ashore have no bottled gas, nor any fuel on board. In practice, this rule is honoured in the breach. It is true that a partly filled tank is more likely to show any leaks in the fuel system than one that is completely empty. However, tanks for fuel or water that are not empty cannot always have the inspection plates taken off and, even if the manholes are on top, liquid in a tank prevents full inspection. For the fullest possible survey, all tanks should be lifted right out of the hull, not just so that the tanks can be tested and their undersides examined, but also to allow the area of the hull normally hidden by the tanks to be seen.

Occasionally the engine is taken out to be inspected fully and to look at the caverns normally hidden by the machinery. These hidden areas are almost always dirty and the sensible owner uses the opportunity to clean and paint the newly exposed parts of the boat.

Ideally, all floorboards and lining should be taken out. However, this could prove a long and expensive job and it is quite usual to lift only the centreline floorboards. Sometimes only alternate pieces of lining, or possibly every third piece, are taken out. A lot depends here on the age of the vessel and her intended use. Before a major voyage it is good practice to strip out all the lining and examine the entire hull. Sometimes the surveyor may find that he can just detect what looks like potential trouble behind a piece of lining that has not been removed. In that case, he will call for a shipwright to take down the sealing that is blocking his view. The rule here must be: when in doubt, take everything out.

It is not universal practice to remove keel bolts and skin fittings before the surveyor arrives, partly because some practitioners defer this work until everything else has been done. They work on the principle that if the vessel has serious defects, the buyer will not wish to incur the expense of taking out fastenings unnecessarily. One trouble with this approach is that some keel bolts are difficult to remove and the surveyor may have to visit the boat a second time a few days after the main inspection to check the principal fastenings. Internal ballast should be removed, though in practice it is quite usual for 30% to be lifted. It may be necessary to make a plan to show how the ballast is stowed, so that it can be refitted correctly.

When a wooden boat is laid up, it should have the bung removed from the lowest part of the bilge so that all water drains away automatically. If this has not been done, it may be necessary to pump the bilge; and if this is done in the presence of the surveyor, it gives him a good opportunity to assess the effectiveness of the bilge-pumping arrangements. Any very dirty bilge should be cleaned out to give the surveyor a chance to see the structure low down.

· ·

SURVEYING NEW BOATS

There is a widespread feeling that new boats do not need surveying – the theory being, 'they are new, so they must be fine'. How different things are in practice. Nothing made by human hands is perfect – and when the hands involved are bored because they have completed 700 identical craft, there are bound to be a few things to worry a surveyor.

Typical sources of defects in new boats are:

● design and building errors in the prototype

which are then passed on to the production line. (Once a surveyor has a list of these for a particular type, he will know what to look for every time he sees another of the class.)

- New ideas are not always fully developed, so they have 'snags' that are not eliminated.
- Cost-cutting techniques are sometimes given priority over quality and safety. Typical is the hatch that has no hinges and depends on a pair of little barrel bolts, or something similar, to keep it in place. It should have at least one totally reliable safety line as well.
- Craft designed and built for one region are sold in other areas where the weather and other adverse factors are more severe. A classic example is the boat designed and built far up a sheltered river, which is then sold for use on the rumbustious ocean.

I have surveyed new boats from good builders and written six-page closely typed reports on things that need attention before the boat is launched. Some defects are common and obvious. These include such things as undersized bilge pumps that are not strongly bolted to a good stiff piece of structure, are located badly, and have portable handles that are not secured by safety lines. There may be no strum box, or there may be one that cannot be cleaned, or it may be secured by a thin piece of light alloy that will corrode in the first season. It is usual to look at new boats and find that structural parts like the bulkheads are poorly fixed in place with just one or two runs of thin narrow glass tape. Even more common is the practice of bonding in furniture with the thinnest layering of glassfibre, which the builder knows will survive for the first 12 months of the boat's life. After that he feels he can wash his hands of the craft, and when the owner complains he will perhaps say that stress of weather or careless handling is the reason why the join has failed.

A badly secured furniture panel was the cause of an accident on a brand new cruiser. She had just been christened, and was craned into the water. The owner started the engine, took in the warps, coiled them, and dropped them into a cockpit locker. The inboard side of this locker was a piece of ply held by three small screws. These failed when the warps thumped against the panel, and the ropes slithered into the bilge. One was against the propeller shaft coupling, so when the engine was put into gear the rope wrapped itself round the shaft in an ever-increasing tangle. This built up in diameter and jammed between the hull and the shaft. The stern gland could not stand the strain and was torn adrift. Water poured in, but the helmsman did not know what was happening until one of the crew noticed the cabin sole was submerged. Fortunately, the launching crane was still in place, and lifted the boat out just in time.

Inadequate fittings

There is one widespread problem that surveyors have when looking at new boats. It concerns the fittings on deck, on the spars, on the locker doors and so on. It is this: the builder, anxious to keep the weight of the yacht to a minimum so that she will be fast, uses the lightest winches, cleats, door hinges, and so on. He finds this approach doubly attractive as a small winch or ventilator or compass can cost half the price of one that is a sensible and practical size. The total saving of money if every fitting is one size below the correct level is enough to undercut rival builders and secure sales galore.

It might be thought that this skimping is not really all that bad, and only occurs intermittently. Proof of how serious this problem is comes from a well-known wholesale chandlers. The managing director has said that a substantial proportion of his sales comes from owners who have bought new boats and found that many parts are too small or flimsy. They have to strip cleats and winches off spars and cockpit coamings and replace them with new ones, sometimes two sizes larger.

There was a time when most standard production yachts, apart from those made for the top end of the market, had sheet winches that were inadequate. This problem is not as bad as it was, but is still found. It is not helped by those winch-makers who are too optimistic about the power and efficiency of their products. On a family yacht, the winches should be powerful enough for the weakest person on board to use with reasonable ease because everyone else may be laid low with seasickness.

Though sheet and halyard winches are now usually up to their job, anchor winches are usually suspect. The price gap between say, type C and the next size up, type D, in any manufacturer's range is usually substantial. Owners jib at paying out a lot of extra cash just to have an anchor winch that will work well in all conditions. If the one fitted as standard on a brand of yacht seems fine for normal weather, when the crew are all fit and well, why (owners ask) go to the considerable extra expense of having a bigger one that will deal with emergencies? The answer comes when the next crisis arises. It is usually at night, in wild weather, on a lee shore, with flat batteries and tired crew. Anyone who has dealt with fraught situations knows that 'just big enough' is not adequate. Gear on boats needs to be weather-proof, fool-proof and panic-proof.

Flimsy door and locker furniture is still a source of friction between builders and owners, not to mention surveyors. Plenty of well-known production yachts have locker hinges that are $1\frac{1}{4}$ in (30 mm) long held by three tiny screws in each flap. These cannot stand up to even the most moderate handling. In the ordinary hustle and bustle of cruising in windy weather, these locker doors come adrift. This presents the surveyor with a problem, because the builder will say that this type and size of door furniture is standard on his product, and always has been. He may add rather vehemently that he would go bankrupt if he upgraded it. The surveyor may let the builder (or his selling agent) have his say, but all these protestations do not make the fittings adequate for their purpose. The surveyor's job is to point out risks and hazards, and though this often upsets builders and salesmen, the surveyor must not be put off.

Delivery defects

A new boat is usually handed over to her owner many miles from where she was built. If the journey from the factory is made by sea, it may be that the delivery crew are careful, and make a list of snags that have arisen while under way. There are some delivery firms that do this automatically as part of their service, and the surveyor, if fully involved with the yacht, will find it worthwhile to use such an organisation.

There is nothing like a maiden voyage for showing up defects, especially in the plumbing, instrumentation, sail handling and electrical equipment. Things that work when the yacht is upright and stationary may fail when she heels and bounces about. Low fiddles and locker doors that refuse to stay shut show up when offshore; windows that are tight when in harbour sometimes leak when the tension of the standing rigging distorts the hull.

When a boat is delivered to her home port by road all sorts of faults are generated, from scratches along the topsides to loosened bulkheads. When the cradle or supporting shores are inadequate or do not spread the hull weight evenly, the jolting of the vehicle may loosen furniture and other structure. If there are leaves or broken twigs (or perhaps even small branches) on deck when she arrives, expect bent pulpits and stanchions, broken windows, gouges on deck and on the cabin top. If the vehicle carrying the boat has stopped en route, perhaps while the driver has a meal, look for signs of pilferage. A bright yellow life-ring hanging on the rail is a temptation that thieves may not be able to resist — and even if it has not been stolen, it may have been blown off.

When my father was building flying boats he sometimes had to send them from the factory by road. He first sent a reconnaissance party along the route. They rode on a platform the size of the aircraft, built on top of a lorry. When they came to a roadside tree with branches that might bash into the aircraft, the men on the platform lopped off the overhanging timber. On one occasion the foreman of this gang asked my father what he should say if the owner of a tree objected. 'Tell him,' my father replied, 'that this time we will trim his trees free, but next time we will require payment.' No one these days sends a party ahead of a boat, and every year a few get damaged. Some of the special vehicles used for boats only have two or three support legs each side, and if there are major pot-holes in the road the hull may be indented and cracked in way of the support legs.

Safety gear

This is seldom comprehensive on new boats. The owner will have just paid out a lot of money for his elegant new boat, and will be reluctant to run up his overdraft further — even supposing the bank manager will permit it. Friends and crew who come aboard bearing gifts to celebrate the arrival of the new boat think that a gold-embossed log-book is the correct thing. It's a pity that they do not buy some big fat flares instead or a sensible size of sheet anchor, which is what many new boats lack.

The builder's fitting-out staff do not always have safety in mind when they are completing the rigging of the boat. Instead, they are probably thinking of that case of beer that they hope the owner will broach without delay. Even if they are the most conscientious people in the industry, they may not have been told to wire up all the rigging screws and tape over all the sharp ends and edges on deck to prevent the sails from snagging, or secure the ends of halyards, or lash the anchors down, or hose test the deck-edges and windows.

It is hardly the surveyor's job to check the charts when going over a new boat, but it would have helped in one celebrated case. This vessel was built to the highest standard by a famous and meticulous builder. The owner's wife smashed the bottle on the bow, and the boat touched the water for the first time. A very few hours later this gleaming new yacht motored out of harbour in perfect weather, in broad daylight. In perfect visibility the owner steered her through a gap in a series of steel pillars outside the harbour, thinking there was a clear passage. There was, but he chose the wrong gap and his boat was holed and sunk within sight of the builders – all for want of a large-scale local chart.

When looking over a new boat a surveyor will find many of the defects seen on mature craft. The gel coat may be rumpled or blotchy, the deck may not be perfectly even, bolts through the deck fittings may not pass through the backing bolts, the weatherboards may jam or be too sloppy, and so on.

The survey of a new boat will take as long as one on an old boat, and may show up as many problems. The sad thing is that so few buyers commission surveys before setting off on the maiden voyage.

. . . .

PARTIAL SURVEYS

There was a time when partial surveys were rare. This was before buyers were more anxious about the cost of the survey than the content, and before insurance companies required an inspection before they would underwrite a policy on a middle-aged boat. Nowadays, plenty of partial surveys are carried out. They include those done afloat for insurance companies (who do not seem concerned about the condition of the hull below the waterline) and surveys of the hull *only* on the outside below the waterline. The latter are usually done for buyers who are not prepared to pay for a full check-up, but want to be sure there is no osmosis on the craft of their choice.

The trouble with these half-done jobs is that they are unseamanlike, unsatisfactory from a safety point of view, and often poor value for the money. However, there are occasions when they make sense. For instance, if a buyer is uncertain about which of a small batch of craft he should select, a good case can be made for spending a fixed number of hours on each boat. The same major items are examined on each vessel, and at the end of the job it is usually easy to pick out which one should be bought. Sometimes a simple 'points system' is used, with the condition of the hull bottom outside being marked out of 10 or 100; the same is done for the structure inside – the rig, engine, and so on.

Partial surveys are sometimes done afloat to save the cost of hauling the craft ashore, or beaching her at low tide. The principal problem here is that one of the most important areas is not seen. There may be galloping osmosis below the waterline, as well as a propeller riddled with electrolysis, a prop shaft almost corroded through, a bent rudder bearing – and no one finds out about them.

There are also difficulties working round outside the topsides when the boat is afloat. An ordinary dinghy is an unsatisfactory platform since it is too mobile and lacks stability. It also bumps the boat being inspected and may cause damage. A rubber dinghy causes no harm unless a metal towing eye or something similar makes scratches. This type of small boat is marvellously stable, but it still needs a second (and ideally a third) person to work it round the topsides, holding on firmly while the surveyor does his work and takes notes. He also gets his feet wet, but this is a standard hazard when in many inflatables, and he is not expected to notice such minor discomforts – even in mid-winter. Even an inflatable dinghy has lots of disadvantages, though. It is useless for getting right under a long counter, or for reaching 3 or 4 m (10 or 14 ft) up the topsides of a large vessel. Also, spray splashes up between the dinghy and the large vessel when there is any sea or another craft goes past. The surveyor is inured to being saturated, but he does hate water all over his note-book and in his dictating machine.

An old-fashioned painters' raft is a stable spacious platform for working round a boat afloat in very calm waters, but the surveyor still needs help when moving this unwieldy craft. It is not good in a strong tide, and the whole job is difficult when there is much current. In severe weather the operation can be a nightmare, with the added embellishments of pinched fingers and a chance of drowning.

Some insurance companies accept surveys afloat with no inspection round the outside of the hull. Alternatively, they may be happy to have a survey done with the boat beached and checked over when the tide has left her high and dry. This sometimes means putting her against a sea-wall, so that the inshore side is largely inaccessible. On other occasions the keel may be deep in the mud, but still the survey is acceptable for its purpose.

It does seem as if insurance underwriters just need a broad indication of the type of craft they are being asked to insure. They certainly know from experience that the vast majority of all boats, large and small, are far from perfect. They also know that certain types have well-established defects: racing yachts have delicate rigs, and inshore fishing boats are notoriously under-equipped with ground tackle.

Partial surveys tend to be worthless unless they cover about 65% of the important parts of the vessel and at least 40% of the lesser factors. A survey of this extent will almost always indicate to a technically qualified person the general state of the craft. When buying an old commercial launch (so often tatty and

battered, dented and dilapidated), this sort of survey seems to be acceptable. Of course, not even a full survey is 100% complete. It is only possible to give a totally comprehensive report if every part is completely dismantled and sections are cut out of each component at close intervals. This would provide all the knowledge needed, but result in a large bill for dismembering work. The craft would then need a major rebuild, which again would take up a lot of time and more money.

Professional organisations that guard surveyors' interests are all against partial surveys. It is not just that the fees are reduced, and the surveyor is running extra risks. There are so many dangers, and the person commissioning the survey may not appreciate the number and importance of the things not checked. Surveyors' associations recommend that a complete list is made of everything not inspected. Since the principal objective of having a partial survey is to save time, and listing is time-consuming, maybe it would be better to have a full inspection. What can be said in favour of partial surveys is that they are vastly better than having no survey at all, and they do give a reasonable *indication* of the quality, level of maintenance and safety standards of a particular vessel.

SEAWORTHINESS AND ASSESSING ABILITY

Surveyors are at times asked to sign certificates of seaworthiness. These documents are needed for some passages along certain rivers and canals because if a vessel sinks in one of these narrow waterways the traffic can be seriously held up. They are also called for by insurance companies in some specialised situations. For instance, they are sometimes required when a vessel is to be towed, even if the voyage is quite short.

For such a passage the towing facilities have to be excellent, and it may be necessary to recommend that new bollards and fairleads are secured to the foredeck. Towing, especially in bad weather, is notorious for being troublesome – the warp chafes by the bow of the towed craft; when there are severe waves the snatching load causes the bollards to rip out; and if there is no one to steer the towed craft, she

may sheer about so much that she almost overtakes her tug. Then the towing line may pull sideways instead of forwards, and can capsize the towed vessel. For a long tow, a surveyor should call in specialist help. Because of the potential problems, the surveyor will probably recommend that there should be a full crew on the towed boat so that she is always steered. These people will need safety gear as well as full living facilities, and may have to have spare towing warps and gear secured on deck, in case the first set breaks.

Before issuing a certificate of seaworthiness the vessel will need a careful (but not total) inspection. The hull and seacocks, the decks and skylights, the bulkheads and floors all have to be in good order, but the engine and some of the deck gear is not going to be used, so their condition is unimportant. It may well be advisable to have the exhaust outlet sealed with a bung or blanking-off plate, and some (or all) the windows and hatches may need to be strongly covered over. Deck equipment such as stanchions, anchor winch and the mooring equipment must all be perfect.

Often, the vessel that needs a seaworthiness certificate has aroused someone's suspicion, otherwise the request (or demand) would not have been made. A surveyor with any experience gets a feeling after an hour aboard a small craft as to whether she is capable of dealing with bad weather. If he finds nothing, but his internal alarm still warns him that he is on a boat that cannot be trusted, he should insist that one or more powerful mechanical pumps are put aboard for the passage. These pumps need their own power source with plenty of fuel. Such pumps are easy to hire, and will be carried well lashed to strong points on deck, or down below if the exhaust can be led overboard. They will be fully set up and tested before leaving harbour, with suction and discharge pipes securely rigged.

During any passage that requires a certificate of seaworthiness the safety and communication equipment has to be in plentiful supply and good order. Relying on a single VHF set seems unwise, especially as these radios are now cheap and can be hired for short periods. Each VHF set should have its own separate power supply. In the same way, the fire extinguishers need a special check. There should be no extinguishers layered with rust or with an ancient date of manufacture.

When signing a form like a certificate of seaworthiness, a surveyor should consider limiting the proposed passage to fine weather with a good four-day forecast. Now that meteorology has harnessed space technology to give such good long-term predictions, there is seldom any need to make a short voyage without knowing what the weather is going to be like. The required standard of crew skill and experience should also be stated, because seaworthiness can only be defined in terms of the ship plus crew. The best vessel afloat is dependent on the crew, and accidents afloat are often the result of inexperience or lack of training and knowledge. This is shown up by the remarkable voyages made by old and creaking boats that win through by the talents and determination, the cleverness and the know-how of the people on board.

Before signing a certificate of seaworthiness, a surveyor may reflect that the Royal National Lifeboat Institute, the US Coast Guard, and the rescue services of every maritime country spend small fortunes each year building and servicing their own rather special small ships and boats. The finest workmanship and materials, the cleverest designs and the latest technology are poured into these craft. However, there are widows in every seaport who will testify that even these craft are not entirely safe when the sea is at its worst. So certificates of seaworthiness are not to be signed lightly, and should be hedged about with limited and defining clauses. There are times when a surveyor is better to forgo a fee than take on a job that makes an impossible demand on his ability to predict the future. Lifeboats and coastguard cutters with all their assets have proved vulnerable, so the average small craft is proportionately less safe. The latter can seldom be described as better than moderately seaworthy.

Just as dangerous, from a surveyor's point of view, is a request for a prediction about a vessel's ability. Will she do 10 knots, and will she roll? Will she win next year's race series, and will it be easy to change headsails when going to windward? The questions are many, and there may well be no firm answers. How can one define seakindliness or comfort afloat? There are techniques, but they apply to big ships and they are not universally accepted. Just as difficult are questions like: Has she adequate water capacity, or fuel, or bottled gas storage? It's tempting to say no on all occasions to this type of question, because some people wash five times a day and motor flat out everywhere while cooking four-course meals; others live like hermits or use their boats as day racers and never fill any of the tanks more than a quarter full. Here we have a situation that is akin to the problem of seaworthiness, and to give an accurate answer it is essential to know a lot about the crew as well as their craft.

Some surveyors offer opinions about a boat's ability without being asked. This seems to be inviting trouble sooner or later. All boats are subject to many outside influences, so a boat that seems fast may turn out to be slow because she is badly tuned. One that looks pretty now may be ugly when the new owner has changed her paint scheme, slightly altered the cabin top, added a bowsprit, and cut the mast height. A buyer may ask if a yacht will have weather helm. The surveyor may remember that she has been designed by a master craftsman whose products are easy to steer, but it may be that the boat in question is one of the designer's earliest works – completed *before* he learned how to make a boat docile. Just to make the situation more confusing, some design offices expand so much that relatively junior draughtsmen are responsible for the lines of some of the secondary boats. If the maestro himself happens to be away on holiday or ill when the hull form is settled, it may be inappropriate to have his name on the design.

If assessing qualities like weather helm and stability are risky, predicting speed is wildly dangerous. Any boat can lose 10% of her speed because a propeller has been wrongly specified or made, or become damaged. For the same reason, sister ships do not always make the same speed. I have come across a twin-screw boat that appeared to have a pair of matching props, but careful measurement showed that one had a 12% error in the pitch, and the other was 23% adrift. Pursuing the matter, I then found that neither propeller had the diameter specified by the designer.

Speed is also affected by displacement, and most boats over the years get heavier as a result of the build-up of extra gadgets added by successive owners, and gear that accumulates in lockers. Hidden pockets of bilge-water and general soakage also add to the weight. This all nibbles away at the speed, and so makes it dangerous to predict how fast any boat will go. Yet another factor is the engine's performance. Even before ageing sets in, plenty of propulsion units do not reach their maximum theoretical rotational speed, and thus the horsepower is reduced.

All in all, the surveyor who makes comments aloud or in writing about a boat's ability or performance, even after he has thoroughly looked over her, is risking his reputation and his professional indemnity insurance.

. . . .

WHAT IS FLIMSY?

After a couple of decades, a professional surveyor can wander through a boat and give a useful opinion as to her strength, provided he can see the structure. However, the practice of covering the whole of the inside of a boat with lining, much of it glued in place, is causing a lot of problems. No one can give an opinion of structure that is well hidden.

Years spent in close proximity with small ships, yachts, fishing boats and launches implants in the mind a scale of soundness that automatically evaluates everything. Even when they are not working, surveyors cannot help looking around when in or on any craft, whether it is a racing yacht or a barge. This may make surveyors seem rude, but it is as natural as the way a plantsman's eye wanders when in a garden, or a coffin-maker automatically measures (in his mind) the height of everyone he meets.

Over the years a surveyor learns to assess the worth of different hull parts and equipment, rigging and spars, chain and anchors. He knows when something is too thin for the job it is expected to do. He learns that a shortage of strength and an inadequate factor of safety result in cracks, leaks and breaks. He knows that the futher below the safety limit anything is, the sooner it will fail, and the worse will be the consequences.

A weak component throws an unfair load on the adjacent structure. A window frame that is too delicate overloads the coaming in which it is set. The coaming will split at the corners, and crack where there is a change of section. I remember surveying a famous offshore racer that had a rudder down the aft end of her keel. The rudder was thick enough by normal standards – or would have been if there had been the usual number and spacing of rudder straps. However, to cut down every interruption to water flow the designer had omitted all straps. Inevitably the rudder bent in the middle when the helm was put over and the yacht was travelling fast. The wear at the bottom bearing was serious, and unusual in appearance. The owner complained that the rate of wear was disconcerting, even though the best material was used. This is a reminder that even the best designers err, or hand over some of their detail design work to lesser men and boys.

An experienced surveyor relies on his years of experience and usually knows instinctively what will stand up to a force 11 gale. He goes offshore often enough, and in a sufficiently wide variety of craft to know what it is like beyond the horizon when a destructive gale is testing the strength of everything afloat. In some ways I regret the popularity of roller headsails because they make it unnecessary to go forward to change headsails. Nothing sharpens a surveyor's awareness like a difficult half-hour on a wave-swept foredeck.

To be a successful, a surveyor has to learn to judge the thickness and spacing of scantlings by eye. He can look at a bulkhead or shroud or coaming edge and write down the thickness before he checks his guess with a gauge. He knows the width of his hand span, thumb span and the thickness of his little finger, and uses these crude measures to speed up his work.

He uses the rules put out by regulatory bodies such as Lloyd's, the American Bureau of Shipping, Bureau Veritas and Norsk Veritas to gain a knowledge of the correct thickness for different parts of a boat. These organisations publish books of scantlings for fibreglass, steel, aluminium and wood construction. There are also government bodies in various countries that lay down the scantlings for fishing boats and commercial craft. These are useful for a surveyor, as he builds up his personal data bank of knowledge. Experience teaches a surveyor to recognise that some craft like tugs and fishing boats need greater factors of safety than racing yachts, and he soon learns that too many racing yachts are built

with scantlings that cannot withstand the buffeting that a boat may experience in a lock or dock.

One of the dilemmas surveyors have to face is what to say, and what to write in a report, when faced with a delicate boat. There is no doubt that many racing craft are built to win regardless of safety. Some suffered in the famous gale during the Fastnet Race of 1979, when so many lives were lost, and a handful of yachts did not return to harbour. However, the opportunity was missed of having a wide selection of the offshore racing fleet at least partially surveyed after the race. One result of this is that owners and crew racing in deep water seldom realise just how small are the factors of safety in their boats.

A surveyor faced with what appears to be a very lightly constructed boat has to remember two principles:
1 The force of a breaking wave is not lessened just because the boat beneath it has been designed for racing.
2 In order to win a race, it is first necessary to finish — which no one does very often in an over-flimsy shell.

If a boat is to be based on an inland lake or river she can be lighter in construction than a sea-going equivalent. Boats built for day sailing do not need massive scantlings, but such boats tend to have short lives and need extra maintenance.

DAMAGE INSPECTIONS

. . . .

DAMAGE SURVEYS

(This section should be read in conjunction with the next one, 'Surveying after Grounding'.)

A damage survey involves a close inspection of all the affected parts of a boat. This work should be done after finding out how the accident happened, and after getting as much information as possible about the incident. Without background knowledge, ancillary problems on the boat may be missed. Where the trouble arises from a failed mooring, underwriters sometimes ask for a report on the ground tackle.

The report on the boat (and the mooring for that matter) may list the repair techniques, the material to be used, and the precautions to be taken during and after the renewal work. Surveyors disagree about this detailing of rebuilding work; some say it is best to leave the specification of repairs to the boatbuilders doing the job. This can be risky if the yard is short of skill, experience or honesty.

Some people specialise in this type of survey work. They seldom venture out except to view a shattered hull or buckled mast. While specialisation has advantages, it also has its dangers. Unless the surveyor takes trouble to know about changing building techniques and the current manner in which boats are used, he may not fully appreciate the background to the damage he is inspecting. All surveyors have to beware of losing touch with changing times and techniques. It is easy when overworked to stop reading technical magazines and going to lectures. Keeping up with the necessary ongoing education can be hard for surveyors who often work on their own and have to run an office with the minimum staff. There are indications that anyone who does nothing but damage surveys is in danger of getting out of touch with the various changes that sweep through the boat industry.

There was one celebrated surveyor who got into a dangerous groove. His main activity was working with damaged craft and he therefore realised that he had to keep on good terms with insurance companies. He tried to do this by beating down quotations from boatyards, always saying that they were too high even when they were fair. Almost every damaged boat under his charge was the subject of a disagreement, since he invariably told the yard manager that unless the price for the repairs was reduced by 12% or 20%, the boat would be taken elsewhere to be mended. After he had taken this line for a few years he was rumbled. From then on all the local boatyards waited before making up the price for repairs to see if this fellow was going to be in charge of the case. When he was, the quotations were inflated by a substantial percentage. The yards then reluctantly agreed (during heated discussions) to lower the price by a modest amount, thus pulling the wool over the eyes of this surveyor and ending up well in profit. It took a few years for the underwriters to realise that this surveyor was putting up their costs by his lack of up-to-date knowledge and current boatbuilding experience.

Even when the surveyor is retained by an insurance company, he has a duty to the owner of the craft. Where a boat is needed back afloat quickly, the owner's interests may be served best by fitting a doubler or patch, or doing a quick, strong (but inelegant) repair. Particularly on old wooden boats, it is often bad practice when effecting a repair to take out frames or knees that have been in place a long time. Far better to put in a new scantling close by, through-fastened to the existing structure. On occasions where there is damage on the port side, it may be sensible to put a new piece on port *and* starboard sides to match and so end up with a good appearance plus some extra strength. For instance, where there are elegant wood cockpit coamings that are fitted in a complicated way, doublers on both sides may produce a neat practical repair. Rooting out or patching only one coaming can result in an uneven appearance.

When specifying renewal work, it is a case of 'horses for courses'. The work has to suit the type of craft and its use, as well as its future schedule. A contractor's launch is usually wanted back in service in a hurry: there are seldom reserve boats available and no one is going to mind about a fancy finish. In contrast, a nearly new yacht should be restored to pristine condition. A principle of insurance is that the person making a claim should end up in the same condition as before the accident, with goods that are neither better nor worse than they were before the event.

This important guideline can be a great help to surveyors who sometimes have to negotiate a deal for the owner or the insurance company. At times both sides will be happy to set one little advantage off against another small loss. For instance, an owner may want both sides of his vessel repainted, even though the damage is only noticeable on one side. The insurance company might turn this request down until the owner offers to do all the early dismantling of the furniture and clean out all the mud and rubbish that got inside the hull during the grounding. Surveyors learn to spot the owners who are honest and prepared for a little 'give and take' on both sides, in contrast to those who try to get a whole spring refit out of the underwriters when they are only due a limited repair.

Where a fibreglass hull is badly damaged, the owner may ask for a new hull, while the underwriters want to do a major rebuild of a shattered side. The final agreement may involve a cash payment to the owner, or he may get a new hull fully equipped with the original gear provided he agrees to some sort of concession. This might involve the owner himself taking all the old equipment off the original hull. The work of removing a complete set of fittings is time-consuming, but some owners will do it willingly in order to end up with the craft they want.

Insurance companies sell off badly damaged craft to specialist shipwrights and amateur boatbuilders. This sale partly offsets the cost of providing a new boat, but the buyer of one of these fractured hulls should be someone with experience and plenty of time, patience and skill. The mended craft may look perfect from the outside, but inside there are likely to be signs of repairs – though these may be covered by lining, panelling or furniture. The repaired boat is liable to have a lower resale value than an unblem-ished boat, which is why owners prefer new boats even though they have to contribute to the cost.

One of the surveyor's skills is in assessing whether it is cheaper to repair a seriously damaged hull or sell it off and provide a new replacement (or a cash payment). Sometimes the owner and underwriter cannot agree. They may fall out if the underwriters select a low-cost firm to do the repairs. The owner may know the company is not sufficiently skilled or experienced to make a good job, while the underwriter is principally interested in paying for the cheapest refurbishment. Surveyors take trouble finding out which boatbuilding companies are good at the different type of repair. One will be brilliant at fibreglass renewal – until perhaps the foreman retires or moves elsewhere; another will make a good job of steel repairs, but be inept at fibreglass renewal work. It is worth looking at all sorts of repair work while it is being done and when it has been completed, even though the boats in question are being monitored by other surveyors.

One aspect of repair work that causes controversy is the extent and strength of repairs. Some surveyors insist that the finished job should be stronger than the original structure, and I share this view. Other people insist that the renewal work should exactly match what was there before. This is fine on a racing boat, where added weight is a handicap. However, in all other cases there is bound to be a risk that the new joins are not quite perfect, so it is logical to extend the new work at least a little beyond the extent of the damage, and finish with thicknesses that are at least slightly greater than before. As a crude rule, I like to have about 15% extra thickness. This does not cost anything like 15% more, because there is often surplus repair material lying about, so it might as well be used up. The additional cost is often tiny – for instance, when making a fibreglass repair the actual layering on of the new glass is a relatively small part of the total work.

Apart from other considerations, it is good boatbuilding practice to make a repaired boat stronger than she was formerly in the area of the damage, and this principle is based on centuries of experience. When adding stiffness, regardless of what material is being used, the edges of the new material should be tapered out. Special care is needed to avoid 'hard spots' and sudden changes of strength. This is particularly important on light high-performance craft. It is sometimes found that an otherwise excellent shipwright or foreman may not appreciate the importance of this fairing out at the ends and edges, just as some do not realise the importance of staggering joins, and the need to avoid long straight lines of close-spaced fastenings.

When asking for changes or special features in a repair, a young surveyor needs tact. The people on the job may be old enough to be the grandparents of the surveyor, and have been doing boat repairs before the surveyor was born. However, there is another aspect to this matter of using tact: just once in a while the surveyor may be baffled about some aspect of a casualty. It may be hard to be sure why an accident happened, or what was the primary cause. A loose P-bracket can be caused by a rope round the shaft, a bump against flotsam, a worn shaft bearing, a misaligned engine, a pair of broken engine holding-down bolts, a loose coupling, a shaky engine bearer, or a combination of any of these. On occasions like this a quiet talk with one of the shipwrights doing the dismantling may suggest a line of inspection that makes the surveyor look like a brilliant detective.

Good surveyors take special trouble to discover the true cause of a failure because this is the one way to be sure that the defect does not reoccur – perhaps within a matter of days. One sees broken and bent stanchions frequently, but not everyone has the

experience to check the socket when arranging repairs. If the socket is the straight type, and the deck is well rounded, the top of the stanchion may be outboard of the topsides, and therefore vulnerable. Simply replacing the stanchion is not very clever. Either the new stanchion should be given a bend at the bottom to make the main length vertical, or a wedge should be inserted under the socket flange to make the tubular part vertical, or the socket should be changed for one that has a 'tilt-in' angle between the tube and the base flange.

When sleuthing around trying to discover the prime cause of a perplexing accident, it is tempting to leap gleefully on all sorts of easily seen evidence. A long thoughtful pause, followed by a careful search in and all round the damage, may throw up some surprising information. I'll always remember the time I discovered a small motor-cruiser sank because she had a slit between the cockpit drain outlet flange and the hull. The drain was well above water level, but only in calm water; however, this was a lively little boat, and she danced about when the waves played with her. Each time she threw up her bow and a wave went past her stern at the same time, that drain went under water and let in a cupful. In the course of a prolonged gale, this fault was enough to sink her.

. . . .

SURVEYING AFTER GROUNDING

Fibreglass boats have a variety of assets, but they are not good at withstanding bumps. The material, design and construction are not resistant to accident damage. In particular, the normal modern sailing yacht, with its steep-fronted short fin keel, seems especially designed to ensure the maximum of trouble when the boat goes aground.

In our office, when fibreglass first came out, we told owners to make sure they had reduced speed to 4 knots or less before a grounding occurred. However, within a year we were saying, 'If you think you may run aground, slow down to just 1 or 2 knots.' By the end of that year, our experience had changed our advice to, 'Don't run aground. Keep further offshore than you have done in the past. Consider fitting two echo sounders. If your yacht has its ballast encapsulated in fibreglass, think about padding the bottom of

the keel with extra chopped strand mat and woven roving epoxied-on.'

Short, deep fin keels, especially if made of incompressible iron, hit the sea-bed with a horrible crack. If the impact is on rock, the boat has to stop in a short distance, so the deceleration is frightening. The damage is often extensive, and much more severe than the first inspection indicates. The first inspection after a grounding can be an unsatisfactory business, because until it has been completed no one knows how much of the furniture has to be taken out, and which lining removed. Once the shipwrights have stripped out all the components that prevented a full inspection, the surveyor can get a better view – but not always a full view. So here we go again – the surveyor has to do a difficult job balancing the requirements of the owner and insurance company within the limitations of time, money and access inside the boat. The boatyard is expected to come up with a firm but competitive quotation for carrying out full repairs. Insurance underwriters and owners hate being told half-way through a rebuilding job that extra work has come to light when the damage is cut back.

In the middle of this fog of conflicting demands and financial interests, the surveyor has to maintain a balance. He also has to make sure that *all* the damage is put right. Everyone concerned, from owner to repairer, from underwriter to the local lifeboat crew, gets upset if the boat starts to fall apart again a few weeks after a repair. So when a surveyor is going round a boat that has run aground, he takes special note of cracks that disappear under a piece of panelling, or snake in behind the glassing of a bulkhead. He also looks at the seating and securing of everything heavy – and even things that are not so heavy.

A sudden stop when the yacht was bowling along under a tight-pressed spinnaker is likely to shift the mast forward. The bulkhead or glassed-in ply floor forward of the anchor chain may also jolt forward, fracturing the boundary join. This break may be right round the perimeter, or just at one corner, and may be hidden because it is filled with mud or covered by a glued-on flexible lining. It may be impossible to spot until the chain has been put overboard and some furniture, as well as some trim, has been eased out.

When a fin-keeled yacht grounds, the ballast may pivot about the top forward corner, so that a tear appears where the top aft corner jumps up. Sometimes the aft top corner acts as a pivot point, and the top forward corner swings down so that the hull shell tears here. Sometimes the forward top corner goes down *and* the aft corner goes up, so the hull has two breaks. These areas of damage vary according to how the hull is built, and what local reinforcing there is. An inexperienced surveyor may expect tears athwartships, so he will not spend time looking for rents that run fore and aft. He will not be surprised to find that the floors near the fore-and-aft ends of the fin keel having peeling glass, especially at their ends. In practice, if one floor has failed it is common for others to go. If there are six floors and three have clearly come adrift, the assumption must be that the others have at least been weakened, and all six should be strengthened during repairs.

Sometimes the muck in the bilge makes it hard to spot areas where the glassing-in has failed in a subtle way. Life is easy when there is a slit into which a

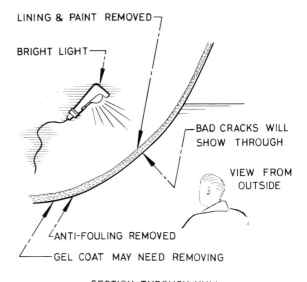

Fig 2 Detecting cracks in hulls

After an accident it can be hard to see cracks, especially if crack detecting fluids cannot be used. When cracks are strongly suspected, or there is a small area of cracking visible, it is logical to check the extent of the trouble by stripping off the anti-fouling, and setting up a strong light inside the hull. A standard 240 watt bulb, as used by photographers, gives out an intense bright light. It also generates a lot of heat.

If the damaged area is above the waterline it will be necessary to strip off the gel coat, and the same procedure may be needed on the underbody. Once a single crack has been detected, others should be expected, forming a pattern of concentric rings, or roughly parallel lines, or lines radiating out from the central point of impact.

surveyor's spike slithers confidently. It is more difficult when the glassing has not lifted up or visibly come away, and *appears* to be tight, snug and strong. If the keel bolts show signs of movement, in one way the surveyor's job is easier. All the bolts have to be taken out and their holes remade. Even a slightly ovalised hole cannot be left unrepaired. The hull shell along the centreline will require thickening during repairs, and if this means that new longer keel bolts are needed, this is good. Bolts that have been subject to a severe jolt may have hidden faults.

Of course the underwriters may say that new keel bolts should in part be paid for by the owner, especially if there are signs of corrosion. In the same way, if the mast has cracks at such places as the gooseneck or crosstree rivets, or where the runners are attached, the underwriters may point out that the mast is several years old, and therefore a portion of its life has been expended. They may insist that a proportion of the cost of a new spar is paid for by the owner. This requirement can apply to any component that the insurance organisation considers is being improved to the advantage of the owner. This replacement of a new part for one that has suffered use is known as 'betterment'.

Mast steps and support pillars suffer damage when grounding occurs at speed, or when the boat pounds on the shore. The mast acts like a battering ram working vertically. Bulkheads are always vulnerable to grounding, but especially when they are close to a mast. Isolated mast support pillars buckle, top and bottom flanges bend or break, padding under these flanges gets compressed or split, fastenings through the heel support as well as the pillar become twisted, or break, or become loose. Occasionally, the deck supporting the mast is forced down into a slight hollow. Splits and cracks may be found where the mast passes through the cabin top, especially (but not exclusively) forward of the mast. The tube of the mast may be dented here, or by the gooseneck. Racing boats are built lightly for speed, so when they ground they are likely to suffer far more damage than less lively boats.

The engine is a dead weight, and when the boat stops suddenly it tries to continue onwards. A few well-built large craft have special chocks forward of the engine feet to stop this tendency, but this precaution is seldom seen on craft under 46 ft (14 m). Even if there are blocks to keep the engine in place, they may not work – especially if the engine mountings are of the flexible type. Where there is a big gap between the top of the engine bearer and the underside of the strong paws on the engine, it is likely that the whole mass of the engine will lurch forward as much as the mountings will allow – or perhaps more.

After a severe grounding, the engine feet, the flexible mountings, the bearers and any floors in the area are all suspect. If one flexible mount fails, it is usual for the others to have to take an overload, so they break too. When they go, this puts unexpected strains on pipes linked to the engine, and also on control rods, the exhaust, and so on. Nothing can be cleared until it has been fully checked, and it may be advisable to check the engine alignment even if there seems to be no visible trouble. It is certainly important to have a full engine trial when the boat is put back in the water after repairs.

The ends and sides of the engine bearers sometimes have cracks or peeling glass. Holding-down bolts or coach-screws sometimes punch their way

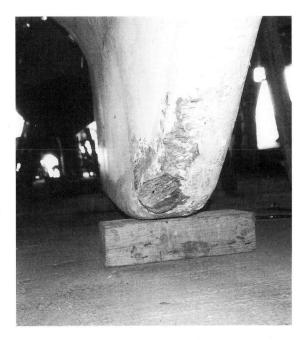

A large dent on the toe of the keel shows that there has been a violent grounding. It is possible that there will be other troubles associated with this type of accident such as loose tanks, and the engine may have sheared or bent holding down bolts. This traditionally built wood yacht needed attention to her keel bolts.

forward, so that they are no longer tight in their holes. It is conceivable that the coupling or its fastenings could be damaged. In a very severe accident the propeller shaft may slide forward till the propeller is bashed against the stern-bearing housing – with all sorts of severe results.

Tanks are trouble-makers. The current trend is to fit them with what is considered to be just adequate securing arrangements, but the person who does this 'considering' is not always the original designer – or anyone with adequate engineering experience. He may be someone who is trying to reduce production costs, or speed up the hull building. Too often he thinks that a tank-holding strap is properly secured if it has just one bolt at each end, or he does not know that wood wedges and chocks need full securing in place. Short flanges or lugs on tanks fracture easily, and fastenings through them sheer through, or tear out or bend. If the tank is partly held in place by the pipes that lead to it, there may be breaks at the welded joins, or at flexible joins. The structure at the fore end of a tank is vulnerable, and if it is a thin bar it may break or bend so much that its end fastenings fail.

It is important, when listing the damage that occurs on any boat, to get a full description of the accident from the crew. This may throw up valuable nuggets of information. If the helmsman has gone to hospital with broken ribs, it is worth checking the steering wheel for subtle bends and it may be that some of the binnacle base bolts have failed. If one of the crew was standing in a hatchway when the grounding occurred, he may be in pain – and so forget to tell anyone his weight broke the hatch-top or its handles. Deck fittings are not likely to suffer much, except perhaps the runner and backstay chain plates. However, when the boat is hauled off the ground, damage frequently occurs. If the rescuing craft is large, heavy and unwieldy, she may cause more damage than the original grounding, especially if she ranges alongside to get a tow-line on board.

If the craft giving help touches the grounded boat there will be scratches to the topsides or worse. A severe bump will shift internal bulkheads and furniture. In any case, even when there is no other vessel involved, the edges of the bulkheads have to be checked to see if the glassing-in has peeled off or fractured. The bulkheads themselves sometimes distort out of line, or move forward. One or more may even shift backwards at the fore end of the vessel where the hull tapers outwards as it runs aft, and so forms a wedge that tends to force loose bulkheads backwards. Doorposts and corner posts on bulk-heads may be split or wrenched off, perhaps at one end only. When this sort of failure occurs deep down in a bilge or above the deckhead lining, it can be hard to see – especially if the boat has been holed and there is a lot of mud on board, as well as discoloration as a result of saturation. A survey after grounding cannot be rushed.

Furniture is normally lightly secured, so it may be split or cracked in unexpected places. Where it is attached to bulkheads that have moved, there is almost bound to be a need for repairs. If the floors have been jolted up, the settee fronts are likely to need reseating and resecuring. Anything heavy fixed to the forward face of a bulkhead may have torn free, at least partly. A heavy fire extinguisher that is secured to a bulkhead by a few little screws may become detached when the boat halts suddenly.

To sum up, a grounding may not at first seem severe, but in practice there is often much more damage than the first inspection indicates. The inspection should be comprehensive and not just in the areas of obvious damage. Often the examination has to be in at least two stages: the first when the boat is slipped, and the second when she is opened up. It is not unusual for a fin keel to damage the hull to the extent that it has to be taken right off to allow the shell to go back to its correct shape, and make it possible for the shipwrights to reinforce the hull in way of the keel.

DIAGONAL DAMAGE

There is a special type of damage that happens in all types of small craft. It can occur regardless of whether the boat is well or badly built, and it is found in vessels of all materials. It is called diagonal damage, and it can be the result of a collision with another craft, or bashing into a quay, or toppling over while on shore.

When a wooden packing case is kicked hard at one edge the rectangular form becomes diamond-shaped. All four edges change from right angles; two become more than 90 degrees and two become less as shown in Fig 3. The same trouble occurs in boats when there is an impact.

A surveyor doing an inspection after an accident has to check not only the area that has incurred the bump, but also the area diagonally opposite. A crack in a dinghy at the port edge of the transom may be matched by damage on the starboard side forward. Sometimes there will be damage on both sides of the transom and on both sides near the stem. Perhaps the surprising thing is that when a boat falls over ashore she can have damage not just at the turn of the bilge that crashes on to the ground, but also at the opposite bilge. This problem is seen especially in lightly built wooden craft with bent or sawn frames. If the accident occurs when the boat is drying out along-side, the damage on the side that hits the water or mud may be less than on the 'uphill' side. There have

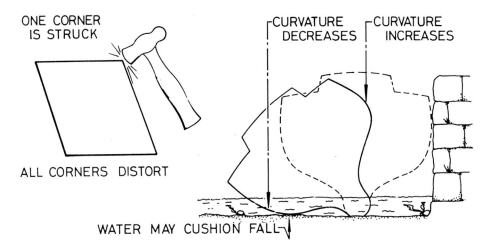

ONE CORNER IS STRUCK

ALL CORNERS DISTORT

CURVATURE DECREASES

CURVATURE INCREASES

WATER MAY CUSHION FALL

Fig 3

Whenever a boat is found to have damage at one edge or corner, the opposite edges and corners should be examined. A structure distorts when it is in collision, and fractures occur at any line of relative weakness such as an edge or sharply curved region.

A typical example occurs when a boat falls over. The side that strikes the ground occasionally has little or no damage because the water and mud cushion the fall. The frames are sometimes found to be fractured at the opposite turn of bilge because they have been jolted into a tighter curve. This trouble occurs particularly when the boat has a tall mast.

---

been instances of boats that have fallen over without any damage on the downward side because it was cushioned by the water or mud. On the other side, as the curvature has increased suddenly and perhaps quite sharply, frames have broken and seams opened.

Sometimes a stiff scantling such as a strong bulkhead is given a severe nudge, which may cause damage at both sides. A severe blow that causes cracks along the bottom of a cabin coaming on the port side may be matched by less marked, but still serious, fracturing on the starboard side. Though fibreglass is a flexible material and it often absorbs blows, it cannot totally avoid the effects of this diagonal damage. When an impact causes any sort of

damage, the inspection should extend all over the hull. The sort of trouble to expect is vertical cracks down from the gunwale, roughly opposite to the place where the main damage is seen.

In the same way, if a mast support pillar sags, it is not enough to seek damage on the cabin top deck where the mast heel sits. There may be cracking or distortion at the outer edges of the cabin top deck and at the bottom of the coamings. If one leg of a pulpit is torn up, there is liable to be trouble near the deck flanges of the other feet. In short, damage often spreads not just outwards from the point of impact, but is found in separate and quite remote areas, often with no linking cracks or signs of trouble.

The topsides and deck edge of this small cruiser have been badly gouged. When surveying this type of accident it is necessary to remove the cabin lining to see the extent of the damage. In practice, the full extent of the trouble cannot always be assessed until damaged parts have been dismantled.

TOOLS AND EQUIPMENT

. . . .

PORTABLE LADDERS

Without a ladder, it is usually impossible to get on to a boat. More ladders are stolen than wear out, so owners chain them to something strong. Boatyards seldom have enough of them, so the sensible thing is for the surveyor to have his own. It has to be long enough to reach from the ground up to the average deck height, but small enough to fit inside a car when folded. This is one reason for having an estate car, and an excellent reason for avoiding a very small vehicle. If the ladder will not go inside the car, it will have to go on a roof rack.

The ideal ladder is a folding aluminium one that lasts for ever, is light, does not corrode, and is cheap. When opened up it will deal with most situations if it is 4 m (13 ft) long, but to be safe, the 5 m (16 ft) size is best. The surveyor must purchase the type that locks firmly when open in order to avoid accidents.

The top needs lots of padding. This can be made from pieces of carpet or closed-cell foam plastic or cloth. To make sure the padding stays on in spite of rain, hard work and general abuse, it needs bolting in place. All the bolts have to go across the ladder, in line with the treads, so that they cannot protrude and scratch the hull against which the ladder rests. Bol-ting on may not prove easy, and strips of duct tape over rags work fairly well, but need annual renewal. The top of the ladder should have a pair of 1 m (3 ft) long lines, about 6 mm ($\frac{1}{4}$ in) in diameter. These ropes are spliced on to the top tread, and used for lashing on to stanchions or cleats. The surveyor's name should be painted in big letters on the sides of the ladder partly to let the world know who is about and how careful he is to have the best equipment, but also to deter thieves.

Anyone who has a problem getting a sufficiently long folding ladder might make do with the longest available, but also have a wood or metal flat-topped sea-chest for carrying the survey gear. If the chest is strongly made and about $750 \times 450 \times 450$ mm ($30 \times 18 \times 18$ in), it can be used to stand the ladder on for extra height. A fiddle along the middle of the top will stiffen the lid and prevent the foot of the ladder from sliding off. This size of chest will also carry all the tools, wandering leads, spare batteries, bulbs and flashlights, as well as note-books, that a surveyor could possibly need. It should have a lid with a lip all round so that rain will not run inside, and a carrying handle at each end.

. . . .

LIGHTS FOR SURVEYING

Mains lighting

The best type of lighting for a surveyor is a wandering lead or fully portable light. Some of my American friends call it a 'trouble lamp', which just about sums up this useful tool. If one is surveying in Europe it is handy to know that the French word is 'La Balladeuse', which literally means 'A ballet-dancer'. This is highly descriptive because this lamp does flit about lighting up everything it looks at.

Even the best flashlight can only be described as a moderately adequate substitute for mains lighting. Ordinary shipwrights' lights in a boat, which are fixed up under the deckhead and are not portable, are not satisfactory. These days it is common to see long tube lights in each cabin, giving the people working on board a good light environment. However, a surveyor needs a beam of illumination directed into the

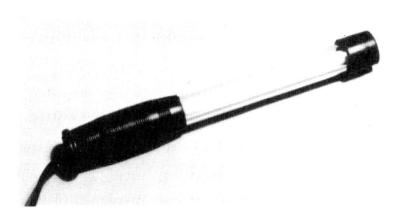

A shatterproof portable neon light makes a good surveyor's torch. It needs an ample length of cable, so that it can be lowered into deep bilges and tanks.

dark remote corners, down small spaces between structure, under engines, and in the depths of small lockers. Therefore he needs a wandering lead.

Mains lighting is so much better than flashlights that I have considered carrying a small portable generator in my car. I do in fact take with me a long electric cable that will stretch from one end of a large boatyard almost to the other end — so that what starts out as 240 volts, trickles into my lamp at a rather more feeble level due to voltage loss. This long lead is useful partly because one so often works on boats that are located far away from electric sockets, partly because all adjacent sockets are often already occupied by other users. I also carry two-way plugs so that I can share a socket with someone else.

A well-protected wandering lead is needed with a wire guard over one side of the bulb and a shade over the other to prevent the light shining back into the surveyor's eyes. In spite of the guard, light bulbs more often break than wear out, so two spare bulbs have to be available. For most jobs, 60 watt bulbs are best, with transparent glass so that when the light fails it is easy to see that the filament is broken, and no time is wasted tracing blown fuses and the primitive connections found in some boatyards.

The type of lamp that has a clamp or spring-loaded alligator clip is best. It can be put on a bulkhead edge, gripped on to a fiddle or grab rail, or on to a bunk front. Care is needed to prevent the clamp from damaging furniture. It may pay to glue on layers of cloth or soft foam plastic to give a soft grip if the clamp has sharp teeth.

It is possible to get wandering leads that have tubular or neon lights, and sometimes these are almost unbreakable. They may also be quite small in diameter, so they can be lowered into small spaces.

Some boats have their own wandering leads, and it is possible to get the type of light that works off a car cigarette lighter or directly off the battery. It is important to watch for a falling voltage, otherwise the boat may be left with no power to start the engine. A car can have the same trouble, and I have taken care to park on a hill before now, so as to start the car by running down the slope.

The combination of low voltage and low amperage combined with a loss of voltage along the wire results in poor illumination. However, one of the best lights I have ever used was in an aircraft hangar; it was specially made for the aircraft industry. The light body was constructed of aluminium, complete with a clamp and shade. The whole thing was compact, but gave superb illumination using mains electricity converted to a low voltage for safety. The light beam was directed and not over-diffused, and the unit could be easily slid into cramped spaces. Unlike normal wandering leads, it did not get hot after an hour's use.

Flashlights

Two torches are needed because they live a rough life, run out of battery power, and get dropped into water-filled bilges. When working in engine compartments, grease gets on to tools, and torches may slither out of the grasp and end up far below and unreachable.

The type of rubber torch that has a ring in the end to take a wrist loop has advantages. However, even rubber torches rebel after they have been constantly dropped or trodden on. One of the skills a surveyor learns is to use the flashlight with the opposite hand to his writing hand, so he does not have to remove the line looped round his wrist every time he makes additional notes or uses his dictating machine.

Some people buy the cheapest flashlights because they reckon the life expectancy of flashlights is short. Others buy the best and hope that the torch will be tough enough to stand the pace. I once bought a superb railwayman's torch, as big as a brick and twice as tough. It was bright yellow (so not easily lost) and made of a light alloy with plastic skin to prevent corrosion. The battery lasted for ages, but cost a lot to replace. I was delighted with it till I noticed how many people tried to acquire it, by fair means or foul. It seemed to 'fall' into other people's kitbags. It got 'mislaid' when I had finished a survey, so that I had to spend too much time finding which locker it had been tidied into. People 'needed to borrow it' to find lost tools in the back of their car, in the bilge of the adjacent boat, and in boat stores at the other end of the yard.

I prefer a very good-quality flashlight, because it tends to have a bright concentrated beam. Expensive torches have powerful bulbs and effective reflectors, which improve performance. My rechargeable Black and Decker gives good service, but does not have a warning device to indicate when the light is about to fail. However, its modest weight and relatively low price are assets in its favour. I like rechargeable batteries for the ordinary tubular type of flashlight, as they save a great deal of money over a year's hard surveying. Miners' lights, which fix on to a hat or on to a band round the head, have never attracted me, but they appeal to some people. The modern light-weight type is best, with the rechargeable battery attached to a belt. These rather specialised lights are sold in some sports shops, and by some engineering wholesale suppliers.

· · · · · · · · · ·

Tools

Spikes and screwdrivers

A good all-round tool for surveying many types of material is a 200 mm (8 in) screwdriver with the blade end sharpened from the normal 6 mm ($\frac{1}{4}$ in) down to a round point of about 1 mm ($\frac{1}{16}$ in) diameter. Fig 4 shows the sort of taper that seems to be just right for so many jobs. The end will need regrinding after a large number of surveys. This tool is fine for checking that fibreglass stringers have no weak points, such as where the cloth has not been properly lapped. It is ideal for sliding down the faces of glassed-in bulkheads and furniture to make sure that the edge of the fibreglass is not peeling. For wood, it is unrivalled – as it will tell the difference between a soft grade of timber like spruce and wood that has lost strength, but not yet got galloping rot; and where there is rampaging rot, it shows up the trouble without leaving a trail of marks that will make the boat unsellable. The owner will not be able to accuse the surveyor of doing excessive damage either.

Different people like different handles. I prefer a smooth screwdriver top, with no serrations, ribs or other finishes that are supposed to improve grip, but just raise blisters after a hard day's work. A cork is needed on the end when the spike is not in use, to prevent puncturing clothes and people.

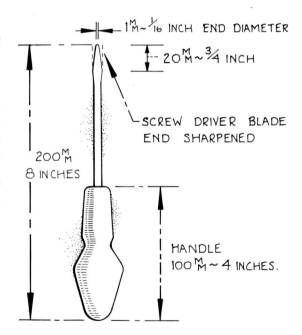

Fig 4 General surveying tool

A standard plastic-handled screwdriver with the blade end ground to a rounded point makes a good tool for surveyors. It makes it easy to detect peeling glassfibre and rotten wood, it is handy for lifting tight floorboards and it is useful for scraping anti-fouling off rudder edges and many similar jobs.

Another screwdriver, similar to the long-handled electrician's type, with the end less sharpened, is handy for reaching under engines and into awkward distant corners. This tool is typically 325 mm (13 in) long, with a blade about 5 mm ($\frac{3}{16}$ in) in diameter. It too needs a cork over the end. Surveyors who wish to impress their clients use champagne corks!

These two spikes are good for prising up floor-boards, but for heavy work a large screwdriver is needed. This needs to be about 350 mm (14 in) long with a blade diameter of around 10 mm ($\frac{3}{8}$ in) and a blade end roughly the same. This tool is good for taking out big screws, lifting loose paint off, easing lining edges gently away from deckheads, and so on. Some surveyors use a jemmy for this and other more strenuous work, and find it excellent for prising up seized sole boards. It is simply a small crow-bar with the end bent over. It is favoured by burglars, so it might be inadvisable to wave it about too much in public.

It seems to me that the use of bradawls is no longer as widespread as formerly, but of course surveyors rarely work as teams, so it may be that this little spike is as popular as ever. It drops under engines and into the bilge easily, so there should be two or three in the surveyor's tool-bag. For recovering tools from deep bilges, a powerful magnet on a length of line is another tool to take along.

Using a knife for surveying can be risky. It may cut in where there was no fault. When used on wood, the difference between the feel of the blade going in across or along the grain is disconcerting and mis-leading. Most blade ends are too sharp to detect the difference between soft wood in good condition and hard wood that is beginning to soften. Shipwrights often use knife points to test boats in a few places, but this intermittent exploration is not to be com-pared with a full day-long survey.

Hammers

A hammer with replaceable striking surfaces at each end of the head is used for fibreglass and wood ves-sels. A semi-hard rubber nose can be used on plastic hulls, but if a metal hammer is used serious damage will be done to the surface. For wood, a hard nylon hammer face is excellent. It can be used on good paintwork without causing damage, provided it is not plied with excessive energy. This type of hammer nose is also useful on aluminium.

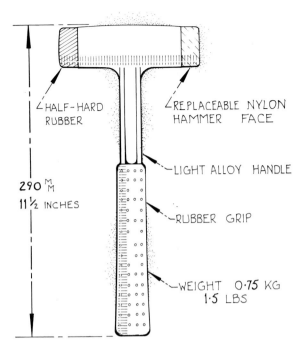

Fig 5 General purpose soft hammer

For testing the strength of a fibreglass hull, a rubber-nosed hammer has many virtues. It will not damage the hull shell unless the structure is exceedingly light – almost certainly too light to go to sea. It leaves no mark unless the face has become gritty or the hammer is used with excessive force. The nylon end is good for testing wood hulls for rot. It can normally be used on a freshly painted hull, provided the paint has had time to dry hard, and the blows are kept down to a firm but not excessive 'round-arm swing'.

For testing fastenings, one wants a conventional steel-headed hammer that gives a bit of punch. A swift tap on a nut or bolt head with a 100 g (4 oz) hammer – one of those long-handled small-headed tools that is sometimes called a pin hammer – will sheer off the bolt end if there is serious corrosion present. On a vessel over, say, 12 m (40 ft), a larger hammer, about 0.75 kg ($1\frac{1}{2}$ lb), is needed for this job. The same hammer is useful for testing steel plating on hulls, tanks, and so on. Some surveyors use a 1.8 kg (4 lb) hammer on rough craft like rugged fish-ing boats, both wood and steel. Using this weight all day is demanding, and the surveyor may run out of steam and alertness so that his concentration fades. This is a dangerous condition.

Hammers, like all surveyors' tools, need sympath-etic handles. The grip must be easy, but not slippery. Working high up on staging or over a deep bilge there should perhaps be a loop at the end of the handle to slip over the wrist, so that the hammer is not dropped. This precaution can be added to other tools. Balance is important in all tools, but especially hammers. For steel surveying, I had a superb bashing tool, specially made. Its basis was an ordinary steel hammer head taken from a 0.75 kg (1½ lb) standard conventional affair. The wood handle was removed and a stainless steel tubular one substituted, complete with rubber grip. On top of the head a 'centre-pop' was welded, with its sharp end outwards. A 'centre-pop' is a tapered rod of hardened steel with a sharp point. It is intended for such jobs as marking metal, for instance where a hole is to be drilled. This sharp point would find weaknesses in steel plating with a speed and efficiency that makes ordinary hammering seem primitive.

I have tried using a tiler's hammer. This has a small striking face at one end of the head and a curved sharp-ended beak at the other. The bend in the sharp end is a nuisance and I have had to grind away part of the pointed striking nose. This hammer is adequate, but nowhere near as good as my special hammer.

Drills and gauges and measuring rules

Generally speaking, a shipwright will be called in to do any drilling that is needed, especially on a metal boat. This is because the surveyor will seldom have time, and also because there may be limitations about who can do what in the boatyard. However, in some out-in-the-wilds locations, the surveyor may have no help and will have to do all the work himself.

For metal hulls it is best to use 10 mm (⅜ in) diameter bits, and electrically powered drills. There are times when it pays to drill a small pilot hole first in order to speed up the work. A 12 volt drill used off the boat's battery or a car battery can be useful, but these tools tend to lack muscle and the work can be slow as a result. Cordless drills are a great asset. They are rather bulky, and sometimes even with a traditional compact electric drill one needs a right-angle drive on the end to get into an awkward corner of the bilge.

The surveyor needs a gauge that will measure the plate thickness in the drilled hole. It can be a hook rule or small vernier caliper. Some calipers will not go through a little hole until the end has been ground away.

For general measuring, a steel self-rerolling 2 m (6 ft) tape is best because it lives comfortably in the pocket in spite of the hectic life of the surveyor, as he goes down into deep dark holes, up masts, and into impossibly small lockers. The traditional shipwright's folding rule will not last two surveys without being broken — unless of course the surveyor is not trying hard enough, and not getting into those inaccessible holes. This self-stowing rule is handy for measuring headroom, berth lengths and widths where these seem inadequate, and so on.

A long tape is needed for major measurements, with 1 m (3 ft) of light line on the end ring for securing the tape. This is used to measure the boat's length, beam, and so on. A roll of coloured plastic electrician's tape is handy for sticking down a tape end, repairing tools, marking defects, and so on.

· · · · · · · · · · · · ·

MIRRORS

In most boats there are areas that are inaccessible. This means they seldom get checked, and the structure (as well as fittings and furnishings) are neglected. Hidden crannies are not dried or painted or even cleaned. This is a recipe for trouble and these unreachable areas are precisely where a surveyor should try to pry. Sometimes the only way to peer into these recesses is by using a mirror.

A suitable mirror must be large enough to give a good view, but small enough to squeeze into the limited space. Those mirrors made for women's handbags are easily obtainable and about the right size. To give a good reach, the mirror is taped on to a stick. Ordinary electrician's plastic tape works well and helps to protect the mirror a little. The stick can be a broom handle or stiff sail batten. Typically, it will be 60 or 120 cm (2 or 4 ft) long, and strong enough to stand up to the rugged life of surveying. More mirrors are broken than wear out, so a good case can be made for having two or three in the kitbag. Unbreakable mirrors are available, but not easy to find. The best thing is to have a selection of different sizes, each with a soft protective bag to fit on before stowing the mirror away. A small flashlight can be taped on, facing the same way as the mirror, to illuminate the awkward corners.

It takes time getting used to working with a mirror, especially in places like the deep bilges of steel craft where everything tends to be the same matt washed-out rusty colour. Spotting corrosion where there seems to be nothing but slimy mud and bilge-water requires experience. Everything seen in a mirror is (not surprisingly) a mirror image and this can be confusing.

It can help to have one or two extra-long-handled tools to use with the mirror, such as a spike and hammer. To be ideal, these long-handled tools need to be in sections so that the end 20 or 30 cm (8 or 12 in) can be turned at an angle and clamped. They can then be used to tap and poke round distant corners where the mirror suggests something interest-ing is happening to the structure. Such things cannot be bought and have to be made up specially.

Under and behind engines are places where a mirror is handy. Behind and beneath tanks there are often quite large spaces that can only be inspected with a mirror. Sometimes it is possible to lower a wandering lead or flashlight on a line into the hidden space to give a good view.

There is a temptation to use mirrors instead of climbing into lockers that are accessible but awkward. After a gruelling day's work it is easy to feel that a quick glance in a mirror is good enough. However, it is never as effective as a straight line of sight inspection, especially if the mirror has become muddied during the day's work. Not every surveyor uses a mirror. Some are wary of them; some feel they are a waste of time. Surveying is as much an art as a science, and not all artists, or scientists, use the same equipment.

GROUND SHEETS AND WATERPROOF NOTE-BAGS

Many surveys are done in the winter, out in the open. The ground is wet or muddy, or covered in snow, but the surveyor has to get down on his knees to see the lower parts of the boat, and sometimes lie on his back to view the underside of the keel. He is human: he does not like getting soaked and muddy early in the day, so that he is filthy and cold for the remaining long hours.

If he is old and wise he obtains a ground sheet. This is a piece of strong, wide waterproof cloth that is tough enough to stand up to gritty ground. It is sometimes possible to buy these sheets in camping stores, or a piece of boat cover may do. I prefer a special sheet, made from the sort of rugged PVC cloth used for mainsail covers. This material comes in widths of about 2 m (6 ft), and a length of about 3 m (9 ft) is ample. If it is too big it will blow about in gale conditions. It does not need seaming round the edge, but I prefer to have this sewn edging, so that metal eyelets can be hammered in at 500 mm (18 in) intervals all round. Then, if it is seriously windy, one edge can be lashed down to the boat trailer or to pegs driven into the ground. No sheet or anything made of cloth should be lashed to individual boat props, otherwise a gust may cause the prop to be whipped out from under the boat and she could topple over.

In continuous rain a ground sheet with reinforced holes all round can be rigged over the boom to form a cockpit tent. This is a wonderful asset in torrential conditions, especially if the surveyor is using a dictating machine, or he wants be on deck to make notes about the cockpit and surrounding fittings.

Many sailmakers stock PVC cloth, and will sell you a short length. If the material is available in widths of about 1 m (approximately 3 ft), a sailmaker will stitch up a couple of widths and waterproof the seam. Pockets may be sewn on at each corner to take heavy stones that will hold the sheet down in windy weather. Heavy-duty polythene sheeting, as sold by building suppliers, can be used for ground sheets, but it does not always withstand hard usage for very long. However, it is cheap – provided a short length and not a complete roll can be bought. Some suppliers call it '1500 gauge'.

Writing notes in wet conditions is a discouraging activity. If the paper gets soggy it disintegrates, and biros will not operate on damp surfaces. There are ways round this problem, such as using waterproof paper and special 'underwater' biros. However, both of these are expensive and not universally obtainable. One answer is to use transparent plastic bags, big enough to hold the note pad, and with enough space inside to write as well. The bag has to be held with the opening facing downwards all the time, otherwise drips will run down the sleeves and into the bag. Experience demonstrates that it is best to have three or four bags and a supply of writing paper kept dry in the car, in case one bag does get water inside.

Another technique for taking notes is to use a rainproof marker pen on stiff plastic sheets. This works fine for a limited amount of writing, but I usually end up with more than 20 pages of closely packed scribble – and sometimes as much as 60 pages on a 24 m craft (an 80 footer) – so I need lots of writing space.

KEELS AND BILGES

· · · · · · · · · · · · · · · · · ·

Ballast Keels

There is often a non-stop battle between surveyors and boat brokers. The latter claim that surveyors stop sales going through by being unnecessarily fussy about alleged defects. Some brokers are only interested in the profits they make in the current month and do not appear to worry about selling dangerous craft. Others seem oblivious to the need to build up a reputation for selling only good craft that will delight their new owners and not cause any trouble.

Surveyors worry a lot about the vast range of problems that can arise in anything that floats. They also agonise about the possibility of being sued for missing some real or imagined defect. It is one of life's injustices that untrustworthy brokers seldom get sued. Surveyors, who have a job that is difficult and sometimes impossible, get sued far more often.

The design of keels and the ballasting of sailing yachts causes endless disputes between surveyors and brokers. The latter often say that surveyors should only report on galloping rust, rot, serious corrosion, cracks and similar easily seen defects. However, surveyors are always aware that their job is to save life and property. If a sailing yacht cannot fight her way off a lee shore in a gale, the crew may be killed or injured and the boat lost or damaged. The keel is critical in this matter.

The ability to go to windward in severe conditions depends to a great extent on the depth and weight of the ballast keel. If a surveyor thinks that a yacht is seriously short of ballast, he should mention this in his report. Ideally he should give figures. As a crude basic rule, the ballast should form at least one-third of the total weight of the whole craft. It is usual to state the condition as: the ballast ratio should be at least 33%. Racing boats often have ratios above 50%.

One reason why some ferro-cement craft perform so badly is that they have heavy hull and deck shells, and thus cannot carry enough ballast. The same used to be said of small steel sailing yachts, but with the coming of epoxy paints their scantlings can be thinner – and so a bigger proportion of the total weight is ballast. Shallow draught boats, very heavily built cruisers, motor sailers and extremely cheap boats are liable to have dangerously low ballast ratios. These are all vessels that tend to be at risk in gales when land is too near. These boats lurch to leeward each time a wave breaks under them, or a squall blasts down, because they have no 'grip' on the water.

A reliable engine, or better still two, does give a factor of safety in bad weather. This is why a motor sailer, especially a large one, may be classified as safe even if she has a ballast ratio of only 25%. Even here, though, it is important to take a cautious view, because the propeller must be well immersed and at least relatively slow-turning.

Of course an estuary cruiser may be considered satisfactory with a fairly low ratio, on the basis that she is never far from safety. However, this type of yacht tends to be small, and the smaller the boat, the more important it is to have a high ratio. Besides, there are widely differing views about what an 'estuary cruiser' is. There was one class of mini-cruiser that seemed to everyone (except the designer and builders) to be under-ballasted. When the mark II version came out, no one was surprised that it had more ballast. The mark III pattern had even more ballast. The sales leaflets handed out at boat shows described how two of these tubs had made ocean crossings. The implication was that these were 'go anywhere' boats. However, many surveyors were convinced that they were no such thing. When inspecting them on behalf of buyers, they said – or hinted broadly in their reports – that these little craft were under-ballasted and dangerous. Many brokers protested vociferously because there were hordes of these boats around and constituted a steady trade in the secondhand market.

If the ballast can be seen, it is sometimes possible to work out fairly easily what it weighs, but this is not much help unless the total weight of the vessel is known. Experienced surveyors build up a knowledge of typical boat weights, and this makes it possible to spot a blatant case of under-ballasting. There are other factors that have to be taken into account though, such as the hull size and shape and the effect of the crew's weight on the weather sidedeck. On racing boats it is common to see a row of people perched along the deck-edge where their combined weight helps the yacht to stand up to the breeze, but when this boat can no longer win races and is sold off – perhaps to someone who wants to do long-distance cruising – there may no longer be a big crew on board.

It can be impossible to decide how much ballast there is in an encapsulated keel. Even if the ballast can be clearly seen on top, down inside a steel fin, it can be impossible to be sure what the total weight is. Some builders mix lead and iron, others mix iron and cement. Some use heavily rusted iron that 'weighs light', and not all builders follow the designer's instructions. A few designers do not appreciate the importance of ample ballast when battling off a lee shore.

Damage to a keel that holds internal ballast must be described in detail when making out a survey report. Fibreglass that shows signs of delaminating, with the cloth layers separating, needs extensive and very careful renewal. There may be widespread cracking that is not visible to the eye. When detailing the repairs it is usually best to ask for the finished job to be thicker and stronger than the original structure. This is partly to cope with the next accident, partly to ensure that unseen damage is dealt with, and partly for the peace of mind of everyone concerned. After a bad grounding the encapsulated chunks of ballast may be seen, half falling out of the keel. Sometimes there is a hollow, showing that some ballast has been left behind where the boat grounded. Before reglassing, new ballast has to be forced in to fill the gap, but first the whole area needs careful cleaning to get rid of every trace of sand, mud and salt water. The weight of a bolted-on fin keel is hard to assess without taking a lot of measurements and thicknesses at different points. Some fins are a mixture of materials, which increases the difficulties yet further.

If a boat is seen to have a lot less ballast than a sister ship, this can be a useful indicator that all is not well. Where one boat has lead and another iron, the latter must be treated with suspicion until there is proof that she is satisfactory. Lead weighs nearly twice as much as iron, which in turn is nearly four times as heavy as cement. The latter is only twice as heavy as water and is often unsatisfactory as ballast. It is used because it is cheap and convenient. A surveyor's dilemma when he finds a shortage of ballast is sharpened because he cannot simply recommend an increase in the total ballast weight. Extra stiffening may be needed to support the additional load. Additional frames and floors are needed, or occasionally more stringers.

The outside surface of an exterior keel is not important on most commercial craft, and on many cruisers. However, on racing boats it is critical and has to be as smooth as the rest of the hull. Getting an iron keel smooth is not too difficult, but if it is to stay smooth for years it should be grit blasted down to the bare metal. It is then painted with epoxy, and filled with an epoxy compound just like any other steel or iron surface. There must be a proper build-up of paint with the anti-fouling put on after a suitable base or barrier coating. The timing intervals of all these layers has to be exact, as laid down by the manufacturers. Sometimes a surveyor finds peeling paint or small areas of rust. This can be the result of applying the paints wrongly, or in too cold a temperature, or when there is moisture in the atmosphere. Sharp edges on an iron keel will not retain paint, so these should be faired off to at least a small radius before the grit blasting is started. If the keel is of lead, it is fairly easy to smooth off by taking off the protuberances and filling the hollows. However, this can be a slow job and therefore expensive, because of the awkward location.

A gouge in the lead tells the surveyor the boat has been aground. If the jagged rent is at the fore end and deep, it suggests the grounding occurred when the yacht was moving fast, so there may well be other damage. It should be expected in the hull by the top corners of the fin, at the mast heel because the spar sometimes jolts forward, on the engine beds, and where heavy tanks are secured. If there is denting only at the heel of the keel, the yacht may have bumped the sea bed when she was at anchor, and swung into the shallows. This may cause trouble where the top aft corner of the fin touches the hull, or at the floors or bulkheads. Gouges in lead are a hint that the surveyor should peer inside and outside the hull for further damage. Lots of criss-cross scratches on lead, or a polished appearance on an iron keel, suggest there have been plenty of meetings with the sea bed. This in turn indicates the owner is inept, careless or unlucky. Whichever it is does not much matter so far as the surveyor is concerned – he knows he can expect ample other trouble throughout the vessel.

When a severe grounding occurs, the whole fin or lump of ballast may have shifted. In very bad cases the keel bolts can be seen to have tilted, or to have torn their round holes into slight ovals. There will probably be leaks at each bolt, though sometimes the bedding between the ballast and the hull is so soft and pliable it continues to keep the water at bay. In passing, it is worth noting that a keel bolt hole that has become even slightly ovalised needs filling and redrilling, or a larger bolt may be fitted. It is important that all the keel bolts fit their holes very snugly.

Just because the ballast does not appear to fit well does not mean that the boat has run ashore violently. Plenty of quite well-constructed craft have ill-fitting keels, so that the stopping on the mating surface has to fill notable gaps. The surveyor may have to make a decision as to whether the ballast was originally badly fitted, or was made with a top surface that does not match the underside of the hull, or has been bashed badly and moved slightly. One cruiser class has had the position of the ballast fin keel shifted forward since the first batch of boats was built, because it was found they trimmed down at the stern. All the subsequent boats looked better afloat, but the top of the fin keels do not exactly fit the hulls. The shipwrights making these boats tighten the keel bolts energetically, and the fibreglass shell is partly pulled down to the keel flange by force. Copious bedding fills the rest of the gap.

It is a good idea when surveying to check other boats of the same class (if there are any in the same boatyard) to see how well their keels fit, or whether they have the same signs of poor matching. However, as the above anecdote shows, not all boats of the same class are built in precisely the same way.

A study of the keel bolt washers inside sometimes tells a tale. Cracks emanating from the side of a keel bolt washer suggest there has been a violent grounding, as do washers that have moved. The indications here will probably be very subtle, but, if a washer has apparently shifted just a fraction, this is something that needs urgent investigation.

Where the ballast is encased in a fibreglass, steel or aluminium hull shell, there must be an excellent

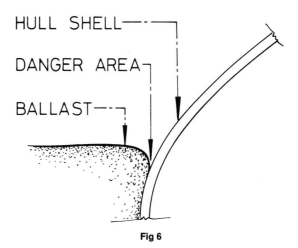

Fig 6

Any type of hull that has ballast inside should be examined very closely around the edge of the top seam. If there is a depression at the edge of the covering over the ballast, water tends to lie and cause trouble. Steel, aluminium and fibreglass hulls all suffer from defects of the shell if water can lie in this type of depression. The cure is to clean out the gutter and fill it with a compound that adheres well to the hull and ensures that any puddle left in the bilge is on top of the ballast sealing and drains away from the shell.

seal over the top. Water that seeps down to ballast causes a batch of problems. Rust takes up more space than unaffected metal, so something has to 'give'. A fibreglass shell can be distorted out sideways. After the top sealant is forced up, more water gets in and the process speeds up. If a boat is turned over in a gale, the ballast will come out if it is not tightly secured. The top glassing-in should be strong enough to hold the ballast, but if rust is at work destroying the top cover, the ballast may just be waiting for the boat to roll over, so that all that weight can come tumbling out on top of the crew.

Water that penetrates down beside the ballast may freeze during the winter lay-up. It then expands and this increases the damage. Water lying on top of encapsulated ballast will in time seep through an epoxy filler, even a thick one. This is just one reason why bilges should be kept dusty dry all the time. It is also why there should be a sump for the bilge pump suction pipe end. Ideally this sump should be lined with stainless steel or bronze to keep away from the fibreglass that last drop of water that the bilge pump cannot suck out.

Materials less resistant to water penetration than epoxies allow moisture to soak through even faster, so a surveyor should always expect trouble with encapsulated keels, especially on old boats and on craft that have been afloat without regular care for long periods. Power craft sometimes have keel bands along the bottom. They are called 'shoes' or 'worm shoes' in the United States, where they are often made of wood. As metal bands take a lot of punishment, they do not last long — especially if they are made of ungalvanised steel. Bronze is the best material, but it is not often seen in Britain because it is so costly. Whatever material is used, it needs looking at with care, so the surveyor will have to lie on his back in the mud to peer upwards. Expect to find trouble at the fore and aft ends, and by the fastenings and at joins. In fact, expect trouble generally.

When a keel band corrodes, many owners look the other way because they know it is expensive to repair. The boat sits on keel blocks, so these have to be hauled sideways out of the way in small batches to allow shipwrights to get at the keel band. Only limited lengths can be worked on during each stage of the job. As much as is accessible is renewed, before shifting the support blocks. It is tempting to do a patch-up job, but this is almost always a mistake. It does not help that the fastenings corrode faster than the band, and are usually very difficult to extract. They also bend when they have wasted away, and sometimes the heads come off, so that there is nothing to grip when the shipwright tries to get them out. Getting the new ones in is also awkward, and involves working upwards — often while lying in the mud!

· · · · · · · · · · · · · · · ·

KEEL BOLTS

Taking out a keel bolt is seldom a job that can be done swiftly or cheaply. This is why the surveyor usually completes his inspection of a boat and, if he does not find much trouble, the buyer then instructs the boatyard to extract the keel bolts for checking.

One defect of this procedure is that the bolt inspection sometimes gets forgotten. I once did impromptu 'market research' among the owners of a wooden one-design class that has iron ballast keels and steel keel bolts. My questioning showed that, though these boats change hands at a steady rate, no one had examined the keel bolts for some years. A few weeks later, while having a quiet drink with some people who owned boats in the class, I suggested that trouble could be brewing unseen in their vessels. With only a little grumbling, three owners pulled out keel bolts. What they found gave them a severe fright, and since then everyone in the class has taken care to find out how much metal still binds the ballast to the rest of the yacht.

Few defects are as easy to see as this one. The fore end of the fin keel is right away from the under side of the hull. Has the keel been forced down when the yacht ran aground, or is the hull so light that it is distorting? Are the keel bolts pulling out, or are they too few and too thin? Seeing a fault is just the first stage in a surveyor's job.

It is hard to lay down rules about how often keel bolts should be examined. In certain racing classes it was the practice to examine at least one bolt every year. Considering these boats had lead keel and bronze bolts, this does seem to be over-cautious, but the loss of the keel means the loss of the yacht — and maybe the crew as well. A more usual approach is to remove at least two bolts every time a yacht changes ownership, and examine every single keel bolt prior to a lengthy voyage. A boat used for normal limited cruising should have two bolts out every four or five years. It is not a good idea to pull just one bolt out; it may be the only good one.

Traditionally, keel bolts have a factor of safety of about 12 or 15 and, broadly speaking, if two bolts are in good order the keel should stay on (provided the yacht does not strike the ground), even if all the other bolts have corroded away. Of course, traditional practices are dying out and some builders have cut the safety factor to 8 or less.

The surveyor must select which bolts are to be withdrawn, and he should not choose the most accessible, because these are the ones that will always be picked by any unsupervised shipwright who has to do the job. In the same way, if a yard manager is instructed to take out a number of bolts, he will tend to go for the easiest ones. Where there are ballast keel fastenings under the engine or beneath a tank, these should be taken out during any of the limited periods when they are accessible, otherwise decades can come and go and no one will check the condition of these bolts.

Bolts that have fibreglassing over the top can lie undisturbed for generations. There are two schools of thought here: one says that the glassing keeps water and oxygen away, so corrosion is unlikely (and hopefully impossible); the opposing view is that the glassing is seldom if ever totally watertight, and by harbouring stagnant water the bolt heads never dry and erode away unseen. What is certain is that the material used for bolts is critical. A few naïve builders claim that by using stainless steel they are playing safe. As stainless steel comes in dozens of formulas, only a few of which are suitable for use in salt water, no one should assume a stainless steel bolt is safe. I have seen advanced erosion in bolts that were only six months old. Steel bolts give far more trouble than bronze ones. Some builders coat all bolts with lanolin before putting them in. The aim is to make them slide in more easily, and repel water once they are in place.

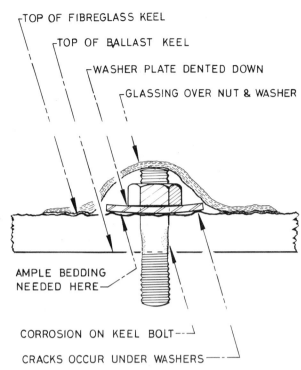

TOP OF FIBREGLASS KEEL

TOP OF BALLAST KEEL

WASHER PLATE DENTED DOWN

GLASSING OVER NUT & WASHER

AMPLE BEDDING NEEDED HERE

CORROSION ON KEEL BOLT

CRACKS OCCUR UNDER WASHERS

Fig 7 Ballast keel bolts

Some keel bolts are glassed over, partly to prevent water getting in past them, partly to lock the nuts on. The nuts and bolts corrode under the glassing, so after a survey it is good practice to strip the glassing off at least two bolts and withdraw them for inspection. If there is even a small amount of corrosion, wise owners insist on having replacements. There should be washer plates (not conventional washers) under the nuts and these plates should be too thick to be distorted and bent down when the bolts are tightened.

Bolts that have nuts or washers of a different material are likely to cause trouble. Unfortunately, a visual inspection will not always tell a surveyor that conflicting materials have been used, and that corrosion is likely once salt water gets near. Even when all the parts are made of an identical material, there may be trouble because there are likely to be at least a few impurities in the main body of the metal. These set up electric currents that result in erosion. Admittedly, the rate at which metal is eaten away is slow, but if it goes on continuously all year (as it can if the bilge is not dried out when the boat is ashore) the end result can be disastrous. If there is the slightest indication of trouble at the visible end of the stainless bolt, it should always be taken out — together with at least one-third of the others holding the keel. Some of the so-called 'mysterious' capsizes, caused by lost keels, can be traced to the way some stainless steel has this dangerous tendency to disintegrate rapidly in sea water.

When the ballast is in the old-fashioned form, outside on a lengthy keel, the bolts may only be removable if the yacht is lifted high, or if a hole can be dug under her in way of each bolt. Bolts made with a nut on both ends can be taken out upwards, but there must still be room to wield a hammer under the keel or slide in a hydraulic jack to force the bolt upwards.

Modern fin keels often have flanges at the top that are held on to the fibreglass hull by short bolts. These may be countersunk, heads downward, with nuts in the bilge. Alternatively, the bolt may be tapped down into the top of the fin keel. This kind is sometimes called a metal thread, or threaded rod. It consists of a length of bar threaded the full length. To extract this type of fastening, the nut on top is slackened slightly, then a second nut put on top. The second one may be taken from another bolt. The two nuts are forced tight up against each other, so that they lock together and lock on the threaded bar. A spanner on the bottom nut should turn the bolt, so that it comes out without undue effort.

It has to be admitted that of all the jobs in a boat, extracting keel bolts is one of the least liked. There are many potential snags. The bolt may have corroded nearly through, so that it breaks when an attempt is made to take it out. Or it may be located where no large spanner will reach – and I have seen some where even a small spanner cannot go. Because yard managers know the various problems that can arise, some will not quote for this job, and some quote very high to err on the safe side. This is why the job is often left till the surveyor has made sure that the rest of the craft is in good order, and her sale is going to go through.

On modern boats the keel bolts may be of mild steel with no protection against rust, so corrosion may be rapid. A few surveyors tap the bolt ends, and if some bolts make a dull sound they assume these have wasted badly, but this is seldom a reliable test. Visual inspection is needed. On some lightly built craft the keel bolts may be quite thin. Twin fin boats, sometimes called bilge-keelers, are found with bolts that are not much thicker than those used to hold down a modest diesel engine. It makes sense when inspecting this sort of craft to have two bolts out of the front and two out of the back of each keel.

Once a bolt is out, it is cleaned off and examined in a good light. Some surveyors ignore surface corrosion, and some work on the basis that there is a factor of safety in the keel-securing arrangements, so that a little local thinning on a bolt is acceptable. Maybe they are right, but a safer approach is to renew all bolts that are not in 'as new' condition. Of course a bolt that has only corroded slightly over a long period is a known factor. A new replacement bolt may be made of an inferior material and may corrode rapidly, and so be more of a hazard than the bolt that was thrown away. This confirms the need to buy keel bolts from a reliable source, and fit them with a waterproof compound over the outside to prevent moisture getting at the head. There should be plenty of waterproof material in the hole before the bolt is put in, with more of this 'gunge' under the big plate washer. The aim here is to prevent water getting into the bolt hole or, if it does, getting up the length of the hole. If it succeeds in doing that, it should be thwarted by a final waterproof barrier at the top.

Steel or iron bolts that have deep rust visible at either end should be replaced. Rusty nuts should be replaced, not least because once the rust bites deep, getting the nuts off becomes difficult. Rusty washers should be replaced because when they get weak they dent downwards and can crack the fibreglass. Under all the nuts there should be big plate washers, at least four times as wide as the diameter of the bolt. When a bolt is out, the structure covered by the washer plate is examined. Cracks here are serious, regardless of the hull construction material. Before putting the bolt back, a little waterproof grease on the thread helps to prevent corrosion and makes the work easier.

On wooden boats it is often advisable to get extra bolts on the centreline structure extracted for inspection. The ones low down and those hard to reach should be inspected first. If the vessel has been kept in the same yard for years, someone somewhere may have a record of which bolts were extracted during the last survey. A few excellent owners keep records of which bolts (and seacocks and chain plate fastenings) have been taken out in past years, and their condition, who did the work, and who supplied any replacements. I have always assumed that such owners go straight to heaven in due course.

There is a technique for inspecting keel bolts without taking them out, using X-rays. Specialist firms advertise this service in marine magazines. They point out that it is often, though not always, cheaper as well as quicker than physically extracting the bolts. This work is done without disturbing the

A typical corroded keel bolt is shown at the top. When one bolt is found like this the surveyor will recommend that all the keel bolts should be replaced. Bottom left is a bronze keel bolt that has become badly corroded and broke off short when an attempt was made to take it out. The two small bolts started life in an identical condition and were fitted within a few inches of each other. The wasted one was near a brass fitting and electrolytic corrosion has occurred. This shows the importance of testing more than one bolt in each area.

interior of the yacht, and without even lifting the sole boards. The cabin cushions do not get dirty, nor is a trail of mud left in the saloon, as happens when some unkempt shipwrights clamber about. The work can be done in the spring when many boatyards have no spare labour, and it can be done if the vessel is not even in a boatyard. The technique can only be used on ferrous bolts, and the vessel must be out of the water. Prices vary but typically are about the same as 'a good lunch for two people' for each bolt.

There is one snag: the X-ray photos have to be interpreted, and the inspector can make a mistake. All safety systems should be 'fail-safe', so that if an error is made the bias is towards pessimism. This means that any mistake indicates that there seems to be more trouble than there is. A good example is a fire alarm that is set to go off at too low a temperature, so that it sometimes rings when no fire is present; this is better than not sounding off when there is a fire. Unfortunately, examining keel bolts by X-ray works the other way. The person viewing the results may not notice trouble, or may feel that marks on the bolts are not significant. The process is therefore not 'fail-safe', but it can be useful as a back-up, especially if at least half the bolts are examined. It is vastly better than the normal arrangement whereby the bolts are hardly ever checked.

· ·

CEMENT AND PITCH IN THE BILGES

When the cabin sole is lifted, the bilge may be found to be covered with cement or pitch. This discovery is rare in fibreglass boats, except occasionally where there is an encapsulated ballast keel. The normal and acceptable practice is to cover the lead or iron ballast with fibreglass, but at least one series of cruisers built in the far East had cement poured in over the iron. I examined one of these craft and found the cement had cracked, allowing water to seep down to the iron which had started to rust and expand. The fibreglass was not able to resist the severe pressure of the expanding rust, and troubles were multiplying.

Infills in the bilge are fairly common in old wooden boats, especially fishing craft. Cement or pitch is also found in a moderate number of steel hulls. The material run in may be to seal over the top of internal ballast, or to stop leaks, or fill over depressions and pockets so that all the bilge-water trickles to a central well. Any surveyor will have a lot of sympathy with the shipwright who tries to keep a boat free from puddles, because long-lying internal water does all sorts of harm. It attacks metal parts, insinuates itself between the laminates of fibreglass, rots the bottom of bulkheads and furniture, as well as filling the boat with unpleasant smells.

When the infilling material is put in to ensure the bilge-water flows to a central pump-out well, it is likely that the cement or pitch will be in small amounts. It is typically triangular in section, against each athwartships obstruction such as the floors. It is needed particularly if the original builder has forgotten to make provision for bilge-water to get past floors. Much of the keel length, or what serves as the keel, or hog in a timber ship, is often visible.

Where pitch or cement is put in over ballast this is almost always an indication of low-cost building. It is often a signal to the surveyor that he should look for the consequences of 'corner-cutting' and practices that are not listed in the best books on boatbuilding. On the other hand, builders sometimes use infills for acceptable reasons, such as adding a small amount of internal ballast that is cheaper and more easily available than lead, and that will not rust like iron. The trouble with this technique is that cement is not particularly heavy. To increase the ballast weight, the builder may add some pieces of iron, but, unless the correct cement is used and trouble is taken to seal all the metal fully, rust weeps are likely.

Sometimes filling material is put in new craft, especially fishing vessels. Careful builders make out a certificate stating that the cement was put in before the vessel was launched, and they occasionally get a surveyor or naval architect to countersign the paper. They may even pin on a copy of the construction plan showing the bays that have to be cemented. By the time the ship is ten years old, the certificate has usually been lost, and a surveyor who comes new to the boat may have a lot of trouble working out why the cement was put in. Fishing boats have to be hosed out after every voyage, and a smooth, fully cemented bilge makes life easier for the crew, whereas one that is a maze of scantlings criss-crossing the bilge will seldom get efficiently washed. Fishermen love a smooth bilge, but they seldom repair cracked or chipped cement to prevent water getting underneath.

If the cement is properly mixed and put in carefully, it helps seal leaks. However, no internal filling is ever as efficient as a proper leak deterrent technique applied on the *outside*. Cementing inside to stop persistent leaking is often a desperate measure. Pitch works better, but it is too often a failure when put in the bilge for this purpose. Leak-stopping work should be done from the outside, so that the water pressure forces the sealant into the seams, not away from them. If pitch is applied on the inside, the boat must first be hauled up, washed through with fresh water, dried out, and warmed inside. The pitch used should be the type that stays slightly flexible, not the brittle type. Any infill in the bilge should remain free from cracks, flaking and powderiness. It should also adhere tightly to all surrounding structure. If even the tiniest gaps appear between the filling compound and the hull sides or frames, water will seep in to the opening. If the fissure is tiny, when the rest of the boat dries out the water in this mini-crack will remain. When it freezes it will expand the crack, so that more water will get in next time.

The top of any filling, whether of cement or pitch, should ideally be hollowed down in the middle to prevent water lying at the edges. Moisture at the edge of an infill tends to rot frames and planking, and rust steel. It is common to find frames that are in reasonable (and maybe excellent) condition a short distance above the bottom of the bilge and below the infill, but in a bad way at the surface of the cement or pitch. A classic danger sign is a crack across cement edged with red rust. This is one of those handy pointers that even a beginner in the surveying world is likely to spot, unless a lot of bilge-water has caused the red tinge to fade. It suggests that the iron ballast or steel floors, or bolts beneath the cement, have been attacked by water, and the cement is likely to be damaged at an increasing rate. The enlargement of the crack may proceed apace.

The only way to tell if there is trouble beneath a filling material is to excavate. This is normally a slow job, and therefore expensive. If mechanical tools are used, they need careful handling, otherwise scantlings which are covered get damaged. It is rare for the work to be completed during a survey, unless it is requested as soon as the surveyor arrives on the job and the vessel is a large one. In practice, it is usual to ask for one bay in four, or perhaps every other bay to be dug out first. If no troubles are discovered, everyone tends to assume that the spaces that have not been cleared out are fine — and generally they are. However, if the vessel is going to make a long voyage, or if she is an old one, cautious surveyors ask for all the filling to be taken out.

FIBREGLASS CONSTRUCTION

. . . .

SURVEYING FIBREGLASS

Fibreglass boats are hard to survey because:

- Many of the faults are hidden, and cannot be detected either by eye or with instruments.
- Large areas are covered with lining that cannot be removed.
- Even when the lining can be removed, sometimes the buyer or seller refuses to agree to it being taken down.
- Areas not lined are often covered by internal mouldings, furniture, or tanks, an engine, sealed-down cabin soles, etc – the list is endless.
- Where there is access, the structure may not be typical.
- Few owners or sellers permit any sort of destructive testing, or allow samples to be cut out of a hull, deck or internal moulding.
- Quality testing is not cheap, and few buyers are prepared to pay for it.
- Even when quality testing can be carried out, it does not tell the surveyor about the whole hull – only about the area being tested.

Faced with this list, a surveyor can be forgiven for being discouraged. What he has to do is examine all the areas he can reach and get a broad view of the quality of construction. He has to gather as many clues as he can that indicate how well (or badly) the boat has been put together.

Small things matter, because it is usually only an accumulation of hints that will tell the surveyor whether the vessel is safe. Rarely does he come across a gash right through the skin below the water-line, dramatic tears in the fibreglass made by keel bolts, or a rudder tube 10 degrees out of line. Even when he does find these startling defects, he still has to discover what caused them in order to prevent a repetition.

When gathering the little bits of information that are going to give an overall view of the boat, and an

assessment as to whether she should be bought, cost-saving ideas are taken into account. A few short-cuts to save man-hours or materials may be acceptable. However, if the whole boat is a mass of gimmickry designed to produce the cheapest possible craft, the surveyor's normally suspicious nature should be particularly wary. The list below gives an idea of the

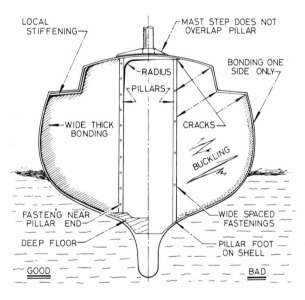

Fig 8

Good and bad mast step construction are shown here. On the left-hand side are the correct techniques. The pillar has close-spaced fastenings with bolts near the top and the bottom into the bulkhead. This in turn is very fully glassed on both sides to the hull, to the cabin top, to the deck, etc. Perhaps most important of all, the foot of the pillar lands on a floor that spreads the load down to the keel and well up round the reverse turn. The mast step itself extends beyond the pillar, and the underdeck doubler has no sharp angles. On the right-hand side these precautions have been omitted, and the signs of trouble will be in the form of a buckling bulkhead, cracks at high stress points, possibly signs of distortion, and even leaks.

way designers and builders think when trying to produce a craft at below the going market price:

- Beams, frames, stringers, sole bearers, etc are widely spaced and omitted wherever possible.
- The fin keel is designed for easy building, but it is poor hydrodynamically.
- The same applies to the rudder.
- Afrormosia or a similar wood is used instead of teak for the trim.
- The stanchions are 2.75 m (9 ft) apart.
- The hatches have no hinges – and sometimes no safety lines either.
- There is only one bilge pump and it is portable, and has no strum box. It often looks more like a toy than an important piece of safety gear.
- Screws are used where there should be bolts.
- The hinges, handles, drawer pulls, locker clips, cleats and fairleads (in fact, all the fittings) are too small and flimsy.

A vessel can have many of these cost-cutting techniques and still be adequate for her job. However, she will not be a good boat, she will be vulnerable to small incidents, and she is almost certain to have a mounting toll of trouble as the years pass. Surveyors learn to be wary of these skimped products, which are often built by people who put no name-plate on the hull. When the name-plate on the craft is an unknown one, this too is a warning.

Basic procedure and weather

The surveyor starts at the bow and works his way aft examining everything: the surface, fittings, fastenings, etc. He does this on the outside of the hull, then along the deck and cabin top, and then does the same inside the vessel.

If it is raining when he arrives at the boat, he works below until the rain stops. If the boat is in the open, he tries to avoid surveying in a gale and he has to give up when the wind freshens to storm force, because surveying calls for concentration. Working afloat, it is hard to do a good job when the motion is severe. I have found that when solid water starts breaking over the bow, it is definitely time to try and get ashore and complete the job later. Opinions vary about snow. A steady fall does not worry me, but I live in Scotland where it seldom stops raining except when it starts snowing. For most surveyors, the job is probably best not done in snowy conditions because such weather is distracting. Also, I have to admit I

work below when I cannot keep the deck reasonably clear.

A good light is needed when working inside any hull, even one that is only partly decked over. So when surveying before dawn or after dusk, it is best to concentrate on the inside of the hull, and leave the outside and deck for the daylight hours. However, even on a sunny day the underside of the keel may be in deep shade, and here a good flashlight or wandering lead light is often needed. A light for the outside of the boat can also be essential on a dull winter's day, when she is closely surrounded by other craft that obscure what little sunshine there is, and the surface is hard to see properly.

Unevenness is usually a sign of bad building. This applies both inside and outside, and also on the deck and rudder. The surface throughout any well-built

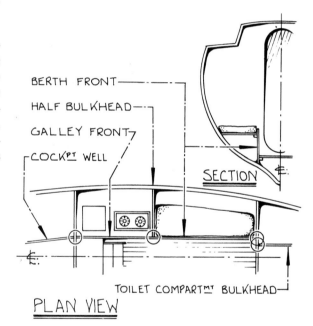

Fig 9

Any part of fibreglass hull stiffening should be tapered away at the ends, or should butt on to another stiffening member. The aim must be to avoid hard spots where a stiffening member stops suddenly. The surveyor should look closely at the way the hull is stiffened and very carefully check round any potential hard spots.

This sketch shows how the berth and galley fronts are butted on to bulkheads, with the partial bulkhead forward of the galley linked to the galley front. The toilet compartment bulkhead does not line up exactly with the berth front, but this is not important because it does butt on to a main bulkhead.

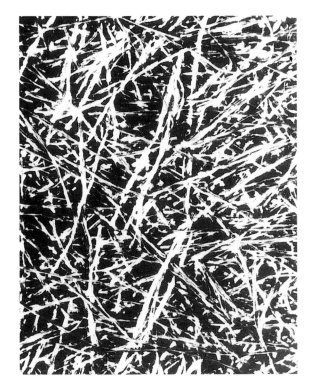

When a surveyor sees this condition in fibreglass he knows he has probably found serious trouble. It is sometimes called 'dry glass' and sometimes 'leaching'. It can be caused by using the wrong resin, or resin that has not been properly cured. A thin watery resin that is slow to cure can run out of the glass cloth and leave this sort of weak and defective structure. The defect may also be caused by exposure of the fibreglass to exceptionally severe weathering. *Photo: Scott Bader.*

The common crazing on the surface of fibreglass tends to occur after years of exposure, and can therefore be a pointer towards the vessel's age. It occurs on the deck more than the topsides as the angle of the sun's rays affects the deck more. It tends to be more even than the crazing shown here, and with far less curling along the cracks. This crazing is a result of resin richness and the use of the wrong resin. It also occurs when the resin is too hard for its thickness. *Photo: Scott Bader.*

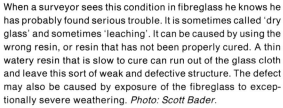

craft has a constancy about it that borders on the boring. The topsides and all surfaces such as the rudder and skeg are smooth and have no undulations, apart from those clearly put there on purpose. The inside of the fibreglass is consistent. There are no deep glossy areas with a complete absence of glass strands. Such a sight shows the resin has been applied too thickly and the fibreglass cloth or mat too thinly. What is sometimes called a 'jewelly' appearance is undesirable, since it indicates resin-richness, which is the same as mat-starvation.

The opposite of this is resin-starvation, and it shows where a spike pulled across the structure tweaks individual strands off the surface. If the trouble is bad, little tufts of fibreglass mat come away. If the spike goes deeply in without effort, the trouble is extremely serious. A spike should not penetrate even a lightly built area of the hull shell or a frame, stringer or beam. This is true even where there is just a thin paper interior or unresisting spongy plastic core to a scantling, over which the fibreglass has been applied. Admittedly, a tough surveyor can drive a sharp spike through the stringers and frames of a delicately built racing machine, or a special lightweight boat such as one designed to be trailed behind a small car.

When looking for clues, it is important to think like a good engineer, and apply his standards. Structural members should taper out, not end suddenly. This applies to frames, stringers, beams, spray rails and bottom stiffeners, moulded-in toerails, engine bearers, and so on. Even better than a tapered end is one that comes into another strong scantling. Beams ideally should terminate right at the deck edge, floors run up to a stringer, and engine bearers link on to bulk-heads at each end. Where a strong part does end

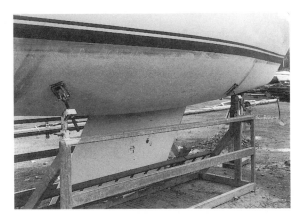

Many modern boat cradles have only two support points on each side. If the support pads are forced against the hull, or a severe storm blows from one side, there may be damage near the pads. This damage is most likely to be inside the hull, and may take the form of loose or distorted framing, stringers and furniture.

suddenly, the area is searched for signs of cracking, peeling or tearing glass at the fillets, and distortions in the shape. When tapped with a soft-nosed hammer, the area just beyond the strong structure may be weak, or even floppy and dangerous.

A soft-nosed hammer is used all over the bottom, to find weak areas that will collapse inwards when struck by flotsam. The same hammer cannot always be used above the waterline as it may cause damage to the fine surface. However, the hammer is used on the skeg, rudder and propeller to find weaknesses that will not stand up to the rough and tumble of life at sea. The surveyor is looking for signs of accidents such as cracks, which are described in a separate section. He peers closely at the hull where it is shored up, to see if the props have indented the shell. If he is unsure, he holds a straight edge against the bottom and this will show if there is an inward curve, or if the sweet sweep of curvature is distorted.

CLASS FAULTS AND PEDIGREE

Boats are built in factories that turn out rows of identical craft. When the sales director reckons he is not finding enough buyers to make a profit, the model is changed, and another ten, hundred or thousand boats emerge from the factory door in due course. Throughout this time, there may be changes of designer, manager, foreman and moulder that are likely to affect the boats being built. However, the factory has a momentum of its own; and though the quality will vary, most changes are likely to be slow – even when an important person in the chain of command leaves or gets promoted.

This situation helps surveyors. After a very few years of looking at a variety of craft, a list of 'standard' defects expected on certain products is accumulated in his personal organiser or laptop computer. Typical examples of defects regularly found are the poor metal fittings on the early imported Far Eastern yachts – and many of us know about the factory that puts 'toy' hinges on the locker doors. As soon as we get into the cabin, we check to see how many doors are coming adrift.

Lists of 'standard' defects are no more than guidelines, for not every boat in the class will have them. Some owners know about potential troubles and forestall them. Others suffer these problems in the first few years of ownership and deal with them, so that when the surveyor comes on the scene the defects have been cured. Like many other owners, when I bought myself a Sigma 33 I spent the first two winters routing out the 'gremlins'. Anyone who surveys that boat now will not find the normal defects for which her class is known – bar one. Mild cracking appeared in way of the backstay eyebolt before I could wriggle into the very small space ahead of the transom and fit a large washer under the nut in place of the stupid little one the builders have been using since production started.

The best builders improve their products each year. Over five hundred modifications were worked into the Nicholson 32 during the early stages of production. Unfortunately, not many builders go to that amount of trouble to erase defects, and some are happy to let things be – even when they know that all is not well. The surveyor's job is complicated because factories sometimes deliberately change production methods, and not always to improve the product. Publicity leaflets are sent out describing this or that alteration, and indicating that from now on the boat will be even better value, or faster, or more comfortable. The truth may be that the specification is being downgraded to reduce production costs. Sometimes mistakes creep in and are perpetuated from then on. On some occasions the shipwrights on the job alter something to make their work easier, and this results in a stronger, more reliable vessel. At still other times feedback from the owners results in changes of design or fabrication.

There was one class with a deep narrow skeg that formed an integral part of the hull. It was impossible to make this bit of the hull shell properly, regardless of the skill and experience of the fabricators. No one could reach in to the bottom of the mould to coax the glass mat and cloth down into small skeg. Nor could

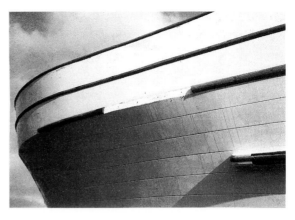

The wood rub rail of this motor cruiser has broken away, showing that it had fastenings which were too small and too far apart. Also the joins of the rub rail were vertical butts instead of the more effective common scarfs. There may be trouble inside the hull in way of the fastenings, and possibly even peeling fibreglass at bulkhead edges or damaged framing and furniture.

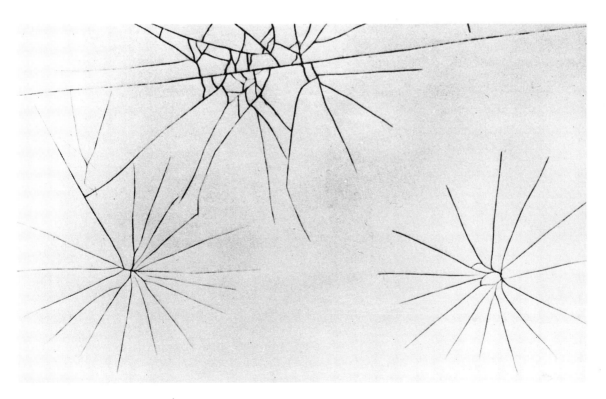

One of the most common fibreglass defects is star cracking. It happens when an anchor is dropped, or when a spinnaker pole bangs down too hard on the deck. It also shows on the outside when the material receives a knock on the inside. In mild cases there is often little damage to the laminates, but in severe instances the glassfibre may be ruptured right through. This can be discovered by taking off the gel coat and examining the material beneath. *Photo: Scott Bader.*

they smooth out the glass, or make well-staggered joins. No one could be sure that the resin wetted out all the glass, and if the resin collected in a puddle, no one could see it. This collection of defects was only cured when a skeg broke off at sea. The unlucky owner created a considerable fuss and the moulding technique was changed. From then on, the skeg was made separately and bonded on when the hull had been completed. Now surveyors all worry about the boats built before the one that fractured its skeg. It is a warning to waggle skegs hard, to see if they are loose or weak or starting to crack across the top.

An even worse history of bad building occurred when a small company found it was losing money. It had built 18 boats to a well-known designer's plans, but to reduce construction costs the next 50 were built with *no floors at all*. As a result, the fin keel moved disconcertingly in bad weather. The firm then went bankrupt and was taken over by a new group who restarted production, putting in the correct number and size of floors. However, the new regime had also underpriced their boats, so they soon cast about for ways of saving money. Presumably they were still employing the same charge hands, because the new management also decided to leave out the floors. It is no consolation to a surveyor that the new company also went under.

What makes this whole sad saga so difficult for surveyors is this: Boats No 1 to 18 are fine, at least so far as the floors are concerned. Nos 19 to 50 are dangerous, but hard to put right – and besides, is anyone sure they did stop at No 50? When firms are getting into financial difficulties, such matters as careful record-keeping get forgotten. Production of the first batch under the new management was fine as far as the floors were concerned, but then things went wrong and another batch (size unknown) was put together with no floors.

There is more to this sorry tale and it makes things even worse. The floors were put in below a fibreglass moulded-in tank, so they are invisible (always assuming they are there, that is). Without some advanced surgery it is impossible to tell whether a yacht of this type has the floors or not – unless of course the keel is clearly weak and too flexible, in which case those who know the class can guess the reason. Someone somewhere possibly knows exactly which boats can be trusted and which have no floors. But it is unlikely he is going to let on, as he will not want to be linked with such a disaster.

One conclusion can be drawn from all this. When starting a survey, the pedigree of the boat should be established. On virtually all except small cheap boats, there is a builder's name-plate; this will normally show:

- The name and address of the builder.
- The boat type or class.
- Its yard number.

Sometimes there is more data, such as the year and month built, the local agent, and perhaps a separate hull moulding number. There may be a separate plate detailing the name and address of the organisation that has supervised construction or the hull moulding. Lloyd's hull moulding certificates are the most famous of these. Part of a surveyor's 'armoury' is his knowledge of which builders are reliable, and to what extent each manufacturer can be trusted. He knows when he is looking at a boat from a particular factory that she is almost bound to be safe, though he is always wary in case he finds himself looking at a 'lemon' – that is, a dud from an otherwise reputable firm. These aberrations occur because foremen go on holiday and leave someone less able in their places, or defective material is supplied by an otherwise safe company, or a quality manager has a row with his girlfriend and does a less than perfect job next day.

Identification markings

On the outside of the transom there may be letters and numbers moulded in. They are occasionally in reverse, or mirror image, but easy enough to read in spite of that. Certain builders put their own numbers on one side, and a Lloyd's or moulder's number on the opposite side. A surveyor should record these as they are similar to a birth certificate number, and not easy to change or fake, or add after the boat is several years old. Some manufacturers incorporate the month and year the hull was built, and this is normally easy to identify.

If the boat is being made for the US market she must have a 'Hull Identification Number', known as an HIN. It is on the starboard side of the transom, or aft on the starboard side of a canoe-sterned craft. There will be three letters, which are often the builder's initials or taken from the builder's name. The next five digits show the hull class and serial number, and the following four give the month and year of manufacture. There may be additional private builder's numbers as well.

Some hulls, especially older ones, have their numbers inside marked on the moulding, often in a cockpit locker or on the transom. This method of numbering is not convenient for everyone concerned. At times the surveyor, trying to read the number, finds himself struggling into a stern locker too small for a mouse on a diet. Another place to find the boat's data and the builder's name is on the switchboard or electrical panel, normally located above the chart table. The name-plate, or lettering on the panel may be a secondary source of information. For instance it may not have the builder's name at all, but instead the firm that did the electrical work, or acted as sales agent when the vessel was new. It can even have the name and address of a firm that renewed the electrical equipment long after the boat was new.

Any information that can be jotted down at the beginning of a survey report to identify the craft is a positive help. Most surveyors have some horror story to tell about the time they (or a rival) spent a long time gazing at the wrong boat or mast. Very occasionally, the wrong boat is actually surveyed. Plenty of boats have no name on them. Just as important, we have to beware of surveying any craft with a common name without first double checking. It is astonishing how often there are two craft with the same name in a boatyard.

Much more serious, aluminium masts do not vary nearly enough. One seldom knows before starting a survey whether the boat's spars are gold or silver anodised, so this is no help. The name should be on the end of the mast – but which end, and is that end accessible? There have been plenty of instances of surveyors inspecting the wrong mast. Old hands note in the report exactly how the mast was identified, and add a few technical details such as the number of crosstrees, winches (and their size as well as type), and also the maker's name and number. Establishing pedigree can be difficult, and it makes sense to cut down the risk of errors.

This whole matter of genealogy is important because good builders produce good boats and a surveyor likes to know before he starts work if he is on a safe vessel or a dangerous one. He wants to be able to check defects known to be the hallmark of a particular builder. He wants to be able to build up a bank of information about regularly made mistakes for future reference. As boatbuilding companies climb up or slither down the ladder called 'Quality', a surveyor wants to be able to update his existing lists of 'standard' faults. Just as important, he wants to establish precisely which vessel he inspected. Just because the key fitted the lock on the cabin door does not mean he spent the day looking at the boat the buyer had in mind!

· ·

TESTING FIBREGLASS

One of the surveyor's principal conundrums is the true quality of fibreglass hulls, decks, cabin tops and rudders. He can scrape off the anti-fouling and study the gel coat. Inside the hull he can peel back glued-on lining or 'unbutton' furniture and study the surface of the moulding, but his eyes cannot tell him what is below the surface. What a surveyor wants is a sample taken from the hull and examined in a laboratory, and this can be done when the boat is built of materials other than fibreglass. There are specialists who can, with very little delay, give a technical analysis of the wood, steel or aluminium used in a vessel. Provided the job is done intelligently, the samples taken out of a wood or metal hull will seldom affect the strength or watertightness of the boat.

With fibreglass, though, things are very different. For a start, few owners, buyers or sellers will agree to sampling. The one time a surveyor gets co-operation from an owner with regard to sampling is when a vessel is going to be used for a major voyage or an especially severe job such as rescue work in storm conditions. Even then, things are seldom straightforward, and the number of samples is almost invariably limited. It would be a help if the builder made sample panels when moulding the hull and deck, but this rarely happens. Besides, such samples might be made with loving care and precision – which might not be similarly lavished on the main structures.

A good opportunity occurs when a new seacock is being fitted, as a circular piece of the shell has to be cut out, and this makes an excellent sample for use in a laboratory. The thickness of the shell where the sample is taken is easy to see, and this thickness should tally fairly closely with the information on the construction plan. If it does not, the surveyor has a right to be suspicious as to whether the correct thickness has been used elsewhere.

Getting the construction plans can be difficult. Some fabricators will say they no longer have the plans as the current boat is No. 300 and, since they have put together 299 previous identical craft, everyone knows how to build the latest one without drawings. Other firms will say drawings are superfluous as the foreman is so knowledgeable. It is reasonable to ask how the moulders manage when the foreman is ill. I was once told by a well-known builder that they had drawings, but they were out of date, and no corrected ones were available. Having seen plenty of boats built with lots of mistakes even when there are copious well-prepared drawings, I am now suspicious when I come across this firm's work — especially as they subsequently went bankrupt. I also discovered that one of their hulls had dead leaves glassed in under the floors. If the hull thickness is found to be in excess of what is called for on the plan, this is not necessarily a good thing. Some craft are built with a fixed total amount of material, so if there is too much at the location of the test sample, there must be a shortage somewhere else.

The hull thickness can be measured by taking out existing skin fittings. Allowance may have to be made for local hull thickening or doublers in way of the hole. Prior to a major voyage, careful owners sometimes improve the quality of the seacocks and this may involve fitting larger ones. This means that though no new hole is being made, existing holes are being enlarged. A hole cutter should always be used when fitting a new skin fitting, but especially if a sample of the fibreglass is wanted. The cutter produces a neat disc, whereas a drill or boring bit generates a pile of shavings, which are far less satisfactory for making tests. A piece of wood should be pressed against the hull on the inboard side, so that the hole cutter makes a neat job. Without a backing block, the exit can be rough. Before taking the sample, the cutter should be tested to ensure it is sharp. A power drill is needed; it should not be pressed too hard against the hull, otherwise it may separate the laminates, particularly as it is emerging at the end of the cut. This is where the backing block also helps. The cut is made from the outside, after a small pilot hole has been bored from the inside to locate the hole accurately.

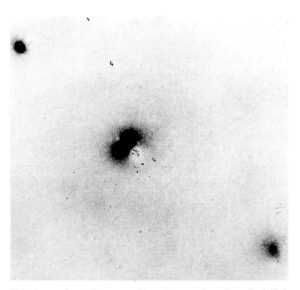

This type of spotting on a fibreglass surface is called 'fish eyes'. It occurs when the gel coat is too thin, and shows up as pale-coloured patches typically less than 8 mm in diameter. Another form of the same defect is seen in straight lines, showing where the brush strokes occurred as the gel coat was applied. As with most gel coat defects, it is not the loss of strength that matters so much as the poor resistance to water penetration and the disappointing appearance. *Photo: Scott Bader.*

The trouble with taking a single hull sample is that it may not be representative. In way of the test, the hull may be too thin or thick, whereas a short distance away, and throughout the rest of the structure, the thickness can be precisely right. Of course, if the hull seems seriously defective over a large area, taking several samples is logical and necessary. If the shell is so weak that it is floppy, or if it indents alarmingly when given a firm but not excessive thump with a soft-nosed hammer, cutting out a selection of carefully selected pieces is going to be essential to discover what the shell is like below the surface. It may be saturated, delaminated, or so lacking in resin that it is like straw-board, or just dangerously thin.

While it is seldom practical to take more than one or two samples from the hull shell, specimen discs can more often be cut from several floors, or the engine bearers, or even from the edges of the bulkheads at the glassing-in. These test areas will not tell a surveyor much about the main hull shell, but they can indicate the quality of work that the builder has turned out. Repairs after removing these cuttings for examination are not difficult, especially as it is normal practice to select areas that are not important, but are accessible. In a few cases, the holes in places like the bulkheads may be left to improve the ventilation. To prevent moisture getting in, the edges of the holes should be sealed with resin. Samples are sent for testing to such firms as the makers of the raw materials, or to a university or commercial laboratory. Because of its close connection with the small craft industry, Southampton University (in the UK) undertakes this type of testing. Before dispatch, each sample should be labelled with the name of the craft and its owner, the precise location from which the sample was taken, and the person requiring the data.

No one should take a cut-out sample without getting the owner's permission in writing. The job should be done in a proper fabrication shed, under controlled conditions so far as humidity and temperature are concerned, so that repairs can be carried out correctly. The cost of taking the samples and having them analysed is normally borne by the person who commissions the survey. It makes sense to get a quote for all stages of the work, including the laboratory testing. The laboratory work can be expensive and it is an extra over and above the normal survey fee. This is why it is not done until the rest of the survey has been completed and its results con-

sidered. If the boat has endless defects, it may not be worth going any further in the process of discovering how seaworthy, well built and well maintained she is.

Of course if the vessel is a lifeboat or service craft, or if she is going to do some onerous work, it can make sense to take plenty of samples, even though the subsequent replacement work is costly. The test work establishes if the correct resin-to-glass ratio has been used in the construction. If there is lots of glass, the structure will be strong, but if there is too much there will be gaps between the glass strands into which water will seep. Too much resin often makes for a good appearance; it gives watertightness and resistance to weathering. However, if this is overdone, there will be a lack of strength, which is serious when the hull has a bump, or a wave breaks massively against it.

The normal test consists of ashing part of the sample. Before and after this, the piece is weighed. This shows the amount of glass and resin, and hence the ratio. Examining the edge of the sample before burning gives a good idea how well the laminates are bonded together, and what voids there are in the lay-up.

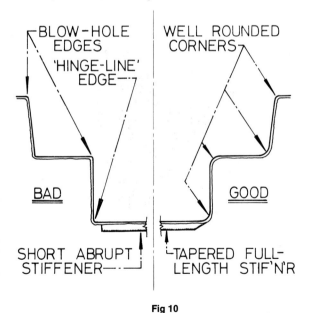

Fig 10

Edges and corners on fibreglass hulls should be well rounded, both for strength and to avoid blow-holes. A well-rounded edge is also less likely to chip or be damaged. On the left, poor practice is shown, with indications where trouble is most likely. The right-hand side shows how these high-risk areas should be treated, with regard to both corners and stiffeners.

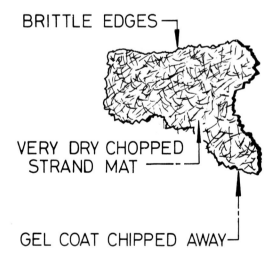

Fig 11

If the gel coat on a fibreglass hull has become chipped away, exposing an area of dry chopped strand mat, the condition is likely to be serious. The surrounding hull should be tapped with a pricker handle to discover the extent of the defect. It is likely that the cure must be the cutting out of the defective area and reglassing, as for damage.

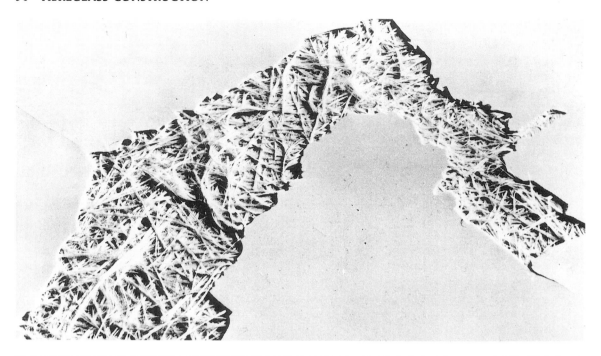

On the inside of a glassfibre hull this sort of defect has to be treated seriously, especially if more than one patch like this is found. It is caused by a shortage of resin which means there is a lack of strength. Just as worrying is the fact that water will get into the interstices and work its way through the laminates. If it then freezes it will expand and force the layers apart. *Photo: Scott Bader.*

There have been decades of research into this matter of testing fibreglass, and to date no simple reliable set of trials has been discovered. At present the amount of data from the skilled examination of a sample is still fairly limited. A surveyor has to use his eyes constantly and without rushing. He looks for the unusual, the break in uniformity, and he often has to be a detective from then on. He is lucky in one respect: if there is a serious defect, it is seldom the only thing wrong. A weakness in one place transfers working loads to adjacent areas which may give warning that they are being overstressed.

It is rare that a fibreglass moulding that forms part of a boat is seriously under-cured. If it is, it makes a dull noise when tapped with the edge of a coin and, in very bad products, the coin leaves an indent. A Barcol Impressor, or Hardness Tester, can be used, though there are plenty of problems here, and its effectiveness is not universally accepted. It does give a clear indication if the laminate is seriously under-cured. A figure of under 25 means that there is so much wrong with the hull, or deck, or whatever is being tested, that it has to be rejected.

ULTRA-THIN FIBREGLASS HULLS

There is one worrying situation that a busy surveyor meets most months in the spring, and often enough during the rest of the year. This is the extremely thin-skinned fibreglass hull. These delicate shells are found in racing yachts of all types, especially under 9 m (30 ft), and also on cheap motor boats up to about the same length.

It only takes a firm nudge with the shoulder, and the topsides dimple in by a startling amount. If a soft-nosed hammer is used, the surveyor gets the

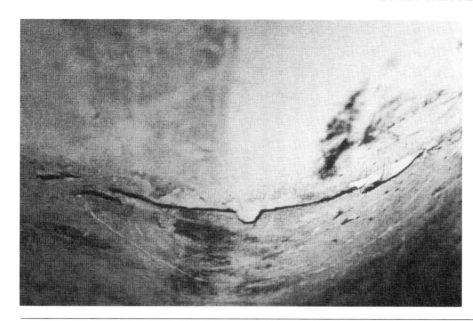

An example of a bad fibreglass repair which is peeling off at the edge. A surveyor seldom gets such a clear-cut warning of trouble; this type of defect is usually quite subtle in the first stages, extending only over one or two inches at first.

feeling that he is about to do widespread damage – even when he gives a very delicate tap. Surveyors new to the job jump back in alarm after the first bop with the hammer because the effect is so disconcerting. This problem is almost always worse on the topsides than the bottom, as the latter has curvature and hence 'shape-strength'.

What the designer and builder have done is to make the hull as thin as they dare. They know that fibreglass is a relatively expensive material. It is more or less 'petrol standing up', so the less used, the cheaper the boat. She will also be light and therefore fast – provided she holds together long enough, that is. The hull is in effect an envelope to keep the water out, not a strong structure that will withstand a certain amount of punishment and moderate accidents. Part of the thinking is that if the boat hits a wave, the blow will be spread out over a wide area, and the deceleration will not be instantaneous if the hull indents to absorb the blow. This is fine provided the hull knows it has to 'outdent' and go back to its original shape after the wave has passed.

One reason why surveyors should go to sea in all weathers is to experience the excitement of being down below in the foc's'le of one of these craft as she batters her way against brick-shaped waves. A hand laid flat on the topsides feels an unnerving pulsation. The movement of the glassfibre shell is sometimes clearly visible, and the noise is frightening.

Anyone selling this sort of boat will say that 50 or 5000 of the same sort have been built, so they must

be all right. This is not a sound argument. The insurance companies may have had to deal with five sinkings in the last month and the type may now be uninsurable. The builders may claim that they have never had a complaint. True enough, because drowned people seldom turn up at the factory to discuss their dissatisfaction with the boat's integrity. On one occasion we acted for an owner whose boat had sunk. The builders were adamant that there was nothing wrong with the craft because they had completed nearly a thousand of them. In vain we repeated: 'But she *did* sink. And no one hit her. There are *no marks* on her.' We knew this because we salvaged her. Eventually we proved that there was no proper supervision in the factory, and the boat had been fitted out wrongly. So an argument about numbers built is no guarantee of safety.

A more difficult builder's defence to deal with is the one that says: 'We build to the class rules. These lay down the thickness of the topsides and bottom. All the boats are identical. And this *is* an international class.' Yes indeed – and all the boats in the class may be equally dangerous. Their insurance premiums may be double or treble the average. Two of the class may have been sunk by trivial accidents that should not have scuppered a child's inflatable toy.

Wise surveyors usually make some remark warning buyers about these thin-skinned craft, even if it only points out that the boat is a lightly built racing machine and she should not be put in a risky situation. The trouble with this type of delicate sailing yacht is that she may drift on the tide with no steerage way and be carried broadside into a navigation buoy. The crew can do little if there is no wind, and may in any case only recognise the danger when it is too late. When the topsides meet the steel buoy the hull may be cracked open from deck to waterline. Down she goes in a very few minutes, leaving the crew to scramble on to the navigation buoy – if they are not swept downtide first.

The same sort of thing can happen to a flimsy motor-cruiser in a marina. These craft have little grip on the water and lots of windage. It is hard to prevent them going sideways and a gust may push the boat against the sharp corner of a walkway that crunches through the topsides. This sort of split travels down to the waterline easily and, once a little water has poured in, the boat heels towards the side where the damage is. This causes the water to flood in ever faster.

When an inspection shows that a 7 m (23 ft) boat has a topsides thickness of 3 mm ($\frac{1}{8}$ in), the surveyor is bound to wrinkle his brow. If the boat is not constructed for racing her weight is not so critical, so it can be suggested that additional strength should be built in. This can take the form of layers of glass inside to thicken the shell, or extra structure such as frames or stringers. The latter sometimes hold water on top, especially where the hull has flare, so frames may be better. I have seen them put in diagonally to give the advantages of both types of reinforcing. The best strengthening may be a combination of extra overall glassing as well as some new frames.

To give powerboats more strength, light internal bulkheads are sometimes fitted, running fore and aft a short distance in from the topsides. Foam plastic is poured in between these thin partitions and the hull shell. This is equivalent to sandwich construction, but much thicker, and with the added advantage that if enough foam plastic is put in, the hull will float even when holed. A comparable technique is used in some racing sailing craft, but the buoyancy is in the form of inflatable bags, as used in racing dinghies. These bags are cheap enough, but they do need efficient strapping in place. On more than one occasion the upward force of several large buoyancy bags has been enough to prise the deck right off a sinking boat. This leaves the owner with a deck and some flotation bags, but no hull or keel.

Whatever is used to ensure the boat stays afloat when holed, there has to be enough total buoyancy to cope with the weight of keel, engine(s), heavy tanks, winches and so on, with a good margin to spare. Without this safety factor the boat may float so low in the water that she cannot be handled, and may be impossible to tow to safety. For stability, the buoyancy has to be high up and spread well athwartships. If there is ample buoyancy, the insurance premium may be reduced – or at least kept within reason.

Two useful figures to remember are:

- 35 cubic ft of buoyancy will support a ton.
- One cubic ft of buoyancy will support a little over 60 lb. Armed with these figures, it is not difficult to work out what capacity of buoyancy is needed for most boats.

CRACKS IN FIBREGLASS HULLS

Cracks that are not dramatic are hard to see on a fibreglass hull, especially in a bad light, and particularly below the waterline when covered with antifouling paint. However, once a single crack has been found others are less difficult to discern, because they tend to be in a pattern.

If the cracks are due to a blow, say the severe nudge of a round fender when the boat bumps against a quay wall, the pattern will be circular. The cracks tend to be in roughly concentric rings, but each crack may appear to have discontinuities, and there will be wiggles, radial cracks from the centre, and other deviations from the pattern. This sort of cracking has been likened to a spider's web, but that is misleading on two counts: webs have all the strands fully continuous and apparently of the same thickness; they also have lots of lines running from the centre, whereas the crack pattern may have none.

Another common pattern is a set of roughly parallel cracks. These lines tend to spread out at each end.

They start off running more or less parallel in the middle of the arrangement and then decide to spread out away from each other. This pattern may be mirror-imaged, so that there is a second comparable set of cracks a short distance away. The two sets will be separated by an area of strength on the inside of the hull.

A third common pattern extends from a bolt hole or the corner of a cabin top, and is often seen by stanchion base flanges. It is a fan of cracks extending from the high stress point outwards. Like all patterns, it helps the surveyor find other troubles by looking at comparable places, and looking beyond the obvious cracks to comparable places adjacent. If one bolt at the bottom of a stanchion has cracks emanating from it, others may have too — as will other stanchions.

Cracks are most likely to be found at the widest point of the hull, because this is where bumps occur when lying alongside a quay. Another common area

The vertical deck-edge flange of this fibreglass boat has cracked right through. It has been repaired and then cracked again, suggesting that there is local overstressing. Possibly the forestay fitting is not properly secured and is causing the damage. It does not look as if the defect was caused by a head-on collision, since the stemhead roller fitting seems to be unblemished.

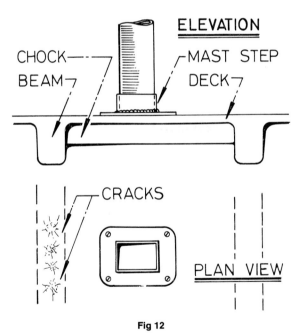

Fig 12

Cracks on the surface of fibreglass tell different stories. Near a deck-stepped mast a row of cracks is sometimes seen. Careful measuring is likely to show that these cracks occur over the mast support beam, suggesting that in heavy weather the bridging arrangement between the beams is inadequate. One cure, which is particularly attractive because it is so simple, is to extend the sides of the mast step well fore and aft so that they overlap the beams. The mast step then forms a bridge and helps the chock under the deck to carry the load on to the support beams.

is forward above the waterline where most hulls are flattish. Here there is little 'shape-strength' as there is not much curvature. Often too, there are few frames or stringers stiffening the topsides. Bashing into a head sea, this area is one moment out of the water, the next deeply immersed, so there are reversing strains that can be severe at high speed. This is also where flotsam is likely to be hit.

When examining the topsides of any craft there may be scratches and cracks. The former can look like cracks, but if there is no pattern the first conclusion is that scratching is the trouble. Even when scratches are roughly in line, they tend to run for only short distances parallel, or nearly so. Human hairs, often found under berths and in the bilge, can look like cracks, but they give themselves away because they are on their own, and even when there are two or three they do not lie in a pattern. A finger rubbed over the area moves the hair and gives the game away. If the line is a crack, and the finger is grubby, dirt may go into a crack and make it easier to see.

On the outside, where cracks run down to the waterline, they sometimes seem to die away around the boot-top. This is because paint has been put into them. Once the paint has been removed the cracks will show up well enough. If the hull has hit some flotsam, the cracks will possibly be worse below the waterline, even though this is far from clear during the initial inspection. The difficult cracks are those that are new, those on dark hulls, and those on a boat laid up in a dimly lit shed. A set of cracks can go unnoticed on a dark hull for years, until someone glances obliquely along the topsides against a bright – but not dazzling – light. This is how the surveyor spots troubles of this sort. His problem is to get into a position where he can see along the hull shell obliquely. In a crowded shed with lots of craft packed tight together, there may be too few places where the surveyor can get a diagonal view along the hull from bow and stern, and from amidships towards the ends.

Generally it is easy to spot old cracks on a white or light-coloured hull. Dirt lodges in the lines, the edges of the cracks minutely chip away widening the fault lines, and more dirt goes in. The ends of a crack may taper down to a width less than the diameter of a human hair. Muck and mud cannot get into such a fine fracture, and even if it does there may be no easily visible sign of it. This brings up one of the great difficulties of surveying: cracking almost always extends well beyond the visible signs. Along the run of cracking the trouble may extend at each end for a distance equal to the lengths of the visible part. This means that a 2 m long crack, which is bad enough, can extend 6 m. This will only be discovered when suitable tests are made. At right angles to the general run of cracking, this 'times three' rule of thumb does not generally apply, but the true width of defective glass may be twice the easily seen area. So what looks like a 2 × 0.5 m area of cracking could be six or more times that extent. Anyone who quotes to do a repair just 1 × 0.5 m and then finds he has so much more work to do, is going to be most unhappy. When an area of cracking has been discovered it is not a good idea to test it with a softnosed hammer as this may extend the problem. A firm but

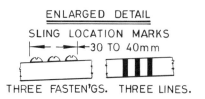

ENLARGED DETAIL

SLING LOCATION MARKS
├── → ┤←30 TO 40mm

THREE FASTEN'GS.   THREE LINES.

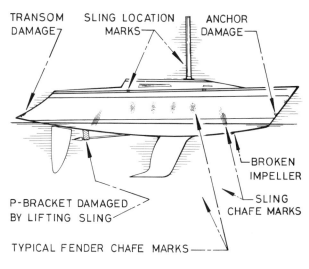

TRANSOM DAMAGE

SLING LOCATION MARKS

ANCHOR DAMAGE

BROKEN IMPELLER

SLING CHAFE MARKS

P-BRACKET DAMAGED BY LIFTING SLING

TYPICAL FENDER CHAFE MARKS

Fig 13

Far too few boats have any labels or marks showing where they should be slung, when they are being lifted out of the water. The enlarged sketch, top left, shows the indicators that may be seen on some craft. Three fastenings very close together, or three paint or tape lines, should be marked, port and starboard, forward and aft.

Where there are no such marks there may be trouble. A sling will destroy a log impeller and may force a P-bracket up inside a boat, or bend a propeller shaft, or damage a propeller.

This sketch shows other common faults on the topsides. It is rare to find a yacht over five years old that has been used much for cruising but does not have either fender chafe marks or chips on the bow caused by an anchor.

controlled push against the area may show it is floppy. This is a warning that the repairs have to be extended well beyond the obvious area, and may be an indication that the hull was weak before the accident. A small batch of short cracks that are so narrow they can only be seen with a magnifying glass may seem trivial. It is worth remembering that a cut in a chain severs it and destroys its strength. Regardless of whether the cut is made with a thin or thick hacksaw blade, the effect of the cut is the same. This also applies to cracks in any structure. The width of the crack is of little importance, but the length matters a lot. A very fine crack will draw in water by capillary action, but a warm wind may fail to suck the moisture out. In cold weather the water will freeze and expand, enlarging the crack. A wider crack may take in water, but discharge it when the atmospheric conditions encourage drying.

Once a crack has been detected, or is suspected, its full extent can be found by using crack-detecting fluids. These come in spray cans and aerosols, and are sold by engineering suppliers as they are used to discover flaws in welds. (A surveyor may use them for the same purpose.) These fluids cannot be used in the rain, but little experience is needed to apply them. The area has to be cleaned, using fresh dry rags. The fluid leaves the cracks showing up as thin red lines that are very hard to eradicate, so there is every chance that the repair firm will do a comprehensive job. Until the repair is complete, the red traces are unsightly – so not everyone will give permission for crack-detecting fluids to be used. Obviously the cracks will be rather hard to see on red hulls.

Generally, it is excessive local force that causes cracking: solid dinghies bumping the transom, anchors swinging against the bow, and topsides pressure due to rafting up with too many other craft are all crack-makers. Heat sources also cause problems so that cracks are found around hot exhaust outlets and by stove chimneys. Minor cracks have to be filled, and this can only be done when the humidity and temperature are right. Major areas of cracking need grinding back or cutting right out, just like an area that has been bashed right through in an accident.

LOOKING FOR OSMOSIS OR BOAT POX

The surface of a fibreglass boat should be as smooth as a well-made bottle. The topsides should be glossy and unblemished and pleasing to the eye. The bottom will be similar when the boat is new and has not yet been afloat, but normally the anti-fouling paint covers the bottom.

Some treatment is needed on the bottom when the boat is new, to make the weed-resisting paint adhere. Sometimes the surface is rubbed down with fine glass-paper; sometimes it is abraded more severely; and sometimes a chemical is used to etch the surface. These 'attacks' leave the surface with varying degrees of roughness, but no tiny pimples, blisters or subtle little ridges. If such blisters are found, the chances are that the surveyor is looking at osmosis or one of its relatives. At first the bumps are small and well spread out. In the early stages they can only be detected by scraping off patches of anti-fouling paint. This scraping is done with care so as not to damage the gel coat, because until the abrading is complete no one knows if there is osmosis, and how bad it is.

This 'disease' affects fibreglass boats only. It has been likened to cancer in human beings because it strikes young and old, it is impossible to predict (though certain types seem more likely to get it than others), and it sometimes inspires more fear than seems justified. Osmosis is the correct technical name for this problem, but its nickname 'boat pox' is widely used – especially in the United States. Sometimes the blisters are so tiny that they are not visible, but may be felt by a delicate finger. A bad light or a thick layer of bottom paint both hamper investigation. When 'mature', the bubbles can be as big as the span of a large man's hand. The malady may extend over a small area or cover the whole of the hull. It is almost always on the outside of the hull below the waterline, but it also occurs on the topsides and, more rarely, inside the shell. It is common inside fibreglass watertanks – for instance, in Nicholson 35s tanks, below the saloon sole. In its early stages it is hard to detect in a poor light when covered with thick layers of anti-fouling.

From a surveyor's point of view, osmosis is central to his life's work unless he specialises in wood or steel craft. Some boat buyers will commission surveys that cover *only* the examination of the hull for this defect. This raises all manner of complications relating to such things as ethics, legal liabilities, professional conduct, the way a business should be run, and so on. For instance, what does a surveyor do if he has been told to do no work except check for osmosis, but he sees that the lifelines are defective? If he says nothing, someone may lean against the lifeline and fall overboard when it breaks. Remembering that the chances are poor of being picked up after going overboard at night offshore in bad weather, no surveyor can blithely walk away from any perceived danger on any vessel.

If it was only a question of dangerous lifelines, the surveyor's life would be fairly simple. What if he spots indications that the rudder bearing is worn, or the P-bracket is just beginning to work loose? If he spends time on these problems he is not earning his living, and may well receive abuse for interfering in areas where he is not welcome, and for which he is not being paid. Some experienced surveyors get round the problem by accepting commissions to examine the hull for osmosis only, but they go aboard and make a brief check for other defects. Being old and wise so far as their job is concerned, they can see half-a-dozen things that need attention before the vessel is commissioned, and these they list – not in great detail, but with just enough information to make everyone concerned take notice.

This approach will add an hour or several on to the day's toil, as far as the surveyor is concerned, but it will sometimes get him additional work when the buyer realises that 'osmosis only' surveys are seldom sensible. It also protects the surveyor to some degree if he emphasises in his report that the additional defects listed (apart from the notes on osmosis) are not comprehensive, have not been charged for, and were just a few of the vessel's problems that were noticed in passing.

Osmosis is a well-known phenomena in science. Research has been going on in this field for years because it has all sorts of applications – for instance, it is used for making fresh water from sea water. It is in theory very simple, though in practice (when studied in depth) there are plenty of complications. It works like this: take two different liquids and put them into a container with a barrier wall between, so that they cannot touch. Make the barrier of a material that is porous, and the less dense liquid will seep through into the other fluid. The two liquids work together to try to even up the density.

From this simplified explanation, all sorts of logical consequences follow. To give just a few examples: if the difference between the densities is great, the flow will be fast, and if the porosity of the barrier is minimal, the flow will be slow. Furthermore, if the two liquids are left on each side of the barrier for a long period, the flow must go on all during that period. As the flow builds up on the 'gaining' side,

the level of fluid on that side will rise ever higher. The practical application of this is seen in trees that take water from the soil and by osmotic pressure force it right to the topmost branch.

Fibreglass is not totally watertight, being more or less porous according to how it is made, precisely what materials are used, and so on. On the outside there is water, and inside the fibreglass hull shell there are liquids left over from the fabrication process. The water oozes through into the fibreglass very slowly, mixing with the globules of fluid in the hull material.

Not all osmosis is caused by the water mixing with fluids in the fibreglass. Water also filters into void spaces in the hull shell material. These are little pockets of air that the fibreglass fabricators have failed to fill when forcing resin into the glass cloth.

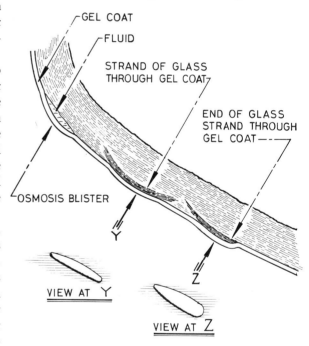

Fig 14 Osmosis and wicking

This is a section through a hull, with an osmosis bubble on the left, and two types of wicking further down the hull. The osmosis shown is the type that occurs right under the gel coat, but some kinds occur deeper inside the fibreglass lay-up.

Normal wicking is seen on the hull surface as slight ridges that stand just above the surface. Those 'lozenges' are roughly parallel sided and may be quite a bit thinner (compared with the length) than shown in the view at Y. Where the wicking is caused by fibreglass strand ends sticking up, the view of the defect on the hull is called 'pear-shaped', as shown by the view at Z. However, it can be more like a wedge with rounded corners.

The rolling-out process, whereby the resin is forced into the interstices between the glass strands, is sometimes less than perfect, and this results in little hollows being left that in the course of time the water fills. Tiny puddles become bigger – and bigger.

The increase in volume shows itself when the liquid has filled the available space and continues to grow in size. It pushes the outer skin of the hull outwards, forming a bubble on the surface. As more water from outside the hull gets through the barrier of the outer skin, the bubble must increase in volume, and so from outside the visible size of the bubble gets larger. The bubble cannot expand inwards because there is a wall of fibreglass preventing it. In theory, one can have a single osmosis bubble on a hull, or a very small number of them. They can be so few or so small that no surveyor will detect them. A few months or even weeks later they may have increased in size and number and be easily seen.

When and where to expect osmosis

Though research into osmosis continues, a good deal is now known about it. The factors that affect it include:

1 The warmer the water, the more likely there is to be osmosis. This follows logically, since warm water is less dense than cold, and so it is more enthusiastic about seeping through the barrier. Incidentally, these porous walls are called semi-permeable membranes, and they are in some respects baffling. For instance, if a bag is made from a semi-permeable membrane and filled with water, there will be no drips visible on the outside of the bag – at least for some time. Osmosis does not act like a raging torrent, but like a subtle sneaking snake moving with infinite slowness through tiny holes that are invisible to the naked eye.

2 The fresher the water, the more likely there is to be osmosis. Again this is obvious, since rainwater is less dense than salt sea water and therefore more eager to do its worst on a fibreglass boat. One consequence of this is that anyone who keeps his boat in a marina with a freshwater stream flowing into it should avoid berths near that stream. Another point that follows from this factor is that the inside of freshwater tanks are likely to have osmosis even when the rest of the vessel that floats in the sea has no trouble. A third factor is that rain on the deck or topsides can cause osmosis even when the underwater parts of the hull are free from trouble.

3 Since osmosis works 24 hours a day all the year round, when the right conditions are present, boats that lie afloat all the year round are more likely to have osmosis than boats that are slipped for the winter. Arguing on from this, boats that are under cover in the dry all winter are less likely to have the trouble than craft stored in the open and that become wet with rain or snow. Thinking further, if a boat has a winter cover made of a waterproof material such as PVC, water will stay trapped between the cover and the hull even when the rest of the boat has been dried by the wind. So where the cover touches the topsides, osmosis can 'grow' even when the boat is ashore. If the cover is dark it warms up more than a light-coloured cover when the sun shines on it. This warmth will heat the trapped patches of moisture that consequently insinuate their way through the gel coat and cause osmosis.

4 Since osmosis is in some respects affected by time, the older the vessel, the more likely she is to have this trouble; and the more winters she has been kept afloat, the more likely she is to have osmosis. If she is hauled out each winter, but very late in the year, with an early launch each spring, she is afloat a large percentage of her life, so osmosis is more likely.

5 Cheap boats tend to be built quickly with low-cost materials. The speed of construction means there may not be enough rolling out and forcing of the liquid resin into the glass mat, so air bubbles are left. These encourage osmosis. Cheap materials in general tend to be more porous, so water gets through more easily and osmosis starts sooner. However, some cheap boats have well-made fibreglass hulls, perhaps fabricated by a different firm from the one that does the final completion; and expensive boats may have hull shells made by inefficient fabricators whose work is not up to the standards of the organisation that does the fitting out.

This means that though as a basic rule the cheaper the boat the more likely there is to be osmosis, there are many exceptions to this rule. Some well-known builders have a reputation for osmosis troubles, while some inexpensive builders have the reverse.

Getting below the anti-fouling paint

When the bubbles on the hull surface are large, numerous and easy to see, the world knows about them and talks about them. Nothing spices boat conversation like a lurid tale of osmosis, especially if it is in a famous boat. A surveyor may be told about it before he sets out on the inspection – perhaps by the buyer of the craft, or by the broker, or by anyone he talks to who is connected with boats. The broker will probably explain that the osmosis is not really important and that a vast allowance has been made in the price of the boat; his aim is often to make the surveyor gloss over or minimise the osmosis in the report.

Sometimes the bubbles turn out to be paint faults, and when the anti-fouling is removed there are no signs of bumps underneath. On these occasions it is essential to check and recheck that the paint really is the trouble because osmosis bubbles sometimes reduce and flatten after weeks ashore in the dry shed. To get a good view of the hull, whether or not there are bubbles visible, the anti-fouling needs to be stripped right off in small patches.

The work may be done by the surveyor, but if he is busy, or has only a short time to inspect the whole vessel, it may be done by the boatyard. As with all work done by professionals, it is best to get a written quotation for the job, not an estimate, which is nothing more than an educated guess – sometimes by a person short of the appropriate technical education. Even a written estimate is not binding, and the person making it can always say, when the final bill is much larger, that certain factors were not allowed for when the estimate was made. Or he may say that unexpected factors affected the job, which then increased the price after the estimate was sent out.

The patches of underwater paint that are removed should be well distributed, on both sides, at bow and stern as well as amidships, and also near the waterline and near the keel. The area of each patch is a matter of personal preference and is typically 100×25 mm (4×1 in) or larger. To save time, a long narrow scraping is likely to be made more quickly than a square area. The rudder and skeg should have small areas cleaned off as they are vulnerable, and are sometimes made using materials and techniques that vary from those used on the main hull. Skegs are sometimes moulded separately from the hull and added when both have cured.

The number of patches scraped clean varies according to who is doing the job and the likelihood

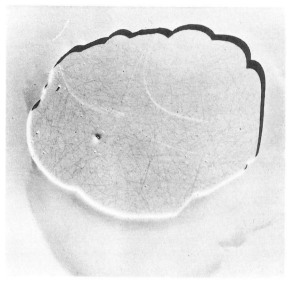

It is not often that a whole piece of gel coat comes adrift from the surface of fibreglass. However, if there is a fairly large blister or an undulating patch of the surface (usually on its own or with a few others) this may be a warning that the gel is not adhering well to the substrate. More gel will probably come off in time, especially when the boat is moved by road or otherwise shaken up. This defect is not to be confused with an accidental bump, where the underlying fibreglass also shows signs of damage, as well as the peeled gel coat. *Photo: Scott Bader.*

that there is trouble. When looking at a 25-year-old boat that has only been slipped briefly each year for repainting, and has been kept near the warm waters of a power station discharge pipe, one expects trouble. The inspector beavers away till osmosis is found or he has proved that it has not yet started, or it has occurred and been cured. His cleaned-off patches may be less than 1 m (3 ft) apart.

A boat that has all the appearances of a lovingly kept mistress, with not a blemish in sight, and all the signs of youth shining forth, will normally be given a less searching examination. The scraped areas may be 2 m apart, well staggered. On a large vessel, the spacing may be twice that distance. As this boat will almost certainly be under cover, the light will be poor and the surveyor will have to spend longer on each cleaned-off patch. He may reasonably be inclined to look at fewer areas, provided each one he inspects is free from osmosis.

Once osmosis is discovered, the situation changes with a vengeance. Now the surveyor wants to know if it is all over the hull, or only on the port side (as sometimes happens), or only near the waterline, or only on the rudder, and so on. If he finds patches generally, he does not then scrape off all the anti-fouling, since he knows that most of the boat has the malady. Even if 40% or even 65% of the boat seems to be sound, the whole hull still has to be cured.

Maybe it is coincidence, but my experience is that the most usual place to discover osmosis is near the waterline, with the aft end more likely than any-where else. As to how many craft have the illness, there is evidence that much depends on the area and the surveyor making up the figures. Anyone who is known to specialise in this problem naturally gets asked to inspect boats that are suspect or known to have osmosis. He soon comes to the conclusion that 25% or more of all craft have it at least slightly. Someone operating mainly on newish boats, with a sprinkling of steel and wood boats in his annual work list, may believe that the figure should be nearer 10% or even less. If he is in an area where the water is cold, his figure may be substantially lower. If he spends a lot of time surveying craft in particular classes that seldom suffer this trouble, his figure can be lower again.

There is no agreement as to the best tool for cleaning off the hull. Anyone worried about damag-ing the gel coat should err on the safe side and use something like the sharp square cut end of a broken fibreglass sail batten. This end will need recutting

often to keep it sharp, but it is unlikely to damage the hull surface. An ordinary wood chisel is often used, but it must be kept sharp and used with care and skill, otherwise it will dig in. A broad-bladed screwdriver is useful and widely available, but it only scrapes a narrow band with each stroke. The same applies to an ordinary surveyor's spike used sideways – that is, at right angles to the length of the blade.

Used with care, various forms of paint scraper work well, and I use a traditional form of paint scraper. It is made from an old file, heated and slightly flattened, then bent over at right angles and ground sharp. The quality of the steel is ideal, the width of the blade gives a broad scrape at a single stroke, sharpening on an electric grinder is not often needed and is easy, and the tool has just the right amount of weight to give it momentum in use.

Having found signs of osmosis, the first job is to 'log' the defect in the note-book or on the dictating machine. It is no good using chalk or indelible pen round the areas, because the marks may get washed off or deliberately removed. Also, a few owners strenuously object to markings. A better system is to describe the affected areas using references such as the distance below the waterline or above the keel, the fore and aft location relative to the stanchions that are easy to see, or relative to seacocks, or the ends of the waterline, and so on.

TYPES OF OSMOSIS

From a surveyor's point of view, osmosis is an irritat-ing problem because the knowledge of its causes and cures is constantly developing. Research continues and provides improving techniques, but the cost of the cure seldom comes down. One result of this is that surveyors are asked to suggest cheaper methods of dealing with defective boats. There are few short cuts to a full repair, though a lot of money can be saved if the owner and his crew do some of the work, because though the materials are expensive, all re-pairs involve a substantial amount of labour.

What makes life complex is that osmosis is not a single, clearly defined problem, and there are over-

lapping areas – for instance, where a vessel may have more than one type.

Osmosis in young hulls
Some surveyors will say that boats over ten years old may be susceptible to osmosis. They base their findings on their records kept over the years, and a few claim that the odds of finding the trouble are over 50%. Other practitioners put the figure even higher. Much depends on the surveyor's 'parish' or battleground. Those who live in warm areas find far higher numbers than those who put on two sweaters and a quilted overall before starting work.

Recent research suggests that osmosis that occurs as a result of glycol in the fibreglass is not related to the age of the vessel in any way. This glycol has a sticky, greasy 'feel' and it attracts water through the gel coat. The water builds up in quantity. Soon the available space cannot hold the water, so the containing space must expand outwards. It cannot go inwards because of the thickness and strength of the inner layers of fibreglass. The expansion results in blisters on the hull surface.

What is universally agreed is that osmosis discovered within the very early years of a vessel's life is bad. Unless the boat has been left in exceptionally warm fresh water almost permanently, with no epoxy coating or other defences, then the indications are that the hull has been poorly built. The trouble may stem from one cause or a combination of them:

- The resin may have been wrongly made.
- The cure may be incomplete.
- The fabricators may have spent insufficient time rolling the glass to get the resin into the cloth and air excluded.
- They may have worked their rollers hard in one area, but missed another, so that though the total rolling time may have seemed ample, patches may have been left porous.
- The rolling may have begun too early, before the resin has soaked into the glass mat and cloth.
- Solvents that attract water may have been left in the hull.
- Too much radiant heat during the cure may cause blistering in early life.

One obvious conclusion to all this is that skill, experience and dedication are needed to make a good product using GRP. The myth that fibreglass boatbuilding requires little or no skill dies hard.

Limited blistering

When only a small area of little blisters has been found, the owner or buyer of the vessel will want to know what he should do. One school of thought says leave the matter to develop fully, then do a comprehensive job putting the trouble right once and for all. The other approach is to cure the localised defect, and keep an eye out for future developments, which may never arise. This is probably the best approach for a buyer, who will not want to own a craft that is less than pristine, and not quite blemish-free. Pride of ownership is an important consideration for many people.

Some people are prepared to leave a minor case of osmosis untouched, but want to know when repairs must definitely be carried out. The answer cannot be precise, but, as a rough rule, blisters that are between 4 and 8 mm are a sign that a full overall treatment is now definitely due. If the bubbling covers more than a twelfth of the hull surface, it certainly cannot be left untouched.

Whether repairs are carried out right away or deferred, it is usual for a seller to reduce the price of the boat by enough to pay for the renewal process. Sometimes he concedes the full repair cost, sometimes half or three-quarters of it. It depends on how keen or desperate he is to sell, and how enthusiastic or relaxed the buyer is. However, if the boat is on the market and the osmosis is mentioned in the list of

This is wrinkling on the surface of fibreglass. It occurs when the resin binding the glass fibres is wrongly made. It is fairly rare, but may be seen in a small area when for instance most of the resin has been correctly made, but a final little batch is unsatisfactory. If warm air blowers are used in the boatbuilder's shed, and if they are directed over instead of away from the mould, they can cause this trouble. *Photo: Scott Bader.*

particulars, then the defect is 'built in' to the price. The owner is admitting to potential buyers that there is something wrong with the craft, and the asking price is seldom thereafter negotiated on the cost of the osmosis cure. In practice, it is usual for some other defect discovered during the survey to result in some negotiating. Whenever a vessel is being bought, the final price is often different from the one agreed prior to the survey.

Serious and extensive blisters

Where there are blisters more or less all over the hull below the waterline, or where the bubbles are big, there is one school of thought that says in effect: 'To hell with it – this hull is like an old car that is very rusty. Such a vehicle can be driven into the ground as long as the engine goes on working – even if the doors have to be welded shut, I can always climb in and out of the windows' – and so on. This is not a safe analogy. A hull that is being seriously attacked by osmosis is gradually becoming softer and weaker, and boats that lack strength eventually sink. Also, they do not always choose the most convenient time and place to do so. Advanced osmosis should not be allowed to 'take its course'.

There is plenty of evidence that a hull that has massive blistering can be given a useful future. There have been boats that have been left afloat and neglected for years, so that they have become 'osmosed' to a sensational degree. With skill and care, time and determination these boats have been scoured off on the outside, examined, carefully dried, rechecked, epoxy treated, filled and faired, then given more epoxy coatings. This is the standard rejuvenation procedure. The results have been encouraging, and these boats now seem to be safe. One would not suggest that such a craft should be used to circle the world, but they do seem (on the available evidence) to be reliable enough to use for normal coastal cruising or commercial operations in settled summer weather.

The cure may be as dramatic as a good thriller. The hull may have to be reduced to half its original thickness by the surface grinder or 'peeling' machine, followed by grit blasting. A surface stripper has been likened to an 'intelligent' sanding machine, as it follows a curved hull surface automatically. Some technicians say it seals over the surface in places, and they prefer a 'peeler' which has a sharp cutting blade. Everyone agrees that grit blasting is needed after either of these machines. Used on its own, a blaster may have trouble getting deep enough below the surface without using excess pressure and causing damage when it comes across a hard surface such as an old epoxy repair.

In places, this power-blasting may go right through the hull, so the furniture, cabin sole, tanks and such like should mostly be taken out. It will almost certainly be necessary to support the hull at close intervals when the shell thickness is reduced substantially. Common sense suggests that when the hull is being renewed it should be made at least a little thicker than the original specification. The extra thickness might be substantial. Any experienced surveyor will have his own private list of owners who are ruthless hard drivers – men and women who only

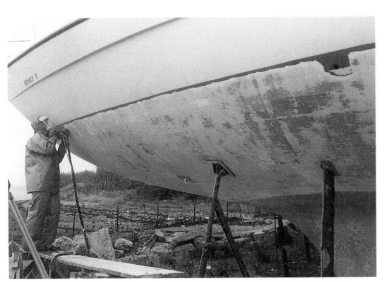

A hull peeling tool is being used to slice off the gel coat on a boat with osmosis. This exposes the outer layering of fibreglass, which is then washed, rechecked, fully dried, filled and coated over. The peeling tool makes less mess, is more controllable than grit blasting, and is quicker than hand stripping.

reef when the wind speed indicator has been blown away. When rebuilding for anyone, but especially for this sort of person, it is best to recommend a hull that ends up 15% or, on occasions, 30% thicker than when new. In very special circumstances, the additional thickness may be even greater. This rebuilding should be to a high standard, with all the edges carefully tapered away so that no one can detect that the hull shell thickness has been increased. Where it is hard to build up extra thickness, there should be some reinforcing such as additional frames or stringers or a higher grade of material than common fibreglass.

For really massive additional ruggedness, one would go for both internal stiffeners and extra shell thickness. When in doubt, it always makes sense to increase the strength of any structure in circumstances like these. The added structure will be concentrated mainly forward, also round the mast step, in the area below the sole amidships, where keel loads are, in the area of the engine bearers and by heavy tanks.

Wet blisters

When a bubble on a hull is pricked it sometimes exudes a fluid. The pressure in the blister may be high and the liquid sometimes comes out in a little spurt. The fluid may be checked with litmus paper to confirm that it is acidic. This acid is formed when the emulsion adhesive that binds chopped strand mat together (and also acts as a wetting agent) breaks down with water. If the boat is properly constructed, the wetting agent will have done its job and will not be available to combine with water.

Things are likely to be made worse because a lack of wetting through suggests local shortages of resin, and hence voids into which water will seep. This can occur even when the builder has used the correct *total* amount of resin for the vessel. There may be too much resin in some areas, and not enough in others. For instance, runny resin sometimes flows down to the bottom of the mould. A quick check along the keel line to see if there is resin richness here may help to explain, at least in part, why there is osmosis elsewhere on the hull shell.

If the characteristic sticky, greasy feel of glycol is detected, the surveyor must insist that the cure is thorough and elaborate. Glycol attracts water, so it is important that after a hull being repaired is scoured off, it is washed thoroughly to get rid of the acid and glycol. Heating alone is no good because glycol has a

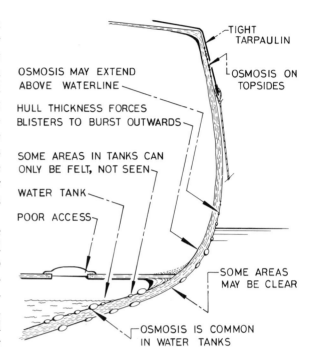

Fig 15 The spread of osmosis

Though most osmosis is found below the waterline, it sometimes appears in other places. If it is on the topside, as a result of an area being kept damp, the bubbles are likely to be small and the area limited. Osmosis below the waterline often extends about half a hand's span above the flotation line. Very occasionally bilge-water causes internal osmosis. Inside water tanks osmosis is extremely common, but not always visible. Fingers have to be run delicately over the surface to feel the bubbles in the areas not directly below the inspection hatches.

high boiling point. A pressure washer is needed to get rid of this pollutant, and it should be fed with hot water to ensure it combines with all the glycol. Some specialists recommend steam cleaning, but this is not universally popular because it requires additional equipment and careful handling. Current recommendations are for repeated washing with warm water every two or three days for two weeks. However, some osmosis repairers claim that as boats cannot be left in expensive sheds for long periods, the washing can be carried out daily for one week. When using a water jet, the pressure is typically set at 3000 psi, but it can be up to 6000 psi. Any pressure higher than this will damage the hull.

Drying after this washing needs to be carefully carried out. Electric heaters of the 'black tube' type are put inside the hull at about 6 m (20 ft) intervals. Externally the drying must not be rushed. The level of moisture is lowered first by using dehumidifiers, with heaters being brought in later. To check the moisture levels, one of the best instruments to use is a moisture meter made by Tramex Ltd of Chamco House, Shankill, Co Dublin, Ireland. The moisture level should be down to 14% or less before the build-up of epoxy coatings can begin. The moisture level in the hull has to be checked daily, and it should fall steadily. It will not do this if glycol is left in the fibreglass. Even on a torrentially wet day the moisture level should not rise much, as the boat is under cover and protected from the outside atmosphere as much as possible.

Different paint makers ask for various procedures, depending on the precise formulation of their products. The cleaned, dried fibreglass should be coated with solvent-free epoxies, otherwise solvents may get trapped in the build-up of the protective coatings. In this case, osmosis may soon reappear. The fillers that are put into the hollows and crannies of the fibreglass also have to be solvent-free. They go on between layers of the paint build-up.

Dry blisters

When a set of blisters is opened up and found to be totally dry, the surveyor may not be looking at osmosis. These bubbles may be due to a pigment that has not been properly mixed. If the pigment is in little lumps it absorbs moisture. On the other hand, osmosis can cause bubbles that grow and grow, then burst, releasing the fluid inside. In time these popped blisters can dry out, especially when the boat is ashore in a dry well-ventilated shed. However, it is unlikely that all the blisters will be totally dry in these circumstances, so the search has to be long and thorough.

The normal cure for a *limited* area of dry blistering is heavy abrasion to level the surface and remove the bubbling, followed by the filling and fairing, after the first epoxy paint coat. Three, four or five layers of epoxy paint are applied after the filling. This should prevent further trouble in the treated area, but the problem may arise elsewhere. It has to be admitted that epoxy is not totally effective as a water barrier, but it seems more efficient than other practical compounds tried. The rate at which it lets water seep through is extremely slow, but the edges of the newly painted area are a danger point. That is why the area treated extends a metre beyond the bubbling at each side, also above and below. In all osmosis repairs, where the trouble extends to the

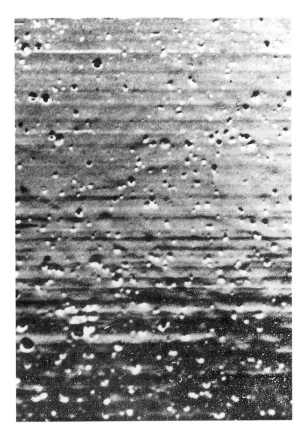

Pinholing is a fairly common defect on the surface of glass-fibre, especially in repairs that have been done without proper skill. It is caused by entrapped air bubbles in the gel coat or repair material. In practice it is often less dramatic than this, and may be in a small area or batch of areas. If there is no dirt in the holes it can be hard to spot, especially on a deck or topsides saturated with torrential rain. *Photo: Scott Bader.*

waterline, it is usual to carry the repairs about 200 mm (8 in) above the waterline.

Some owners leave small areas of dry bubbles untreated, on the basis that the trouble is going to spread, and a full cure should not be made until the problem has worked its way through the hull. This is seldom a good plan as moisture will get deeper into the laminates and cause assorted troubles. These include the separation of the layers of cloth and mat. Once this happens, the hull progressively loses strength.

Soft hulls and curing

The hull of a fibreglass boat should 'ring' when tapped with the edge of a coin. If the coin makes an indent, the hull shell is almost certainly under-cured, and likely to be weak. Osmosis may well be present, or in the offing. In a very serious case, a thumb-nail may cause a tiny mark on the hull, but it is rare to find a situation as bad as this.

There was a time when an instrument called a Barcol Hardness Tester, or Barcol Impressor, was widely used for determining the quality of the fibreglass surface. Opinion now seems to be swinging away from using this device, though some surveyors continue to use it regularly. Part of the reason why it is not so popular is that there is no unanimity as to what is a satisfactory standard. A figure over 50 on the Barcol scale is widely accepted as satisfactory, but some people will accept 40. Most agree 25 is too low and 20 is dangerous. To complicate the issue, there have been special 'soft' resins, developed to withstand wear and tear, and these must give low Barcol readings. A principal reason why Barcol testing is not universally popular is that the results will vary according to what 'fillers' are added to the resin. Also, fibreglass strands near the surface (which admittedly may in themselves be a defect) can give misleading readings.

When checking a brand-new boat, it is important to confirm that the hull, deck, cabin top and other GRP mouldings are more than a month old, so as to be sure they have fully cured. One proof that cure is complete is that the smell should have disappeared; this will not happen if there is no ventilation. Chemical smells are not popular with owners, and in the early days of fibreglass, a wash of vinegar, or vinegar and water, was used to get rid of the odour. Nowadays a domestic air freshener or scented compound sold in hardware shops is more often used. If a smell inside a hull persists, and it has been established that the cure is complete, the usual cure is to paint the interior with 2-pack polyurethane paint.

Wicking

(Strictly speaking, this is not osmosis, but it is almost always linked with it because the symptoms and cures are related. See Fig 14.)

When the blisters on the hull are long and thin, the problem is called 'wicking'. It is the result of water getting into the strands of fibreglass that lie near the surface, just below, or sometimes in the gel coat. This defect is easier to detect on colourless hulls, once the anti-fouling has been stripped off. Pale lines are seen running randomly in all directions in the gel coat. Sometimes the end, rather than the middle, of a bunch of thin glass fibres is through, or deep into, the gel coat. Water seeps through the thin outer 'skin' and into the glass. There is a natural tendency for the water to be sucked along the fibres, bulking them out. Any expansion has to be outwards, as the solid backing and strength of the hull shell prevents swelling inwards.

If the weather turns cold, the trapped water freezes and increases in volume. When warm conditions return there is every opportunity for more water to filter in; and of course under 'melting' conditions there is usually plenty of moisture about, running down the hull and in the air. Even without the additional destructive effects of freezing weather, wicking is likely to occur if the strands of glass are not adequately covered over by resin during the hull fabrication. Where the ends of a strand are near (or on) the surface, the long thin blister will be thicker at one end. Instead of appearing as a thin parallel-sided ridge, it may be more like an elongated egg, broader towards one end.

An owner with this defect has the consolation of knowing that there is less likely to be weakening voids and, provided a suitable surface is built up, that will normally be the end of the problem, although the hull surface should be rechecked annually. Where there are hollows in the hull structure (as there are with so many forms of osmosis), there must always be a worry that even the most careful grit-blasting to open up the cavities has not penetrated deeply enough into the thickness of the shell.

Wicking should not be treated lightly. It can suck in water month by month, and this separates the layers of fibreglass. It pays to remember the symbol of the Romans: a bundle of sticks tightly tied together. The ancients realised that each stick on its own was weak, but bound in a bundle they were unbreakable. So it is with layers of fibreglass. As long as they are bonded well, they form a strong hull. Once the layers have peeled apart by the ingress of water, they result in a floppy, flimsy, frightening hull that cannot stand up to rough weather or bumping into flotsam.

BULKHEADS in FIBREGLASS CONSTRUCTION

A fibreglass hull is 'all of a piece', to use an old boat-builder's expression. It is in some ways like a welded steel shell, in that the structure is all one part, and the strength continuous, without joins from bow to transom except where the hull meets the deck. It differs from a planked hull, which has a lot of strong parts held together by fastenings, each of which allows a tiny movement.

Whether or not there are stringers and frames in a fibreglass hull, the rigidity is fairly uniform all over. Into these relatively flexible hulls it is normal practice to fit plywood bulkheads that are in several respects more rigid than the surrounding fibreglass. This is especially true if the bulkheads are strengthened with door-posts or pillars vertically, as well as beams and sole bearers athwartships.

Bulkheads are fitted to divide up the cabins, but they have a more important purpose: they give the

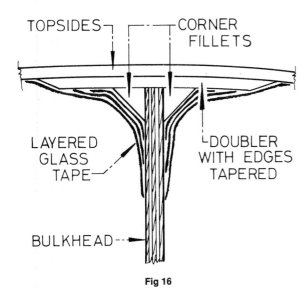

Fig 16

This sketch shows the way a good builder will fit a bulkhead into a fibreglass hull. The doubler is to prevent the bulkhead from imposing a high local loading on the shell and the fillet wedges are to avoid sharp angles for the glass tape to bridge. Not all boats have all these details at each bulkhead edge, but the more the builders have departed from this arrangement, the lower the quality of construction and the more likely resulting defects.

hull strength and stiffness. They prevent the topsides and deck from distorting when buffeted by the waves or nudged by other craft in the harbour. They help to retain the shape, and are good for holding heavily loaded fittings such as the chain plates. The best bulkheads are full depth and width so that they hold the cabin top up, support the sidedecks, stiffen the topsides, prevent the turn of the bilge from flattening out or increasing in curvature, and they resist the panting of the lower part of the hull, which is pressed in by water pressure, especially when pounding into a head sea. To do all this, a bulkhead has to be fully and carefully bonded on all round, on both fore and aft sides.

If for some reason a bulkhead does not extend right up to the underside of the sidedecks, or right down into the bilge, or it is only glassed in on the aft side, this should be mentioned in a survey report. It is a clear case of potential strength being thrown away. And if there is one thing that can be said about the majority of modern (and not so recent) craft, it is that they are not wonderfully strong. 'Adequate rather than rugged' is the way hardened boatbuilders think of current vessels.

Any boat that is being surveyed prior to a long voyage across wide oceans needs all the strength available, and it is a good idea to make sure that the entire perimeter of all bulkheads is fully, continuously and strongly bonded on to the hull on the forward and aft sides. A single row of glass tape is always inadequate, and even on a small boat two thicknesses is too little. On the small cruisers and decked motor boats, three runs is common and widely considered just enough. For serious offshore work, four runs is the minimum for peace of mind. Large craft, over 11 m (36 ft), need more.

The way bulkheads are glassed in tells a surveyor plenty about the boat's builder. If the fore side of the forward bulkhead is not bonded in with strips of fibreglass (and plenty are not), the builder has saved money by avoiding work in an awkward location. It so happens that the bow is where many of the heavy stresses come, and it is here that there is often a lack of 'shape-strength' because the topsides are flat. Lacking the strength of well-curved panels, the for-

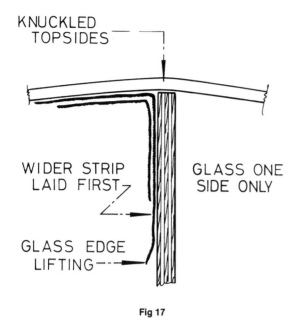

KNUCKLED
TOPSIDES

WIDER STRIP
LAID FIRST

GLASS ONE
SIDE ONLY

GLASS EDGE
LIFTING

Fig 17

Typical defects of a badly glassed-in bulkhead are shown
here. These troubles will not extend right round the perimeter
of the bulkhead except in really bad instances. Trouble is most
likely where the work is most difficult of access, namely high
up under a deck-edge and deep down in a confined bilge
space.

ward sections need all the reinforcing that a bulkhead
can supply. Glassing on one side reduces the potential strength by more than 50%. Cured fibreglass
such as the tape around bulkhead edges bends easily
enough, and acts like a slow-moving hinge. This in
turn peels the glassing off the inside of the hull, or off
the bulkhead, or both. An additional reason for
applying fibreglass on both fore-and-aft edges of each
bulkhead is to exclude water from the ply. Moisture
quickly soaks in when it reaches a bulkhead edge
because at least half the plies have exposed end grain.
Where the line of the hull is angled diagonally across
the runs of grain, all plies are vulnerable to soakage.

Most years a busy surveyor will come across rot
at the bottom of a bulkhead, where bilge-water has
slopped up and soaked in. The darkening and discoloration normally make the defect easy to see,
especially if there is some form of fungoid growth. If
the deterioration appears from the outside to extend
over 20 cm diameter, it probably affects an area
30 cm across. Rot is also found where water can
lodge, especially if there are fastenings into the ply.
Places like the tops of berths, cabin thresholds, settee
tops, and along sole end bearers are the places to

look. This is where we peer, expecting to find the
tell-tale darkening and perhaps the glint of moisture.
Condensation, leaks through windows, drips from
the deck at the chain plates, and spray through
hatches are all culprits. Sometimes there is no rot, but
a subtle softening of the wood, and perhaps flecks of
black mildew, indicating that trouble is brewing. The
outer laminate of the ply may be split, or peeling, or
uneven where it has swollen with the damp. On
other occasions the outside layers of the ply are fine,
but the inner ones are slightly soft – or even totally
lacking in strength. Probing with a spike will reveal a
lot about the condition.

The common fault on glassed-in bulkheads is failure of the bonding. It sometimes peels off the inside
of the hull shell, but far more often the glassing
comes adrift from the bulkhead. There are assorted
reasons for this. The glassing may lack adequate
width, the wood may be badly prepared and, in some
cases, not even cleaned and roughened. I have even
seen the glassing applied to the shiny smooth
slightly oily plastic Formica-type laminate. There is
little chance that the fibreglass will bond well and
stay tight on such a smooth surface, which is in every
respect so unsympathetic to glassing-in.

Peeling glass is usually easy to see, as there is
often a light patch, sometimes slightly greenish or
yellowy, with the individual strands of glass clearly
visible. Where the glass is holding on tightly it is
translucent, and the wood can be seen, or sensed,
through the layers of fibreglass. When peeling is present, there is normally a tiny gap between the wood
and the bonding.

A spike is pushed down the bulkhead at intervals
and, where the bonding has let go, the spike slithers
into the gap. Wise surveyors use a 25 cm (10 in) or
longer spike, partly to give a good reach to awkward
corners, but also to keep the hands well back from the
sharp serrated edge of the fibreglass tape, which cuts
flesh so effectively. It is unusual to find a single short
length of deglassing, so once one area has been discovered the surveyor knows he is on the right track.
He ferrets away until he has tested the opposite face
of the bulkhead, also the adjacent bulkheads; and
where the first trouble is found on the port, he
expects to discover something similar on the starboard side. He also tests the nearby furniture, sole
bearers, and so on. Peeling glass is, as it were, conta-
gious. Where there is a little, the surveyor should
suspect it has been spreading for months. There is a
certain logic in this. If the glass was poorly applied in

one area, the same shipwright probably made other mistakes, resulting in more weak points. Good shipwrights are good all the time; sloppy ones leave a trail of troubles.

In addition, when the glassing fails at one point, the adjacent areas have to withstand higher stresses, so they are more likely to peel off in their turn. This is a principle that applies in any structure and is a useful guide when doing any surveying. The cure for deglassing bulkhead edges is normally straightforward. All the peeling glass is ground off, and the preparation carried a hand span or more further along on to the good glass. The hull and bulkhead are carefully cleaned, rechecked and prepared for new glassing. This should be wider, thicker and stronger — also, it should be bonded on using an epoxy resin.

A surveyor may come across a bulkhead that has popped right out. This happens when the glassing fractures or rips off right round, so that the whole bulkhead moves inside the hull. Naturally a forward bulkhead moves aft, and an aft one forward, as this is the way the hull tapers. A less dramatic event is when just one side of the bulkhead comes totally adrift, and lurches right out of its proper home. I understand this sort of high drama occurred inside one or two yachts in the Fastnet gale of 1979. It takes a lot of pummelling to shift a whole bulkhead a visible distance. Racing yachts that do not have much internal furniture inside are more likely to have this sort of trouble. In cruisers there is so much in the way of berths and lockers fitting tightly between the bulkheads, so that serious movement is difficult — unless of course great chunks of furniture are dislodged, as happens when a severe grounding takes place.

It is not easy to make an entirely reliable firm bonding of fibreglass on to the ply bulkhead, especially if the labour force is short of skill, experience, motivation and supervision. To get over this, and to give some extra strength, builders put bolts fore and aft through the bulkhead and glass tape. They often degrade a sensible precaution by locating the fastenings 35 cm (14 in) or more apart. A spacing of 25 cm (10 in) or less for inshore craft, and half that for ocean-crossers, is better. It is common practice to use roofing bolts because they are threaded up to or near the head, so the total thickness of the bulkhead plus its glassing is immaterial. Ordinary bolts only have a short length of thread on them. Roofing bolts are cheap, which is partly why they are selected, and they have broad heads. However, they need large washers under the head and nut. They are electro-

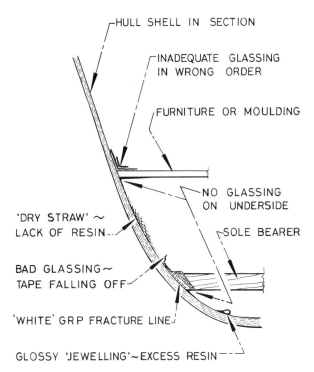

Fig 18

The quality of a fibreglass hull is hard to discover, but tiny clues always help. If there are areas where the resin has not fully wetted the glass cloth or mat, this shows up as 'dry straw', while below there may be regions where the resin has run down into puddles or 'jewels'; this suggests poor workmanship.

Glass tape put on with the narrow bands on top of wider ones indicates poor supervision and inexpert fabrication, as do places where the edges of the tape have peeled off or have never been rolled down firmly. Breaks in the glass where it has been used to hold in bulkheads or sole bearers and such like can be hard to see. They sometimes show up as pale (almost white) lines, which often run along the sharp interior angle of the glassing-in.

plated against rust, but this form of defence is not even moderately effective at sea and rust can be seen here in boats only two years old. It is good sense to suggest in a survey report that the bolts together with their nuts and washers are well painted and kept so, as they rust soon, swiftly, and with evident enthusiasm.

A ploy used by a few careful builders to get a good permanent bond of glass to ply involves drilling holes round the perimeter of the bulkhead. These holes are typically 30 mm ($1\frac{1}{4}$ in) diameter, and spaced perhaps 250 mm (10 in) apart. They are deeply countersunk on the fore and aft sides of the bulkhead, then glass cloth is fed through. Extra strands of loose glass are also poked through the holes, and plenty of resin wetted into the glass. This bonds the glass tape on the fore side of the bulkhead to the aft side. It is a time-consuming job, and not popular with anyone trying to build swiftly or cheaply.

When looking at bulkheads it is worth thinking about the ship's ventilation. It is rare to see vent slots or gratings in bulkheads, and the only way air can get past, when the door is closed, is below the sole. Some bulkheads extend right to the bottom of the hull, which gives good strength but no air-flow. Even when there is a gap between the hull and the bottom of the bulkhead, there is seldom an adequate flow of air in the bilge. This is principally because the sole is secured tight down all round and sometimes sealed at the edges.

Bulkheads should not bow or bend. A straight edge held vertically or horizontally should touch along its full length. Where it does not, there may be overloading, due for instance to the downward pressure of a deck-stepped mast. Sometimes these bends are caused by poor joins, where two sheets of ply have been fitted edge to edge. A bolted doubler or, better still, one on the forward and one on the aft side of the seam, should cure this trouble. This is a typical situation where years of experience recommends thick reinforcing pieces with lots of through bolts, staggered or zigzagged, and half a hand's span apart.

Overstressed bulkheads tell of their problems by forcing door frames off, opening up seam joins, coming away from pillars, and so on. If there is a door through, sometimes it will not shut or, when shut, it can be the very devil to open. The bulkhead near the mast on a sailing yacht sometimes distorts when the rigging is tightened, or when the vessel is pressed hard on the wind. This is shown by the way the door can be closed in harbour, but not at sea, except in the calmest weather.

It seems to be current practice to accept this degree of bulkhead bending for craft that stay within 'shouting for help' range of the shore; but for deep-sea vessels that must look after themselves in all weathers, such flexing can hardly be considered acceptable. Whatever type of craft is being checked, there should be ample width of bulkhead between the doorway cut-out and the edge of the bulkhead. Just what the minimum width must be will depend on the size of craft and the hull thickness, and so on. As a rough guide, 15 cm (6 in) is probably a minimum.

Strengthening weak bulkheads is normally straightforward. Stiffeners of metal or timber are bolted on, athwartships and vertically. Existing reinforcing, such as doubling pieces and beams, are made to work more effectively by fitting extra bolts, properly staggered. Few builders use bolts in this location. Often there is nothing but widely spaced thin screws holding a chunky beam to a bulkhead. Subtle gaps between the ply and the beam show where the screws are failing to do a proper job. Where possible, some epoxy glue is run in to these fissures before closing them with bolts. If the bolt heads and nuts cannot be dowelled over, they should be of a decorative type to go with the adjacent furnishings. When adding extra wood stiffeners, glue as well as bolt is used – provided the bulkhead is not covered with a plastic laminate such as Formica or Wareite, or something similar.

It is seldom easy to confirm that a bulkhead is exactly at right angles to the centreline of the vessel, and surveyors seldom make any tests unless a bulkhead is obviously misaligned. A quick check can be made by measuring from the fore side of the adjacent bulkhead to the aft side of the doubtful one. Another measurement is then made from the bulkhead forward of the questionable one. The dimensions taken are as near as possible fore and aft parallel with the centreline, right out to port and then to starboard. Of course, the bulkheads being used as 'controls' can be misaligned too, so, to be safe, a whole series of measurements has to be made right through the vessel. Slight misalignment is seldom important, though it does suggest that the standard of construction is not high.

If the whole matter is of importance, a taut line is run through the hull, fixed at each end on the centreline. The surveyor has to borrow or make up a really large set square or Tee square. These instruments are found in boatyards and sail lofts, and are typically a metre or so in length along the sides. They can be useful tools here and elsewhere, but they are not often used, so few surveyors own them. Using one of these large 'squares' it is not too hard to see if the bulkhead alignment is accurate, provided the circumstances are propitious. Among the problems that arise are:

- There are offset doors in the bulkheads, so the taut line cannot extend right through the boat on the centreline.
- There are no facilities for securing the line and drawing it very tight.

- The cockpit or some such obstruction gets in the way of the taut line.
- A helper, or some sort of jig or support is needed to steady the square against the taut line.

Surveying is seldom straightforward, and getting round these difficulties will involve drawing on that stock of ingenuity that all good surveyors have.

When the hull is viewed from outboard it should be impossible to detect where the bulkheads are. If the builder has put the bulkheads in without proper preparations, or into a hull that is still 'green' and not fully cured, the topsides may have a subtle knuckle in way of each bulkhead. Thin fibreglass hulls need some doubling in way of each bulkhead to prevent local distortions to the hull shell. A great many builders do not put in doublers. Instead they fit the bulkhead with a gap all round, and apply fibreglass tape round the edge to secure the ply in place, and also to act as a 'spring-loaded' join. This avoids hard spots, provided all goes well. If the bulkhead touches in just one place, the hull shell may end up with a hard spot there, as a lot of stress may be concentrated in a small area.

· ·

BALLAST KEEL SUPPORT STRUCTURES

When the cabin sole boards amidships are lifted, the structure that comes into view may look like part of a crossword puzzle pattern made in fibreglass, with the smooth gel coat finish facing upwards. This grid consists of one, two or three fore-and-aft fibreglass upstanding ridges or bars, and a number of athwartships ones. The structure is a separate moulding that has been made after the hull moulding was completed. It is fitted before the deck and furniture go in. This strong grid is principally designed to support the weight of the ballast keel, but it has secondary purposes that may include acting as sole bearers, tying in and holding settee fronts, securing and stiffening the bottoms of bulkheads, and strengthening the lower part of the hull.

This important strength unit has various names, including 'octopus' (because it has lots of arms), 'spider' (for the same reason) and 'waffle'. The latter name is used in the United States, and it is the most accurate. However, it is a little misleading, because waffles have cross-bars that are all the same size, whereas in a fibreglass boat the fore-and-aft parts tend to be wider than the athwartships ones, and a waffle for eating is rectangular, whereas one in a boat has, as a rule, slightly curved sides. This 'octo-spiwaffle' carries the keel bolts, spreads the loads from the keel (and sometimes the mast heel), and adds strength to what is usually a fairly lightly built hull shell. It is bonded inside the hull at flanges that run fore-and-aft as well as athwartships. It may extend up the sides of the boat outboard of the settees, and it should certainly be longer than the keel.

The whole idea seems elegant, and at first sight appears to be good engineering. However, the troubles these 'waffles' cause are numerous, subtle and sometimes impossible to detect until the problem has become well developed. If the bonding on to the hull fails, the openings may not be at the edges, and so they are completely out of sight even when all the furniture and obstructions have been removed. Admittedly, any peeling of the hull is likely to start at the edges, but it still may be inaccessible because it is covered by a tank or settee front or some such. Even when a slot is detected between the hull and the 'waffle', it is seldom possible to tell how far this dangerous separation has travelled. A narrow flexible knife blade can sometimes be slid into the fissure, and it may show how far the bonding has cracked open — or it may not.

Recommending repairs is hard until the whole boat has been opened up fully amidships. Often the only safe procedure is to assume that once the bonding has failed in one place, it is about to do the same all over. It may seem over-cautious to recommend taking out the entire 'waffle' or 'spider' just to make sure a small break has not extended far across or along the whole structure, but any partial repair is risky. This structural component is as important as any in the hull, and if it fails totally the keel may tear off and sink the boat swiftly.

A 'waffle' largely depends for its effectiveness on the bond between it and the hull. This bond is made up as a resin or paste or cement and applied to the flanges that touch the inside of the hull. The people who put the 'octopus' or 'waffle' in place have no way of knowing if the flanges are in good contact with the hull, nor can they be sure that the bonding material has cured correctly all over. They cannot even be sure if the bonding is continuous, or has air bubbles, or has been made so liquid that it has all drained down to the low point in the hull. They can calculate the theoretical strength of the bond, but what they cannot be sure is whether the bond is strong enough to work in a rough sea. The builder is trying to secure a discontinuous surface that is curved in both directions, and the 'end product' is out of sight except round the edges.

The principal consequence of a failed bond is that the hull lacks strength in way of the keel. This is shown up when the yacht is hauled out. The hull bottom is seen to dent inwards port and starboard, fore and aft of the keel. Instead of the hull being flat or convex outwards at the keel, it is concave. Sometimes the indent is only seen at the forward or aft end of the fin keel, suggesting that the 'waffle' has failed at that end, but is still holding on at the other end. However, it may mean that the hull is well supported by a bow or stern cradle or chock, and supported elsewhere by the keel, which is distorting the shell inwards.

A straight edge, which can be just a length of wood planed exactly straight along one edge, is laid on the bottom of the boat, first athwartships at the front and back of the keel, then fore and aft on each side of the keel. If daylight shows in the middle of the straight edge, the hull shell is being pressed inwards by the keel. There are builders who say that a little indenting and flexing here is acceptable, but would they say the same if they were on board – with the boat fighting off a cliff-bound lee shore in a Force 11?

A 'spider' or 'waffle' is designed to absorb the loads as the keel shakes and jolts when the yacht pounds to windward, or races down a wave-face under a bulging spinnaker. It is seldom strong enough to take the wrench when the boat runs aground, especially if this happens when going fast, or even at a moderate speed. On lightly built racing machines, a grounding at 2 knots can cause extensive damage if the front of the keel is nearly vertical, the sea-bed is rock, and the scantlings are extremely thin. Sometimes the crew do not realise there is slight damage, so they press on, driving the boat with that well-known race-bred enthusiasm. What they report as 'a very slight grounding – we hardly felt a thing', may have produced just enough damage to start tears in the 'waffle'. Subsequent straining can extend these rents right through each part; and when one 'bar' of a 'waffle' fails, it throws a great load on the next one, which may in turn fail, and so on to the next.

A fracture shows as whiskers of fibreglass strands in a jagged line where the gel coat has chipped away. A spike goes through the line of the break effortlessly. Once the boat has been fully opened up, the trouble is easy to see; but if there is a cabin sole made of an internal moulding over the 'waffle', it may be impossible to get anything but a glimpse of 1% of the structure. One thing is certain: if a single crack is seen, the whole structure should be made visible as it is likely there will be several breaks. As these fractures are so important, and as they can creep because there are no crack-limiters built in, this is an area where no risks can be taken.

Repairs consist of three jobs:

1 The boat is opened up and made accessible.
2 The damage to the 'waffle' is repaired.
3 The furniture, tanks, wiring, and plumbing, etc are put back.

It can be seen from this that to do one basic repair there are three sets of jobs, of which the first and last are not productive. This is why this type of renewal is so expensive. It is tempting when mending a 'waffle' to layer on the new bonding thickly. This is an admirable trait, but it needs controlling. The adhesion of the inside structure to the hull shell is critical, so the gluing compound must dry out and harden at the right speed, and without distortion. Also, the top of the 'octopus' must be at the same level as it originally was if it supports the sole.

There may be limber holes in the 'waffle' and these form weaknesses where cracks are likely to be found. During repairs, these holes must be kept clear so that water will flow through, but they often need strengthening with layered glassfibre over the top. If there are no limber holes, the keel bolts may lie in permanent puddles, and so corrode. When replacing a 'waffle' after mending it, the keel bolt holes have to be lined up exactly with those in the hull, and the bonding material must not fill the holes.

The nuts on top of the keel bolts are sometimes down in the hollows between the bars of the 'waffle' and sometimes on top of the bars. Alternatively, they may be recessed into hollows on top of the bars to allow the cabin sole to fit on top of the 'waffle'. Cracking at the edge of the washers under the nuts is an indication that the yacht may have run aground, and suggests that a very full inspection is needed, with all the adjacent sole boards (and perhaps some furniture) removed.

· ·

FIBREGLASS FLOORS

In traditional boatbuilding terminology, regardless of the material used, the 'floors' are the athwartships strength members across the centreline structure. On wood and metal vessels they form the links with the bottoms of the port and starboard frames, and tie the frames to the strong backbone running fore and aft.

Fibreglass floors have much in common with those made of other materials, except that they often do not link on to framing. They are generally vertical flat-sided pieces of fibreglass with a horizontal top, which means they taper out each side as the hull shell rises up towards the turn of bilge. Their top edges tend to have wooden battens secured on, to support the cabin sole.

Whatever the material, floors are important. Often they do not get the care they deserve when being designed and built. Construction varies, but quite often plywood is used as a former and core. It should be covered all over with chopped strand mat. It is a mark of bad building if the ends of the floors are not totally glassed over and well bonded on to the hull shell or berth fronts. Sometimes the core is paper tubing or a light foam plastic, and occasionally it is metal angle-bar with the flat flange drilled for the keel bolts. Metal is not popular because of its expense, and the difficulty of getting the fibreglass to adhere well and bed down tightly.

If there is one consistent weakness in fibreglass boatbuilding, it is the lack of strength amidships in an athwartships direction. This is what fibreglass floors are intended to·cure, but time after time surveyors find that there are too few floors and they lack strength. This flimsiness is partly caused by the lack of depth. It is basic engineering know-how to appreciate that a deep floor is vastly stronger than one that extends just a few fingers thickness above the keel. Designers and builders want to keep the cabin sole as low as possible to give lots of head-room, so they sacrifice the strength of the floors – and live to regret it.

It would not be so bad if there was plenty of fore-and-aft thickness to compensate, but it is usual to find that 12 mm ($\frac{1}{2}$ in) ply has been used as the core, and the spacing is often such that there are only three or four floors along the full length of the ballast keel. In the same way, floors are seldom extended far outboard. It is quite common to terminate them at the berth fronts, and tie them to these parts of the structure, even though the width between the berths is small. Of course it is much more trouble, and therefore more expensive, to slot the bottoms of the settee inboard faces and run the floors up to the turn of bilge. However, this should be done if there are widespread signs of weakness in way of the keel. Also, the floor ends should not be in a straight line if they do not link on to a structural part like the berth fronts.

Rarely seen is a technique that combines traditional building with fibreglass; here the floors are made of thick wood fully glassed all over and the keel bolts pass down through the floor, with a great big washer plate spanning the full siding (the thickness) of the top of the floor.

In practice, it is depressing to see how often the keel bolts are not even close to the floors. Just occasionally a builder restores an aged surveyor's faith in mankind by doing something like fitting angle-bar plate washers under the keel bolt nuts, with the vertical flange of the angle-bar bolted to a floor. Just as rare is good drainage past the floors. Limber holes need to be bushed with tubing to be sure they are not filled with stray ends of glass and drips of resin during construction, and further sealed by debris in the bilge. These holes should be in pairs, port and starboard and clear of the centreline.

Floors are hard to see over their full length, especially when the sole consists of an internal moulding with nothing but small access panels by the keel bolts. Faults to expect are:

- Glass peeling off where the floors are bonded in.
- Cracks right down from top to bottom, roughly vertical.
- Glassing torn off at the ends.
- Lack of total glassing all over.
- Water seepage into the core.
- Blocked, badly made or non-existent limber holes.

The first three items are often caused by grounding. Whatever the trouble, repairs should be beefed up so that the same trouble does not happen next month. It is good practice, when several floors are in poor condition, to recommend that intermediate extra-thick floors are fitted between the existing ones. It is good practice to make them wider than the existing set and taper the ends out slowly. All this work may be difficult if the internal lining and moulding is widespread and obtrusive, but it often turns a flimsy, frightening boat into a proper sea-going craft.

A principal problem when repairing floors is that the whole area is usually saturated. It needs opening up, cleaning out, drying, grinding back, then drying again. To gain access it may be necessary to carry out lots of surgery inside the cabin to get down to the basic structure, but it's certainly worth the effort in order to get some rigid guts into the boat.

FIBREGLASS DECKS AND BEAMS

The first test for a fibreglass deck is to walk over it. However, I cannot recommend jumping down on it from a height to see if it is tough enough, because one person who tried this went right through. The owner took the joke badly.

A poor deck feels spongy and it may even be possible to see the top surface dent down under the pressure of the foot. It is no good expecting a great hollow to appear, even under the tread of an over-weight surveyor. The deck will subtly sag the smallest amount, but can be detected by the surveyor himself. On other occasions it is just discernible by an assistant who is lying nearby with his eye low down or holding a straight edge along the deck surface. This dinge down is the result of a lack of deck strength or having beams spaced too far apart, or beams made without enough material in them.

Careless boatbuilders conveniently give themselves away when putting beams under fibreglass decks. Good beams extend each end right out to the hull moulding, or very close. If the beam end is attached to a hanging knee, the builder is probably good at his job. If it stops well in from the topsides, he is trying too hard to save money. Beams that terminate 400 mm (16 in) from the deck-edge are scandalous, and those that stop 150 mm (6 in) from the edge are often inadequate. Beam ends should either be glassed at each end to the topsides or tapered out and neatly glassed over. An abrupt end results in a local 'hard spot', and in time the beam is likely to peel off the deck or the deck may crack. Where the beams are too widely spaced, the deck is likely to sag if trodden on clear of the supports. As a broad generalisation, it is a good idea to be suspicious when the beams are more than 500 mm (20 in) apart.

Beams need testing like bulkhead edges, with a spike that is slid along the underside of the deck against the beam sides. If the glassing of the beams has failed, and this is most likely at the ends, the spike slips between the deck and the beam. A beam that has been overloaded may crack right through, then the two broken ends come together again, so that the crack is hard to see. It may show up as a line of glass strand ends, almost white in colour, the line probably being roughly vertical and slightly zigzag down the depth of the beam. If a spike end is pressed against this line, it goes right through. If one beam is broken or peeling off the deckhead, the adjacent ones probably have the same problem.

Excess flexiness in a deck is usually found at the aft end of the foredeck and the forward ends of the sidedecks, and also on and around the forward end of a cabin top. Sometimes there is a local indent or downward hollow. This is seen by anchor winches, at forehatches and, above all, where a deck-stepped mast is supported. If the mast is not up on a sailing boat and there is a soggy feel round the chain plates, this is almost always a sign that there are profound problems.

A deck is tapped to find the same defects as on the hull, such as bad lay-up, thin areas and unevenness in the fabrication. Many decks are of sandwich construction, with a thin layer of fibreglass on the top and bottom forming the 'bread' of the sandwich. The filling may be balsa wood, cut so that the end of the grain abuts on the fibreglass, or a foam plastic. On racing boats and others built without regard to the total cost, there may be a honeycomb material between the glassfibre layers. As long as all three layers stick together, everything is fine. Once separation starts it is liable to spread, sometimes fast. The three layers on their own, with no secure bonding holding them together, are disconcertingly weak. Practical tests have shown that if an area more than 40 mm ($1\frac{1}{2}$ in) in diameter lacks a binding glue, the deck is noticeably weak. As the diameter that is unglued increases, so does the deck weakness – to a serious extent.

Water that gets into the sandwich may freeze and force the layers apart. Even without freezing, water in a three-layer deck can do all sorts of damage, including:

● Rotting the balsa.
● Weakening the glue.
● Corroding deck fitting fastenings, etc.

Any unevenness on the top of any deck is cause for concern, but with a sandwich deck it rings the alarm bells extra loud. A deck that has lost its camber needs prompt and thoughtful attention, especially if there are signs that the hull has been affected by being forced outwards as the deck has sagged down.

Repairs to multi-layer decks are dealt with in the secion on sandwich construction (p. 87). It is important to bear in mind that the foredeck is subject to severe loads when a big sea breaks aboard, or when the whole crew stand on it to try and force out a fouled anchor. Also, when the boat plunges her bow deep into a wave, the sides are forced inwards and this transfers a side or edge loading onto the foredeck. To make matters worse, cabin tops often extend deep into the foredeck, further reducing the

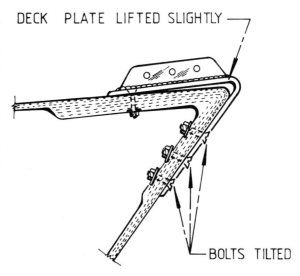

DECK PLATE LIFTED SLIGHTLY

BOLTS TILTED

Fig 19

A glance over the bow may show that the bolts holding the stemhead fitting are tilted slightly. Then peer closely at the flat plate on the deck, and see if it has pulled up just slightly. This means there will be leaks through the deck, and in time the whole fitting may come adrift. Also, check the backstay chain plate for tilted bolts.

strength of the structure. For all these reasons, it is often a good idea to recommend hanging knees be fitted. These should join the beam ends to the topsides. The bottom leg of each knee should taper away to a thin tail, or additional stringers may be glassed in linking the bottoms of the hanging knees on the port and starboard sides. Sometimes the knees can be terminated at an existing stringer to avoid hard spots. These knees are normally made of marine ply layered over with glass cloth, wetted with epoxy resin, after first preparing the underside of the deck and the topsides.

If the top surface of any fibreglass deck is worn so that it is no longer rough and safe, there are various techniques available. A non-slip paint can be applied, or self-adhesive strips of tape with a gritty top, such as 'Safety Walk', though the latter is expensive. Alternatively, Treadmaster may be glued down in sections over all or part of the deck. This is a useful way of covering or disguising a repair.

Where the deck has a rough non-slip surface made during the moulding process, there may be pin-holes. They are usually at the top of each little upstanding piece of fibreglass, but they can be in the hollows. They are caused by the resin not flowing into the interstices of the mould, or contracting as it hardens.

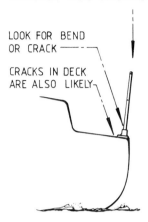

STANCHION TILTS OUTBOARD   **Fig 20**

LOOK FOR BEND
OR CRACK

CRACKS IN DECK
ARE ALSO LIKELY

Stanchions should be vertical, otherwise they will be forced inwards when the boat comes alongside a quay wall. Either the deck should have a horizontal area to take the stanchion base flange, or there should be a tapered wood wedge fitted under each stanchion base to ensure the stanchion stands upright.

Most surveyors draw attention to this defect, but do not recommend repairs unless the trouble seems extensive and deep. Where these little holes clearly cannot be ignored, a thorough clean-off followed by a gel coat application is often enough.

A faded deck does not look smart, and painting over is the commonest cure; before this is done, chips as well as minor cracks need filing and fairing. These blemishes are common and easy to see when they are old, because dirt gets in, and the fracture lines are black or at least grey. New cracks can be extremely hard to spot, even when conditions are good. If the surveyor is working in a gale with driving rain, it is difficult to concentrate – and even the finest pair of eyes will miss a thin crack. Where there seems to be a crack but it is not certain, some surveyors take a lump of mud and rub it over the area. This acts like a cheap form of 'crack detector' fluid, as the silt lies in the crack, making an easily seen line when the surrounding area is wiped clean.

At stanchions the cracks are usually like spokes of a wheel, emanating outwards from the bolt holes. If the deck is weak there may be general cracking under the stanchion. In extreme cases there may be total failure, so that the fibreglass has broken right through. This is easy to spot as the stanchion wobbles like a drunken yachtsman and all round the stanchion base flange there are sharp needles of glass waiting to pierce the surveyor's fingers. A really big repair is needed, with an extensive backing pad under the deck in way of each stanchion.

This type of total failure is occasionally discovered at winches, cleats, bollards and other places where excessive force has been applied – or where the deck structure is too flimsy. Adding extensive

strength on the underside can be difficult. For instance, where sheet winches are sitting on top of wide hollow cockpit coamings it may be almost impossible to do a good job of adding fibreglass cloth in the limited space underneath. Wetting it out effectively (even with a small roller), to ensure air is excluded can be impossible, or so difficult that the job needs as much supervision as man-hours doing the actual work. This doubles the cost and so an alternative is worth considering. One technique is to add extra strength using hardwood pads full length on top and inside the coaming. They are secured with a pattern of well-spread countersunk or dowelled bolts and the edges are well rounded. Between the wood and the fibreglass coaming there should be a copious amount of a waterproof sealant, which also has bonding properties. Sikaflex or some similar compound works well here.

If there are cracks radiating from a chain plate that is secured through the deck, this rings loud alarm bells, as it suggests the structure is not strong enough to support the rig. If the deck has cracked right through, or even deeply, there is probably a massive loss of strength. Some repairers add something like 50% of the deck thickness in new fibreglass on the underside. This in effect means the chain plate – or whatever the fitting is, since other parts can have this big loss of support strength – is held by new fibreglass that is not much stronger than half the original structure. And this has already proved inadequate. The moral of this is that when making repairs at and around deck fittings, thought must be given to the consequences of another break.

It is clear that repairs must result in a deck that is much stronger than the original structure, to ensure the normal and crisis strains can be handled. On the foredeck, cracking is found near the anchor chocks, where wet cold hands have let an anchor drop. It may be a good idea to suggest that after repairs the deck is protected by Treadmaster, or strips of teak, to deal with future accidents and cover the repairs neatly.

The deck as a 'lid'
Considering any small craft from the point of view of an engineer, the deck forms the lid of a box. It can also be considered as the top flange of a hollow beam. At sea, when the vessel rides over the crest of a wave, the bow and stern are partially unsupported. Sometimes when beating into a steep sea, the bow for a long-distance aft is totally out of the water. Under these conditions the deck is in tension. In the

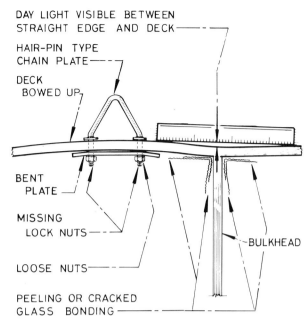

DAY LIGHT VISIBLE BETWEEN
STRAIGHT EDGE AND DECK

HAIR-PIN TYPE
CHAIN PLATE

DECK
BOWED UP

BENT
PLATE

MISSING
LOCK NUTS

LOOSE NUTS

BULKHEAD

PEELING OR CRACKED
GLASS BONDING

Fig 21 Hair-pin type chain plates

These are fitted through the deck, and sometimes cause it to bow upwards, even though there is a plate beneath the deck. The plate may be too small, or may bend with the deck. Glassing on to an adjacent bulkhead or other component may come adrift on one or both sides.

The distortion of the deck can be checked by laying a straight edge on top, first fore and aft, then athwartships or diagonally if space is limited. The amount of daylight between the bottom of the straight edge and the top of the deck shows the amount the deck has been pulled up. Allowance must be made for deck camber and the shape of the sheer. A check should be made for looseness of the chain plate, lack of bedding, loose nuts, and missing locking nuts.

trough of a sea, the reverse applies. The ends of the hull may be deeply immersed, with tremendous buoyancy lifting the weight of the vessel, while the middle is partly unsupported. This condition also occurs when the bow plunges deep into a wave face. Now the deck is in compression.

These reversing loads can cause havoc. One large racing yacht had extra circular holes cut in her deck in way of the cockpit, port and starboard, for extra compasses. No one thought of checking with the designer before making these holes. In a gale the deck tore across, because the compasses were located in an area where there was only just enough strength.

Decks, like other structures, are weakest at changes of shape or section, or where holes have been made. Sharp interior angles, such as at the corners of hatches and cabin tops and cockpits, cause loss of strength. If the angle is sharp, the loss is likely to be serious, especially if there is no doubling up or thickening in the area. Cracks in cockpit corners and at cabin entrances are common, and I have seen them in new boats that have suffered nothing more than a 500 mile journey on a lorry. Cracks at the ends and sides of moulded-in toerails are seen often, especially on craft that have been in a marina during a bad gale, when the topsides have been bashed about. Cracks at deck-edge flanges are found mainly at the bow and top corners of the transom.

It is broadly true to say that when looking at an old or badly built boat there is, more often than not, at least one defect in the deck. A surveyor just has to keep beavering away, working his duodenal ulcer into a rage, until he finds it.

FIBREGLASS DECK EDGE JOINS

In the early days of fibreglass boatbuilding, the deck-to-hull join caused problems. Even today, it is an area where surveyors have to spend a little extra time. I once surveyed a fast motor-cruiser, which initially looked well put together. When I studied the deck-to-hull join I became suspicious because it was uneven. In some places the bedding between the two fibreglass mouldings was a thin line that almost disappeared. Elsewhere it was thicker than a thumb.

At the bow the overhanging deck flange was deep, and it was hard to see how the join had been put together. I went inside the boat up forward and pushed a coin up the aft face of the stem, till it was near the deck. The coin never reached the underside of the deck, but disappeared into a cavity at the stem-head; I heard it fall with a clink on the concrete outside. The joint probably had a wad of stopping but hammering into waves had caused it to drop out.

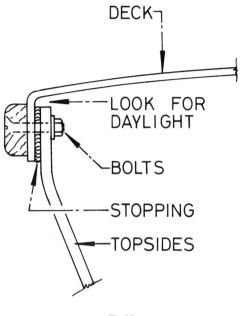

Fig 22

Fibreglass hulls are joined in many different ways to GRP decks. A typical method is shown here, with stopping between the two flanges. This stopping sometimes hardens and drops out, or dries and cracks. Occasionally the stopping is not used in sufficient quantity, so that there are gaps where water can get in. Hose testing from outboard and below is not always possible, but the surveyor can look all round the deck-edge for slits of daylight coming up through gaps in the stopping.

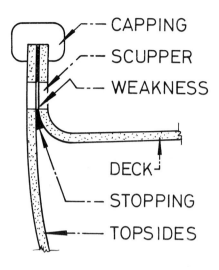

Fig 23

Scuppers cut through an upturned fibreglass deck flange can be a source of leaks. Where the hull and deck flanges are secured and bedded over a reasonable width, no leaks occur, but below the scuppers the depth of stopping is often quite limited. The stopping forms a wedge, and if the deck moves relative to the topsides, this wedge may drop out beneath the scupper, letting water into the hull.

Deck-edge joins, where visible, should be even. Where there is a variation in the way the flanges abut, this should not be great. A slow tapering in and out, as a result of such factors as the thickness of the fibreglass lay-up and the subtle variations in the curve of deck and hull shell, is acceptable. Missing lengths of stopping are bad even if the hull is well glassed to the deck inside. Just as bad are open slits, like gaps in seams, beside the bedding. A tweak with a spike will often cause another lump of sealing compound to drop out. Another bad sign is water dripping out from joins, as it suggests that there is a trapped puddle.

Whatever shape and section the join has, it should be totally and definitely watertight. Dribbles seen running down the inside cannot be dismissed as acceptable because the boat is small, or old, or only used for local racing. This is where hose testing is carried out. It is rare for a surveyor to carry out hose testing during his inspection, but he will often recommend the job be done, and may at a later stage be part of the team that does this important investigation. It needs a good light inside the boat, someone outside with a controllable hose or buckets of water, and lots of patience. It also requires time. This is not a test that can be rushed, nor can it be done in a gale or rain.

The water is applied at the lowest point and the hose gradually directed along the sheer, or whatever part is being tested, at a higher and higher point. This is because water runs downhill and one must test the lowest section first. It is so important to detect that glint of moisture as the first drip comes through that I have used my children's sharp eyesight to help me make the critical sighting. If one is slow to detect the first droplet as it creeps through the join line, the precise location of the leak will not be known.

Surveyors have to know about current and past boatbuilding techniques, so that they understand how the deck is joined. Sometimes there is a downward turned flange to fit over the top edge of the hull. Some designers like to turn the deck-edge up inside the topsides and fit a capping. On other occasions there is an inward or outward flange along the sheer, with the deck fastened down on this, and so on. Whatever system is used, there should be nowhere for the puddles to lie. This applies especially where there are upward turning flanges, because water here will freeze and force the deck away from the hull and leaking will follow.

One attraction of this type of join is that the upstanding flange of the deck-edge forms a toerail. However, scuppers have to be cut and here one gets leaks because they are, or certainly should be, right down at deck level. The filling material on the underside may be thin or friable or badly supported. A bump when coming alongside is enough to cause the filling to become loose or drop out. Flange edges are covered by aluminium, rubber or plastic extrusions, or wood edging pieces. These get damaged when in contact with the shore or other craft. Short lengths of edging material tell the surveyor someone has had an accident and made a poor repair. Even a mild area of damage should be repaired by a full-length new extrusion from bow to stern on small craft. On larger vessels the repair extends between existing joins, just as in traditional boatbuilding.

These deck-edge materials are designed to protect the topsides and deck-edge from damage, so they take the wear and tear themselves. Except on new or carefully kept boats, there are always scratches and gouges, and also sometimes splits and loose fastenings. There may be dents upwards, downwards or inwards. These may look quite mild, but there may be hidden leaks in way of them. On their own, a lightweight extruded moulding plus some bolts joining the hull to the deck is seldom enough except on small runabout motor boats and such like. A full and continuous internal seal with fibreglass strips is needed on every sort of craft.

This glassing-in should be thick, continuous and even in appearance. It should certainly not stop at the bulkheads, or appear thinner in locations that are hard to reach. It should be smoothed on to the hull and underside of the deck, and clearly be several layers thick. Testing with a spike should discover no weak points, hollows, peeling glass, discoloration, dry glass or excess resin. 'Dry glass' is seen as cloth or mat that has not been saturated in resin, so that a spike will effortlessly pull off tufts or individual strands of glass. Excess resin gleams like thick jewels, with no sign of glass strands in it. Anyone who has seen an insect or flower cast in resin will at once recognise excess resin.

Mechanical fastenings such as bolts or rivets are used to hold the deck and hull together before the glassing is applied, and to give additional mechanical strength. There is controversy about these fastenings. Some designers and builders say they are temporary till the glassing has been completed, and are only left in place because it costs money to take them out. Others say they form an important part of the join. I tend to the latter view.

Rivets should only be used on the smallest craft, up to about 6 m (20 ft) long. They should be close together, typically at 75 mm (3 in) centres. Where bolts are used, they are sometimes spaced 600 mm (2 ft) apart, but in my opinion this is too large a distance, even on large vessels. I like to see bolts at least 6 mm ($\frac{1}{4}$ in) diameter for every 6 m (20 ft) of boat length. They need glassing over very fully, partly to ensure that the deck-edge join is strong and water-

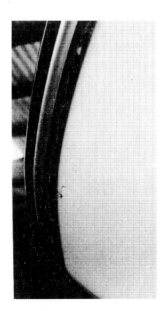

The deck flange of this motor-cruiser is so badly fitted that water can easily get between it and the hull moulding. The fibreglass flange has been bolted to the top of the hull, but long lengths of the bolts are visible from below, where the stopping is missing.

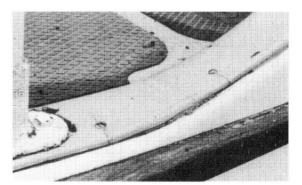

The fibreglass deck-edge flange has cracked at each fastening. Stopping below the flange has fallen out, so leaking here seems inevitable. Before recommending repairs the surveyor has to determine the reason for the cracks. It may have been overtightening of the fastenings, but the indications are that the deck flange never matched the hull, so the cracking occurred when the two were pulled together.

tight, and partly to stop water getting at the fastenings and corroding them.

One reason why the fastenings are so important is that items like chain plates are often secured to the deck. Loadings will tend to peel off the glassing, and a few extra bolts in way of the chain plates suggests the builder is conscientious. One surveyor told me about a boat he inspected just after she came in from a weekend's sailing. The crew had noticed the mast leaning over, and the lee rigging going very slack. They hurriedly dropped the sails and motored home to call the surveyor. He stood on the sidedeck, and pulled the rigging up vigorously. The chain plates seemed secure enough until he jumped on to the quay. Now that he was no longer standing on the deck, he gave another energetic upward pull on the rigging. The deck-edge curved up towards him away from the hull!

THE HINGE EFFECT IN FIBREGLASS

When fibreglass was becoming popular as a boatbuilding material, I was able to do some experiments in association with the Mechanical Engineering Department of Glasgow University. These showed, among other things, that if two thick cured panels of fibreglass were joined by one or two runs of glass tape and resin, the join could act like a stiff hinge. We went on to do other experiments, and from these developed the idea of the 'hinge effect'. It is something a surveyor comes across a lot.

Wherever a panel, which incidentally need not itself be stiff, is secured to another piece of structure by thin fibreglass, the join will flex if loaded. Whereas a hinge can take a million 'swings' back and forth because that is what it is designed to do, fibreglass has a limited life and resistance in this situation. The first sign of trouble is usually a surface crack, or a row of roughly parallel cracks, extending along the 'hinge' line. The most common place to find this problem is at the base of a cockpit well, both port and starboard where the bottom meets the sides. Sometimes the trouble occurs along the edges of a deck, especially just forward of a cabin top, and at the fore end of sidedecks.

Sometimes the argument is put forward that decks or cockpit panels that flex are safe enough, and the movement is merely taking up the loads being applied. It is true that any structure bends at least slightly when a load is applied – a massive bridge sags just a tiny amount when a kitten walks across. However, the amount of the bend is relevant. As far as fibreglass structures are concerned, there should not be a great deal of visible movement when the crew wander about. If there is, cracks are likely to appear, and from then on the structure deteriorates at an accelerating pace.

Builders of cruisers intended for estuary use sometimes claim that a delicate deck that sags noticeably under the weight of two people is acceptable, because the boat is not going to get a big breaking sea on board. This strikes me as a dubious contention. I have seen 11 m (35 ft) yachts swept by breaking seas inside estuaries that are reckoned to be well enclosed and safe. There are also the times when the owner decides to have a party on board, and a lot of people are standing on deck. It spoils their enjoyment and spills the drinks if the deck fails suddenly.

Where the longitudinal cracks are seen at the bottom of a cockpit, an inspection of the underside will show:

- no stiffeners, or
- stiffeners that are far apart, or
- stiffeners that are thin, or
- stiffeners that are not full width, or
- stiffeners that are peeling off – or
- a combination of any of these problems.

If the hinge effect is allowed to develop, the whole panel may drop out. This is rare, but does occur on the bottoms of high-speed motor boats. Here the whole surface pulsates in and out at each impact with the sea's surface. The reversing strain, occurring thousands of times each day, cracks through the gel coat and sets about fracturing the glass fibres.

This situation can arise in sheltered waters, where the waves are quite small but closely spaced. The impact with each individual wave may be quite modest compared with the crash into a big sea offshore. However, the frequency of the reversal of loading on the bottom of the boat is so high that the glass cracks through more quickly than when the vessel is used offshore. This particular trouble is found especially with sandwich construction. If one of the fibreglass skins does not continue to grip the core, the trouble may develop quickly. It is worst if the outside fibreglass fails, but the failure of the inner bond is nearly as devastating. The first indication of the hinge effect is a single approximately parallel crack (or a series of them) along the 'hinge line'.

Bulkheads fixed in place with fibreglass bonding only on the forward or aft face may have a comparable problem. If the bulkhead is of thin ply with no stiffeners or strong door framing, the whole ply panel can 'oil-can' or bend in the middle, allowing the hull to be pressed inwards at each side. The trouble may still occur if the bulkhead has glassing all round on both faces, but it is likely to be less severe.

An extremely lightly built boat with a long cabin top and lengthy cockpit can suffer from a shortage of strength athwartships at deck level. In effect, she needs more beams and stronger beams. She may pant, and this can result in the hinge effect where the deck meets the topsides, along the inner edges of the cockpit seats, and also where the cabin coamings meet the deck.

On racing dinghies the hinge effect is seen along the inside edges of the buoyancy tanks, where they meet the hull bottom. Another place is each side at the bottom of the centreboard case, with extensions forward and aft along the backbone stiffener. The cause of trouble here is the flexing of the bottom of the hull. As the boat pounds over the waves, the bottom can be felt moving in and out appreciably. When the crew move about in the boat, their feet also force the light shell down slightly. I have seen this trouble on a batch of racing dinghies less than a month old. These boats were of a well-known class with sail numbers above 60,000. This defect may not worry those dinghy owners who feel that they have proof that their boats are not too heavily built. They rightly value a hull built right down to the minimum weight allowed by the class rules. It is universally agreed that extra pounds lose races. What these enthusiasts don't appreciate is that a hull that flexes and distorts is slower than a stiff one. Also, five cracks today become 25 cracks next month.

Recommending a cure is not easy, because the total weight of the dinghy must not be increased if she is to remain competitive. If the trouble is far advanced, the most satisfactory procedure is to get a new hull that is properly built with gentle sweeping radii where the buoyancy tank sides meet the hull shell, and local reinforcing on the inside of the hull to take the tank boundaries. The same approach − gentle sweeping radii at least 50 mm (2 in) and, better still, 75 mm (3 in) − has to be used where structures meet along the centreline backbone.

A typical repair will consist of stiffening the hull by frames with knees on to the centreline structure and inboard sides of the buoyancy tanks. However, this adds obtrusive extra parts that get in the way during a race − and good crews do so hate any sort of distraction. The best repair, though, often consists of taking from the damaged hull all its fittings, spars, sails, foils, etc and transferring them to a new, properly built hull.

WOOD ENCLOSED IN FIBREGLASS

A purist will say that wood should not be embedded in fibreglass because the two materials have different rates of expansion. When wood gets wet it swells a lot, and this is likely to cause trouble. Even a change in temperature will have a different effect on the two materials.

However, boatbuilding is seldom a matter of pure science. There are many practical considerations, such as cost, the availability and ease of working the materials, and past experience. When the chips are down (if the pun can be excused), wood is so handy, so widely available, and so easy to use − so no wonder it is widely found inside fibreglass fabrications. Typical locations are:

- inside deck beams,
- as sole bearers,
- as doublers in way of deck fittings, bilge pumps on cockpit sides, and at chain plates,
- in floors and stringers,
- inside engine bearers.

As a general rule, engines should not be held down by coach-screws, but there are times when lack of access makes it impossible to use bolts. Provided the engine is small (5 hp might be taken as the top limit), the job is well done, and the coach-screws are thick as well as long, they can be acceptable. This is where wood engine bearers fully covered with at least four layers of fibreglass makes sense. Just occasionally, engine beds are made of wood, but only glassed in round the base, in the same way that bulkheads are secured with fibreglass tape round the edges. This building technique usually involves ply bearers, which are high with hardwood top 'flanges' or stiffeners to take the engine holding-down bolts. Along the bottom there should be heavy glassing on to the hull, and some arrangement to prevent the bearers 'tripping' or tipping sideways. Both ends of this sort of bearer are secured to bulkheads or deep floors, or tapered out over a long length down to thin ends.

Normally a wood insert needs a full covering of fibreglass all over because it must hold the wood securely in all directions. More important, it keeps water away from the wood. Admittedly, moisture does seep through in time, but, provided no puddles lie against the GRP, the penetration is slow and the quantity that gets through is tiny. The wood should not have sharp edges or corners, because this makes it difficult for the fabricators to persuade the glass cloth to lie right up on the timber. Wood insert pads are often bevelled 45 degrees along all sides, to help the glass lie snugly. Where this is not done, a surveyor may see hollows and air gaps along the boundaries of these pads. It is especially easy to detect this fault under decks where clear uncoloured resin has been used.

The ends of beams should be very carefully glassed over. This is where there are high stresses, especially if the beam is not fully tapered and does not end very close to the topsides. Where beams are not glassed neatly all along the length and round the ends, a careful search should be made for peeled glass. Sometimes the whole deck sags or loses some of its camber, as the beams are not doing their job. If one end of one beam has come adrift, there is a good chance that the adjacent beams are in trouble too.

Even when the fibreglass is layered on all over the wood, water can get in through bolt and screw holes. Fittings secured to pads or beams should be extra-well bedded down, so that the waterproof compound can be seen all round the base flange. If there is a tiny black line between the flange and the deck, this suggests that the bedding is either inadequate, or has come out, or was never put in during construction.

Once a little water gets at the wood it starts to swell. This can be devastating as wood can easily grow a millimetre in thickness for every 20 mm depth or width. The fibreglass may start off tightly bonded on to the wood, but it soon gives up under the forces generated by swelling. Water lodging between the wood and fibreglass causes more and more swelling. If freezing occurs, the force prying the wood off the fibreglass is massive – the ancients used it to split big rocks. Quite apart from the ingress of moisture, the separation of the wood and the fibreglass weakens the structure because the two materials no longer work together. Where the wood is accessible, it should be tested with a spike to confirm that it is hard and not moving inside its casing of fibreglass.

In way of wood inserts, the fibreglass should not show signs of crushing. There should be no local change of colour round the washers of the through-bolts. This change is usually almost white in contrast to the translucent adjacent glass that has the brown wood showing through. There should be no sharp splinters of protruding glass fibres or signs of fractured surface cloth. A spike pushed hard against the surface glass should not penetrate through to the wood anywhere.

FASTENINGS & CHAIN PLATES ON FIBREGLASS

From a surveyor's point of view, fastenings through fibreglass make life a little easier. They often show the standard of construction of the vessel, and if she has had hard use there may also be signs of this at the fastenings. We look for cracks at the bolt holes, elongated holes, corrosion on the fastenings because of trapped water, bent washers, and other signs of deformation and destruction.

Broadly speaking, and with lots of exceptions, it is true but pedantic to say that metal fastenings should not be put through fibreglass; and if they must be used, there should be special preparations and special washers. In practice, things are very different; builders save money by taking few, if any, precautions here. It is usual to see complete sets of deck fittings secured straight on to fibreglass with just a little bedding, the minimum or no reinforcing, and not much effort is made to reduce the risk of cracking and other defects.

Fibreglass is a brittle material that dislikes high concentrated loads, so a metal fastening is likely to cause cracking unless precautions are taken. Ideally, holes for bolts should be bushed with plastic tubing that is markedly softer than fibreglass, so that the shank of the fastening is not directly against the fibreglass. In practice, this precaution is very seldom taken. However, where a bolt is likely to be very highly loaded sideways, and there has been or may be troubles from this intense localised pressure, then this is the way things should be done.

On a superbly built boat every bolt through fibreglass will have washers that are three times the bolt diameter under both the head and the nut, with half-hard washers under the metal washers. These semi-hard washers compress slightly and distort, so they exactly follow the contour of the fibreglass, spreading the load evenly. This avoids the situation where the metal fastening impinges on a tiny area and cause cracks from that point. On cheap boats the washers are sometimes less than double the bolt diameter, and on the cheapest there are no washers at all.

As a basic rule, metal fastenings should never be put through laminates that are less than 3 mm ($\frac{1}{8}$ in) thick. The glass should be built up to a greater thick-

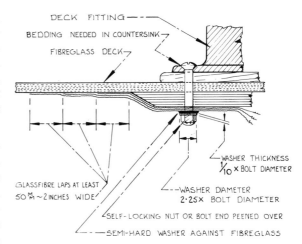

Fig 24

This shows good boatbuilding practice and some details that US Coast Guard inspectors look for when assessing a vessel's soundness. If no bedding is put under bolt heads there may be corrosion here as a result of the proximity of different metals. The washer diameter is about standard on most boats, but where the loads are large and the structure soft, extra large discs, called 'penny washers', are needed. It is rare to see locked nuts or peened bolt ends in this location on yachts and fishing boats. The lap of successive laminations of glass is recommended practice regardless of the size of vessel and the number of cloth layers.

ness. Wherever metal fastenings have to be used, the fibreglass should theoretically be thickened in way of the holes to compensate for the loss of strength, and this reinforcing ought to be tapered away at all the edges. In practice, for fittings like genoa sheet lead tracks it is usual to fit a wood doubler (or, less often, a metal one) under the deck. This reinforcing is sometimes glassed in place, but not often on cheap craft, or boats under 9 m (30 ft). Where metal fastenings are used, it is fairly common to find cracks emanating from the holes. These cracks are seen on top of the deck, but seldom on the underside.

The fibreglass may be dinged in by the pressure applied when the fastening is tightened up, but this is a fairly rare defect. In bad cases, the glass may have cracks along a line of fastenings. It is not enough to mend the cracks, because they can recur even if the glass is made thicker. In way of a deck fitting, a good crack-by-a-hole repair will consist of:

- Reglassing with perhaps 33% extra thickness of glass on the underside.
- The crack(s) on top are repaired in the usual way.
- A wood pad on deck is fitted between the fitting's base and the fibreglass.
- A bigger, better pad underneath the deck.

Practical politics dictate that rather less comprehensive renewal work is usually carried out, and of course even then the trouble may return.

Both pads should taper in thickness at the edges all round and have rounded edges against the fibreglass. Wood pads and metal washer plates have to be thick enough to stay flat and not bend in way of the fastenings. A useful rule of thumb is that the pad on deck should be between 10% and 25% longer and broader than the base of the fitting, while the underdeck pad should be quite 50% broader and longer. It is rare to see an underdeck pad large enough for extremely severe conditions, even on well-built craft.

Keel bolts carry particularly heavy loads, so the area round them must be checked for cracks, especially when bolts are removed. The top of the fibreglass keel in way of keel bolts is seldom level or flat, and the washers for these bolts should be large. Therefore something is needed to take up the unevenness between the top of the fibreglass and the underside of the washer. Some builders use layers of wet fibreglass on which they harden down the nuts. The theory is that the glass will exactly mate with the underside of the washer before hardening. This is being optimistic – and besides, it takes no account of the changes that may take place as the glass hardens or the future life of the yacht; for instance, the washer may corrode or bell downwards under pressure. A better technique is to fit a compressible waterproof material spread over the whole area of the washer, and extending a little all round the edge. The washer plate should be so thick that there is no risk it will bend, however much the nut is tightened. This extra metal thickness will also cope with corrosion. Screws can only be used in fibreglass for minor items such as the framing round small windows, to hold beading down along the front of a main hatch hood, to hold the 'garage' over the fore end of a sliding main hatch, and so on. If it is found that deck fittings like cleats are screwed down, this is dangerous and clear proof of low-quality building.

In theory, fairleads should not be screwed down,

but in practice they almost always are on craft up to about 12 m (40 ft) because of the difficulty of getting bolts through right out at the deck-edge. Fairleads that are not out close by the topsides are less than fully effective. Besides, the loads on fairleads are mainly horizontal along the deck, so screwing down is widely accepted. One or two of the worst builders screw down mooring bollards. They may argue that using big screws makes this practice acceptable. The only thing that is acceptable is the surveyor's fee when he sorts out the damage after the bollard has pulled out, and the boat gone adrift.

On small boats it is quite usual to find cabin top grab rails that are screwed in place. This is not the best practice, but most surveyors accept it provided that roughly the following conditions are fulfilled:

- The screws are at least 12 gauge size.
- They extend at least 30 mm ($1\frac{1}{4}$ in) into the wood.
- They are no more than 350 mm (14 in) apart.
- There are at least five of them in each handrail.

Even though screwed-on handrails are common, for extended offshore cruising experienced mariners prefer bolts.

Chain plate bolts are heavily loaded and sometimes suffer jerking loads that are twice as bad as a steady pull. Modern rigs impose heavy stresses because the shrouds are at a small angle to the mast, modern sails are made stronger and more efficient each year, and also crews are learning how to sail faster in gale conditions. So what was adequate a few years ago is no longer acceptable. There must never be less than four fastenings in any chain plate, even on a tiny cruiser. Five is normally the accepted minimum.

Sometimes chain plates are bolted flat on the outside of the hull. This rather primitive approach is seen on 'modern traditional' or semi-replica craft, and on cheap boats. One consequence may be cracking by the plates at the deck-edge. The topsides cannot always prevent the plates from being pulled inboard, and unless there is a wood pad or some such here, damage is likely after a few seasons. This problem is seen just occasionally where chain plates are secured to the cabin top coamings. Here the chain plate should not be near a window and should extend down almost to the deck. If the chain plates extend through the deck, and this is the usual way of fitting them, local cracking may occur on the inboard side, especially if flat bars are used and are not exactly

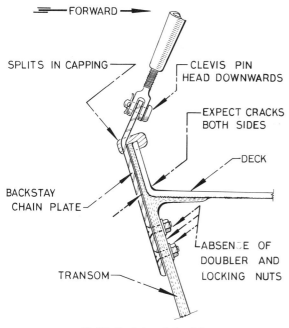

Fig 25 Backstay chain plate

The type of chain plate that is bent in over the edge of the deck is liable to cause cracking, especially if there is an upstanding toerail made of fibreglass. The rail capping is also vulnerable. Just occasionally shroud chain plates fitted by the mast have similar problems. The absence of an inside doubler inside the hull, and the inverted clevis pin that will fall out if the split pin fails, are other notable defects.

aligned with the shrouds. The first sign of trouble is often a leak, and the usual reaction of owner, boatyard and everyone else involved is to splash a lot of flexible waterproof stopping around. This may stop the leak, but it does not always cure the whole problem.

There are two possible sources of trouble here: the flat bar chain plate may be bolted athwartships, with the flat area of the bar extending fore and aft – or the flat area may be athwartships. In the former case, the bend at the top of the bar causes trouble as it flexes under load. The bend may be slightly too low, so that the bar presses heavily on the deck. Or it may be too high, in which case the vertical part of the bar may flex against the deck and cause cracking or chipping. If the bar is secured to a bulkhead (so that the flat broad side is athwartships), leaking and deck cracking is less likely. However, if the bolts work slightly loose or twist sideways under load, leaking follows. Where the bolts are small and there is no long backing washer, it is quite usual for the chain plate to shift just slightly – which is enough for water to seep in. A common sight, especially on small yachts, is a row of bolts with the nuts tightened so that the washers are biting deep into the ply bulkhead.

A good way to cure chain plate leaks is to fit a flat plate on deck, entirely surrounding the chain plate. This plate is typically between 3 and 6 mm ($\frac{1}{8}$ and $\frac{1}{4}$ in) thick, and it extends 25 or 50 mm (1 or 2 in) all round the chain plate. It is screwed or bolted down, with lots of non-hardening bedding underneath. Here, as with all these waterproofing jobs, the bedding must ooze out all round so that there is no risk of water seeping in through a gap.

FOAM SANDWICH CONSTRUCTION

Surveyors have to know about engineering, to appreciate how boats are built, and why they fall apart when things go wrong. Foam sandwich building is simple in concept, complex in practice, and it can be a surveyor's nightmare – for all too often he has to guess what is going on inside a sealed structure.

One of the simplest tenets of engineering can be summed up in the phrase 'basic beam theory'. This explains how beams work, and how strong they are.

In engineering terms, any structure that is held at each end or one end, and that supports a load at right angles or obliquely on to the structure, is a beam. An engineer will look at a sole bearer or frame or carline and call it a beam, because these structural members are firmly held in position and have to cope with forces acting down or obliquely on to their length.

The way to make a beam strong is to have the maximum possible depth, and to have as much of the material that forms the beam at the outside edges of the structure. A standard steel I beam is an excellent example of beam theory at work. These beams are strong for their size and weight, because they are deep and have thick flanges at top and bottom, but a relatively thin central web joining the flanges.

When a boatbuilder wants to build a strong hull, he sometimes applies beam theory in a subtle way. He makes the hull shell out of a strong inner skin, bonded to a light, weak and 'just adequate' core, with another strong skin bonded on the outside. The inner and outer skins act like the flanges of the I beam and are made of fibreglass. The light core is like the web, and is made of a foam plastic material, or a 'honeycomb' material, or balsa wood — which lacks strength, but is incredibly light. There are other core materials that can be used, and they are all light, usually short on strength, but good at holding the inner and outer skins well separated. This form of boatbuilding, which has such excellent theoretical advantages, is called foam sandwich construction. The sandwich has thin layers of fibreglass instead of the bread, and the filling or meat in the middle is the foam or balsa core. The butter on the bread is replaced by the bonding material holding the fibreglass skins to the core. In boatbuilding, this bonding is usually the weak link.

Nothing is straightforward when you try to make a craft that will stay afloat and stand up to the battering of waves — so it is with foam sandwich. A great deal can go wrong with this basically simple concept. The layers may come apart because the critical bonding between them may be too weak or badly made, the inner or outer layers may crack because they are fairly thin, the middle layer may crumble or soak up water or be compressed by an unfair strain, the edge seals may fail — and so on. A surveyor finding cracks in the inner or outer fibreglass of a foam sandwich hull or deck must buckle down and spend time looking for other troubles, and for the reason why the cracks have occurred. It may be that the fibreglass was made too thin, or it has been bashed, or the core no longer supports it, so that a quite moderate force against it caused fracturing.

Though enthusiasts for this form of construction will cry 'Foul!', it has to be said that foam sandwich boatbuilding is risky. It is too easy to make fabrication mistakes, either by accident or because some small precaution has been forgotten. It is too vulnerable to common accidents, and too often small areas of damage cause a disproportionate amount of trouble before repairs are started. Like flying, foam sandwich boatbuilding can be frightening when it stops working.

A friend of mine bought a dinghy of fibreglass foam sandwich construction. It had an extra thick middle layer that formed buoyancy, so the dinghy could fill to the gunwales, but would still stay afloat with all her crew. Alas, despite the high hopes of the owner, this little boat only lasted two years. The inner and outer fibreglass layers came away from the core. What started as one quite strong boat became three very flimsy, crumbly ones! This separation of the three layers has for years been a major problem with sandwich construction. Techniques to prevent it include:

- The use of expensive adhesives.
- A pattern of little 'pillars' or 'tie-bars' of fibreglass extending from the inner to the outer layers.
- Internal frames bonded on to both layers.
- An arrangement of quite large solid inserts in the soft core.

Decks are often built using the sandwich technique and one reason why they last is that there are hard core inserts in way of each of the numerous deck fittings. These solid core pieces are essential to prevent the bolts that hold the deck fittings in place from crushing the sandwich deck as they are tightened up.

It is seldom easy to get hold of the construction plans of a vessel built by this technique, but it is worth taking trouble to do so. They should show what precautions have been taken to prevent delaminating, and where the solid chocks are located.

Even if the engineering is good, separation must be suspected. Old sandwich boats suffer a lot from this defect, and sometimes the lift-off of one layer from the core is so big it spans a cabin. The extent of the air bubble or void between the fibreglass layer and the core may be so large that it is hard to detect, because the contrast, where adhesion has not failed, is so far from the area being examined. Places to look for trouble are where the stresses are high, such as the bottom forward where pounding takes place, in the area of the mast, by chain plates and backstay plate, by the keel and engine, and also at the point of maximum beam where pinching occurs when lots of boats are moored up together.

The most dramatic example of this defect I can remember was on an 80 ft (24 m) sloop that had been driven hard for too many years across gale-torn seas. The deck appeared to be just slightly more cambered forward of the mast than elsewhere. When I first went on board, I assumed that the naval architect had designed in this extra curvature, possibly to direct water coming aboard at the bow to torrent off sideways rather than cascade aft. Treading on the foredeck was eerie, because the top fibreglass surface was thin and largely unsupported. It was fine when walking along the edge, but as the footsteps progressed inboard, the deck seemed to sag. Little by little I realised that this large sailing craft, with her tall rig, was very short of deck strength. My first reaction was to tip-toe stealthily away and hope that the mast would remain upright until I was out of range.

Delamination is seldom as dramatic as that. It is usually necessary to sight obliquely along the hull and deck to see areas where the fibreglass has bulged away from the core. Anyone who does not have a good 'eye' for this sort of distortion should take a long batten and lay it along the topsides, and on the deck. Circumstances vary a lot, and affect the best size of batten. For a large craft, a batten perhaps 3 or 4 m long and 50×20 mm in section will be fine. (That is, 10 or 12 ft in length and $2 \times \frac{3}{4}$ in in section.) For small boats, a better size will be 1 or 2 m long and 30×8 mm (about 3 or 6 ft in length and $1\frac{1}{4} \times \frac{5}{16}$ in).

Using a batten on the inboard side of the hull is seldom possible as there are too many obstructions. In any case, a batten only shows where the fibreglass has bulged up. Often the bonding fails, but the GRP skin remains close to, if not touching, the core material. This is especially true on the inside of the hull where the general shape is a concave curve. The surveyor presses with the flat of the hand to try and detect 'bubbling up'. If the thin fibreglass skin 'pings' in and out, it has almost certainly lost any adhesion on to the core. All over the hull and deck the inspector presses to see if he can produce local movement. Sometimes hand pressure is not enough, especially on craft over 12 m (40 ft) long. A firm thrust with the foot will be used on larger craft, to try to detect separate movement of the fibreglass independent of the full hull shell thickness.

A valuable tool for further testing is a light hammer or big coin. It is used for tapping all over, but especially in highly stressed areas and on large flattish panels. These are where problems are most likely. When examining racing craft, the areas that pound in heavy seas should be scrutinised very carefully. The bottom, where the hull comes pounding down ferociously, and where any flat panels take extra punishment, are fully checked.

Work by Giovanni Belgrano of SP Systems has shown that the vulnerable areas are from the bow to about station 4.5. This is based on the normal division of the yacht's length into ten stations. The research shows the loading is high near the bow and back to station 4.5, then it drops steeply to station 4.75. Logically one must expect that these areas will flex most, and there may be cracks caused by local flexing from the bow back to stations 4.5 or 4.75.

Tapping the hull and deck, as well as the cabin top and cockpit, is only effective when there is no other noise to obtrude, so it should not be done afloat in windy weather, or ashore near noisy machinery. The hull on the inside and outside should give a ringing tone. Areas where the fibreglass has peeled away from the core give a more dead or hollow sound. A steady firm pressure applied, and then released, on the hull or deck made of sandwich construction may produce a noise like scratching or crackling. This is an indication that the core is not adhering to the facings, but has sheered. It suggests that the glue holding the skin has held on, but the weak core has failed, so that there is an internal break bounded on each side by core material. A pumping pressure causes the two faces of the core to rub together – hence the 'sandpaper' sound.

All this testing produces evidence that there are spaces or gaps where there should be none. To be effective, sandwich construction must be solid, tightly bound, from inside to outside. When defects are suspected, the way to be sure is to drill the fibreglass, and this is done after getting the owner's permission. Unimportant hidden areas – such as in lockers – are chosen if this suits the test requirements, so that the appearance of the vessel is not spoilt. A drill bit just 3 mm ($\frac{1}{8}$ in) diameter can sometimes be used, but it is seldom satisfactory because it does not give a sideways view into the hole. However, if the drill first meets solid material as it goes through the fibreglass, then plunges deep in with no effort – this suggests there is a void under the fibreglass layer. The difficulty here is detecting the difference between an air gap and the very soft core that presents so little resistance to the drill. If the core is honeycomb material for most of the area, there will be no resistance to the drill once it is through the fibreglass.

The attraction of using this small size of drill is that it does little visible damage, so some surveyors use it first, and only go on to a larger drill when the required information is not forthcoming. A good technique is to use a drill bit at least 8 mm ($\frac{5}{16}$ in) diameter, and ideally somewhat larger. This chops away a reasonable piece of fibreglass and lets the surveyor look obliquely into the hole. He can see if the fibreglass layers are tightly bonded to the core. If the fibreglass is just very slightly away from the middle layer, the bond is totally broken, and there is little strength there. It is as if a flange of an I beam has come away from the central web. Any gap, however tiny, is catastrophic. Some boatbuilders say that small areas of separation do not matter, but how do they know the size and number of the broken bonding without taking off a whole fibreglass skin?

Another general weakness of all sandwich construction methods is that the edges are vulnerable. They are often highly stressed, but are areas least able to stand heavy loadings. They are subject to sideways bumps that they are not able to resist adequately. This means all accessible edges need to be studied with dedication.

Some core materials blot up water like sponges. Balsa wood is absorbent and blackens when wet, then often starts to rot. This trouble is seen, for instance, where a balsa core sandwich deck has a ventilator hole. The whole perimeter of this hole should be comprehensively sealed with resin, but sometimes this precaution is forgotten or not done with enough care. Even when there is a seal, it is usually thin and easily damaged. Water gets in at many vents, and even when the boat stays in harbour there is usually enough moisture to start up the process of mildew, which may be followed by rot.

In extreme cases, a deck or cabin top or cockpit sole may make squishy watery noises when walked over. On occasions, bubbles and dribbles are seen at deck fitting fastenings when a heavy foot treads nearby. Where there is a lot of water about, repairs have to be carried out in such a way that the moisture is removed first. This tends to make the job time-consuming and expensive.

At each deck fitting a check is made to see if the top or bottom surfaces dent in. If the builder has forgotten to put in a solid core material, when the bolts holding the deck fitting down are tightened, the inner and outer skins are pulled together, since the normal core has no strength against this force. In practice, few builders forget more than one or two solid cores, but these areas can cause trouble that spreads. Anyone adding a fitting after the boat has been built may omit this essential tough inner core piece or construct it inadequately.

Misaligned core pads are common, and result in deck fittings that tilt sideways slightly because two of the four bolts are through a rigid material, but two others have just missed it. When the latter are tightened, they tilt the fitting – and, in extreme cases, crack one or both of the fibreglass outer laminates. These troubles occur less often where skin fittings are put through sandwich hulls. One reason for this is that solid inserts in the hull tend to be extensive, so if the fitting is slightly misaligned, it still 'picks up' its solid core and does not extend over the edge.

Any cautious surveyor supervising the building of a sandwich hull will ask for *outsize* solid inserts. He will insist on these extra-big pads in way of the chain plates, mooring cleats, fairleads, tank filler caps, seacocks – in fact, at every fitting. This ensures that minor misalignment is not damaging. He will also suggest that some spare inserts are fitted on deck and in the lower part of the hull. They are for extra deck fittings and seacocks that may be required in future years. The precise location of these pads is marked on the hull and on the plans.

Delamination is less likely in way of bolted fittings partly because the fibreglass normally bonds well on to ply inserts, partly because the bolts hold the three layers together, and partly because the ply can withstand heavy sheering forces that will shatter lightweight core materials. However, vulnerable areas are found near the edges of all hard core inserts because there is a sudden change of strength. This is in every sense of the phrase a 'hard spot'. When using a coin or the hard plastic handle of a spike for hammer testing, there is a solid ring in way of hard inserts. Where the glassfibre is transparent, it is normally (but not always) easy to see the inserts, provided the light is good.

Repairing delaminated sandwich construction is seldom easy and sometimes uneconomic. Before work commences it has to be assumed that if the trouble appears to extend over an area 1×1 m, opening up will probably show that repairs are needed over 2×2 m – or more. If a technique is used that does not involve opening up, or slicing off one of the layers of fibreglass, the repairs should be made over much more than the region that is obviously defective. One such method involves drilling a pattern of holes in the fibreglass skin and injecting epoxy resin. This method of rebonding separated layers works best on horizontal surfaces like decks and the bottoms of dinghies.

When pouring in resin, the temperature and humidity must be correct, and the space being filled must be dry. This may involve using fan heaters after the drilling. The deck must be warm on both sides and, generally speaking, one wants the epoxy resin to be slightly warm so that it easily runs into all the crevices. However, there is a theory that the resin should not be too runny as this means it dribbles effortlessly downhill and leaves voids. The way round this dilemma is to start with a very fluid mix and when it has trickled into the remote interstices and set, a second batch of more viscid epoxy goes in. After the resin has had plenty of time to set, an extra batch of trial holes may be drilled to confirm there are no voids left between the fibreglass and the core.

This all sounds fine in theory, but any practical boatbuilder can list a dozen snags that are likely to make the job hard or even impossible. The deck-edge may be unsealed on the underside, so that resin trickles copiously down inside the hull and on to lining, furniture and everything else — resulting in a sensational mess. An attempt may be made to seal the edge with adhesive tape, but several layers will have to be used to be safe. Also, if the seal is ineffective, the discovery tends to be rather late — after repairs have been started.

Other potential problems include trapped water, air blockages that stop the resin reaching some parts, intermittent sealing due to premature hardening of the resin, sealing between the upper fibreglass and the core, but no seal between the core and the bottom fibreglass, and so on. In addition, it is not easy to prevent the top of the deck being damaged and ending up with hard resin droplets. A good cure is to clean off and reseal the top of the deck then cover it with Treadmaster, or a similar deck sheathing material, or wood deck planks. If only a small area of the deck needs repairing, it is not necessary to cover the whole deck with the new sheathing, provided the work is done in a professional way so that it looks purposeful and is identical port and starboard.

Instead of making a pattern of small holes, it is sometimes possible to make just two large ones, the first near the deck-edge and the second at the top of the camber. Resin is run in at the lower hole, using a tube that is sealed at the deck and has a funnel at the top to direct the resin down the tube. If all goes well, the resin will in time appear at the breathing hole, so pouring can stop. In practice, resin may come in sight of the top hole, then subside. It reappears when more resin goes down the tube and eventually all the cavities are filled and the resin in the breather hole stays level with the top of the fibreglass.

There are plenty of occasions when the people involved are not happy about drilling a pattern of holes in the deck and pouring in a bonding resin, because they are not sure how strong the final structure will be. It is easy to sympathise with this attitude, especially if the vessel is a big one, or liable to be driven hard, or if she has a large rig or powerful engine.

A more radical repair technique involves cutting off the top layer of fibreglass except for a rim round the edge of perhaps 75 mm (3 in). Next, the light inner supporting material is checked all over. This core has to be removed if it is rotting or soggy balsa wood, or crumbling foam plastic. The whole cavity has to be carefully cleaned out then dried. If the core is removed, the bottom layer of fibreglass is accessible and is examined all over. If the core is defective, a new one is fitted and marine ply is good for the job. The largest possible pieces are fitted, consistent with following the deck camber and the sheer. This ply is heavy compared with balsa, but the total increase in weight is seldom serious. The aim is to have a strong reliable deck, and the extra weight is a small price to pay.

When mending a delaminated hull shell, it is seldom enough to run in resin. Normally the inside layer of fibreglass is taken out and the core replaced as needed. Ideally the fibreglass removed should be cut into small or medium-sized panels, with horizontal and vertical bands left in place. These intact pieces meet with radiused corners to retain the maximum amount of strength. It may be necessary to make hull repairs in layers working from the bottom. The job can seldom be done swiftly or cheaply, and of course anything in the way, such as lining or furniture, has to be removed first, then put back later. It is the old problem: to do a repair job there are the preparation and restitution stages, each of which can be almost as expensive as the repair work.

New techniques are being developed all the time, and it is a good idea to get in touch with the specialists in this field for the latest information. One firm that makes the repair resins and gives good advice is SP Systems of Eastgate House, Town Quay, Southampton SO1 1LX.

LEAKERS

When fibreglass boats were first made, the builders said they had banished leaks forever. This turned out to be a rash claim, though some GRP boats are still sold without bilge pumps.

Surveyors have their private lists of boat types that leak round the windows, and those that let in water through the main hatch – not to mention those that have dribbles at the electric glands by the mast. There are others that build up a decent level of bilge-water on a beat because the cockpit locker lids have drains sloping down inboard at 15 degrees, whereas these boats often sail at 20 degrees or more – and so let in water along the outboard edges of the locker lids when spray and rain builds up in the angle between the cockpit coaming and the seat. Finding leaks can be frustrating, especially if they only occur when the boat is heeled, or only when she is lying in a marina with her stern to the wind and rain.

The recognised technique is to wait till the leak is clearly happening. Next, dry the boat out, then look for the return of the leak, shown up by signs of glinting water. What is needed is a strong but not blinding portable light, with a shade round an arc of 270 degrees (or even more) so that none of the illumination shines back towards the surveyor. Once the first gleam of water has been found, it is dried off and studied in order to see where the renewed seepage comes from. Working in the bilge, it is sometimes necessary to begin amidships, and gradually progress 'upstream' till the point of ingress is discovered. On an 80 footer, this may be more than an afternoon's work. Help is often needed to shift sole boards, and perhaps unscrew furniture or lining and move tanks.

Leaks occur mostly, but not exclusively, at joins and where fittings are secured to the hull and deck. Runnels where incoming water has left little tracks of dirt or discoloration, or even softening wood, indicate leaks from above. Sometimes salt crystals give a clue as to where there is trouble, especially at window bottom corners. Damaged varnish on the wood trim is often seen at hatch corners, telling of weeps due to failed waterproof bedding or perished seals.

Some overhead leaks show near the sheer, whereas the point of ingress is well inboard. This trouble occurs when water is channelled outboard by the deckhead lining, and drips of this sort are found on modern fibreglass boats as well as older vessels built of other materials. No one should ever assume that the place where water is first seen inside a hull is necessarily where it gets through the hull, deck or cabin top. The most sensational 'leaker' I ever examined had more than 94 leaks through the deck, and she was only an average-sized cruiser. The builders had omitted almost all the waterproof sealant under the deck fittings and in way of the toerail bolts. It was always a mystery how she got past the builder's inspection, especially as she was put together by a company that previously had a good reputation.

Leaking at stress points like chain plates and runner fittings is fairly common, particularly if the boat is old enough for the bedding compound to have become aged. When each pulpit foot consists of a threaded rod through the deck, with a nut on the underside and a small flange above deck, leaking may well occur early on in the life of the boat. Eyebolts that have serious side loading leak badly and should be replaced by eye-plates of the type that have two fastenings or, better still, four.

Sliding hatches that do not clamp down tightly will leak, especially when there is a strong wind blowing from aft the beam. In general, most cruiser owners accept a certain amount of dribbling round the main hatch, at least in severe weather. Leaks round forehatches are less acceptable, except on old boats with wood hatches where dribbles used to be almost compulsory.

Hull leaks in fibreglass craft are most common at the stern gland. Occasionally water seeps in at a keel bolt or seacock, or at the transducer of one of the electronic instruments. Leaks around the rudder gland are common in old boats, but they are rare where the stock is in a tube that extends up to the deck. If the gland is hard to reach, it never gets tightened or repacked, so it is only a matter of time and use before water seeps in here.

Leaking at the top of P-brackets is now quite fashionable and in some classes seems to be part of the builder's specification. It is often caused by bad

Leaks often give themselves away. The driblets from this bolt show quite clearly where the water is coming in and suggest that the bolt is rusting and should be renewed, with plenty of bedding round the replacement. The breasthook above has been painted, but rust is breaking through and regalvanising is overdue.

installation, with inadequate glassing round the vertical stem-plate of the bracket. It may be started by the poor installation of the engine, which causes the shaft to vibrate ferociously. Where there is a flimsy structure round the bracket, leaking will start if the propeller hits some flotsam.

When a boat is being lifted ashore, the aft sling may be put round the propeller shaft accidentally, but no one will see this until the boat is clear of the water. In these circumstances half the weight of the craft is taken by the prop shaft and hence by the P-bracket. This can cause subtle or galloping leaks – and also perhaps a slightly bent shaft that may not be noticed until the engine is next put into gear. The resulting vibration can loosen the P-bracket even if it was firm beforehand.

Although this chapter concentrates on fibreglass construction, whilst on the subject of leakers we should have a look at boats built of other materials.

Old wooden boats leak when driven hard to windward because the tension of the windward rigging and the downward drag of the ballast tend to open the plank seams. This effect may be so subtle that it is hard to discover which seams are giving trouble. Alternatively, it can be so bad that the pumps have trouble keeping pace. Cracked frames and weak floors speed up this process. Sometimes the deck is pulled away from the top plank. In sensational cases one sees daylight from inside, which is a real worry if the weather forecast is predicting double-figure wind forces. In severe cases, when the whole boat is being tortured by heavy seas, the stopping may become loosened as the planks work. An even more extreme form of this trouble occurs when the planks spew out the caulking. Ragged ends of caulking hanging from seams, and lengths of open seam where the stopping is missing, tell the surveyor all he needs to know when he sees the boat hauled up.

Mature wood boats become soft around fastenings without having what can be classified as proper 'rot'. It is all part of the ageing process, and it is sometimes seen in low-quality boats only a few years old, especially if they have been kept continuously afloat. There may be subtle weeps, not even a discernible regular drip, at fastenings that are no longer lodged in firm strong wood. Where there are enough of these fastenings, there may be a regular build-up of water in the bilge when under way, even though there are no signs of leaks when on moorings. Tracing leaks in mature wood cabin tops can be difficult. The water may enter at a forward corner post and run down the carline. From there it may run outboard along a half-beam, down the back of a lining panel, and then past a seacock (which promptly becomes suspect) and so into the bilge.

To find this sort of leak, or indeed any dribble through the deck, two people are needed. The one on deck plays a slow-running hose gently on the suspected area, starting at the lowest point and working

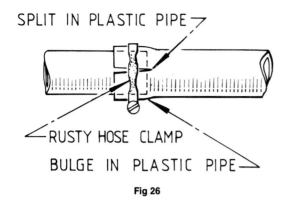

Fig 26

Plastic pipes forced over metal pipes sometimes split causing subtle but dangerous leaks. If a plastic pipe has a bulge where it joins a metal one, this is a danger sign. Likewise, rust on hose clamps is a sign of trouble because sooner or later the clamp will break.

uphill. The second person is inside the boat with a strong light, watching intently for any sign of a glint as the first droplet comes through. It is important to start with the whole cabin dry, perhaps using a big fan blower to remove all dampness; and it may need two people inside to catch that first subtle gleam of moisture. This technique is used on all types and sizes of craft, regardless of what the construction material is. Some boatyards have sonic testers that work in a comparable way using sound waves instead of water to find fissures that need sealing up.

A leak may be the result of defective plumbing. For instance, if a bilge pump outlet is below the waterline, it is possible to get syphoning back after pumping out. The conditions for this are:

1 The pipe has to be full of water throughout its length, as it often will be after the pump has been used.
2 The outlet at the hull side has to be higher than the inlet in the bilge. Even when the craft is well heeled, it is almost bound to be higher.
3 The pump must be designed so that water can seep back through it. In theory, the modern diaphragm pump has two watertight valves, and these should stop water running back through the pump. However, on occasions quite tiny pieces of rubbish can prevent both of these valves from closing tightly.

The same trouble can occur with toilet outlets, sink drains, and so on. Experienced designers locate outlets well above the waterline, and this is fine provided the boat is not heeled. Of course, owners love

to add extra gear every year, so seacocks and discharges that were once clearly above the waterline are now well and truly submerged. I once examined a famous yawl in Italy and found she had so much extra gear on board that the numerous seacocks that were built into the original boot-top were all now out of sight below her new waterline. Her old pumps were so worn that a small fish could have swum on board through the barely effective pump valves.

Regular leakers sometimes give themselves away. If the bilge has a series of well-established 'high tide marks', this is suspicious. The bilge may have nails that have rusted deeply and scraps of paper that have a pulpy or bleached look. The whole bilge may have a bland dirty appearance, with a general lack of contrasting colours. Sometimes the sole and its bearers may be saturated or even soft. There may be a high tide of oil, but this can be misleading as it could just indicate one event when the bilge filled when there was oil in it. If the boat has more than one electric pump but she is under 11 m (36 ft) long, or if the hand pumps show signs of excessive use or are coming adrift from their brackets, it is time to become suspicious. Finding leaks can be difficult and time-consuming. A surveyor who quotes a fixed price for doing the job may find he has badly underestimated

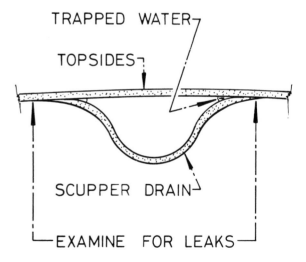

Fig 27

On fibreglass shells the drain scupper edges should be examined to see if the top-hat section has been forced away from the topsides, either by a bump alongside or by frost. Sometimes the drain scupper has an internal pipe, but this is not always 100% watertight at top and bottom, so water can get between the pipe and top-hat section and become trapped.

the number of hours the job takes. I have known cases where a leaking boat has been taken ashore, repaired, and put back afloat three times before she was pronounced fully watertight.

Then there was the aircraft company that had to buy a launch for a coastal project and decided to get an aluminium one because everyone was familiar with the material. This boat lay on moorings for a number of months, and then she sank without warning. She was salvaged and taken to the company's headquarters where engineers examined her, using all sorts of advanced electronic equipment. They were unable to find out why the boat sank, and called in a boat surveyor. He asked for a large bundle of dry absorbent rags and the help of one labourer. He got his helper to clean off and dry the outside of the boat, then slowly run water into her from a hose.

The boat was set up on trestles, so the surveyor had no trouble crawling under her with a bright light. He warned his helper to run the hose slowly, as he did not wish to damage the hull by overloading it, or be squashed if it collapsed on him. Just as important, he wanted to see the first dewy sparkle under the hull as the water rose to the level of the leak. There was sensation when the surveyor found four leaks,

because the staff of the aircraft company had found none. The mystery had to be solved fully, so the surveyor started to ask lots of questions.

He discovered that the launch was on a mooring near a fairway, so she had to have an anchor-light on each night. This light was linked to a battery and an automatic 'electronic-eye' switch that came on as the daylight faded. There was also an echo sounder on board connected to the battery, and the main battery switch had to be left on all the time for the anchor-light. Stray electric currents had wandered about this launch, eating away tiny pinholes that were invisible to the naked eye, especially when covered by anti-fouling paint and the usual mild fouling that builds up on the bottom of even well-kept boats. Normally the crew of a boat turn off the main battery switch when they go ashore, but this was impossible on this launch because of the anchor-light.

This trick of putting water inside a hull that is ashore needs to be used with caution. A big internal weight will distort a hull, even a steel one. All hulls alter shape at least slightly when ashore, and any added weight will accentuate this. Boats that leak when ashore may not do so when afloat, and vice versa.

METAL HULLS

· · · · · · · · · · · · · · · ·

Steel Craft

(For a full study of steel construction, see my *Small Steel Craft*, published by Adlard Coles Nautical in the UK and International Marine in the USA.)

A great gulf exists between large ships and small craft built of steel. However, there is another substantial difference between steel boats and those built of other materials. In many ways steel is a good-tempered material, and in small craft it seldom fails without giving ample notice. There is no equivalent to that sudden splitting that occurs in wood, and wood rot is much faster moving and more insidious than rust. Troubles in steel are often, but not always, easier to see than those in fibreglass. Steel craft seldom suffer from a lack of strength, though in the past this has been because scantlings have had to be large to deal with corrosion; now that we have reliable paint systems, parts like frames and plating are made thinner, and we will have to be more careful. Denting will be more of a problem; rusting less of one.

The surveyor's principal activity is to discover the extent and depth of corrosion. A secondary set of problems concern denting and distortion, but these defects are usually easy to discover and less worrying, though not always easier or cheaper to repair.

The four testing techniques used are:

1 **Visual inspection.** This is always the first line of attack and nearly always the most valuable. It is beaten, though, by lack of access.
2 **Hammering**. This is usually used even when the other methods are employed. It is hampered by fine paintwork that must not be damaged.
3 **Drilling**. Owners do not always allow this, and some surveyors rarely use it. It is time-consuming and requires a variety of skills, such as the ability to work in awkward locations and sharpen drills effectively.

4 **Ultrasonics.** This is a most valuable 'weapon', but one that is too often believed to be infallible. It can be misleading, but it gives a great deal of information for relatively little effort and moderate cost. It makes a steel survey more reliable than one on an equivalent fibreglass craft.

Hard hammering

Hammer testing is hard work, and professionals learn to alternate, using first the right hand, then the left, so that they can keep going without getting tired. When the plating is 6 mm ($\frac{1}{4}$ in) or more, it is difficult to be too strong with a 1 kg (2 lb) hammer. Plating only 3 mm ($\frac{1}{8}$ in) thick can be dented by over-enthusiastic battering even when new, so care is needed.

The surveyor wants to know when the plating varies in thickness, so he listens for a different note — thin plating and thick rust sound duller than new, clean, corrosion-free plating. The classic 'sound test' of plating that has become too thin is to compare the noise of battering on it to the sound of a hammer on a tin of baked beans. The latter is a soft, soggy, tinny, thin, dead, 'ding' noise. Thick plating rings and clangs more like a bell.

A surveyor watches to see if the plating has become so thin that it dinges inwards under his blows. Where he finds this happening, he turns the hammer over from the flat 'nail-hitting' side to the sharp pointed side to see if it will go right through or make a localised deep dent. As it *may* go clean through the plating, this sharp-ended hammer must not be used if the boat has been laid alongside a pier and is expected to float off as the incoming tide advances. I have only once gone right through the bottom of a boat — she was strongly built and *looked* sound enough — and the drama that ensued as I fought to ensure she was made watertight before the tide came right in will live with me for ever.

This steel skeg is near a bronze propeller and stainless steel propeller shaft. Extensive electrolytic action has corroded the skeg badly. No sacrificial plate was fitted on this boat.

It is usual for plating to corrode most near the keel. The trick is therefore to use the hammer in a series of blows from the bilge downwards, expecting signs of serious corrosion at the bottom. Good builders fit extra-thick plates below the bilge and even thicker ones by the keel, to deal with this corrosion caused by puddles of water lying for long periods in the bilge.

Hammering is carried out on all the components that can be reached. It has two effects: it breaks away layered rust and it reveals excessive weakness. This is seen where the component dents or bends, and where there is serious pitting on the exposed surface. Almost the only limit to widespread energetic hammering is good new paint. This fine finish should be studied all over, taking plenty of time. It may have been put on to fool surveyors and buyers. However, rust is like an enthusiastic weed, and it pushes its way to the surface through paint and filling compounds. Where there is roughness, bubbles, cracks — or indeed, any surface defect – it is likely there is trouble underneath. The lack of perfection on the paint surface gives the surveyor his excuse to use his hammer, and he is likely to find that the slightly imperfect paint is a traitor, telling the visitor about the troubles that lie beneath its surface. It may be advisable to photograph the defects on the paint's surface before causing more damage, as proof that the hammering was justified.

If the paint inside or out is very new, the surveyor is entitled to ask why it is so recent and perfect. Has the boat been 'dolled up' for selling? Has she been kept like this all her life? Does she have a local reputation confirming she has always been as perfect as her current paint covering? Painstaking searching usually shows up an area, perhaps near the rudder tube, or by a skin fitting, or by the toerail capping where the paint is less than perfect, and this region can be scraped to see if there is corrosion underneath. Once one area has been proved defective, a surveyor is less inhibited in his testing.

Modern epoxy paints are glass-hard, so they cannot be hammered without doing damage unless a semi-soft hammer face is used. Steel craft are grit-blasted when new these days, so that they show bright metal all over when the hull is complete. The glinting steel is treated with epoxy paints that are expected to give a rust-free life of many years. The guarantees vary, but at least 10 years is what most people expect, and 25 years is becoming common. No one voluntarily destroys a skin that has another 24 years of life ahead of it, so one has to go steady with a steel-faced hammer, especially on the topsides. Below the waterline it is easier to touch up bare metal, since the final finish, where the new paint meets the old, does not have to be such a perfect match.

As with all testing, when corrosion has been found in one area the same region on the opposite side of the boat is immediately checked. If, for example, No 7 floor has deep rust, then Nos 5, 6, 8 and 9 are also looked at to see if there is a pattern of trouble. If Nos 6 and 7 floors are in a bad way, but Nos 8 and 9 are under a tank and thus inaccessible, it is likely that the hidden ones will be worse, since it has been impossible to wire brush and paint them since the tank was installed.

Floors and frames rust at the bottom where they lie in the bilge-water. The trouble is often serious right at the bottom, with the metal having been

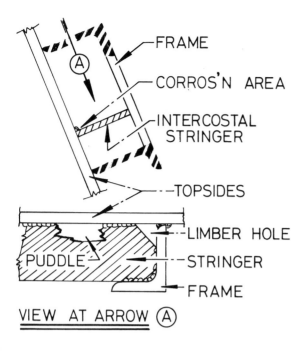

FRAME

CORROS'N AREA

INTERCOSTAL STRINGER

TOPSIDES

LIMBER HOLE

PUDDLE

STRINGER

FRAME

VIEW AT ARROW Ⓐ

Fig 28

Where intercostal stringers are fitted it is usual to have limber holes at each end to let water drain away. Sometimes these limber holes become blocked with dirt and paint so that water sits on top of the stringer and causes local corrosion. On other occasions the intermittent welding collects puddles of water between each run of welding and again local corrosion occurs. Limbers are equally necessary in wood, fibreglass or aluminium construction.

entirely eaten away. In contrast, a short distance above there may be plenty of *surface* corrosion, with pitting in patches perhaps 12 mm ($\frac{1}{2}$ in) in diameter and often a quarter of the diameter in depth. These blotches may be numerous, with little good unblemished steel between. Then, in further contrast, only a hand's span above, the steel may still have its original paint and be well-nigh perfect, with just the occasional spot of trouble where a puddle has lodged in a cranny, unnoticed for many years.

It has to be admitted that even with widespread careful testing and searching, there can be a batch of hidden thin patches on what looks like a sound steel hull. I like to see a good set of hand and power bilge pumps on a steel vessel, appropriate to her size, just in case there is a set of potential leaks that cannot be found even by a meticulous surveyor. But then of course all vessels should have enough pump capacity to deal with more than one dribbling persistent leak. It is a useful feature of steel hulls that they tend to get

tiny weeps at thin places, warning an alert crew that things are not what they should be.

Drilling plating to discover its thickness used to be popular before the coming of ultrasonic testers. It is still a valuable way of getting at the truth, especially as ultrasonic gauges are not cheap – also, they hate being dropped in deep puddles. They require a level of skill that takes time to acquire, and they cannot be used in a deep mucky cramped bilge. On the other hand, drilling is not without problems. It can be very difficult working in a tight narrow bilge, especially if the area has not been cleaned for a decade or two. Sailing craft with hollow fins that reach far down are distressingly inaccessible. More than once I have slid away down into one of these pits and wondered if I would ever get out.

These low awkward unreachable areas are just where corrosion occurs most, so this is where drilling should be carried out. A good shipwright will be able to drill from the outside of this sort of unreachable cavern, having measured down inside to make sure he is clear of frames and such like. He will work as low as he can when making his hole, yet in a position where he can put a sealing bolt in if he cannot weld over the holes he makes. Holes should be as small as possible, but large enough to take the measuring gauge. In practice, 6 mm ($\frac{1}{4}$ in) is too small, and 8 mm ($\frac{3}{8}$ in) suits most situations. It may be good policy to drill a 3 mm ($\frac{1}{8}$ in) pilot hole first.

When working with the boat grounded between tides, time is critical. The comprehensive preparations have to be made well before the boat is put ashore at the beginning of the ebb. Several sharp drill bits are needed, and ideally more than one shipwright. Power drills are preferable to hand-operated ones, and this may mean bringing in a generator or using 12 volt drills off the ship's batteries. These have to be fully charged before the water leaves the engine cooling water intake high and dry, as the tide goes down. Bolts to match the drill diameter are needed, with plenty of spares. Washers and waterproof washers are needed, inside and out. If access is poor inside the hull, arrangements may have to be made to push the bolt through its hole from inside using a long spanner that will hold the bolt head while the nut and washers are put on.

It is easy to miss some of the holes when sealing them by welding or with bolts after the surveyor has measured the thickness of the metal. Before drilling the hole, it should be marked boldly with chalk or a bright contrasting circle of paint. The holes are made in batches of three (or some other convenient number) and the same number are drilled port and starboard to help when putting the bolts in. Anything is important that assists in the job of ensuring that every drilled hole is filled. These precautions are just as vital if the vessel is laid up in a shed. There is no guarantee that the painters putting on the anti-fouling will notice one small open hole; and when launching a boat, not every yard has a reliable bosun who will check the bilge as she goes in, then check it again an hour or two later.

On small craft it may be necessary to have a right-angle drill to get into awkward corners low down. An alternative is to have a flexible extension drive with a chuck on the end, driven off a power drill. Holes should not be close to corners, frames or stringers, otherwise it may be hard to get a bolt in or reweld over from the inside.

Ultrasonics

In many ways the most effective way of examining a steel hull is to run an ultrasonic test all over her. This process uses an instrument like a portable echosounder. There is the test head, which is a small cylinder held in the hand, wired to a gauge in a casing that tells the operator the thickness of sound steel. The test head is held tight against the plating while the thickness is read off the gauge. The instrument is not large or heavy, and though it takes skill to get the best out of it, there is no great mystery in its operation. A typical modern sonic tester is so handy it could be taken aloft to test the thickness of a steel mast.

A small-craft surveyor who does not examine many steel craft will bring in a specialised firm to do the ultrasonic testing while he does the rest of the work. This ensures that the thickness testing is done by someone who is experienced and can interpret the results. He may also ultrasonically check welds and, if his instrument is good enough, the quality of the plates. Before doing these tests or, for that matter, drill testing, it is a good idea to get a construction elevation plan of the vessel. When a specialised printing firm is available, it is an elegant 'extra' to print the plan off the right way round and also reversed. This gives a view of the port and starboard sides, so the ultrasonic results are marked on each print showing the exact plate thicknesses all over the hull.

In practice, many ultrasonic testers use just one elevation drawing, which they make up themselves when printed plans are not available. It is important to have reference points such as portlights or, better still, frame numbers marked on the drawing. It is usual to show the plate thicknesses in red ink for port, and black for starboard, or use some similar code. In theory, the drawings can give as much information as is wanted, indicating the precise thickness of every little patch of plating. If the tester works with the surveyor, they may do a quick set of checks all over, dividing the vessel's length into, say, 10 or 20 parts, then go back over the bad areas where the corrosion has eaten the plates badly.

A sonic tester cannot work properly through paint, layered rust, grease or lining. Before the tests are made, the face of the steel must be prepared. This is best done with a grinder to clean off everything on the surface back to bright steel. Careless work when using a grinder results in the plate thickness being decreased – not the happiest of events, as the whole object of the exercise is to discover how thick the undamaged plates are. Like so much surveying, a little subtlety and skilled hand- and brain-work is needed. Ultrasonic testing is done by non-destructive test companies whose addresses are found in trade magazines, in the Yellow Pages telephone books, and at large public libraries.

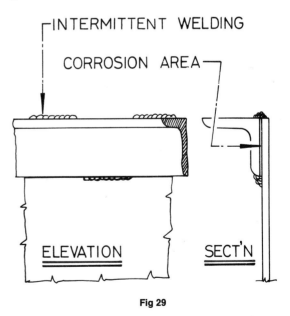

Fig 29

If an angle-bar is intermittently welded to a plate, for instance to stiffen a floor, there is always a risk that water will get between the plate and the flange of the bar. In theory a bar should be toe-welded, but the ideal practice is not always followed.

With all types of testing, it is important to look for trouble in the places it is normally found. These include close by the top of ballast that is inside a 'box' keel, at the edge of cement or any infill in the bilge, outside along the waterline, outboard by skin fittings, and at the bottom of steel bulkheads. The latter are often corroded right through, even when the great majority of the plating is in excellent condition.

Designers specify extra-thick lower hull plating, but on small craft seldom do the same for bulkheads. This so often results in deep corrosion that is very local and low down, where it is hard to see. Logically, when specifying the repairs, the new plating should be thicker than the steel that has failed. When making a repair in most locations, and certainly at the bottom of a bulkhead, the extra cost of new plating that is double the thickness of the rest is tiny compared with the labour and overhead charges. This is a fact that applies in almost every case, on all types of craft, and with all materials. Experienced surveyors tend to insist on plenty of extra material being used whenever damage is being put right – even though they are doing themselves out of future work!

Where the rudder tube is attached to the hull, and all over the rudder, by the skeg and aft end of the keel, expect deep rust. If there is a steel seacock fitted to a steel hull, there may be trouble with both, and if there is another metal in the seacock be sure to have the fitting taken off and checked inside. It may be necessary to cut away plating to gain access. For instance, if a double bottom is too shallow for a man to climb through, the only satisfactory way of finding the condition in this space is to cut out top panels or, if this cannot be done, the hull plating may have to be opened up. At least with steel, reinstating the hull shell is not difficult or too time-consuming.

Sometimes access has been blocked by alterations and additions to the vessel. This is an instance where cutting away structure may be the sensible way to make a thorough inspection. The surgery should be carried out intelligently so that replacement can be made neatly, with the maximum amount of down-hand welding, and the minimum disturbance to furniture and other equipment. When looking at tanks it is important to examine the striking plates under the sounding tubes. These plates are omitted on cheap craft, so local corrosion is probable (see figure on p.183).

Corrosion will be found where water is trapped in narrow interstices. There is often serious rust under wood decks that are on top of steel decks or on steel

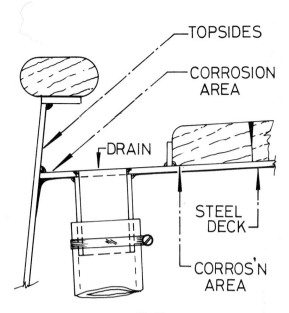

Fig 30

In deck depressions, puddles lie and cause corrosion troubles. A drainpipe cannot be put right against the topsides because a welder would not be able to get round the outboard side of the pipe spigot. As a result, a tiny quantity of water can lie outboard of the drain, and this cases rusting.

Between the edge of the wood sheathing and its steel boundary bar there should be a watertight seal. However, this sometimes has faults in it, maybe only a centimetre long, but enough to let the water get in. This moisture cannot easily dry out, and corrosion starts. Once it gets a hold it tends to force the wood away and let in more water.

margin plates and centreline plates. The trouble feeds on itself here, since the rust crushes into the wood and forces it upwards. This allows more water to get in, and so more rust is generated. When looking for places where puddles have been lying, it is important to remember that a boat's trim or attitude varies. She may be laid up with her keel horizontal, in which case she is likely to be down by the nose, as compared with her trim afloat. A fishing boat may spend time laid up afloat with ballast out and no nets or fuel on board. She may have a permanent heel in towards a quay, due to a pile of chain on the inside deck. These unusual attitudes result in extra sets of puddles, and hence erosion, in unexpected places.

Corrosion tends to be bad where any deck structure meets the deck or cabin top deck. Vent trunks, steel skylights, hatch coamings, bulwarks and their stanchions all corrode fast at the bottom, and sometimes hardly at all a short distance higher up. Trouble must be expected under gratings, because this is where dust collects and holds moisture that generates rust. Where chafe occurs, the rust is polished off, then forms again. This means that deterioration is rapid at steel stemhead rollers, by fairleads, where anchors and chain chafe, and where the keel rubs a lot on taking the ground. A similar place to look for damage is the bottom of bilge keels, if these regularly grind on the sea-bed.

Mild buckling of plates and frames is generally not significant on commercial craft. However, it is less acceptable on yachts, directors' launches and other prestige boats. A serious dent may call for an immediate repair because the welding has fractured. On a working boat, the owner may simply ask for the strength to be replaced by local welding. The appearance may not be restored, as this takes more time and the main object may be to get the vessel back into service swiftly. The good looks may be put back at the next major refit, but, as the vessel is required to make a profit, she may go around with lots of dents for many years. The reverse applies with yachts. The owner normally has enormous pride of ownership and is more interested in having the appearance of damage removed. It is up to the surveyor to make sure that the strength is also put back, with a little extra to prevent the same trouble recurring next week.

In practice, cutting out and welding in a new piece is the best repair, and hammering things back to their original shape is seldom possible.

Dents and other damage may give a clue as to the way a vessel has been handled and treated. There is a class of middle-water fishing boats that all have buckled bows, because their reverse gears are slow to react. They bash into quay walls before the propeller has had a chance to take way off the vessel.

. . . .

ALUMINIUM

Like all boats, aluminium craft are surveyed by examining every accessible area inside and out. The defects to look for are galvanic problems, corrosion, dents and bends, and also welding and riveting faults. This type of vessel seems to be particularly susceptible to troubles in the hull near propellers, especially if powerful engines are fitted. The pounding given by the reversing loads, as each propeller tip hurtles past the hull plating, causes vibrations that are strong and destructive. Additional structure may be needed in this region in the form of intermediate frames, doublers on the back of normal frames, and perhaps stringers as well. In addition, it may be necessary to have extra-thick plating, which is useful in this area to support the A-brackets on the aft end of the propeller shafts. The trouble is not found so often in steel craft, because this heavier metal does not suffer as much from fatigue. Aluminium is prone to fatigue, so it should be extra thick and very well supported when used for engine bearers, propeller shaft tubing, and stern gland supports.

Surveyors like working on alloy craft because large areas are left unpainted. There is no need to paint the 'out-of-sight' areas such as inside at bow and stern, below the cabin sole, and so on. It is quite common for the topsides to be left unpainted on ocean cruisers and all sorts of boats under 9 m (30 ft), especially runabouts and work boats. Soon after the craft is complete the grey metallic surface takes on a rough grittiness. It is somewhat mottled, and perhaps a little unattractive, but it is so practical that commercial users are delighted with it.

Painted areas should be looked over carefully, and small patches cleaned off. Where the paint is crumbling or uneven, a wire brush or scraper is used to get down to the metal and see if there is erosion working deep into the surface. Occasionally a particularly unpleasant type of corrosion occurs: the paint remains intact all over, except for a few tiny places that are subject to intensive local attack because these are the only parts that have no guard against the flow of electric current. There have been cases of electrolytic corrosion acting almost like a drill, penetrating inwards over a minute area right through the plating. When one of these defects is found, it is important to search around for other similar small (but serious) faults. They can be remarkably hard to detect without good lighting.

The inspection has to be all over the hull and superstructure, but the places to look most carefully are:

- At joins, whether they are made with welds, rivets or bolts.
- At the deck-edges, especially if the deck is of wood, or is wood sheathed, or has wood pads on it.
- Along the waterline.
- Around the rudder(s) and propeller(s).
- At apertures, windows, ports and skin fittings.
- Where there are two different metals, even though both may be aluminium alloys. An aluminium P-bracket is most unlikely to be exactly the same alloy as the adjacent plating and framing, for instance, and this can cause problems.
- Where deck structures meet the deck, and at the corners, flanges and the joins of different parts of deck structures. Also, where different metals meet in these structures.

Welding needs much more inspection in aluminium craft compared with steel vessels. Hair cracks are more common, and it may be advisable to use a dye-detection system. If a surveyor finds, say, a dozen frame-to-stringer cracks at the fore end of a boat, he should consider getting help from a non-destructive testing firm that is used to looking for cracks in welds, if he is not competent to do the job himself or does not have the time.

My experience suggests that weld failures tend to be worst at the bow, and taper off towards amidships, with the same pattern (but less marked) starting from the stern. Weld cracks are common in way of the mast at the beam ends, by the carline ends, and where the half-beams meet the carlines. The latter troubles seem more prevalent when the mast is keel-stepped.

Highly loaded parts like chain plates tend to wear and 'creep'. One technique used to prevent the rigging screws and their toggles from destroying the chain plates from the holes upwards is to have a bushing of stainless steel. This fits in the hole that takes the clevis pin of the rigging screw or its toggle. The bushing does not wear, spreads the load, and is out in the open − so it is easily seen each week should corrosion start as a result of the presence of different metals. A thick smear of lanoline before the rigging screw is fitted may stop future corrosion by preventing water from getting at the area.

It is noticeable that good boatbuilders make aluminium chain plates rather massive, even though this means thinning them down locally to accept the jaws of the rigging screw toggles. Except on small craft, it is not good practice to weld the chain plates directly on to the deck. Instead the plate is set right through the deck with welding on top and beneath, and the loads carried down to a strong point lower down. Sometimes the chain plate itself extends down to a frame or stringer; sometimes a thinner bar carries the load on the principle that the deck will take part of the tension. When a chain plate is secured to a cabin top, the load is dissipated down to the deck or beyond, using a bar that may be less strong than the chain plate because it is not subject to wear at the rigging screw clevis pin, and because the cabin top is normally strong enough to bear some of the stresses.

Riveting joins are used when the plating is thin because it is quicker and far easier. The welding of thin alloy plates is something of an art, and needs plenty of practice. Except on minor parts or on craft under 4 m (12 ft), blind rivets or 'pop' rivets should not be used. Rivets become loose due to corrosion and strain. Erosion shows itself by the fretting round the edges of the rivets and the usual white powder that is so often the sign of trouble as far as aluminium is concerned. When the edge of a rivet has been eaten away, dirt takes its place, and this highlights the trouble for the surveyor. It is not often that he is pleased to see grime, but in this case it does make his job easier.

Defective rivets are drilled out and replaced with new ones. If a whole row has to be removed, it is often good practice to fit the next size up, so as to be sure the rivets fill the holes tightly. If in a row there are ten adjacent defective rivets, the surveyor should recommend that something like fourteen new ones should be fitted. The extra two new ones at each end of the line ensures that rivets on the verge of giving trouble are replaced. Riveting joins are made with a bedding compound on the mating faces to prevent corrosion. I like to see the waterproof compound clearly along the seam edge, as I then know it is there in ample quantity. If it is not visible, there is a good chance that the messy compounds of corrosion will be visible instead.

Aluminium is not as tough as steel, so it dents fairly easily. In some ways this is a good thing − a collision results in a dinge inwards, but often there is no penetration of the plating and thus no water gets in. The edges of a dent should be examined for cracks, and the nearby welds or lines of riveting need

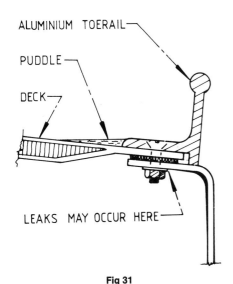

ALUMINIUM TOERAIL

PUDDLE

DECK

LEAKS MAY OCCUR HERE

Fig 31

Where an aluminium toerail is bolted down to a fibreglass deck there may be leaks at each fastening, particularly if the toerail traps water in a puddle and if the toerail has been bumped inwards in such a way that the bolts are slightly loose. All the bolts should be put in with bedding round them and, if self tapping fastenings are used here, leaks are likely.

special attention. Mild dents are often left alone, especially on fishing boats and commercial craft. Even quite large dents may be left alone on the principle that hammering them out may cause more problems, such as cracking. Besides, knocking out a dent can be a slow job, and therefore expensive. Where appearance matters, a view has to be taken before recommending the repairs. A mild dent may be best left untreated except for layers of filling to disguise the hollow. Rather than hammering out, it may be more sensible to cut out the damaged area and replace it with a new plate to reduce the chances of locking in all sorts of latent stresses.

It is logical to expect most problems on alloy vessels to be due to a difference in the location on the galvanic series between aluminium and the other materials used on board. All brasses and bronzes are dangerous, and should only be used reluctantly on an alloy boat. When they are seen, it is advisable to spend lots of time searching all round for trouble, and checking the insulation. The keel of a sailing yacht together with its bolts need well insulating. Though galvanised steel components and those made of stainless steel or Monel should not in theory give trouble, it is best to check round them carefully. Impurities in metals are a source of corrosion.

Engines and generators need total insulation from the hull. This means that cooling water inlet pipes, fuel pipes and exhaust pipes all need non-metallic sections. Even the controls should be given some padding where they are attached to the engine or the hull, or both, to avoid a continuous metal path along which electricity can track. Rubber engine mounts are used to insulate machinery, but it is not easy to get aluminium seacocks, and some of the plastic types have not proved tough enough.

Correctly chosen, aluminium alloys are so good afloat that they are used for tanks even in craft not made of this material. Fuel, water, sewage, 'grey water' and septic tanks can all be constructed in aluminium. Because the material gives so little trouble, it is often found that tanks are not opened up for years on end and dirt builds up inside. By then, the fastenings on the tank doors may be hard to get out. I prefer the arrangement whereby the tank lid is bolted to a frame round the access hole made of angle-bar, which in turn is welded to the tank. The nuts can be cut off or the bolt 'massacred' if the nuts are badly seized on, without damaging the tank at all, and without much expenditure of time.

WOOD CONSTRUCTION

·······

ROT

Rot is found in craft built of timber, but also in the wood parts of all sorts of boats – including those made mainly of fibreglass, steel, aluminium and ferro-cement. Almost every vessel has a few components made of wood, and many fibreglass ones have a lot of important parts made of timber. For instance, sole bearers are of wood more often than not. The person who breaks his ankle because a surveyor has failed to spot that the cabin sole is about to plunge into the bilge, because of rotten bearers, is not going to be convinced when told that 'fibreglass boats do not suffer from rot'.

Only wood can rot, but other materials have their own forms of deterioration that are just as bad and often much harder to detect. In some ways wood is user-friendly, because it gives off broad hints that it is in trouble and losing strength. Rot is often, but by no means always, on the surface. On fishing boats that have been hastily and roughly built, rot is found along the top of the beams – where it cannot be seen without taking the deck off. Rot is totally unaccept-able because it causes progressive loss of both tensile and compressive strength. The weakening can at first be quite slight, but it often speeds up at a frightening rate. Fastenings pull out of rotten wood, and corrode fast because the rot cradles the metal in moisture.

Rot germs are called 'spores' and they travel on the wind, in sawdust, on ropes, on bedding and clothing. If a boat is stored on rotten keel chocks, the surveyor has a warning that there may be rot on board. If the side props are rotten, the wise surveyor walks away from the boat treading gently, and gets the boatyard to substitute reliable supports before he goes on board. He then looks for rot.

So far as rot is concerned, salt water is a mild antiseptic, the accent being on the word 'mild'. This explains in part why rot is more often found in cabin tops than in planking. Boats kept in fresh water need an extra careful inspection, but many harbours and marinas have freshwater streams running into them and so rot has to be suspected everywhere. Cockpits collect rain more than spray, so cockpit bearers that get damp are at risk. If there is an imperfect seal round an access hatch in the cockpit sole, the adjacent bearers need checking. Dampness may have crept into little fissures and frost opened the glassed-over ends of the bearers. The result may be rotten bearers that are no longer held by intact glassing – a real disaster area, especially if a heavy sea fills the cockpit with tons of water.

When looking at a boat stored in a garden, a sur-veyor should be suspicious because it is usual to find the cover is less than 100% effective, and gardens are alive with undetectable spores. These tiny saboteurs are about three-thousandths of an inch long, so they can still get into a boat that is well wrapped up. Wood that is wet and then dry again is more likely to rot than material that is constantly wet. The best technique is to keep all wood permanently dry, which explains why good owners take trouble to have dry bilges and good ventilation throughout the entire length of the hull.

A bulkhead that reaches into the bilge or a wood mast support pillar may be fully glassed in at the bottom. This glassing can act like a cup, retaining water round the wood for long periods. If the bulk-head is made of a soft or low-quality ply, it will rot with enthusiasm. This defect can affect the inner layers and not be visible on the outside for months. In time, the rot makes the outer laminates wrinkle, undulate and split. It takes a keen and sober eye to detect the early signs of unevenness that may be the first warning. Using a spike at a slight angle to the wood to detect peeling glassing should also detect rot.

Sapwood in all species of timber rots first and fastest. The older inner parts of a tree are harder and more resilient and is the only part of the tree that

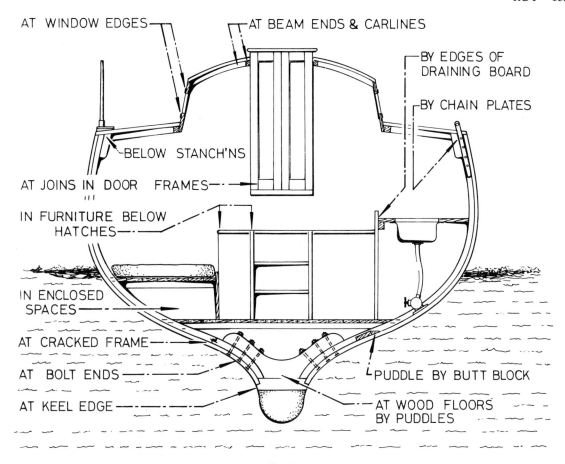

AT WINDOW EDGES

AT BEAM ENDS & CARLINES

BY EDGES OF DRAINING BOARD

BY CHAIN PLATES

BELOW STANCH'NS

AT JOINS IN DOOR FRAMES

IN FURNITURE BELOW HATCHES

IN ENCLOSED SPACES

AT CRACKED FRAME

AT BOLT ENDS

AT KEEL EDGE

PUDDLE BY BUTT BLOCK

AT WOOD FLOORS BY PUDDLES

Fig 32

A search should be made for rot wherever water can become trapped, and particularly where rainwater can seep in. This sketch shows typical vulnerable areas and suggests other comparable danger spots. For instance, stanchions work loose so that rain and spray gets down through their bolt-holes. The same trouble occurs at other deck fittings, especially those which take a lot of punishment.

should be used on marine craft. Lowering standards in the timber and boatbuilding industries have allowed sapwood to sneak into boats. If sapwood is seen, it should be 'spiked' on all accessible sides. Cheaply built boats are more likely to have sapwood in them – indeed, the best builders never allow sapwood to get outside the timber mill. They know it has no use except in the boiler that keeps the sheds warm in winter. It shows up as a light brown or dark cream colour on many reddish mahoganies. In oak the colouring is reversed, with the whiter wood the hard core and the reddish timber sapwood.

A drying current of air is the first line of defence against rot. If the moisture content is below 20% (or, conversely, very high), wood is unlikely to rot. The temperature is important, and must be in the range of 4 to 40 degrees centigrade. This is encouraging in

one way – when it is freezing, at least rot stops its evil work.

Rot attacks young and old boats if the conditions are right. Partly decked boats like wooden Dragons seldom suffer from rot because they have no bulkheads, so air can circulate freely and most of the time the wood is dry. This is especially true if the boat is cosseted and stored each winter in a dry shed. Day-racing boats that have slatted floorboards or gratings can dry out in the bilge more easily than those with tight boards. Careful owners who have boats with spinnaker chutes at the bow take these out each winter and leave the chute hatch or cover off. This allows lots of air to circulate and suck off stagnant moisture.

Good surveyors insist that rot is treated promptly, and not left till the owner has made more

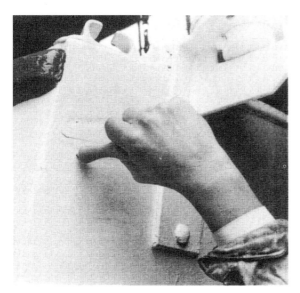

A usual place to find rot is at the top outer edge of a wood transom. The surveyor had plenty of warning of trouble here since the paint was undulating and a graving piece had already been let in.

Since the spike has gone in right to the hilt this rot is severe, and probably plank ends as well as the transom framing and possibly the deck will also be affected.

money for the repairs, or until the cold winter weather is passed. No excuse should be made for delaying a comprehensive repair. An area of rot in the deck may spread towards the bow and the stern, as well as working its way athwartships, towards the port and starboard planking – all at this disconcerting speed. What starts as a small area of softness no larger than the point of the surveyor's spike can be 0.5 sq m (2 sq ft) in area in a month's time.

This speed of advance is one reason why it is risky to suggest remedial treatment rather than total replacement. There are chemicals that halt the spread of rot, but in general it is best to use them copiously on the new wood that replaces the rotten timber. This chemical treatment is also applied to all the sound timber after cutting away the rot and before the new parts are fitted, to kill off rot spores in the area. Sometimes rot is not cut away with sufficient enthusiasm and it reappears next year, or sooner. After treatment and repairs, the area should be checked every three months.

There are various chemicals that are used to prevent rot. One of the best known is Cuprinol, which is available in a coloured form from hardwear stores. If the timber is to be varnished, a colourless version can

be used. Another type of chemical is based on epoxy resins and this soaks into the softened wood to restore strength. This is not always a complete cure and it requires expert application. Its great virtue is that it is cheaper and easier to apply than a 'cut and replace' procedure, which normally calls for the full range of shipwright skills. Soaking with an epoxy is used where there is a small amount of rot in a location that is hard to reach. Firms like Structural Polymer Systems, of Eastgate House, Town Quay, Southampton, England SO1 1LX, supply the material and special instructions.

Chemical treatments need special conditions, with

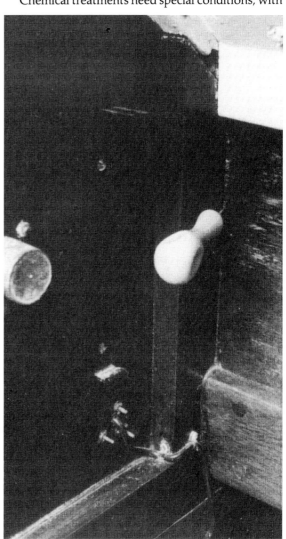

The rot in this cabin coaming was easy to detect because of the discoloration. The aft beam of the cabin top is so rotten that parts have actually dropped out, as is seen just above the spike.

warmth and dryness high on the list. On their own, chemicals may not be enough and some reinforcing may be required. Because no one can be sure how much strength has been lost, it is sensible to put in extra-long, thick doublers well secured, regardless of which curing technique is used.

Dry rot (Merulius lachrymans)

Quite rightly, this is the most dreaded disease found in wooden vessels. It totally destroys the strength of the wood, so that instead of using a sharp spike, a surveyor can poke his finger deep into the timber. Fastenings can be pulled out by hand. Under bad conditions, this rot can spread at about 8 mm ($\frac{5}{16}$ in) per day and the only consolation is that it is relatively rare afloat. Also, it gives itself away by its smell, and it is often easy to see unless it is growing somewhere inaccessible such as in a cramped stern locker.

The external signs are cracking along and across the grain of the wood. Painted wood gets undulations first, then when the rot increases, the paint cracks. There is a total lack of resistance when a spike is plunged in, so that the blade (and sometimes even the handle) may disappear into the hopeless wood.

Every effort has to be made to stop the rot spreading. Infected timber should be removed carefully in plastic bags and kept away from stocks of wood, other boats and buildings. It should be burned immediately, taking care to destroy every piece.

When removing this rot, the whole component should be taken out and the adjacent parts checked meticulously. Where a part is not affected along its whole length, and where it is a large important scantling, the rot is cut out together with plenty of the adjacent timber that appears to be sound. How much is cut away depends on circumstances, but typically half a metre (say 18 ins) beyond the last sign of rot is enough along the grain. Across the grain the rot spreads less efficiently, and a cutback of 100 mm (4 ins) is likely to be enough.

It used to be said that this form of rot was mostly found in Europe, whereas its American half-cousin, *Poria incrassata*, was more likely to be found on the windward side of the Atlantic. However, these days there is so much travel, and such vast amounts of material are shifted about the globe, that one can never be sure which diseases are rife in any area. *Poria* is an unpleasant fellow, and should be treated as ruthlessly as *Merulius*.

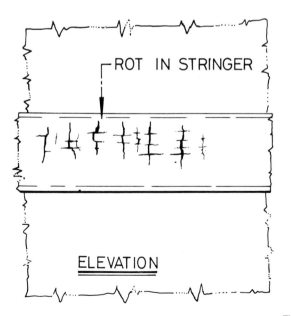

ROT IN STRINGER

ELEVATION

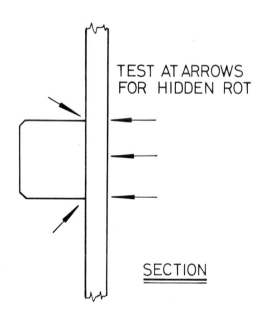

TEST AT ARROWS FOR HIDDEN ROT

SECTION

Fig 33

On the left, a typical area of rot is shown in a stringer. Its characteristic is the cubing that results from cracks both across and with the grain. When rot is found in one piece of wood, the surrounding scantlings should be examined to see if the trouble has spread. If the bulkhead has not been infected, it should be well treated with a chemical preservative when the stringer is being repaired.

Wet rot (Coniophora cerebella)

This form of rot is common where there are leaks above the waterline in wooden boats. It is not so virulent as dry rot, but it shares many of its characteristics. It thrives where there is a lack of ventilation, so it is found at the extreme bow and stern of wood boats, below the sole on any vessel, in corners of lockers, where water dribbles in down chain plates, and in the bottoms of chain lockers made of wood. Where there is a thin gap between two pieces of wood, water gets in easily. It cannot escape, and no air currents can reach into such a tiny fissure, so it lies there indefinitely, a perfect breeding ground for rot. This is why all timber should be bedded with a waterproof compound wherever the pieces touch, to prevent any moisture seeping in.

Wet rot looks something like dry rot, as the timber cracks down and across the grain, almost as if it was being charred, but without the blackening. There may be signs of thin brown strands on bare wood. The same subtle denting and bulging on the surface occurs when this rot first gets going beneath paintwork. As the defect increases, it causes the paint to crack.

Testing with a spike is often sensational as the probe sinks right into the soft timber. The minimum number of test jabs is made to discover how far along and across the grain the rot has crawled. As with other forms of rot, it is common to find adjacent parts affected, and the trouble spreads faster along the grain than across it.

Rot prevention

Boats put in the tombs of ancient Egyptians have survived 4,000 years because they have been totally dry. We can all take the hint, and keep water out or, when it gets in, dry it up promptly. When a boat is being surveyed in a shed in the late spring and water is found in the bilge, the obvious question is: Has the puddle been there since the boat was hauled ashore in the autumn? If the answer is 'Yes', then this hull is not well ventilated and rot should be suspected.

Deck and cabin top leaks are prime causes of rot. When the drips fall on the owner's bunk the trouble is soon put right, but leaks that cause no immediate discomfort may not be seen and, if they are, they may be neglected. An occasional drip that runs down behind lining, or is hidden in the dark at the back of a remote locker, receives no attention. However, it can take its revenge by causing very expensive damage.

To stop rot:

1 Seal all leaks.
2 Ventilate the entire vessel, especially enclosed spaces. Each locker should have two holes, one to let air in, the other to channel it out. The aim is to create a constant draught and have no stagnant air anywhere aboard. Each hole must be at least 150 × 50 mm (6 × 2 ins), otherwise air will not circulate easily. These holes should be at diagonally opposite corners of the locker. If they are both at the top, air will waft in one and out the other, leaving a damp atmosphere at the bottom of the locker. Ideally there should be more than two holes, and they cannot be too large.
3 Pump and sponge out the bilge and keep it dry.
4 Enhance ventilation by leaving locker doors open, cushions tilted up, sole boards on edge, and hatches ajar as often as possible – and certainly whenever the boat is not being used.
5 Buy a powerful light and use it often in all the dark corners.

When a surveyor discovers that the inside of a boat has all these precautions, he is less likely to find rot. However, what he is seeing may be the actions of the current owner, and the previous one may have been less careful. So when the inside of the boat appears to be well-kept and dry, one looks for signs of rot that have been halted. This may be discovered in ply decks under teak, especially near hatches and by stanchion bolt holes through the deck.

WORM

Any craft that has wood components below the waterline may be attacked by ship worm. These dangerous animals find just a tiny exposed area of immersed timber, and dig in below the surface. Some nibble along the grain for great distances, others eat their way inwards. They can do an enormous amount of damage.

These parasites are found principally in warm waters, so the nearer the Equator, the more likely they are to be discovered. In north-western Europe it is probably true to say that less than one boat in two hundred is affected. However, they are a serious problem for surveyors because at the early stages there may only be quite small areas affected, and these can be hard, or even impossible, to find. A few months later the whole hull may be destroyed because the multiplying ship worm may have riddled the planking with a mass of holes, weakening it and causing dozens of little leaks.

Surveyors keep records of their discoveries of this pest because they know that if a boat in one particular harbour has been affected, others are likely to have the same trouble. A regularly occurring rumour suggests that where there is a hot water discharge from a power station in a temperate region, ship worm is liable to be found. Plenty of craft are kept near electricity-generating stations, where the sea is continuously warmed by the waste water. Therefore it is logical to expect the ecology to be different from the cooler surrounding areas.

Though teredo and gribble, two common types of worm, prefer warm water, they keep eating away winter and summer. This means that a boat left afloat for long periods is more likely to have worm than one taken ashore regularly each 'off' season. The probability is more than doubled if she does not have a new coat of anti-fouling every six months. In fact, a general lack of anti-fouling, or indications that cheap paint has been used, is a warning to check for worm.

One reason why teak is such a prized wood is that it has a resistance to ship worm. As a general rule, the harder the wood the less trouble one expects. However, any timber can be attacked, and wood that is in good condition in March can be in real trouble by May of the same year. The first indication of worm may be small leaks that are hard to explain. Weeps found away from seams or butts or skin fittings may be the first clue that there is ship worm in the planking. If the boat is put ashore for the winter or just for a scrub, and the forward or aft deadwood crushes in on the underside, or when hammered, look for worm. If the rudder fittings become sloppy or a seacock seems to be less than perfectly tight in the planking, start using a spike in the affected area.

A good spike for the first inspection is a bradawl with a 5 mm ($\frac{3}{16}$ in) diameter probe. It needs careful handling in soft woods, especially if the boat has been afloat for a long period and is saturated. The spike may sink into sound wood with little effort if used too energetically by a newcomer to surveying; an experienced surveyor has a less robust and more thoughtful approach. The spike should be pushed in near the suspected area, up and down the grain, because most worm damage extends along the way the wood has grown. You may find that the wood surface is sound, then there may be a little tunnel left by the worm, with the inner surface of the wood solid. So a very carefully handled spike meets initial resistance, then nothing, then firm timber again. Of course, the distances involved are small (the burrows may be less than 3 mm ($\frac{1}{8}$ in) across), so at times the surveyor's job is bordering on the impossible.

Once trouble is suspected, the area should be probed extensively, working far up and down the grain, and in the adjacent planks. Once a tunnel has been found, the wood on the outside should be levered off, perhaps with a larger spike, and the tunnel traced extensively. This may not be easy, and when it becomes very hard most surveyors start exploring for adjacent holes. Naturally, the worm takes the line of least resistance, so the holes wander and go round fastenings.

When worm is strongly suspected but extensive spiking has produced no definite results, another technique is tried. Where there are clear signs of leaking through the middle of a plank that is not split, it may be advisable to take it off and cut it across at 1 m (3 ft) intervals, and also to examine the exposed edges of the adjacent planks. Of course, if a plank has a split, worm may have entered at this crack, since there may well be no protection from anti-fouling paint. A more common approach is to shave off about a third of the plank thickness. This is normally done well clear of fastenings unless the trouble is suspected close to one of them. The incision is made over half or even two-thirds of the width of the plank, and over a length of perhaps 15 cm (6 ins). The same process is repeated in several places, at bow and stern, port and starboard. As a general rule, worm favours plank ends, so this is where the main search must be.

Assuming no trouble is found, it is reasonable to suppose that no worm is present, provided plenty of spike testing has been carried out in vulnerable areas. Graving pieces are epoxy glued at the cut-away patches to restore the lost strength. Properly done, the investigation should not weaken the craft seriously, but the owner's permission in writing must be obtained before starting to chisel into the planking. The most likely place to find worm is where the anti-fouling is least effective. Plenty of craft are put afloat with no defensive paint on the undersides of the fore and aft deadwoods, and the bottom of the rudder and skeg. Close-by skin fittings that are low down near the keel of 'flat-floored' vessels is a problem area, because the fitting may have an external flange. A paintbrush will sweep over this flange, leaving no paint by its protruding edge; this is because the painter has such a hard job getting in under the bilge, so he cannot always see what he is doing.

Where there is sheathing, either with traditional copper or one of the modern skins that may be of nylon or fibreglass or some such, the vulnerable areas are:

- On the underside of the keel and deadwood areas, especially after a grounding or careless hauling out on a marine railway, or when the sheathing is old.
- By skin fittings.
- On the bottom of rudder blades, by any rudder fitting, and at the top where the stock joins the blade; also, in any area that has chafe or wear.
- In way of any damage. This can be from ground-

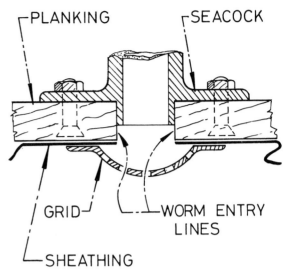

When examining sheathed wood boats it is important to remove grids and gratings over seacock inlets to examine the ends of the planking. Antifouling paint is seldom put on the plank end-grain round the seacock apertures because the grid has to be taken off before the painter can do his work. To prevent worm getting in, the seacock spigot should extend right through the planking or the sheathing should be curved in to meet the spigot.

ing, and may be up the front of the stem or forward deadwood or keel, or it can be caused by flotsam. It may be where the propeller has hurled something against the hull.
- At any join or seam in the sheathing, especially if the overlap has peeled back to show the hull beneath.
- At the top of the sheathing if the boat is floating low on her marks, perhaps due to a bigger engine being fitted, or weighty extra gear on board.
- By sterntubes and instrument transducers — for instance, by the sonic probe of the echo sounder.

Some types of worm can enter a gap in the defences only 1 mm ($\frac{1}{32}$ in) wide, so anti-fouling paint slapped on carelessly can be the cause of massive destruction. This is one reason why at least two coats of this important paint must be applied twice each year. It should be layered on thickly round and into the aperture of all skin fittings, especially where the grain is not entirely covered by the spigot.

PLYWOOD

In fibreglass boats it is usual to use plywood for the bulkheads, cabin soles, sometimes for the lining and furniture, for berth bases, shelves, and so on. There are few vessels that do not have at least a little ply in them, regardless of what the principal construction material is.

Plywood has these special advantages:

- It is consistent in its dimensions. Almost all sheets are made 2440 × 1220 mm (8 × 4 ft) and the thicknesses range from 3 mm up to 25 ($\frac{1}{8}$ in to 1 in). There are fabricators who will produce thinner and thicker material, but 3 to 25 mm is the range used for most boatbuilding.
- There is not much variation in size, especially when ply is bought in batches from one maker.
- Ply arrives ready machined and smooth on all broad faces, which saves time and labour in the boatbuilders' premises.
- The most convenient way to cover large areas, such as cabin soles, is with ply sheets. The labour saved usually more than offsets the higher cost of the material when compared with normal 'tree-wood'.
- Swelling and shrinking are limited.
- As a general rule, plywood can be bought confidently without first being inspected at the maker's factory. Certainly the best ply makers guard their reputation by producing a consistent high quality.
- The strength of a ply panel in all directions is convenient for all sorts of locations, particularly bulkheads.
- The absence of weakening knots and shakes in good-quality ply means that builders can use it swiftly and without spending time looking for weaknesses. There is, or should be, no sapwood, and in general the strength of ply is consistent. These factors suit modern builders who employ semi-skilled labour.
- It comes in a wide variety of types. Some have hard-wearing plastic surfaces that need no painting, some are of decorative woods, and some are extra light for racing craft.

A thoughtful surveyor uses this list when looking at ply to help him find defects. For instance, if he finds buckling in one bulkhead he knows that the strength of the other bulkheads will be almost the same, so they too should be checked to see if they are bowed. If water has soaked into the bottom of the port side of a bulkhead, the starboard side will probably have the same trouble. This saturation depends a lot on the hardness and water resistance of the core material used in the ply, and we expect this to be the same on both sides of the vessel. Bulkheads should be checked all round, but especially in the bilge and by chain plates, because these are places where water often attacks. Few builders take precautions such as coating the edges with a fibreglassing resin, or even a good application of a rot-preventing compound. If one is used, it must accord with any glassing-in subsequently done in the same area.

When the surface of ply is found to be uneven or split, a spike test frequently shows the inner wood has become soft. Sometimes the surface laminates on both sides may be in reasonable or even perfect condition, but the internal ones are soggy as a result of edge soakage. When this trouble is found at the bottom of a bulkhead, it usually extends athwartships because water laps up across the full width of the bilge, and reaches higher on the outboard side when the yacht heels. However, water soaks along the grain in rotting ply, and the saturation may extend above the sole boards even though the bilge-water has not reached that level.

Recommending a repair is not a straightforward job. Some people will insist that the whole bulkhead is taken out, arguing that this is the only way to be sure of a total cure. This remedy is expensive, because furniture and possibly lining has to be taken out, then put back after the new bulkhead is in place. This path is normally followed only when the trouble is extensive.

In practice, the shipwright is normally told to cut out the defective patch plus about 15 cm (6 ins) all round to be sure of eliminating all the saturated soft core wood. A new piece of matching ply is slid in place, and a doubler fitted on the side where it will show least. (Some skilled shipwrights like to scarf in the new piece and do without the doubler, and this is acceptable provided there is definitely no loss of strength.) The doubler is glued and bolted, then reglassed on to the hull along the outer perimeter, with plenty of extra glassing to compensate for any loss of ruggedness. There is a vogue for screwing doublers, but as they and the ply are about 12 mm ($\frac{1}{2}$ in) thick, screws cannot get an adequate grip.

One way to find defects in ply panels is to close the eyes and run the fingertips gently over the surface. Undulations indicate hidden problems, and are most likely to be found near seams and edges. If a little water gets into a join and freezes, the expansion forces the layers of wood apart. Fracturing occurs in the wood rather than the glue, except when the ply is of a low grade or of a non-marine quality made with a glue that is not waterproof.

Cheap boats are sometimes made with what is called 'exterior grade' ply, intended for buildings. It may last in a boat if she is put in a dry shed each winter and well maintained, but its low price is seldom an adequate reason for using it in boats. Many surveyors make a note in their report when they find this material has been used.

Good plywood has a stamp mark on it when it arrives from the factory, showing it has been made to a quality that will stand up to marine conditions. Different countries have their own requirements, and one that is widely used is British Standard Specification No 1088. The mark on each panel is BSS 1088. This lays down the type and quality of wood and glue that must be used, and in general any boards with this code number marked on them are reliable. However, there have been makers who have abused the system and stamped inferior ply with this important lettering and number, so surveyors can no longer rely on the code. Sometimes the numbers can be seen on the ply under a coat of varnish, down in a dark locker, and it is tempting to assume that this is a sign of reliability.

Good marine ply can be affected along the edge in wet and freezing weather – sometimes seriously, but sometimes with little loss of strength. Where the ply has been used for decking, and the defect is seen to be very local, a limited cure can sometimes be suggested. For instance, the wood can be dried out and a fully waterproof covering glued over the top. However, when making this sort of suggestion, a surveyor has to add in his report that the affected area and similar regions have to be checked frequently.

Ply decks are seen on 'one-off specials'. These boats are sometimes fibreglass shells completed by an amateur or a small boatyard for ocean cruising or singlehanded long-distance racing, or an unusual purpose of this sort. The same sort of deck is also found on wooden hulls, and on a few steel and aluminium boats. The edges, butts and seams of these decks need scrutinising, especially where the butt blocks or doublers that hold the joins are less than 18 times the ply thickness in width. Ply manufacturers will scarf up the standard ply sheets, joining two or three panels together; this is the best way to make decks, because it reduces the number of butts or seams.

The joins are normally end to end, rather than side to side, giving long lengths 1220 mm (4 ft) wide. One of these pieces quickly covers a good area of deck and a small batch of skilled men will deck a whole hull in a day. Making a deck with these lengthy panels simplifies the builder's job, but the scarfs must be perfect and should be looked at from above and below. There should be no protruding wood fibres and the join should be undetectable when brushed over lightly with the fingers and the eyes closed.

Ply is not strongly resistant to blows on the edge, so decks need studying all round the sheer. It is common to find some sort of moulding covering the outside edge. This battening is normally the same thickness as the ply, and it seldom lasts ten years without failing over at least a few short lengths. Water seeps between the solid wood edging and the ply, then remains there indefinitely even when the rest of the boat dries off. The first sign of trouble may be peeling paint, or discoloration under varnish. It may only be dirty marks or a subtle softness in the edge of the ply. This loss of strength can at first be very mild, but it should not be ignored for it can develop in about six months. Provided the work is done well, and kept under observation, this can be a place to run in epoxy resin that is truly liquid, so that it flows well, soaks into the wood, and restores firmness.

Where two ply panels are joined on a curve, there should be no 'knuckle' or discontinuity in the sweeping shape. A straight edge placed at right angles to the line of join will show if the curve is broken, and alert the surveyor to various problems. The butt strap may be too thin, too short, too narrow, or not properly glued. Its edges may be secured, but not its middle, or it may need fastenings to help the glue. In bad cases, the backing behind the join may be just a frame or beam that is far too thin to form a substantial joining piece.

An exposed edge of ply is widely considered to be unsightly, but there are exceptions to this 'rule'. From the point of view of long life without loss of strength, an uncovered ply deck-edge that is properly sealed and checked monthly will often outlast an edge sealed by strips of wood, however well the protection is fitted. A good trick is to bevel the ply, so that there is less of an 'end-grain' effect and a better chance that a sealing compound will stay on permanently. Omitting an edge moulding ensures that drying off occurs quickly, and this is a real asset. Inside a boat, exposed ply edges tend to be a sign of cheap building, and an indication of less than excellent quality. However, anyone who has spent a few years in and around small craft will know that there are always exceptions to this rule.

When McGruers of Rosneath built one of their very fine 8 m cruiser-racers, they wanted to save all the weight they could, especially at the ends of the yacht. There was a ply bulkhead at the fore end of the forward cabin, with a large access hole through. Normally this hole would have been edged with a hardwood moulding. To save half a kilo, the edging was omitted, but the ply edge was precisely rounded, so that each layer of ply was seen from aft as a neat circle with no trace of a ragged edge. So accurately was the work done that the visible widths of the laminates did not vary the slightest bit right round the aperture, and of course the wood was totally smooth. This display of virtuosity in woodworking will impress any surveyor, and tell him that the builders have almost certainly done a similarly fine job in the rest of the construction.

The normal tool for testing ply is a spike, but a hammer can be useful, especially when it has been established that the core is soggy and soft. Using a hammer without expending too much energy, the extent of the trouble can be discovered by tapping to see where the 'dead' sound ends. When banged, good wood gives a ring or lively sound. The power of the blow should not dent the good surface of the ply.

One reason why ply is used is to save weight. It is therefore used in the thinnest sheets the designer considers safe. Sometimes he is over-optimistic and a surveyor finds that panels will move when given a firm thrust with a boot. This may be acceptable on a small cruiser used in sheltered waters, or perhaps on a

dinghy, but seldom elsewhere.

Where chain plates or rudder hangings are fitted, there should be a substantial doubler or, better still, one on each side. As the securing bolts are tightened, they tend to pull the fitting through the outer (and sometimes the inner) layers of ply, which consequently lose strength. This confirms the importance of solid wood (not ply) pads. It is important that they extend well beyond the fitting all round and should be glued or well bedded with a waterproof material. A good type is Farocaulk, which also sticks the parts together, adding strength.

Where skin fittings pass through ply, these wood pads are important, but it is rare to have one on the outboard side. The pad on the inside should be bevelled round the edges, and especially along the top, to prevent water lying here. It is details like these that tell a surveyor how good the builder is. This knowledge helps to assess the general quality of the craft. There should be no gaps between stringers, frames or beams and the ply panels that they support. These stiffeners should be glued along the full length, and it is a good sign to see a few screws (or, better still, bolts) to be doubly safe. It's supposed to be bad engineering to mix glue and metal fastenings, but that is a purist view, and one that does not stand up to experience in boatbuilding works and afloat.

It is good to see a minimum of one or two metal fastenings at each end of every supporting batten. Their principal disadvantage is that they pierce the ply and let water seep in round the fastening if the surface coating is not well maintained. The full length and width of each stiffener, such as a frame or stringer, should lie flat on the ply. On shoddily built craft it is common to find that frames right forward jump across gaps, leaving the ply panel locally unsupported just where strength is so important to cope with the pounding when punching into a head sea. Even when stringers do touch, they sometimes meet the ply only at one edge. A cure can be made by 'filleting' with a thickened epoxy resin applied the full length of the stiffener on both sides.

Fast motor boats sometimes have very strong bottom panels, but flimsy topsides. This is to save weight, but it ignores the way life is offshore. In severe weather these craft have to slow down, so that waves break against the sides above the chine, and then the loadings may be too great for thin ply — or any other material for that matter. As this style of boat is normally beamy, the loadings forward are all the greater.

TEST BORINGS IN WOOD

It is not always easy to find out the extent of rot in wood by hammer and spike testing alone. A technique that was once popular, but not used much these days, consists of making test borings in timber. This drilling may be used to confirm the extent of known rot, or to discover if hidden rot is present.

This examination used to be done in heavily built wood fishing boats, especially in the beam ends, tops and bottoms of frames, in the wood floors, and so on. It is sometimes done in the backbone, notably into the stem starting near the deck. If the stem is found to be rotten at the top and for about 60 cm (2 ft) down, the cost of repairs will be reasonable. But if the rot extends to the keel it will cost a fortune to renew the stem. Other borings may be made at a distance of perhaps 15 cm (6 ins) from backbone structural joins. Drilling is done with care and forethought to minimise the damage, having first got the owner's permission in writing. The work needs some skill to avoid leaving a trail of destruction. Each hole in sound timber is carefully sealed with a glued-in wood plug of the same timber. Careful shipwrights line up the grain in the plug with the grain of the scantling, and paint over the area fully.

It is unusual to do test borings in lightly built vessels, partly because the components are thin and rot seldom lurks unseen beneath the surface. Also, unlike heavily built commercial craft, light boats do not have big factors of safety, so it is seldom safe to puncture their beams and frames with holes, even if they are later plugged. As a rule, test borings are made when the rest of the survey has been completed. If the vessel has so many troubles that she is not worth buying, there is no point in spending money examining the insides of the beams. If the investigation has to be limited, the first drillings should be near the ends of the widest beams and half-beams. These drillings are made from forward or aft, and as near the top of the beam as possible to minimise the loss of strength and to probe into the most likely area of rot.

Water trickles through deck seams and lies on top of beams for long periods, starting rot particularly when the sun warms the deck. Clear of the beams, if there is a leak in a deck seam the water dries up on the underside of the planking when the rain stops. Water also gets down beside deck fastenings into beams. Hammer testing may give a dull or lively sound that confuses the inspector. The outside of the beam can be unyielding and solid even though the whole of the core is gutless and powdery. The drill will sometimes work hard at first as it goes into the scantling, then plunge in effortlessly as it meets friable wood, before coming up against more good wood that needs effort in order to penetrate it.

A wood bit and ratchet brace is used for this drilling, never a power drill or a high-speed metal bit. This is so that the shipwright can assess the toughness of the wood as he works into it, and to get big shavings. Rot is subtle stuff, and not homogeneous. Sometimes it is in layers, and it is sometimes almost as hard as the surrounding timber. The wood may be very wet but not yet weak, or it may be dry but totally lacking in strength. An experienced craftsman will be able to tell the surveyor a lot as he works. The normal size of auger will be about 12 mm ($\frac{1}{2}$ in) diameter in a 60 mm ($2\frac{1}{2}$ in) beam and 20 mm ($\frac{3}{4}$ in) diameter in a 125 mm (5 in) beam.

A cloth, newspaper or polythene sheet is spread on the cabin sole to collect the borings as they come out, though most surveyors like to collect them in the hand as they fall from the auger. The smell, dampness and powdery appearance will indicate if there are problems and how bad they are. Even if it comes out in discrete lumps, rotten wood crumbles when rubbed between the fingers. Crackly strong chips that are holding together tenaciously are what the owner and buyer are hoping will emerge from the hole as the drill cuts in. Assuming that crisp, brightly coloured shavings with a pleasant smell come out, the next boring will probably be 30 cm (12 ins) further along, or in the next beam. One tries to avoid drilling at vulnerable places, such as near masts and in the middle of beams. Drilling above deck, except in wheelhouse beams and carlines, is to be avoided as far as possible. As a rule, it is bad practice to take drillings in areas that will be exposed to rain and spray. However, it is even worse to miss rot hidden below the surface.

The minimum number of drillings should be

made, and the work planned in advance so that when the job has been completed and the necessary repain-

ting finished, it should be hard to tell where the tests were made.

· · · · · · · · · · · · · · · · ·

PLANK SEAMS

A conventionally planked boat should ideally have no visible seams after she has been painted. When she is new, or is old but is being expertly maintained for racing, it is often hard to see any trace of the seams, even when a good light is shining obliquely on the topsides. As boats get older, the seams show more and more. If an old boat is moved by a travel-lift or one of the special moving cranes used in marinas, she may not show her seams before the lift, but they may be all too visible when she is put down. This indicates the hull is getting tired and losing strength. It suggests fastenings are no longer in solid hard wood and that frames have cracks, rot or nail-sickness. Of course, it may also show how uneven the terrain is, and suggests that the marina owner should do something about levelling and concreting the ground.

Poorly built boats show their seams in the first week and for the rest of their lives. In some cases this is the result of uneven planking; sometimes because the low-quality wood is 'restless' and constantly changes volume; sometimes because the wrong filler or seam compound has been used. Bad maintenance makes the seams show sooner, and a hull painted a dark colour often cracks her seams when exposed to prolonged hot sunshine. One reason for varnishing the topsides is to make it easy to see the condition of the stopping or splines.

A seam is said to be 'open' when there is a slit down the middle of the stopping or between the filling and the plank edge. These longitudinal slots need looking at closely to see if the sealing compound is brittle or hard. Wood swells and contracts with changes in temperature and moisture. The seams have to accommodate these constant alterations in the plank width. Logically, the seam filling compound should be flexible so that it can come and go, but it must not be runny or friable. It certainly must not fall out of the seams, so it needs to be sticky and adhere well to the wood.

A hard stopping cannot change shape with the wood, so all sorts of troubles occur. The filling material sometimes crumbles and falls out. It may resist the swelling wood and crush the edges of the planks, which then cannot hold the caulking, and become splintered and saturated – rot may then follow. Some hard stoppings are pinched flat when the planks expand. Later the wood dries out and shrinks, while the stopping remains in contact with the top or bottom plank. This leaves a long slot between the stopping and one plank edge. Water flows in and starts to rot the caulking. Sometimes it seeps through the seam and runs down into the bilge.

Ordinary house putty, as used by home builders, is not suitable for filling in wood plank seams. The ingredients are linseed oil (or a substitute) and whiting. After a time the oil leaches into the wood and the remaining material is brittle, crumbly and rock-hard. It falls out in chunks and lets water in. Sometimes a handful of putty is mixed with a lump of mineral grease the size of a walnut, to prevent this drying-out process. The grease is supposed to stay in the putty and not wander off into the wood. The theory is interesting, but has anyone told the grease it is not supposed to chase after the linseed oil into the wood?

The best way to stop in plank seams is to use one of the compounds recommended by a firm that makes boat paint. Following the company's advice, one can be sure the filler and paints will be compatible. Also, if anything goes wrong, there is someone to turn to for advice – and someone to blame! Many non-hardening proprietary stoppings are coloured, which helps the painter to see what he is doing when putting them in. They cannot be used with varnished topsides, unless they match the wood.

From the surveyor's point of view, a coloured compound is useful because most putty is white. However, trowel cement or knifing stopper, which is put on to make the topsides smooth and flush, is often white – and this must not be confused with putty. This cement is a filler compound laid on the planking after the first undercoat or primer. It goes on in thin layers with frequent bare patches where the planking does not need building up, in order to give a perfectly smooth, even surface.

Seam compounds are put in over caulking that is a white fluffy string. It looks like tough angora wool or a soft white rope made from twisting cotton fibres together. It goes dark as it rots. In good condition it is dry, not easily broken, and not hard or brittle. Any of these conditions indicate the caulking is due for renewal. It should be tough and hold together in long lengths. If it can be pulled out in short pieces, it has served its useful life and recaulking is overdue. Caulking should extend neatly along each seam, ideally in one length from bow to stern. It should not be bunched up like entrails. Where a wide seam has to be caulked, the correct procedure is to twist together several strands into a thicker rope. This is done using an electric drill with a hook such as a bent nail in the chuck, and the cotton strands are twisted together as in rope-making.

In practice, the largest seams, such as those found in fishing boats, are caulked with oakum. This is brown, whiskery, almost like tobacco or moss. It is twisted into a crude rope, and again should not be bunched or looped to fill gaping seams. As oakum rots it loses its springiness, becomes friable, smelly, and may be saturated. It is easy to tell when it needs replacing, as it has little strength and is not easy to handle – one does not have to be critical to see that it is no longer to be trusted. It must be replaced when it comes out in short lengths, starts to drop out of the seams, or becomes wet and soggy.

Synthetic caulking materials that are oily or greasy have the advantage of resisting water and rot. They are 'clean', as the term is understood by engineers, and should last well. However, if they become saturated, lose strength or become discontinuous, they must be suspect. Recaulking is only expensive when it is awkward, such as under a nearly flat-bottomed craft in a muddy boatyard in the middle of a freezing winter, or when the vessel is a very large one. As a general rule, caulking will need renewing at least four (and perhaps ten) times in the life of an average boat, so it is not surprising if a surveyor finds that it is due. It can be done by amateurs, and must be considered part of normal maintenance.

Hooking out lengths of caulking is not normally done by a surveyor, but by one of the shipwrights at the boatyard. Like all such work, it is charged to the person who has commissioned the survey, and is often postponed till the main part of the inspection has been completed, in case there are so many defects in the vessel that she is not worth purchasing.

Caulking should not show on the outside, and should certainly not protrude outboard of the planking. If it shows, it means that the stopping is defective, or so much caulking has been hammered in that there is not enough room for the filler. Regardless of the size of boat, a seam compound needs quite 4 mm ($\frac{3}{16}$ in) depth to get an adequate grip on the plank edges. This is a principal reason why thin carvel planking is so difficult, because the seams must be perfect and the caulking done with precision. Signs of caulking on the *outside* suggest someone has been trying to pack in more cotton or oakum to staunch a leak. Where caulking shows on the *inside*, various conclusions wrestle in the surveyor's mind as he tries to work out what has happened to the boat:

- Badly fitted planks do not touch all along all the seams, so the boat has been poorly built.
- The seams may have been well made, but a leak has occurred (perhaps after a grounding) and someone has inserted too much caulking, or driven it in too hard, or both.
- The boat may be feeling her age, so that the frames no longer hold the planks tightly, and heavy caulking has been used to try to keep water out.
- An accident may have damaged some planking that has been inexpertly replaced, so that caulking is required to fill the over-wide seams.
- The planks at such places as the reverse turn near the garboard may have seams that have not been properly 'belled' out or bevelled for correct caulking. Some seams may actually taper together towards the *outside* instead of towards the inside of the planking. This means that as the caulking is tapped in from outside, the seam shape does not compress it, and it takes the easy line – expanding and slipping inboard right through the seam.
- On occasions, several of these factors together explain why the caulking is visible inside the hull.

When caulking is seen inboard, a surveyor has to take a cautious line. There could be serious leaks that are impossible to stop when at sea. A traditional cure is to screw well-bedded chocks over the inside of the seams, but this does not stop leaking in way of the frames, and it is an expensive job if done in more than a few isolated places. Seam battens are often an admission of failure or desperation, and they are not always reliable. The cure may be replanking, or glued splines may have to be fitted first, then new caulking and stopping. Caulking from the inside, where the seams have their tapers the wrong way, is not an option.

Caulking is most often visible on the outside at the garboard. This is the plank that gives most trouble, and so gets most treatment with the caulker's iron and mallet. When two or three attempts have failed to stop leaking in this area, the time has come to fit new planks. These should be of a hard wood, made in one length, carefully fitted after the opportunity has been taken to dry and clean out the bilge and check for other problems in this area. This is a good opportunity to deal with other problems in a region that is often inaccessible.

The decision to fit a new garboard may be a hard one. This is not a cheap job and, as so often, if the port side needs doing, the starboard side nearly always requires the same treatment. When agonising over whether to go ahead, the first thing is to take out long lengths of caulking. If wide gaps of daylight show through the seam, the plank fits badly and should be replaced. If the wood round the fastenings is soft, renewal is due. If the owner complains about the cost, he is told that two (or four or six) new planks are cheaper than a new boat.

Splined seams

Splines are long thin pieces of wood put into seams after the caulking, and instead of the stopping or seam compound. They are wedge-shaped in section and normally of a soft wood, so that they compress when the planking expands. They are fixed into the seams using a glue that (after a few years) will fail. Epoxy glues are not used because they grip too well, and when the time comes to renew the splines, the wood, not the glue, shears off. This leaves a rough surface of wood slivers and hard glue on the edge of each plank. Less tenacious glues start to let go when the splines are due for renewal. Splines are easy to survey because they ensure that the hull is smooth at all the seams until they are due to be replaced, when they start to gape, or split, and stand out beyond the face of the planking. They need loosening at this stage, and this is done with a caulking iron set just below the width of the seam. It is bashed into the seam, and this drives the spline inwards, breaking the glued join. A metal hook pulls the spline out and, after cleaning the seam, new splines are glued in.

Splines should be made too wide athwartships, and when the glue has set hard the excess is planed off flush with the outside of the planking. They last between four and ten years, but some perish sooner and some last longer. As with so many things in small craft, there is always some unsung modern Michelangelo whose work outlasts that of others, just as his planking has a magic smoothness and his frames are so even that they seem to have been laid by a machine. At the other extreme, there are standard splines that do not last a season.

Splines last longest on craft that live a sedentary life. If a boat is hard driven or tends to flex, her splines will work loose sooner. The temptation is to insert glue in order to resecure splines that are not holding on, but this is a bad idea.

Close-seamed planking or glued seams

A small number of boats have no caulking or stopping in the seams. They are usually craft made to a high standard, and are not to be confused with strip-planked boats. This is how the original wood International One Designs were put together. Their Norwegian builders killed off the old tale that one cannot make soft-wood boats with glued seams. There were also a lot of Folkboats built in Eastern Germany with glued seams.

Faults in this type of seam are hard to cure. One trick is to turn the boat upside down and run the glue in. The glue will have to be thickened to stop it trickling right through, and it may be necessary to seal the seams on the inside to retain the liquid glue while it hardens. The same technique can be used using thixotropic glue; this is glue that has a filler to make it dense and semi-solid, so that it will not run or dribble out of the seams after it has been knifed in.

If this type of seam is caulked, the trouble often spreads, so the caulking has to be done reluctantly. It should ideally be done lightly, and from the bow right to the stern. Caulking in short lengths is liable to cure one leak and make two more – one at each end of the new caulking. The original seam may have been made by heavily depressing the middle of the edge of each plank before it is fitted, using a flat tool such as a screwdriver blade. The unpressed part of the plank is left standing up either side of the wide shallow groove, which has been forced into the plank. These upstanding parts are now planed off, and the plank put in place. When it gets wet, the depressed line along the whole length of the plank expands and seals the seam.

Open seams can be a serious problem with close-seamed boats, because putting anything between the planks is negating the original concept. However, if nothing is forced into the open seams, leaks persist. One line to take is to clean out the seams with a chemical cleaner, then run in a flexible rubbery compound, perhaps using an air-powered dispenser or gun. This will fill the gaps with a waterproof material that is easily compressed by the expanding planks; and if the correct filler is used, it bonds on to the plank edges. This can be an excellent way to make an old boat watertight. However, the only trouble is that the filler expands and contracts a lot, so it is almost impossible to get perfectly painted topsides.

DOUBLE DIAGONAL PLANKING

(This section covers treble-and other multiple-layer planking and, to some extent, cold-moulded planking. However, there is also a separate section for that technique (p.126). The sort of defects and repair problems found in two layers of planking are found in three and more skins. Additional information can be found in my *Cold Moulded and Strip-Planked Wood Boatbuilding*, published by Adlard Coles Nautical in the UK and Sheridan House Inc. in the USA.)

Multiple layers of planking are used to give a strong, easily made hull without the problems of caulking and paying. The thin planks are laid with their edges close together. As each skin of planking is relatively floppy, it is easy to bend it round sharp curves, at least in theory. In practice, very tight tucks are awkward and the wood often splits. This is one defect the surveyor can expect to find at all sharp alterations of hull shape.

This style of planking has been used on RNLI boats, because it stands up to bumping on the sea-bed and alongside big ships in a crisis – but of course there is a limit to how much pounding any hull can tolerate. When surveying any multi-layer vessel it is important to see if external damage (such as cracks in the planking) is repeated inside the hull shell; and where the one or more layers of planking are damaged, the nearby frames, beams and other scantlings may have suffered too. This planking is flexible and appears to take punishment without leaking. What sometimes happens, though, is that the boat bumps the sea-bed and there are few if any leaks, so everyone is pleased and no one thinks of spending time looking for hidden problems – such as slightly open seams and cracks that only affect one layer of planking. These defects let in water, and in time the timber softens.

A good repair sometimes involves replanking large areas. When a row of new plank ends is discovered, a second line of new butts must be sought, this being the other boundary of the renewed region. The best repairs to major damage in diagonal planking are carried right up to the gunwale and down to the keel, so that there are no short lengths of planking. This is a big and expensive job. Half or even more of the work may be removing the furniture or machinery (or both), and later putting back all the things that have been taken out once the repair is complete.

There is no doubt that this form of planking is strong. Frames are often much farther apart than with normal carvel planking. Sometimes there are no frames at all, just a few strength bulkheads. If the boat is a 6 m (20 ft) launch or some such, there may be no internal stiffening. On other craft the internal reinforcing may be in the form of a few strong frames plus stringers. There should be no signs of plank movement in way of the internal structure and no open edges on the outsides of the frames. Because this type of planking is strong it remains watertight even when flexing. For that reason, it has been favoured for high-speed power craft and all types of racing boats.

Between 1939 and 1945 various small warships were built using this planking, partly because semi-skilled craftsmen could make an adequate job of it, and partly because the plank lengths are not long. On chine boats, they only reach from the chine to the gunwale or hog, so cheap, short lengths of timber can be used. However, the young and sometimes not fully skilled men who drove these boats were interested in winning the war – or even having fun by simply going fast. They did not always nurse their craft in rough weather, and sometimes the bilges of some of these boats became littered with fractured fastenings. What tends to happen is that the relatively thin flexible hull planking moves a lot, whereas the more rigid internal structure – such as the engine bearers – cracks or tears away and snaps its fastenings.

The seams outside show if the boat has been badly built or if she is old. If she is suffering from age and inept workmanship, the appearance will be awful. This is hard to cure, especially when the outside planking is 'capping' – a malady in which the planks curve or warp across the width.

Leaking is serious because it is so hard to find and to cure. Water will enter at one seam, run along between the plank layers, and come inboard near or far away from the starting point. Even if the water is passing through the two or three layers of planking in a straight line, so that where the water starts to seep in is right opposite the place where it trickles down the inside on the planking, how is the surveyor to know this? It is usually easy to see where the leak is inside the boat, but seldom possible on the outside.

One can put the boat ashore and dry her thoroughly on the outside, then put some water in the bilge and see where it appears on the outside. However, this needs dry weather, lots of patience, and some good luck. The boat has to be fully and carefully supported almost as well as she would be when afloat. Even then, it may be impossible to find out where the leak starts. Besides, the surveyor may find five leaks, whereas there may actually be ten.

Signs of caulking or splining raise the surveyor's eyebrows. Someone has been trying to stop leaks – no one caulks a multi-skin boat unless they are ignorant or desperate. This form of planking is essentially close-seamed, except perhaps along rebates at the stem, sternpost, etc where there is sometimes a caulked seam. Inboard and outboard the plank layers should be tested for rot. Rot can be expected externally around the waterline, and especially at the hood ends. If it is in one layer, it is likely to have penetrated into the next. Any defect in the outer layer need not be serious. The plank is easily taken off and a new one, or new shorter length, inserted.

However, if an inner plank has become rotten, all the 20 or 30 planks that cross it have to be first prised off. This is a long job, which normally means that new planks have to be made unless the shipwrights are lucky as well as skilled, in that they can reuse the old external planking. Between the layers of planking it used to be the practice to apply a cloth impregnated with a water-resistant fluid such as linseed oil.

In time, the oil dries and leaches into the wood, then the cloth rots, or loses the ability to stop water flowing through. This is a common reason why leaks occur.

Double diagonal planking should be fully clenched with four fastenings round every intersection of the inner and outer seams. The rooves, or dished copper washers, are tested during a survey by inserting a spike under a sample, and twisting sideways. Because of ageing and electrolytic action, sometimes the rooves fail, and sometimes the nails let go – and sometimes both. They become brittle and crumble. It is easy for even a newcomer to surveying to see that they have lost most of their strength. Rooves and nails should be checked at bow and stern, port and starboard, high and low.

It is broadly true to say that a small defect in double or multiple diagonal planking is easy to repair. A graving piece or a pair, one inside, one outside, of different sizes can be fitted even where the hull is curved. It may be necessary to fit an internal doubler, something like an outsize seam batten or something similar, but provided the trouble is not extensive, the job is seldom vexatious. When the defect covers perhaps 3% or more of one side of the hull, things tend to become difficult – and expensive for whoever is paying the bill. One does see ingenious patching jobs, with the external planks renewed, the inner ones left with their cracks, and some new planking added inside the hull to put back some of the lost strength. This may be fine for a short period, perhaps to get the vessel back to her home port where a proper repair can be carried out. However, it is seldom the sort of patching that can safely be left for years.

Refastening this type of planking is expensive, because there are so many rooves to go in. On some racing boats there are screws mixed with clenches and sometimes screws alone. The latter are driven from the inside outwards. This looks superb, as the fastenings leave the outside of the hull free from any fastening marks, or filling. On the inside the hull is smooth, the screws being countersunk, then varnished over. However, the screws are so short that they are not strong; they tend to be small in diameter too. So when they start to corrode, there is not much metal to be eaten away. This is one of those situations where an experienced surveyor grabs the right size of screwdriver from his kit and tries to undo a selection of screws. He stops when they start to sheer, and makes a note in his report where replacement screws have to be put in, as well as mentioning the parlous state of the fastenings. Screws that cannot be taken out because they break easily, but do not do their job for the same reason, present what is often an insuperable problem for anyone who wants to make a thorough repair.

Screw fastenings are seen in special craft such as 6 m Class yachts where light weight and a perfectly smooth external finish is essential. These boats sometimes have one layer of planking on the outside laid to follow the sheer. The next layer may be at 45 degrees, and the internal layer follows the outside one. Occasionally, the diagonal layer may be at 30 degrees to the horizontal, the idea being that when the wood swells the movement between the different layers will be minimised. Yet another variation has both layers running horizontally with the inner one covering the seams of the outer layer. The inside seams should be close and even.

There is no doubt that *diagonal* planking on the outside never looks perfect when the seams are visible. The run of planking should take the eye along the beautiful sweep of the sheer. Where short diagonal lengths have been let in by way of a repair, the job looks wrong and makes any surveyor worry about the strength in the affected area.

BEAM SHELVES AND STRINGERS

Finding trouble in these scantlings is not necessarily hard, but putting it right is often awkward. Where there is rot that extends the length of a cabin, the new piece inserted should be half as long again, and how is it to be wriggled in through the bulkheads? A major repair to a beam shelf is almost always difficult without taking off the deck, and that involves removing deck fittings first. Sometimes the cabin top has to be removed as well, not to mention the toerail. This is yet another situation where a limited defect often needs a lot of time and money to rectify.

One way round the problem is to fit shortish lengths, layered in, with lots of glue and fastenings. If the piece being repaired was 48 mm (2 in) thick, the replacement is made of eight layers 6 mm ($\frac{1}{4}$ in) thick with well-staggered butts or joins. The thin parts can be bent in and slithered through small slots in the bulkheads, whereas a piece of wood the original thickness would be unmanageable. Trouble is most often found where rain lies in puddles and where it comes through the deck and hatches. Beneath chain plates and stanchions, under mooring cleats and in way of runner fittings, the surveyor shines his torch and peers closely.

At fastenings there are often signs of electrolysis. This is seen as a patch of wood that may be almost as hard as the surrounding timber, or it may be truly soft. It is tested with a spike, quite gently at first, after rubbing away crumbling paint. The defect is usually right round the metal bolt or screw, but extends most down the grain so that the discoloured wood is lozenge shaped. When this disease is advanced, the wood cracks down the grain and this is a sign that renewal work is essential. Where the wood is only moderately soft, a graving piece may be adequate. The mildest attacks can be treated by cleaning the area and removing the paint or varnish. Next the wood is well washed with warm fresh water to take away all traces of salt. When the region is completely dry, it is treated with a rot-preventing compound, then very fully painted or varnished. As moisture can no longer get at the metal, there should be no further trouble − but a regular inspection is important to make sure that electrolysis is not continuing. The first sign of renewed trouble is usually loose flaking paint or peeling varnish.

This easy 'cure' does not put back lost strength and it is often advisable to fit additional fastenings in the gaps between the original ones. If graving pieces are fitted, it is normally necessary to take out the fastening before the new chock of wood is inserted. It is a good idea to use new fastenings that are one or two sizes larger, and coat them with epoxy paint or lanoline or any suitable compound that prevents water touching them. Graving pieces are not used if the defective timber penetrates more than a third of the way through the scantling. Each new insert of wood extends well beyond signs of trouble and is epoxy glued in place. A graving piece is made too thick, and once the glue is hard the surplus thickness

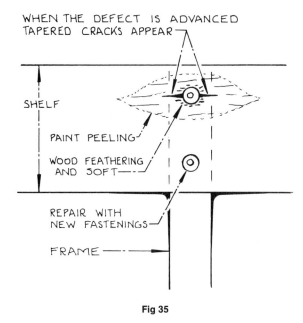

WHEN THE DEFECT IS ADVANCED
TAPERED CRACKS APPEAR

SHELF

PAINT PEELING

WOOD FEATHERING
AND SOFT

REPAIR WITH
NEW FASTENINGS

FRAME

Fig 35

Electrolytic action often causes softening of the wood round fastenings, such as those through beam shelves. Almost always the most intelligent way of carrying out a repair is to put a new fastening in below or above the existing one. Another method is to put in a graving piece, but it is seldom a practical proposition to renew the shelf unless it has been let go so far that no strength is left in it.

---

is planed off. In this way, the repair should be invisible when it has been painted over. If varnish is used, the finished job should look totally tidy.

Ideally there should be a fastening through every stringer at every frame; however, some builders save money and weight by securing at alternate frames. As a rough rule, there should be a screw, or better still a bolt, at 40 mm (16 in) centres or less for craft up to 11 m (36 ft). Where the shelf and stringers are massive, such as in traditional-type inshore fishing boats, quite vicious-looking longitudinal splits are not too serious. However, in lighter types of craft this sort of defect is less acceptable and normally calls for a doubler, or pair of them, to bridge the weakness.

Any crack *across* a shelf or stringer is viewed with deep suspicion. The structure all round is minutely checked to see if there has been a collision. The boat may have been squeezed in a lock, or pinched between a quay and a large vessel, or she may have toppled over. Whatever the cause, the cure must be comprehensive, and end up with more than the original strength. For instance, if a 25 × 25 mm (1 × 1 in) stringer is cracked through, the doublers glued top and bottom ought to be the same siding so as not to

obtrude into the cabin, but should be 20 mm ($\frac{3}{4}$ in) deep, and tapered out each end.

Some longitudinal scantlings are slit vertically with a saw by the builder to make them easier to bend into the vessel. This sort of cut cannot be painted inside and the best builders run glue into the slot to keep moisture out, as well as to restore lost strength. If no provision is made against the ingress of water, this is a place to expect rot. It is common to taper the ends of longitudinal components, and building instructions such as Lloyd's Rules encourage this. It helps the builder twist the wood in place and saves weight near the bow and stern.

On sailing craft the taper should not extend back anywhere near the chain plates, because this is where the maximum strength is needed. Tapering may be acceptable in way of mizzen chain plates on a yawl when the aft mast is small.

The ends of beam shelves and stringers should be secured to the backbone structure and to the transom. Knees are used to make a strong join, and here (as elsewhere) there should be three fastenings in each leg of each knee. In craft under about 12 m (40 ft), the stringers may end with no breast-hook or other linkage on to any adjacent part. In practice, surveyors come across large craft with stringers ending 'in the air' or fastened to a frame that is not always the last one. This may be a hint that the vessel has not been built by the best craftsmen, or it may be a designer's mistake, or it may be acceptable. After years of experience a surveyor learns to view each area of a hull and decide if it is strong enough. He gets some of this knowledge from scantling rules, from studying plans, and from going to sea.

In theory, such things as breast-hooks on each stringer are not needed if the boat is going to lead a sedentary life, but when in doubt they should be fitted. A head-on collision even at slow speed may open up the stem if the stringers are not tied in at each end. Much depends on the plank thickness and fastenings into the stem. In effect, each plank is a stringer. Thin planks need good stringers well secured at the bow and stern. Occasionally, stringers are responsible for frame fractures, because the longitudinal component forms a 'hard spot'. The curve of the bilge is held fairly rigidly along a fore-and-aft line, and when the craft is bumped the frames may break in line along the stringer. When the breaks are behind the stringer, they may be hard to see even with a good light. It is sometimes easier to detect them by touch rather than sight.

CRACKS IN BENT TIMBERS

Cracks, in this context, mean fractures more or less at right angles across the grain, which naturally runs along the length of the timbers. Splits along the grain are not to be ignored, but they are less common and almost always less serious.

Almost all bent-timbered boats have a few transverse cracks in the framing. It is not unusual to find these defects in new craft, because the work of fitting bent timbers is not easy. The shipwrights have to work in heavy gloves to prevent being burned by the hot steamed wood. They have to work fast, otherwise the timbers will cool and harden before they have been forced in place.

No wonder a few pieces crack as they go in, or as they are fastened; and it is not really surprising that some of these cracks are either not noticed or ignored, especially as there is almost always a good reserve of strength. Besides, many boats with bent timbers are made by people who do not claim to be

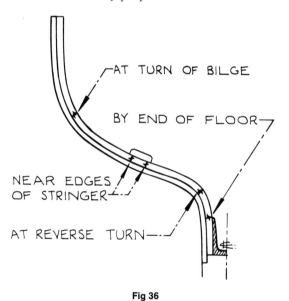

Fig 36

The most likely points to find breaks in timbers are at the area of maximum curvature and at high stress points where other potent structural members abut. If floors do not taper away gradually, they make hard spots at the ends of the floor arms. In the same way, the bilge stringers hold the boat rigid and flexing occurs clear of them, putting an unfair local strain on the frames at the edges of the stringers.

high-flying experts: they specialise in economical vessels rather than superbly finished craft.

When looking at certain types of craft, a surveyor knows he is almost bound to find broken timbers. For instance, Folkboats built in some Eastern European countries suffer from this trouble, because the close-seamed planking (which has no caulking) expands when wet. The frames cannot stretch longitudinally very much, so they pull away from the planking where it curves concavely on the inside – notably at the turn of bilge – and then break. Where the curve is convex inside they break, sometimes in rows with no sound timber left over more than 1 m (3 ft) length.

These fractures are across the grain and are sometimes so sharp that they appear to have been made with a tenon saw. They are normally easy enough to see as they are near the places where the timber is off the planking. Besides, once one has been spotted, the 'bloodhound' is on the scent, and simply has to follow his nose to the next and the next similar broken timber. What is happening here, in part, is that one frame is failing, so its work has to be done by the adjacent two. They are overloaded, so that they let go when under less tension than that which broke the first timber. Once three have failed, the boat may start to 'unzip', so that in severe cases the surveyor finds perhaps 12 broken frames in a row. He should call for extra strength to be put back when repairs are made. The new frames should be made stouter and extra stiffening put in beyond the breaks. For instance, if there are eight broken frames more or less in succession, it is logical to fit a couple of extra doublers ahead and aft of the area repaired.

Yachts like those built to the International 6 Metre Rule, which have a mixture of grown frames and bent timbers, regularly have fractures in the latter. Then there are those lightly built carvel and clincher launches that were so popular before hard chine planing motor boats became all the rage. These pre-chine powerboats were framed with tiny strips of wood that to some people look like thick shoelaces. The turn of the bilge aft was usually sharp, so this was an especially vulnerable area. To make matters worse, these launches were built with light, smooth-running petrol engines. Later diesels were substituted and the boat was expected to stand up to more vibration, more power, more weight and more speed. Something had to give, and the bent timbers usually led the way.

Any boat sitting badly on a trailer, or moved far over rough ground on almost any vehicle, is likely to have broken timbers. The defect is particularly common when the supports are beneath the turn of bilge, and the rise of floor is flat, so that the chocks beneath the hull are pushing almost vertically upwards. Trailers that have strut supports with small badly padded palms on top increase the chances of trouble. At least the surveyor has a handy guide as to where he should start looking for broken timbers. He begins by examining the areas inboard of the supports and, if he finds all is well, he cleans his spectacles, gets out a bigger, brighter flashlight, and rechecks the area.

When he has recorded the damage and recommended repairs, the surveyor should also point out the reason why the boat was damaged in the first place. Most inspectors do not list defects they see in trailers and such like, but where some obvious fault affects the boat, it makes sense to mention it.

In all boats, the most common location of broken timbers is at the reverse turn of the garboard, where the curvature is most acute. This is almost always right aft, often under the engine in sailing yachts. When a boat runs ashore and bumps on passing waves, the keel will be forced upwards as the mass of the hull is dropping down in a trough. This is just the situation that breaks timbers.

When one broken timber has been discovered, it is rare to find it is the only one due for repairs. The places to look are:

- Along the adjacent timbers at the same height, also a little above and below.
- It may be that the next timber is fine, but check the next, and the next, and the next – along the same plank, also just above and below.
- If trouble is found on the port side, check the same place on the starboard side. Also, on the adjacent frames on the starboard side.
- In the most inaccessible places, because that is where the last surveyor did not look – or maybe he did, but he had no mirror, or was too arthritic to get into the cramped corners.
- Where the planking is 'clinkered' or angled at the seam, when seen from forward or aft. If two adjacent planks do not follow the same ath-

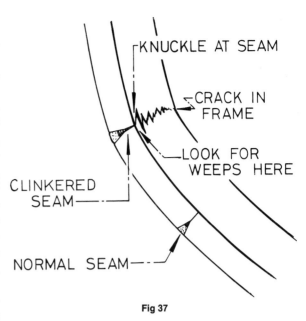

Fig 37

A clear angle along the seams in a carvel-built boat is sometimes called 'clinkering'. The defect can look almost like a very tiny chine, and may be more visible on the outside, although sometimes it looks worse on the inside. It is occasionally caused by a row of broken frames, and on other boats it is the clinkering that causes the frames to crack in line. The bad appearance is secondary; what matters is that leaking is likely all along the seam.

wartships curve, and have a slight but discernible angle between them, the planking is 'clinkered' and so the timbers here have an unfair strain on them. 'Clinkering' can be inwards or outwards; that is, this ugly angle can be at the turn of the bilge or at the reverse turn of the garboard. It may have been built into the boat, or arisen as a result of age or an accident. Sometimes the 'clinkering' causes the timbers to crack; sometimes the breaks occur and then the planking 'clinkers', because it is no longer properly supported.

Not all breaks are easily spotted. I once surveyed a Mylne 38 ft One-design and found 23 broken timbers. The yacht was lying in the boatyard where she was built, and a shipwright was told to repair the timbers. He could only find ten breaks, so the foreman was called in. He found two more, so the manager was called in. He found another two. They all swore I had over-counted, but I had spent a whole afternoon painstakingly running a finger down the front and back face of every timber, using a carefully directed light beam and taking my time. If a crack is only on the outside of the timber, it can be almost invisible, especially if the fracture is jagged and the splinters are camouflaged by the different colours of the wood's grain. A thick layer of paint may hide a break, or copious varnish may fill the slit and make it invisible.

When patience is wearing out, the weather is numbingly cold and the boat cramped inside, the surveyor has to stop work, take a swig of coffee, tell himself that this is just the sort of place that is *bound* to have broken timbers, and go back to a slow search till he finds what he knows must be there. Each frame has to be viewed from forward and aft. Just occasionally a crack will not extend right across the timber, so it can only be found by looking on both sides. When my children were small they were wizards at finding broken timbers, because they found it great fun and could effortlessly get into places I could only reach with difficulty.

Repairs

It is common practice to put a new piece of broken timber alongside the one that has failed, to restore the strength. This new part is sometimes called a 'sister-frame', and I have heard shipwrights talk about 'sistering'. The work is fairly easy, quickly done, and on the whole acceptable – especially in cheap boats and commercial craft.

Each doubler must extend at least three planks above and below the break, and must have two fastenings into each plank, except perhaps right forward and aft where the planks may be too narrow for more than one clench. The doubler ends should be tapered away, but seldom are. It is not usual to fasten the new frame to the broken one, but they should be tight together, and the new one should have its fastenings staggered relative to existing fastenings.

Many boatyards put doublers in that are of the same size as the broken timbers, but this is not logical, and the new part should be 30% wider, or be made of tougher wood – or both. In practice, because the timbers fit under stringers it is usually impossible to make them with a greater moulded depth – that is, with a bigger dimension athwartships. They must therefore be made with a larger siding – the fore-and-aft thickness. The broken timber is left in place, because this saves money and avoids disturbing existing structure – the latter is always advisable when mending old boats. However, the finished job does not look wonderful and the wood at the fracture may rot. The splintered wood at the break holds both rot

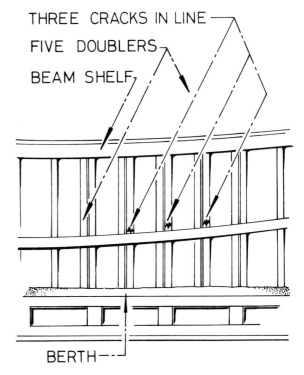

Fig 38

When recommending repairs for cracked frames, it is good practice to specify additional doublers when a series of cracks are in line, in order to prevent a recurrence of the trouble. The doublers are carried up to the beam shelf and down to behind the berth, so that their ends do not show and in order to extend the doubling well beyond the fracture line.

spores and moisture efficiently, so rot has a good starting base. This is a region that surveyors have to check on any repaired craft.

The best repair involves removing the broken timber and putting a new one in its place, using the same fastening holes perhaps with slightly larger screws, bolts or clenches. This requires a standard of skill and dedication not found everywhere. Bending a new timber in place can be impossible even for a brilliant craftsman. In such a case, the replacement is laminated in, using the hull as the former or pattern.

Ideally the laminations should have staggered ends top and bottom. It is always a good idea to make the replacement timber as long as possible and, if possible, right down to the hog. This means that all the laminations end right at the bottom of the bilge, and this solves the problem of how to make a neat termination. The top of the newly laminated-in section may be partly or fully tucked under a stringer, or be hidden in a locker. Well-fitted laminations are lapped on to the existing timber, which is cut in steps to take the new thin strips. This avoids a 'hard spot' or sudden cessation of strength in the timber.

Normally no heating or steaming is needed to laminate in a new length of timber. If the timber has several breaks, so that a new part is needed from deck to keel, laminating is often the only way to do the job. The longest feasible lengths are used and the butts are well staggered. They should so far as possible be kept clear of curved parts of the hull. Sometimes a new piece of timber is scarfed in. Here the slope should be 1:8 and epoxy glue used as well as three or more fastenings through each scarf. The joins are hidden by the best boatbuilders, who tuck the wood in with that miraculous skill that makes it so exciting to watch these fellows at work.

. . . .

GROWN FRAMES

Grown frames are cut to shape from solid chunks of timbers, unlike bent timbers that are heated in a steam box and forced into the hull shape by being pushed in place. One advantage of having grown frames is that no building sections or moulds are needed, which cuts down waste.

However, frames tend to warp, twist or 'move' during and after building. If this movement is about 10% of the moulded or sided dimension of the frame, it is generally considered acceptable, except in very finely built craft. In commercial vessels and fishing boats the movement can be 15% of the frame thickness and still be considered acceptable. These distortions are mentioned in a survey report because they indicate the quality of the original construction.

A more serious problem, which is found particularly on crudely built craft, is a shortage of fastenings. The frames are made up in relatively short lengths or futtocks. Each join should have a minimum of three bolts, which should be well spaced and staggered. The spacing between the bolts must not be too close, so the overlap of one futtock on to the next should be at least six times the siding or moulding of the frame – this figure being the minimum.

Often the wood round the fastenings is beginning to soften. Taking these bolts out is seldom easy and the usual thing is to put in additional ones in the gaps because this is quick and relatively cheap. It also saves dismantling structure, and that is something to avoid in many mature craft. If the bolts are rusting, there is a dilemma: getting them out is almost always a slow frustrating business, but if they are left in they are likely to go on affecting the adjacent wood. This situation can be summed up roughly as follows: the correct thing to do is to take out all the rusty fittings and clean up the adjacent wood; but because this is such a costly business, it is seldom done in cheap boats, and additional fastenings are put in instead. Here we have one of those sad occasions when the surveyor has to state the correct course, but often sees his advice ignored. All the while he knows the owner is probably being commercially sensible, even though he is shortening the life of his vessel or bringing forward the day when new frames will have to be fitted.

Grown frames tend to become soft where two futtocks are edge to edge. Water lodges here, dirt collects, and the resulting mud remains wet when the rest of the boat is dry in warm weather. This is just the place for rot to flourish. The join of the bottom futtock to the floor is especially important. It is near the bilge-water, so it is often wet. It is adjacent to or below the sole, so dust and dirt gets into the slightest opening at the join and this encourages moisture to stay. It is also one of the most highly stressed joins.

There are builders who claim that provided all the scantlings are thick enough, all will be well. This approach does not stand up to scrutiny. In practice, the frames are made quickly and crudely with sapwood and sometimes even bark. This is wood-butchery, not boatbuilding, and rot can be rampant even before the boat has had a bottle smashed over her bow for her first launching. In small fishing boats that are built with all grown frames, this sort of low-quality and no-quality construction is often seen. Where grown frames run up through the deck, rot is very common. It usually starts where rain puddles can lie, and this is at the low point of the sheer, typically about one-third or one-quarter of the boat's length from the stern. If one frame is found to be rotten just above the deck, the chances are that there will be many. It is often quicker to list the ones that are sound!

Where the frames do not run up through the deck there may be bulwark stanchions that are like short lengths of frame, extending from the top of the bulwark down through the deck. These rot just like frames and, like them, need rigorous checking above and below the deck. If there is a lot of lining, it can be hard to get at the frames. A shipwright should be asked to remove areas of lining where defects are most likely to be found. These include:

- Just below the deck, where leaks cause trouble.
- At the sharpest turn of the bilge, where the change of shape makes construction most difficult and the frames most vulnerable.

- Where the bilge rests when the boat lies ashore without 'legs' or side supports, as this is where the frames take a pounding.
- Low down, as this is the region that is wet most often, and where there is frequently no ventilation.

Cracks in grown frames are common. The best repair is to fit a doubler that is bolted fore and aft to the damaged part. The new piece is not always secured to the planking, but logically it should be. The new component must overlap the broken one by at least three plank widths beyond the ends of the fracture, which often extends diagonally down the length of the futtock. A doubler must be at least as strong as the part that has failed, and 10% extra thickness makes sense.

GLUED LAYERS OR LAMINATED PARTS

(For further information, see my *Cold Moulded and Strip-Planked Wood Boatbuilding*, published by Adlard Coles Nautical in the UK and Sheridan House Inc. in the USA.)

Thin strips of wood glued together, often called laminations, are a sign of good building. The best builders ignore the fact that it takes a long time and plenty of skill to glue together extra-thin pieces, so laminations of say 3 mm ($\frac{1}{8}$ in) indicate good quality. However, if there are gaps, or places where the glue has been used to fill spaces between the wood, the level of skill has to be questioned.

The edges and ends of all laminated parts are studied to see if there are signs of glue failure, cracks or rot. The top of a laminated stem is scrutinised, particularly if it is weathered or if there is no protection on top. This is a typical place to expect glue failure. A large number of the Loch Long class have suffered from this trouble, with the top of the stem opening out as each laminate in turn peels away from its neighbour, starting with the front one. As each strip comes loose, it tries to straighten out and the result looks a bit like a monstrous shaving brush.

The cure here, as in many cases of glue failure, is to make and fit a new part. This is expensive and most

shipwrights merely clean the open seams, getting rid of the old glue and exposing fresh wood. New epoxy glue is run in to each joint carefully, under perfect conditions of temperature and moisture. To clamp the wood layers together, bolts are inserted, well staggered and tightened on big washers. Most repairers leave the bolts in, but some take them out and plug the holes when the glue has finally and totally set, as they want to save weight – and be able to use the bolts again. Screws are sometimes used, but they are less effective than bolts. Sometimes when repairing parts like frames a combination of screws and bolts is best. In addition, shores will be jammed in against the opposite frame, forcing the layers of wood together after the glue has been trickled in.

If one laminated part has failed, the chances are others will have the same defect. Parts built in frosty weather tend to suffer glue failure unless proper heating has been used. It is no good turning off the heat when the shipwrights go home in the evening – the hardening glue needs to be kept warm until it has finally set; and it seems to me that some glues dislike freezing conditions even after they have nominally become finally and fully set. As a result of frost, certain types of clear uncoloured glue seem to fail more often than other types.

Laminated frames are expensive to make, so they are usually a sign of good quality. Glue failure is most likely to be at the bottom, particularly where there is a sharp reverse turn down towards the garboard. If there are no floors, or if the floor fastenings are driven fore and aft through laminated frames, a careful check for delamination is needed. Glue failure and opening up in beams is most likely at the ends and where carlines run in to join the beams. It is not easy to introduce fresh glue into the little slits where the layers have parted, because of the awkwardness of 'up-hand' or overhead work and the difficulty of preventing glue getting on furniture, etc. In any case, it is probably safest to fit entirely new beams.

Splits are found where fastenings have been put in along the same plane as the laminations. Some well-made laminated parts have a great resistance to splitting, but in general, because all the grain normally runs in the same direction, laminated components do not have the resistance to splitting that plywood does. When a good glue such as epoxy is correctly used, the wood pieces are more likely to fracture than the glue lines. However, splits can cross glue lines diagonally, and cracks can cross a succession of laminates diagonally or at right angles. In short, expect breakages in all directions. Because laminating is used in light fast craft, there is always a good chance that some of the structure has been overstressed at some stage – either in a race or when running aground.

Laminated tillers should be inspected carefully, as a failure here can be catastrophic. The most likely place to find trouble is at the ends, especially aft where athwartships bolts holding on the rudder stock plates run in the same direction as the layers of wood. Patching up a tiller that is peeling apart is seldom acceptable, especially as it is not an expensive job to make a new replacement. A principal reason for using laminations is to get strength at curves. Laminated hanging and lodging knees are sometimes used, even when there is no other laminated part in the vessel.

Sometimes the shipwright doing the laminating is too ambitious and he tries to get wood that is too thick to work round a tight curve. This is why one finds cracks within the layers of a laminated part, particularly at the tightest part of the bend. It is not always necessary to condemn a part like a laminated knee just because one or two of the inner laminations have signs of mild splitting – provided the outer layers are intact, that is, and there is clearly ample strength in the component.

Rot is rare in laminated parts because the glue tends to halt its spread, and because low-quality wood is seldom used. Also, all sides of a laminated part are planed, so the rot spores have no easy starting point. In fact, it is the resistance to rot that is one of the attractions of this building technique. However, rot is occasionally found – usually where glue failure has occurred, or where there is a crack.

METAL PARTS AND MAST SUPPORTS

· ·

Wrought Iron Floors

This is a name widely used for steel and iron floors made of ferrous strip material. Usually the floor is secured to a pair of frames or bent timbers. If on the latter the floor is normally the same siding (fore-and-aft width) as the frame, or is slightly narrower. The moulded or vertical thickness is typically about one-quarter of the siding, and there is no flanging. There should be at least two vertical fastenings down into the hog or keel, and a minimum of three fastenings up each arm. Of these three, the top one should be near the tip of the floor and the bottom one well down.

The traditional wrought iron floor was fabricated by a blacksmith in a forge. He was often a craftsman who knew about the stresses in a boat, so he would thicken the metal at the angles, and taper out the top ends. These embellishments resulted in a strong long-lasting floor that was slightly flexy at the tips. This meant that the frame was not overloaded locally at the floor end. Modern so-called wrought iron floors are usually made of welded mild steel, and not wrought at all. They have no extra thickness at the change of direction (called the 'throat'), so this is a weak point, and corrosion here is sometimes more severe than at other parts – the reverse of what is wanted. Also, the tips of the arms are not nowadays tapered, so the frames (and especially bent timbers) tend to fracture at this point.

The traditional blacksmith hand hammered his floors to get the extra throat thickness and thin tapered ends. This resulted in each floor being a different length, which in turn avoided what we find now: often all the floors terminate in straight line, so there is a 'hard spot' along one plank. This can cause a succession of frames to break in a line.

An unusual fault in these floors is a type of electrolysis that is hard to detect. It seems to occur especially near engines, and may be localised with intermittent pitting. The floor looks all right in the dim light of the bilge, because the pitting in the metal may be covered by a black mud that can be firm. The floor may seem in good order, even when scraped or lightly hammered. A close inspection can be hard when the floor is right under the engine, but this may be where the corrosion is worst. If there is a drip tray over the floor this may accelerate the problem, and also make the floor impossible to see or test.

This defect sometimes attacks most fiercely at the knuckle, so wrought floors should be heavily chipped here with a sharp spike or hammer. The aim is to pry off any surface muck and show up pockets of erosion underneath. An ordinary flat scraper may ride over the holes, and indicate that the floor is sound. Once the truth has been discovered, all the adjacent floors should be rigorously tested.

If the bilge is kept dry, one essential ingredient of corrosion or electrolysis is absent, so the floors should last indefinitely. There used to be a school of thought that held that water in the bilge was an asset because it kept everything 'sweet', which presumably means fresh and clean. The argument continued: 'Salt water in quantity kills off rot spores, so a slosh of water in the bilge is a good thing.' This theory never did make sense, because the way to keep structures in good order is to keep all moisture away. What is wanted is not lots of water, but copious quantities of fresh air – that is, good ventilation. It is likely that people trying to sell leaking boats started the idea that lots of bilge-water is beneficial in order to dupe beginners!

A good way to repair damaged floors is to strengthen the existing ones, then the same fastening holes are used again. Also, the amount of work and new material is reduced, and the floors will fit back in place accurately after they have been mended, provided of course they were a good fit in the first place. If the floor needs stiffening, this can be done effectively by welding on a vertical flat plate to the

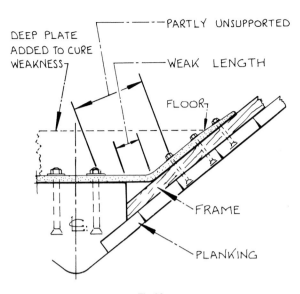

Fig 39

This type of wrought iron floor is common. The arms of the floor are relatively thin in a vertical direction, and spread fore and aft for approximately the width of the frame. As a result, they are weak in the direction of the main stress. The gap where the floor jumps from the backbone across to the frame is particularly vulnerable, although in fact the weak region extends from the fastening into the backbone across to the first fastening up the frame. There is very little resistance against bending in this type of floor and, as a result, the garboard is likely to leak. A cure is the fitting of a deep plate (shown dotted). This plate should be carried as high up as possible, the limitation to depth usually being the sole.

bottom, and partly or fully up the side arms. The welding should be full and continuous, or at least 40% alternate intermittent with welding round the ends. The floor has to be removed before any welding is done, otherwise the surrounding structure will be damaged. Once a floor is off, the previously hidden faces that were against the wood should be inspected.

No one takes out a steel floor without regalvanising it before it is refitted. As a general rule, the fastenings should be increased by one size and this involves drilling larger holes in the floor. Drilling out is also needed to cope with the regalvanising that partly fills all the holes. It is an excellent idea to epoxy paint the floors after they have been galvanised, and this requires yet larger fastening holes to allow space for the paint layer. Before putting on the epoxy paint, a galvanised fitting needs degreasing.

Wrought floors fit across the top of the hog or keel and extend up the inner face of the frames. Sometimes the top of the hog is well above the inner

face of the planking, so that part of each floor on each side is unsupported. This condition is made worse if the fastenings are not near the throat. If the bottom of the floor is fastened down with short coach screws, the situation is worse, especially when the hog has been damp for some years so that the coach screws no longer hold tight. Under these conditions, the floors cannot do their job properly. They no longer bind the vessel's sides and backbone structure securely together, so the job has to be done at least in part by the garboard planks. As a result, these lower planks work loose and leak.

Chronic leaking is often easy to detect: good pointers are the worn hand-operated bilge pump backed up by an outsize electric one with its own big battery, and also 'washed-out' tinges under the cabin sole and the peeling bilge paint. Before recommending that the garboards are recaulked, it is sensible to check the strength of the floors. Their spacing is also important. On the best boats, they are fitted on every frame and bent timber. Less rugged boats have them on alternate ones. If the spacing is on one frame out of three, it is almost certainly too far apart. If the spacing is more than one-fourteenth of the boat's length, it is definitely inadequate, especially in a vessel that is heavily stressed at sea — such as a racing boat.

Weak floors cannot always be strengthened by welding in a deep plate, because there may not be enough space in the bilge. Tanks under the cabin sole prevent this sort of highly effective repair. However, just welding in a bottom strap that is twice as thick as the original one does increase the strength substantially; and if the tank does not extend right out to the frames, sometimes small triangular brackets can be welded in at each throat angle. They can be fitted on the forward or aft face of the floor, so as to be clear of the bottom fastenings.

Where a floor extends right across the top of a hog that reaches from inside the planking on one side to the planking on the other side, there should be a limber hole or two. These holes are made by chiselling a shallow groove fore and aft on top of the hog, and are typically 20 mm ($\frac{3}{4}$ in) wide and half that depth. They tend to become filled with dirt and painted over, so that they soon cease to work and water cannot flow under the floors. This results in puddles adjacent to each floor, so it is no wonder that these parts give so much trouble. Careful owners clean out the limber holes, then gouge them slightly deeper. They run a thin chain or knotted line fore and aft through these holes with a length of shock-cord at each end. Anyone can easily free the holes sufficiently to let water through by grabbing one end of the chain and giving it a series of jerks.

When mending floors it is a good idea to look into ways of improving them, as they do tend to need more repairs than other parts. One technique is to go for a non-rusting metal. I recently inspected an 80 footer that was being rebuilt after 65 years of hard sailing. Her steel floors were badly corroded, and it was decided to replace them by cast bronze ones. This material is more expensive than steel, but no galvanising or painting is needed and the old fastening holes in the planking are easily used, since the floors can be drilled through from outside the planking. There is no worry concerning the possibility that the paint and galvanising will be chipped during refitting, and limber holes can be cast in the bottom part. The casting was cheaper than fabrication, partly because some patterns were used for more than one floor, and partly because the shipwrights made the patterns swiftly and skilfully using machined strips of wood and epoxy glue.

. . . .

PLATE FLOORS

A plate floor consists of a flat plate athwartships, and it looks like the type of floor used in steel vessels. It is strong for its weight because of its depth, and it is good for taking the load of a ballast keel. Sometimes the bottom flange of a plate floor is made extra large to take a ballast keel bolt.

A boat with a deep bilge needs lots of strength below the sole, and this is where a plate floor is so good. The same sort of floor is used towards the ends of a boat because its obtrusive depth does not take up valuable cabin space. Plate floors are used between tanks that are located under the cabin sole, and also fitted to support big engine bearers. They are made of relatively thin plate, and to save weight a lightening hole may be cut in the middle. The bottom is flanged to take fastenings through the hog or keel. Flanges on each side are bolted to frames or the planking. The best of these floors have at least a small stiffening flange across the top.

Corrosion rapidly eats away at this type of floor, because the metal is thin. The trouble starts at the limber holes that are normally cut out at each bottom corner. It also attacks the rim of the lightening hole. In time, the steel becomes so thin that it can be broken away with the fingers. The fastenings may also erode, so that the fitting may be in good order, but not held tightly in place.

A hammer is used to test these fittings, but if there is no space, a strongly wielded spike will show if the steel is paper thin. It can be a problem knowing when to recommend renewal if the floor is mostly in good condition, with only patches of localised rust.

Factors to take into consideration include:

- The age of the vessel. If she is old, she is likely to be due for strengthening, and as nothing is more important than the floors, make a start here.
- Her intended use. If she is going on a long voyage she will not receive major maintenance for some time, and she is almost bound to meet severe weather. Her crew need to know that the hull structure is sound, and renewing the floors allows other structural parts to be closely examined.
- The area where she is used. If it is shallow she is likely to ground at least once a year, and floors resist the severe strains this event imposes.
- The character of the owner. If he is the sort of person who remembers to carry out comprehensive maintenance each year, some repairs can sometimes be postponed for 12 months. However, most owners have so many distractions, and are subject to economic changes that may make them short of cash in future years. So when considering the owner, it is seldom possible to recommend postponement.
- The extent of the defects. If a floor appears to have lost no more than 25% of its strength, it can often be left for another year. Old boats were built with factors of safety of four or more, so a plate floor that was made of 6 mm ($\frac{1}{4}$ in) steel and has widespread pitting down to 3 mm ($\frac{1}{8}$ in) minimum thickness is probably safe for another

season. If there is a patch at the bottom that has corroded right away, but the top and middle is intact, most of the strength will still be there, and one might be tempted to postpone renewal provided the floor is well fixed to the hog. However, modern lightweight craft are built with small factors of safety, sometimes as low as 1.5. Where this design standard has been used, renewal is needed at an early stage.

When 'in the field', there are times when a surveyor feels that part of a vessel is not in a very bad condition, and could be left a little longer, especially if the owner is fully warned about the problem in the survey report. However, not everyone reads reports right through, and some do not understand what they read. Some owners are deliberately over-optimistic, especially if they carry lots of safety equipment on board as well as a couple of radios that can be used to shout for help. So there are times when surveyors have to be extra pessimistic, to offset the way buyers and owners tend to be biased in the opposite direction.

When this type of floor starts to rust, the next stage is a loss of strength through corrosion. If the floors are taken out when rust is just starting to show through, very little repair work will be needed, apart from the regalvanising. This is a good way to save money. It is seldom effective in the long term to apply paint of any sort to cover failing galvanising, especially as the areas that cannot be touched up, between the floor and adjacent wood, are where rust is probably most severe.

MAST SUPPORT STRUCTURES

(Many masts are supported by pillars under the cabin top. These pillars may seem light for the job, and their strength can be roughly checked using the tables in my *Boat Data Book*, published by Adlard Coles Nautical in the UK and Sheridan House Inc in the USA.)

It is common practice for the mast to stand on the cabin top, with a strong structure beneath that transmits the downward force from the spar to the hull. A rough 'rule of thumb' says that the vertical force down the alloy tube is about the same as the weight of the boat when the yacht is going to windward in a fresh breeze. This so-called rule is very approximate, and it does not indicate whether the reputed load is when the yacht is jolting badly or sailing steadily, so we do not know if this is a maximum force or nearer half the maximum. However, these primitive dictums are handy, because they warn a surveyor that he is dealing with a problem that has been crudely quantified, and he knows that there is potential trouble where there are such large loads.

Mast support structures fall into three classes:

1 The mast is one deck, but not above a bulkhead. The supporting structure often consists of a metal tube or, more rarely, a wooden strut. It stands free in the middle of the saloon or other cabin. This pillar extends between the cabin top deck and the top of the 'keel'.

2 The mast stands on the cabin top deck above a bulkhead. There is usually some stiffening on the centreline under the mast, such as a wooden pillar bolted to the bulkhead, and the doorway is offset to one side. Alternatively, there is a centreline doorway with pillars on each side and a strong beam between them.

3 The mast heel may be down through deck. It rests on top of the 'keel' and there is structure designed to stiffen the cabin top or deck on a 'flush decker'. There are severe side loadings where the mast goes through the decking, and these forces need containing.

An isolated pillar

This often suffers from corrosion because the foot of the pillar is in the bilge, often near a low point where a puddle may lie for a long period. Lack of a constant drying draught of air is endemic here. 'Improve the ventilation under the sole' is the advice that a surveyor often gives.

Steel is used for the pillar because it is strong, widely available, easy to work and reliable. It rusts, and this defect is found regularly where the top and bottom flanges meet the tube. Sometimes the tube ends are glassed in, and this seal often fails, partly because of the rust. The corrosion is not always easy to detect when there is a decorative finish on the tube that is carried right to the ends. It is a good idea to get behind the decoration, even if it is well secured.

A pillar should not look flimsy and must be firmly fixed at each end. It should not rattle, bend or flex when grabbed and shaken, and should not give the appearance that it might collapse when the yacht is plunging into a severe sea while over-canvassed in a gusting force 10. We had an experience of this. A yacht importer phoned to tell us that one of the cruiser/racers he had sold had been beating to windward in rough (but not hair-raising) conditions when the mast support pillar in the saloon had buckled slightly. The crew, rightly alarmed at the thought that the deck-stepped mast heel was about to test thickness of the hull bottom, dragged the sails down in something of a panic and motored home. They phoned the importer, who phoned the designers in Paris, who in turn went back to the drawing board and their calculations. The naval architects phoned back, swearing that the accident could not happen, and that the pillar was definitely strong enough. The problem was dumped in my lap, with the proviso that I should not spend any significant amount of money solving it – and also could I produce the answer in two hours please, as the owners were threatening legal action. The broker insisted that it was not necessary to see the boat – all I needed to know was that the pillar was bent and to find out why!

I was tempted to give the matter up, but in the end decided to persist. The first discovery I turned up was that the boat had been designed in Paris, but stylists in the factory in La Rochelle had gone to work on her later. The designers had done the calculations and drawn out the lines, sail plan and such like, but the cabin plan was the work of the builders. Little by little, I gathered other nuggets of information. In the end I got enough data to show that the designers had wanted the boat to be as light (and therefore as fast) as possible. Everything was made as thin as their courage would allow. They had not considered that anyone would secure the cabin table to the mast support pillar, or that two of the crew would fall against the cabin table just as the yacht fell off a

wave. The sideways force on the support pillar was substantial and devastating, but had not been allowed for in the designer's calculations.

The bottom of the tube may be held by screws or coach-screws through the base flange. In theory, there is very little sideways pressure, but the securing should not be flimsy and I prefer some sort of cavity, cup or recess in which the heel of the tube sits. There should be no risk that it can shift fore and aft or sideways.

The top of the tube may be glassed up under the cabin top, and this area often has peeling bonding. I have seen quite a few examples of shocking boatbuilding at the tops of pillars, including:

- Two tiny unsecured soft-wood wedges pushed in between the top flange and the underside of the cabin top because the tube was too short.
- A soft pad, already partially crushed, between the top flange and the cabin top.
- A wooden pad on top of the flange that did not mate even roughly with the underside of the cabin top.
- A wooden pad that was not held in place and was already starting to slide out from between the top flange and the cabin top deck.
- A top flange that was long fore and aft, but not at the same angle as the underside of the cabin top deck, which it touched at the aft edge only. This would have been bad at any time, but the mast heel was clear of the area where there was contact between the top flange and the cabin top deck.

As this area is frequently concealed behind lining, a surveyor has to recommend that some of the decoration is taken down at some stage, even if it cannot be done during his inspection.

The bottom of a pillar should land on a strong part of the vessel. Ideally there should be a floor across the top of the keel area, or some such. In practice, it is now usual to fit the pillar down on to the thick fibreglass strengthening that runs fore and aft over the ballast keel, and consider that enough.

A bulkhead-supported mast

The second type of mast support structure is normally all wood and consists of a ply bulkhead with a stiffening pillar under the deck in way of the mast. This pillar may form one post of the offset door-way through the bulkhead. The ends of the pillar may be glassed-in, and this seal often breaks free from the wood because of the downward pumping action of the heavily loaded mast. In theory this is not too serious, since the glass forms an encasement that continues to hold the pillar in place. However, I always worry about peeling glass, because it can hold moisture that will cause rot. This can happen at the top and bottom of the pillar.

If the doorway through the bulkhead is on the centreline, there are pillars each side of the access, forming door-posts. Sometimes these posts are twinned, with one pair on the fore side of the bulkhead and one pair aft. The same arrangement of two posts, one in front and one behind the bulkhead, is occasionally seen with a centreline pillar. The forward pillar may be much smaller than the aft one, or vice versa. One pillar may be 'disguised' as a corner post to join on another bulkhead or be a door-post, perhaps for the toilet compartment.

It is obviously essential that the bulkhead is strong enough – it is always of ply, but not always thick enough. Generally, if the boat is over 9 m (30 ft) the bulkhead thickness should be 12 mm ($\frac{1}{2}$in) or more. A straight edge laid vertically, horizontally and diagonally will show if the bulkhead is bowing or bending. It may take up a curvature and force the pillars to do the same, or the screws through the ply into the pillar may be loose. Sometimes the bulkhead has not distorted, but there is a thin gap between the pillar and the ply, suggesting that either the original fabrication was sloppy, or these two important scantlings are coming apart.

More and better fastenings are called for. I prefer bolts to screws here, and where I find the fastenings are inadequate I nearly always recommend that new bolts are put in between the existing screws all the way down. Sometimes I ask for two bolts in every gap. This is a place where decorative-headed bolts and 'dome' or other attractive nuts can be used to make a quick and tidy repair, without sinking both the heads and nuts into the pillar. Such recessing reduces the strength of the pillar, quite apart from the problem of getting neat dowels that match the original timber.

As a crude rule of thumb it is generally true to say that the fastenings joining the pillars to the bulkhead should not be more than 250 mm (10 in) apart regardless of the size of yacht. Ideally the fastenings should be staggered or zigzagged for a better grip and to avoid a succession of holes through a line of the grain. Some builders rely entirely on glue here, but they are taking a risk as the glue can be so heavily stressed by a peeling force. It can be almost as if a wedge is being driven between the two joined parts – nothing is so likely to force them apart. Sometimes the glue may hold, but the surface of the wood is ripped off. Give me close-spaced bolts any time – but especially when I'm sailing a long way offshore in a hurricane!

The bottoms of the pillars ought to be supported by something strong that spreads the load effectively. A floor right across the boat is good, and I would be worried if there was not something like this in a yacht over 12 m (40 ft). On smaller boats it is usual to see the pillars stop just above the fibreglass shell, leaving the ply bulkhead to spread the downward pressure on to the hull. Some cheap boats even have the pillars stopped three or four hand spans above the hull shell in order to save money. If the boat is to be taken far offshore, some modifications here are advisable.

When examining a doorway it is usual to find on boats over ten years old that the decorative seal on the edge of the ply is adrift, at least over a short length. This gives a chance to see the condition of the ply, but it does not indicate that the bulkhead has been overloaded. Signs of movement between the pillar(s) and ply (or the top beam and the ply) are often serious, and even when there is just a tiny slit of space between any two components, it is advisable to assume something horrible is about to happen. At the very least, additional fastenings should be recommended, and sometimes there must be dismantling first in order to see what is going on in hidden areas. Strengthening in this area is always a good idea, because the loads are large and the consequences of failure can be tremendous.

Beams tend to be cut away or kept to a minimum depth to give the best headroom through the doorway. This ensures that the boat is fine when inspected at a glittering boat show, but she is weaker than she should be. If there is any doubt about the strength here, a second beam can be added on the opposite side of the bulkhead, or the existing beam can be doubled over, or knees can be used at each end of the beam and against the pillar(s) to reduce the effective span of the beam.

The use of knees holding any two structural components together is something of a forgotten art in the boatbuilding world. This is a pity because knees can be used in a variety of places to make a weak item strong, a poor join good, a highly stressed scantling into one only moderately loaded, and so on. Knees joining a beam to a pair of pillars can be fitted in a rectangular doorway, because people are wider at shoulder level than at head height. So doorways need be only 300 mm (12 in) wide at the top, but have to be 450 mm (18 in) wide lower down. The addition of a knee or, better still, two or four of them at the top of a pillar has the effect of shortening the length of the pillar and so making it able to stand higher loadings. If a set of knees is also added at the bottom, the effect is even more marked – and the cost of this work is often quite small.

Keel-stepped masts

A mast down through the cabin top, or through a flush deck, can be fitted with a gap all round. When this is done there is no stress on the deck, and all the loads come on the rigging (transferred to the chain plates) and at the heel of the mast. At least, that is the theory. In practice, the boat may be built like this, but later wedges are forced in round the mast when she is put afloat for her third or fifth year, perhaps. Suddenly the demands on the deck or cabin top construction are different, and much larger.

Semi-soft rubber wedges or packing pieces may be used where the mast goes through the deck, and it is tempting to think that these pads will compress and there will be no great shove by the mast against the deck. It is risky making this assumption, because the rubber can only be squeezed a certain amount, and then it is in effect solid, and is certainly unyielding. A substantial sideways thrust of the mast then comes on the deck or cabin top deck, which has to be well able to stand up to the loads even when the

yacht is heeled right over and dropping off the tops of the waves.

Most keel-stepped masts are located close by a strong bulkhead. The glassing all round needs an extra careful inspection, especially where it bonds on to the sidedecks, cabin coamings and cabin top deck. Down in the bilge the mast step is often short of drainage holes, so puddles slosh about, corroding metalwork and softening wood. It is hard to get enough ventilation in this area to dry these puddles quickly, because there is almost always a bulkhead close by. Even if a metal mast step is well painted or has a skin of plastic sheathing over it, corrosion is often generated here.

Sailing yachts sometimes have windows in the cabin coamings that are continued upwards so that they cut right into the cabin top deck. This is presumably a fashion gimmick. No other explanation can be offered for such bad engineering, since a far better way of getting extra light into the cabin is to use ordinary side windows in the coamings and hatches in the cabin top deck, with plenty of strong fibreglass between.

These angled-over windows are outrageous, but at least a surveyor knows he must study them carefully. They degrade an important structure that already has weakening features such as two sharp changes of direction at the top and bottom of the coaming, a cut-out for the main hatch, and the severe localised loads from the mast. It is only good sense to search round all these oversized windows for cracks, distortions and fissures. Leaks may be the first warning that something is awry.

RUDDERS AND THEIR GEAR

· ·

FIBREGLASS RUDDERS

The following paragraphs apply to what is by far the most common type of fibreglass rudder. This is made of a metal stock that is almost always stainless steel, with one or more quite thin flat bars welded to the aft edge of the stock. Encasing the stock and the flat plates there is a fibreglass structure made up of port and starboard matching mouldings bonded together. These mouldings are thin skinned – in fact, they are often too thin on fast craft. They give the rudder its hydrodynamic shape and hold the filler material that occupies the space round the metalwork between the side mouldings.

There was a time when boat factories had more problems with this type of rudder than any other component. The trouble was mainly, though not exclusively, seen in the vertical join that extends all round the blade where the port and starboard mouldings are joined. This join is not easy to make, and it is subject to severe stresses when the rudder is working hard, so it is not surprising that cracks occur at the mating face.

A thick layer of anti-fouling may cover an open crack, and it makes sense to scrape away the anti-fouling in short lengths down the front, up the back and along the bottom. It is often impossible to get at the join line along the top, especially just aft of the stock where the loads can be high. Once the paint has been cleared away, the surveyor has to use his experience and intelligence. For instance, a crack may not show, but if there is a line of paint that appears to be inlaid, the inference must be that whoever put on the anti-fouling has applied it deep into a crack. The painter may believe, quite wrongly, that if ample paint is worked into this crack, all will be well.

When the crack on the centreline of a rudder is short, it is usual to clean off the area and fill the crack with resin. The repair is finished off with fibreglass in perhaps five or eight layers to seal over and strengthen the area. This is fine for small boats working

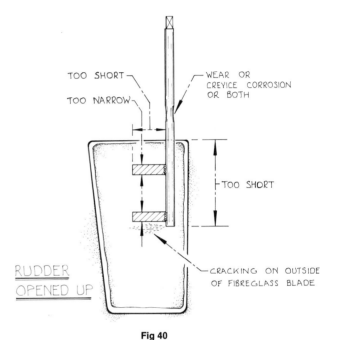

Fig 40

A surveyor starts off knowing that most rudders give trouble, so he beavers away until he finds out which are present, and is surprised if he finds none. Sometimes he is lucky and spots water dripping out of the blade just after the boat is hauled up, and this tells him a lot. If there is no water inside a rudder this must be considered a bonus, because it is rare on craft over four years old.

Just how much damage the water inside the blade causes cannot be known until the rudder is opened up. Welds are made with metal different from the parts it is joining, so there is always a chance of electrolytic action here. The welding of the plate or straps to the stock should extend right round the top and bottom ends for strength and reliability.

close to the shore. However, for more serious situations it is best to open the crack up all round, separate the two sides of the rudder, and examine the inside structure and components. When repairs have been completed, a new fully sealed join all round has to be made. This is a good approach, because the inside of a rudder contains so many potential problems. In practice, few people want to go to the expense of opening up a rudder, because it and the reassembly job are costly. However, before a major offshore voyage, it is a sensible precaution to take.

Sometimes the argument put forward is that if the centreline join has failed, or if the blade has cracks on the surface that do not look too serious, then the wise thing to do is encase the whole blade in a few layers of new fibreglass, and all will be well. Maybe, but this is akin to welding new plates on corroded ones – a technique that may be acceptable in a situation that borders on a crisis. Patching over is seldom good boatbuilding and usually no more than a temporary measure suitable for getting the boat back home, provided she can avoid rough weather.

Small areas of anti-fouling should be scraped off the blade to look for osmosis and cracks. The dreaded 'Os' may not be found on the hull, but may be present on the rudder, and vice versa. It seems to defy logic. Constant vigilance is needed if it is to be avoided and cured before it becomes severe. Where the rudder blade has no heel bearing, there may be a horizontal crack running fore and aft. As always, if they are found on one side, the sharp-witted surveyor nips round to the other side to see if they are there as well. In practice it does not much matter whether they are on one side or both – they indicate that the blade is flexing too much or has been damaged by hitting flotsam or some such. Just because the cracks are low down, it cannot be inferred that floating rubbish is not the trouble: at sea, boats pitch and heave a lot, at times lifting much of the rudder blade out of the water. As a result, a floating log can cause damage quite low down on a rudder blade, or even on the hull for that matter.

The most usual cause of rudder blade fore-and-aft cracking is lack of adequate internal stiffening. If the metal stock is extended down inside for half the blade length, and the boat is driven hard, perhaps planing off the wave fronts, the bottom of the blade may well flex and crack just below the bottom of the metal reinforcing. It will be expensive making an entirely new stock, with a new blade welded on, and a good metalworker will often be able to extend the depth of the stock by welding on an extra piece. The weld has to be long and strong, and not just across the bottom of the circular bar of the stock. The new piece need not be of the same section, but can be a piece of flat bar welded to the forward or aft edge of the stock, as well as across its bottom face.

This rudder has water inside, as shown by the dribbling outwards near the leading edge at the bottom. Ideally such a rudder should be opened up so that the internal condition can be checked properly. A cheaper but less thorough technique is to cut two or three large inspection holes in the side. These should expose the weld of the fore and aft plate to the bar which forms the rudder stock.

A principal reason for opening up a rudder is to examine the metalware inside. It is almost certain that the majority of fibreglass rudders have water inside them after a few years afloat. There is evidence than some rudders take in water from the first day the boat is launched. This water may corrode the stock, or the metal straps welded to it, or (most common) the welds. The worrying aspect of this trouble is that it cannot be discovered without opening up the rudder, though various nondestructive techniques have been suggested for diagnosing distress without going to the expense of rudder surgery. I question these approaches because they are not 'fail-safe'. They do not *guarantee* that they always detect trouble, even though they may accidentally indicate problems when none are there. They work the other way – pointing out troubles over the months they are used, but not being totally certain in every case, so they can miss trouble just once in a thousand tests. This is no consolation to the crew who lose their rudder on a lee shore with no time to get assistance before the vessel grounds.

A common place for water to get inside a rudder blade is at the top, where the stock enters. The seal is almost always dependent on the bond of the fibre-glass to the metal, and this is most unreliable. To make a watertight join here, probably the best approach is to rout out a little trench in the fibreglass all round the stock and clean off the whole area, then fill the trench with a semi-soft bonding material such as one of the rubbery compounds that adheres with total certainty to fibreglass and metal. This non-hardening seal will flex without breaking free when there is subtle slight movement between the metal and fibreglass. To protect the sealant, it is worth adding fibreglass over the top. This final covering is not expected to be permanently watertight. Its job is to guard against the rubbery seal being damaged or eased out of place.

On most rudders it is impossible to carry out the modification just described without first dropping the rudder, in order to get access to the top of the blade. In practice, it is sensible to drop the rudder during a survey, but it is seldom done because the boat has to be lifted high above the ground. Where such a lift is not possible, the alternative approach is to dig a hole below the rudder. If the boat is big, the shipwright has to dig very deep, and it may be worth getting a mechanical digger. I've been in boatyards where it has been necessary to chip down through a layer of concrete to dig the hole, because the boat could not be moved – there were too many laid up behind her.

Before a voyage round the world or some such, the rudder should always be dropped for a full check all over. Because there have been so many rudder problems, and because the consequences are so serious, I have advised ocean wanderers who own standard fibreglass boats to have special rudders made to ensure a big margin of safety. These rudders have had extra-strong stocks with hard-wood blades. Instead of a single plate welded to the stock, there are two, one each side. Fastenings through the plates hold the wood in place. To keep away worm and to keep the fastenings protected from contact with sea water, the whole wood blade and the side plates are

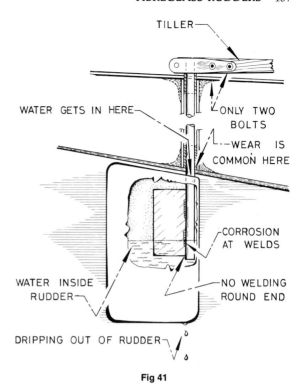

Fig 41

Some rudder faults can only be seen when the two halves of the fibreglass blade have been opened up. However, if the outside of the blades has fore and aft cracks roughly half-way down, a guess can be made about the inadequate length of the stock.

The straps welded to the blade should extend almost to the aft edge of the blade and be deep enough to support a big area. They should also have long welds. Wear or corrosion on the stock may not be visible until the rudder is dropped. If the rudder cannot be taken right out because there is insufficient space below the counter, it can still be worth lowering the blade to expose a good length of the stock.

layered over with fibreglass. In the event of a serious grounding the bottom of the blade may be damaged, but much should remain, so that the yacht can be steered to safety once she has been hauled off into deep water.

Reverting to less far-ranging craft, there is more to this rudder dropping than at first meets the eye. Once the whole affair is off, the boat repairs are much easier, and therefore cheaper. Besides, there may be wear on the stock that can only be detected when it has been withdrawn. When the rudder is in place, wear on the bearings will be found by pushing the blade backwards and forwards, then side to side. If the boat is large, singlehanded pushing will not be effective, so the surveyor looks around for help.

When a surveyor spots something like this he starts asking questions. A metal strap has been fixed vertically up the bottom of the skeg, indicating that extra strength was needed, perhaps to stop the bottom rudder bearing from moving. The strap only has a single bolt at each end, whereas three each end is good engineering practice. This strap is not recessed, so it will spoil the water flow just ahead of the rudder. Perhaps it is a temporary repair.

THESE SCREWS SHOULD BE
REPLACED BY BOLTS

TRANSOM

WIRE TO QUADRANT

WIRE TO STEER^g WHEEL

Fig 42

Sheave cages for steering gear should always be bolted in place. On small craft an argument might be raised for using screws in shear. There is never any excuse for putting screws in tension, as shown in this sketch.

Where there is no available additional muscle-power, he needs to use cunning – such as a swift kick, or the leverage of a large screwdriver. Pads of wood and some care are needed to prevent the blade of the screwdriver cracking the fibreglass.

Worn bearings are endemic in certain classes of yacht, especially where cheap soft plastic material is used. It is advisable to be suspicious of creamy-white nylon-like bearings because these can chafe away to an unacceptable extent in just one summer. Yet a similar type, with suitable wear-resistant inclusions, can last far longer. The additives that reduce wear sometimes give the bearing different colours, such as a pale greeny-yellow shade. Of course, the situation can change in a matter of weeks, and even as I write this there may be a firm that is making a bearing with eternal wear-resistance that is precisely the same colour as the cheap horrible type. For this reason, surveyors try to build up banks of knowledge about each class and manufacture of boat.

Excessive wear is sometimes caused by having a stock that is not thick enough. The lack of adequate diameter means there is a smaller wearing area, and there may be subtle bending at the bearing that will also speed up wear. Traditionally designers have worked out the required thickness of the stock using one of the formulae put out by the organisations that supervise the construction of ships and boats. A few years ago a yacht on an ocean voyage lost her rudder far offshore. The crew were rescued because the owner had taken trouble to have on board a world-ranging radio, so he was able to get help from afar. When he got ashore he started an inquiry into the reasons why his rudder failed, and after a massive search and years of work he discovered that the rudder had been designed to a faulty formula. As this formula was widely used (naturally enough, bearing in mind the reputation of the organisation that circulated it), there are craft afloat that have inadequate rudder stocks.

A surveyor may be tempted to despair when he learns of this situation. If a major regulatory body can make such a fundamental error, how can a busy surveyor expect to detect a problem? So far as the case of his broken rudder far offshore is concerned, the answer found by the owner is of double interest: the overseeing organisation that devised and circulated the defective formula had adopted the calculation without having it double checked. More important, it worked on the outdated theory that a sailing boat will not go faster than about 1.5 times the square root of the waterline length. Plenty of modern cruisers and virtually all racing craft get up and plane at least intermittently. This means that their speeds are far above that given by the 'traditional' formula. When looking at a rudder stock, a surveyor can use one of the formula circulated by the world-wide building supervisory bodies, but he must be sure to put in a velocity figure that takes into account planing speeds. It is fairly common for a lightly built cruiser to achieve three times the square root of the sailing waterline length, and racing craft may get up to double this speed for short periods.

On transom-sterned craft fibreglass rudders have on the whole been more reliable. We do find cracks at the centreline join of the blade, but chafe at the bottom due to grounding is more common. It shows up as chafed and splintered fibreglass. Careful cleaning off and grinding back is needed first, followed by a reinspection to see what sort of problems there are. The interior of the rudder may be visible and a light has to be shone inside. The whole area has to be dried well before repairs can begin, and this may involve digging out some plastic foam core material.

The upper rudder hangings are bolted to the transom and there may be cracks emanating from the fastenings, especially near the bottom of the transom. It is not enough to repair the cracks, because next time a comparable load comes on the rudder the old cracks will reopen, and new ones may show up. What is needed is substantial local reinforcing inside the transom. It will probably be made of marine ply, glassed in place, with washer plates at each bolt. A handy simple formula is as follows: the height and width of the doubler pad should be about one thirty-fifth the length of the boat, so that the load is spread over a big area. The thickness of the doubler pad will be of the order of 19 mm ($\frac{3}{4}$ in) on a 7.5 mm (25 ft) boat, and 32 mm ($1\frac{1}{4}$ in) on a 10 m (35 ft) craft. As always, if the vessel is to make a substantial long-range voyage, the factors of safety must be higher, and so thicknesses, heights, and widths of the doublers must be greater.

Though seldom seen, all the nuts on the bolts ought to be locked or glassed over to prevent them coming off. Under power, and sometimes under sail, a rudder will vibrate, and this motion will be transmitted to the rudder supports, so there is always a slight risk that the nuts will unwind themselves. The gaps between the rudder hangings should not be more than about a metre – 3 ft for those who still use imperial measurements. Big rudders are more highly

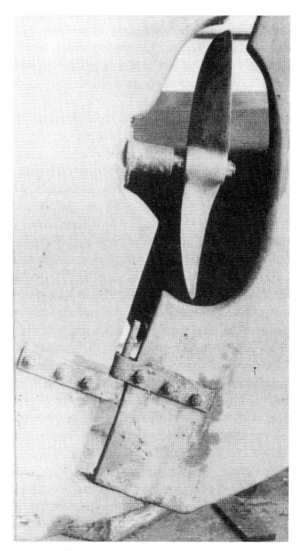

The heel of this rudder is touching the deadwood, presumably because the gudgeons and pintles have worn. Alternatively, there may have been washers on the pintles, which have been removed because a new propeller has been fitted and adequate tip clearance is needed. The tip clearance at the bottom is too small, being less than $\frac{1}{12}$ of the diameter of the propeller.

stressed than small ones, so they need more hangings in proportion to their length, which explains why there is no variation in spacing with boat size.

Wear on the pintles and gudgeons is always worst at the bottom pair, but it is still essential to look at all the sets. If the boat is fairly new and the wear is serious, it may be that the pintles are not properly lined up, or they could be undersized. Another possibility is that the boat goes aground at low tide, on her moorings, so that grit gets caked round the pintle and grinds away the metal. Naturally no one wants to spend money replacing or repairing fittings that have an acceptable amount of wear, so the question arises: What can be left for another year, and what must be renewed right away? If there is 10% loss of diameter on the pintle, renewal is needed right away. If the rudder noticeably rattles, something is wrong. If the wear seems rather subtle, repair work might be deferred till the next fitting-out period. But here, as throughout a survey, it's best to be guided by two rules:

1   If in doubt, get it right immediately.
2   If the boat is going to be used for any work that involves a lot of stress, such as a series of races, a voyage across the adjacent major ocean, or a full season's chartering, then repairs must be carried out promptly.

. . . .

WOOD RUDDERS

A few fibreglass yachts have wood rudders, and all wood yachts have them. Some ferro-cement yachts have them, and a few metal yachts have them. The material is widely available, easy to work and repair, and all this explains its popularity.

Old wooden yachts sometimes have stocks made of wood that may be inside wood trunks. Ample trouble is to be expected here unless the boat has been well maintained by each successive owner. However, wood stocks have to be so large to give enough strength, so that it is possible to slide a flashlight or wandering lead or 'trouble lamp' down inside the trunk to look for defects like rot, splits and distortion.

Wood stocks are normally secured with bolts or metal rods that are roughly horizontal and extend through the whole width of the blade. If the trailing edge of the blade is thin, the bolts terminate a few inches ahead of the aft edge. Where there are signs of rust at the ends of these bolts, or at the vertical seams of the blade, it has to be assumed that these important supporting bars are weak and that new ones need to be put in. It may be almost impossible to extract the old rusty bolts, and it is quite usual in these circumstances to add extra rods between the existing defective ones. Admittedly this is not the best shipwright practice, merely practical politics. Where the rods are long and well rusted, the only way to get them out may be to destroy large parts of the rudder, in which case it will often be cheaper and quicker to make an entirely new rudder.

In this connection it is worth remembering that a well-built strong hull is likely to need more than one new rudder in the course of her life. Any major hull rebuild is likely to involve the fabrication of a new rudder blade, if not the whole affair. Unless the boat is old, the stock will almost certainly be of metal, with a pair of metal straps welded to the bottom. These are bolted to a wood blade, which is tested (like all timber) with a sharp spike. The surveyor looks for cracks in the wood and metal parts, especially near the highly stressed regions such as round a big propeller aperture. He views even quite tiny cracks with more than average suspicion. Rudders are too important and too vulnerable to be left with any weakness.

A wood rudder may have a bend that may be fore and aft, or in the vertical plane. The former causes the boat to wander when she should sail straight, and the latter results in binding at the bearings and fast wear at these points. This warping is not always readily seen, but if a straight edge is laid on the blade, first vertically, then fore and aft, the defect is obvious.

A rudder blade cannot be made up of a single piece of wood, and the joins will be vertical seams. These open up when the boat dries out, but they will normally close again after she has been afloat for no more than a few hours. If the seams remain open, the cause may be due to over-swelling. This can happen if the rudder is made up of dry wood, with vertical planks joined by horizontal bolts and all the seams closed up tight when the craft is new. After the boat is launched the wood swells and, as the seams are already tight, the size of the rudder increases in a horizontal direction. This can only happen by the end nuts of the horizontal bolts being crushed into the wood, or the athwartships fastenings through the planks crushing sideways into the wood. The boat is then laid up and the wood shrinks, so the seams open. Someone now mistakenly puts in a seam filling compound that is hard. The next time the boat goes afloat the wood swells, but the seams cannot close as they are filled with a rock-like material. So the planks swell sideways and the fastenings crush even more into the timber. When the boat is then laid up, the hard stopping drops out and all the vertical planks have been forced sideways along the securing bolts. The seams will not necessarily close up tight when the yacht is next put afloat. The moral of all this is that one should be careful when making remarks about open seams in rudder blades. Where it is felt that some stopping should be put in before the vessel is put afloat, it is best to use a compound that will stay soft and squeeze out as the timber wets and swells.

Instead of internal rods or bolts, the rudder blade may be held by external metal straps, which are usually of flat bar. Poorly built boats have these bars simply laid on the blade surfaces, port and starboard, and through-bolted or screwed. This causes turbulence on the blade and reduces steering efficiency. It also offends the eye. The flat strips of metal should be recessed flush with the surface of the blade.

The ideal method of fastening these metal strips is with clenched counter-sunk fastenings of the same material as the bars. In practice, some builders use countersunk bolts, so the nut stands out, or they use screws. The latter always seem eager to fail through fatigue, corrosion or electrolysis. It's amazing how a rudder that is not many years old will have half its fastenings down to one-tenth their original strength. Testing them with a screwdriver results in the heads or shanks sheering off, often with no effort. In this situation it is important that all the fastenings are replaced – the ones that seem fine are just waiting for the surveyor to turn his back, and then they too will give up most of their strength.

The wood of the blade usually softens first at the bottom and round the aperture for the propeller. This is in part because these areas have exposed end grain, and protective paint in these regions soon gets destroyed. When the boat settles into mud or sand, the bottom of the blade gets chafed so that water starts to work into the timber. The whirling of the propeller can act like a shot-blaster, scouring off paint and pitting the wood with fine sand. Here too, water starts to weaken the wood.

It is usual to have a metal strap or two securing the forward edge of the blade to the aft edge of the

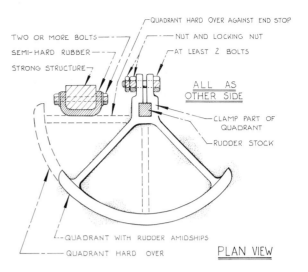

Fig 43

To protect the rudder and steering gear there must be end stops port and starboard to prevent a quadrant going over more than about 40 degrees. These strong points (sometimes called limit stops) must be rugged because if the vessel is going hard astern the loading on them can be massive. To absorb the blow as the quadrant bangs against the stop it is usual to have something like a rubber pad that must be flexible and replaceable. It should be kept in place by two or more greased bolts.

Details to look for on a quadrant are a tight grip on the rudder stock, and at least two well-locked bolts retaining this grip. Even a slight movement between the quadrant and the stock is bad.

sternpost on traditional long-keel boats. These straps occasionally crack at the point of maximum bend or where they meet the sternpost. This failure seldom occurs until the straps have done many years of hard work. The constant load of the moving rudder causes the straps to flex minutely and this causes fatigue. Admittedly this is not a defect one meets weekly, or even every year. It is one of those subtle faults that are easy to miss, especially if there are layers of ageing anti-fouling paint over the cracks. To make this type of trouble more difficult to see, it is often on the inside of the strap.

Where these straps wrap round the blade, wear takes place both horizontally due to the rubbing of the band, and vertically because the bottom bearing wears so that the rudder settles down slightly. The usual first repair is to bush the bearing area with a suitable bronze sheeting. During a major refit, the wood beneath this wrapping of metal has to be examined.

The heel fittings are most often made up of a pin

at the bottom of the blade that pivots in a hole in a metal chock at the aft end of the aft deadwood. Wear here is common, partly because when the boat rests on a muddy or sandy sea-bed grit gets into the socket holding the pin. Rudders move slightly even when the vessel is on moorings or in a marina, and this means the heel pin may be ground away all day every day. This wear is easy enough to detect. The heel fitting takes the greatest load on the rudder, so it

is important to renew the pin and bush its socket before the wear is serious.

Less obvious are the problems that arise with the fastenings that hold the rudder heel fitting and its mate on the end of the deadwood. It is good practice to scrape anti-fouling away round the ends of these fastenings. Corrosion, loose or headless bolts and cracks in the side straps sometimes show up.

· ·

RUDDER TUBES AND GLANDS

Rudder tubes are made of glassfibre on hulls of the same material, though occasionally they will be metal. On wood and metal craft the tubes are metal. Steel tubes are sometimes fixed at the bottom in such a way that a puddle lies behind them. This may cause rust that is hard to see, so that it builds up over the years and eventually penetrates right through the tube wall. The vessel may not sink, because this part of the tube is sometimes just above the waterline. Under way, or on moorings when there are high waves, water will dribble through the corroded area, and this is the reason why some ships have subtle, apparently intermittent leaks from the counter.

Whatever a tube is made from, it should be supported at the top, though there are plenty that do not have this sensible precaution. The logical place to grasp the top of the tube is at the underside of the deck, but this is an area that is hard to reach inside many craft. The glassing-in is 'up-hand', so the resin is liable to trickle out of the glass and drip down. As a result, this is a place where the glassing-in may be dry and short of strength.

Loadings at the bottom of the tube are high, so the glassing-in should be well 'filleted'. This means that the sharp angle between the inside of the hull shell and the sides of the tube should be copiously filled in, giving a well-rounded and thick join that extends up the tube perhaps one-sixth of its length, and on to the hull for the same or an even greater distance. The bottoms of some tubes appear to be well glassed in, but this may be an illusion, as there may be a housing for a bearing that occupies much of what looks like a substantial 'fillet'. My own preference is for the filleting to extend up above the housing for the bearing,

because this can be a weak area, where there is a sharp change in section at the bottom of the tube.

On all but very cheaply built boats, and on virtually all craft over about 12 m (40 ft), there are replaceable bearings at the top and bottom of the tube. The top one is often bolted to the deck; it is necessary to check that the flange has packing to align it with the slope of the deck sheer. If there is misalignment here, or poor workmanship or excessive loads, the flange bolts may be loose. Some of these bearings are self-aligning, so that no packing is needed.

The bottom gland may be the type that is made of bronze, with inner and outer machined castings and 'greasy string' compressed between the two parts. Tightening is by hardening down the nuts on the threaded rods on each side. On large craft there may be four of these nuts, but, whatever the number, each should have a locking nut, or there should be some reliable way of fully securing these nuts. A positive device for preventing the nuts unwinding themselves is particularly important where there is a lot of vibration. This occurs most often in lightly built craft with lots of horsepower. It can also occur under sail when going hard, especially if there is some slight deformation in the rudder, or wear at the rudder bearings.

A glance at the nuts will often show that no spanner has been near them for ages. Anyone tightening down this gland is working in a confined space, so it is inevitable that the spanner will make a few marks on the nuts. No bright glinting scratches implies that no one has been at work here, and the gland probably needs tightening. It may need repacking, and it

A rudder which can turn through nearly 90 degrees can cause a host of problems. At this angle it acts as a brake rather than a turning device. The loads on it are far higher than at the normal maximum turning angle of about 35 degrees, so the blade may be split, the stock bent, the tube loosened and so on. The bottom bearing is likely to be worn.

certainly does if the nuts are nearly right down at the bottom of the threaded rods. Occasionally the nut on one side is seen to be lower than on the opposite side. This may be because of a lack of space for the mechanic to do his work. It is bad, and may well mean there is a crack in the flange or distortion.

The inside of the hull round the bottom of the tube and round a gland should be checked to see if there is that characteristic faded discoloration that is the sign of a leak. The traces of a leak extend forward almost always, because the hull slopes down this way. There may be tiny signs of dried salt crystals; these indicate that sea water has dribbled in and dried up.

On the side of a rudder tube there may be a grease nipple. It is normally out of sight and out of reach, so it is usually neglected. This lack of use can be detected, because there is no shiny grease on the nipple end. Over the months dust settles on the old grease, making the whole nipple dull in appearance. Sometimes the body of the nipple starts to rust — a mute condemnation of the crew's efficiency.

DECK GEAR AND HATCHES

· · · · · · · · · · · · · · · · · · ·

DECK FITTINGS

When a surveyor approaches a job, his first good view of the vessel may be the deck. This is certainly true when he walks along a marina or dock. If the boat is ashore closely surrounded by other boats, his first proper sight of her may be when he reaches the top of the ladder before stepping aboard. So again it is the deck view that makes the first impression.

This initial glance tells him a lot, because there is plenty of detail to see. He usually knows at once if the boat is old-fashioned or new, or old but updated. He can see if she is well kept, because an owner who neglects the obvious items under his nose will certainly ignore what is out of sight below the sole, inside the engine and up at the top of the mast. If the varnished deck fittings glisten, and the guardrails are unkinked, if the stanchions are straight, and the rigging screws are neatly taped up, then at least this owner cares and makes some effort to keep his boat in good condition.

On boats that are raced hard there is a steady toll of destruction, because no one cares about taking care – they only want to win. This shows along alloy toerails where there will be bends and gouge marks, and often the pulpit has had a bump or two. In the same way, on fishing boats there will be broken fittings and welds where patching has been carried out in a hurry between voyages. Cleats are bent and sampson posts deeply scored. The amount of punishment that deck fittings take on fishing boats and the delays before anything is mended are notorious. I have seen wooden bollards on a seine-netter cut three-quarters of the way through by constant wear from warps, yet the crew appear to have ignored the growing danger. It may be that commercial fishing is so dangerous that they learn to accept the risks to life and limb. They tend to repair things only when there is a chance that the catch of fish may be endangered. They depend a lot on the massive size and strength (when new) of the fittings.

General signs of neglect warn a surveyor to expect widespread troubles. The loss of the rubber insert on the aluminium rub rail may not be serious even though it is seen on both the side and transom. But the aluminium extrusion may have been displaced, in which case there could be leaking at several fastenings. Also an old sail makes a poor winter cover.

It might be thought that an individual deck fitting is not important; but if a mooring cleat pulls out because its under-deck pad is too small, the vessel will go ashore, and may be a total loss – all for the want of a good stout pad. If a bent stanchion is not replaced it may break when it is next heavily loaded. This can happen when someone falls against the guardwires, an accident that occurs frequently in bad weather. Should this person go over the side and have no safety harness on, the chances are minimal of being recovered in severe weather at night.

Stanchions should be spaced about 1.8 m (6 ft) apart, and certainly not more than 2.3 m (7 ft 6 in), since they will not offer each other mutual support if they are spaced too widely. It is bad practice to omit a stanchion near standing rigging and secure the

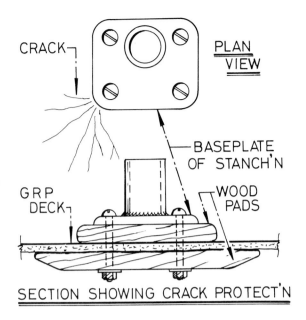

CRACK

PLAN VIEW

BASEPLATE OF STANCH'N

GRP DECK

WOOD PADS

SECTION SHOWING CRACK PROTECT'N

Fig 44

Cracks in fibreglass growing away from a deck fitting tell an obvious tale. The top diagram shows a stanchion base that has been pulled inwards so that one corner has cracked the deck. The bottom one shows how this kind of trouble is avoided, with upper and lower wood pads sandwiching the GRP deck. Both pads have to be well bedded in a non-hardening mastic compound to give a watertight seal.

guardwires to shrouds. Each stanchion base should be inspected to check it is not loose or cracked. If someone climbs aboard without care, hoisting himself up by hauling on the top guardwire, he may cause a stanchion base flange to fracture in way of a fastening or come loose at the deck. If water gets into certain types of aluminium stanchion supports and then freezes, it splits the socket — sometimes just a little at the top so that it is hard to detect, but sometimes right down to the base in the most dramatic way. If one is found with just the tiniest split, all the others have to be checked religiously, because there is little strength left once a crack is established.

With stanchions, as with many other components, the surveyor has to assess their size and strength, relative to the type and size of craft. Pilot boats need herculean stanchions, at least 4 cm ($1\frac{1}{2}$ in) in diameter, spaced no more than 1.5 m (5 ft) apart, each stanchion having a base plate quite 10 cm (4 ins) square with four through-bolts. These stanchions have to be joined by two (or, better still, three) rows of rigid steel tubing. The whole affair has to be massive, even on the smallest pilot boat working inshore.

Finding defective stanchions is an important part of a surveyor's job, but it is not a sensational event. A typical hull in the course of its life may have three or four sets of stanchions, and over the same period seven or ten sets of guardwires. Quite a lot of deck fittings are almost 'consumable stores', in that they needed regular replacement. These include pulpits, which frequently get bent, and 'halyard organisers'. These are sets of sheaves in a common casing or cage, set on the deck or cabin top deck, aft and outboard of the mast. They lead the ropes on the mast back to the cockpit. These organisers suffer a lot of wear, especially on racing boats that are forever hoisting and lowering sails. If the halyards are part rope, part wire, the chafe on the top plate of the organiser is rapid, and replacement may be needed after a very few seasons.

When looking at lifelines some care is needed. I once went on board an almost new yacht lying afloat. The lifelines looked fine, but I pressed hard down on one just to be sure. It gave, and it was only quick footwork that saved me from a ducking. I called to the yard foreman: 'Look, all I did was to lean hard on this lifeline, and it failed – like this. Whooops!' At that moment the second one came apart at the end just like the first, and I just clawed my way inboard without plunging into the sea. We subsequently found that the Norseman end fittings had been used with a slightly non-standard diameter wire. Each lifeline was apparently strong till given a hearty jolt, when it failed suddenly. The boat was about to depart on a long voyage with an owner who sailed singlehanded.

Lifelines need checking at each stanchion for broken strands, kinking and any sign of fatigue. They need inspecting at the ends for any sign of cracking, corrosion or a build-up of crystals, which suggests imminent trouble. The rigging screws here should be locked by split pins or wired up, because stainless steel locking nuts cannot be relied upon to stay tight. End shackles should also be wired up. If there are end lashings, these should not be over 100 mm (4 in) long and should be quite as strong as the wire they hold. They need renewing annually, so if they are weathered or dirty it is time they were replaced.

The wires should in general be 5 mm ($\frac{5}{16}$ in) diameter, though for boats under about 12 m (40 ft) some authorities accept 4 mm ($\frac{5}{32}$ in) diameter. On very little boats, typically those under about 8 m (26 ft), there may be low stanchions, just 45 cm (18 ins) high, and these may be fitted with 3 mm ($\frac{1}{8}$ in) diameter wires. This low standard is not acceptable for ocean voyaging, and is a concession to the racing world and to little boats that would be over-burdened by full-size stanchions. All these wire diameters do not include the thickness of any plastic sheathing. This skin cracks and breaks at the stanchions, and crevice corrosion may follow. The trouble with this type of metal sickness is that a very tiny area under attack is often more serious than a big region. If there is only 1 mm square area open to electrolysis, the volume of metal is eroded nearly as fast as if there were a square metre under attack. Corrosion rate is proportional to the current flowing, and if the accessible area is tiny then the depth it is eroded in a short time can be startling. I have bolts in my office with 3 mm ($\frac{1}{8}$ in) holes in them that go right through the 25 mm (1 in) heads. It looks as if a metal-eating toredo worm has been at work, and this damage occurred in just one summer.

Where there is any cracking, chafe or wear in the plastic sheathing of the guardwires, total renewal is recommended. Any defect in the outside skin traps water that may be doing unseen damage. Handrails and grabrails are often screwed down, so they should be given a hearty jolt to see if they can be coaxed to come off while the boat is snug in harbour. I am not sure how much truth there is in the story that a surveyor gave a great heave at a grabrail along a cabin top, and discovered that it was not safely secured down, nor were the adjacent stanchions – he found out as he fell against them and into the water. With few exceptions, all deck fittings should be bolted down. It can be hard to get under the deck right aft, so flagstaff sockets are often held by screws – and almost as often found to be loose.

Bolts through the deck need large washers under the nuts and good doubling pads to spread the load when the fitting is stressed. These pads are located by the builder when the deck is being fabricated, sometimes not very carefully. Something like one fitting in fifteen is bolted down in such a way that some of the bolts miss the doubler and just go through the relatively flimsy deck. Some of the most famous names in the boatbuilding world have made this mistake – and on occasions sited important mooring cleats so far adrift that all four of the bolts fail to pass through the underdeck doubler.

Sheet lead tracks need very secure fastening as the loads on them can be massive. On yachts where there is no amidships mooring cleat, crews secure warps and springs to the sheet lead cars, imposing a

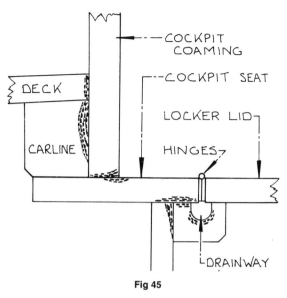

Fig 45

Rot is likely to be found wherever puddles can lie. Cockpit coamings are often subject to severe stresses, particularly where sheet winches are fastened to them, and this may open the joins slightly. Water gets into these small fissures and lies there, causing rot. The trouble is easy enough to detect in a drainway, or at the bottom of a coaming where it is open. But if the trouble has spread to a carline it is very likely to be on the hidden face which is impossible to see. Only drilling will show this up, apart from dismantling some of the structure.

strain that the maker never intended. Old yachts sometimes have tracks that are kinked up between the fastenings, but this is a fault that is dying out. Instead the latest lunacy is to fit flimsy under-deck pads that do not have the guts of a sugar mouse. I once winched a sheet lead track clean off the deck of a lightly built boat. I showed the builder what had happened by demonstrating on the other side, and pulled that one off too!

Old wooden boats sometimes have the sheet lead tracks on the deck-edge, held by long screws down through the toerail. As the wood ages and softens, the screws loosen their grip and the track starts to pull off. This defect usually starts at the end, but any tiny gap between the track and the wood beneath is a warning sign. The carriages, cars, sliders or movable fairleads that work along these tracks are 'consumable stores'. They wear fast and break often. It is usual to find worn sheave axles, damaged sheaves, chafed and bent sheave casings, jammed plungers, and so on. This sort of equipment is seldom repaired because replacement is cheaper, except perhaps at the very top end of the market, where one block costs more than a dinghy.

On some deck tracks there are no end stops, so that the crew can easily fit new carriages or sliders. Racing crews like to carry spares they can put on swiftly. For ocean cruising, a case can be made for having screwed down front and back end-stops to avoid the risk of losing sliders. Main sheet horses need massive cushioned end-stops, and on boats more than five years old half these fittings are either distorted, twisted sideways, or missing. The makers do not realise that a heavy gybe generates a lot of destructive power, which the end-stops cannot take. The traveller needs checking, as it too lives a rough life and wears fast. The rollers get flattened and refuse to rotate, and on the type with built-in ball-bearings crews are careless about maintenance. They strip the fitting down and let the balls drop into the cockpit and thence overboard via the drains.

Surveyors do not strip down fittings. If the sheet and halyard winches show signs of sloppiness or wear or seized pawls when rotated, this is noted. The fact that one or all the pawls may be worn or defective is not important, because the winch has to be stripped fully just to repair one. And if one pawl is worn, all should be replaced. If the winch appears to be sited so that ropes leading to it chafe the cockpit coamings or the cabin top, or indeed any structure, this defect is mentioned in the report. It may be that the winch needs a pad under the base to raise it slightly, or to angle the winch so that the rope comes to it at an angle of about 100 degrees to the vertical axle – that is, the rope in effect comes up from below the winch to pass round the drum.

There was a time when sheet winches fitted by production builders were almost always two sizes too small. Things have got better, but when inspecting an old yacht note that the size of the winch relative to the sail it has to handle should be considered. Undersized winches wear out fast and make the crew's job hard or impossible.

Anchor winches must never be used as the principal mooring point. Where one of these winches is fitted, but there is no stout set of cleats or a big sampson post or bollard, this must be mentioned as a serious defect. I have seen anchor winches sheered off their base-plates, broken in half, torn off the deck, and uprooted complete with the adjacent deck. These winches suffer all sorts of troubles because they do have to work very hard when the anchor catches on the sea-bed, or when the crew forget to sail forward till the mooring rope or chain is vertical, before hauling it in. Common faults are rust and corrosion, peeling plastic protective skins, seized pawls, worn pawl axles, worn bearings, leaking oil baths, rusty and bent grease nipples, holding-down bolts that are almost rusted through, inadequate under-deck strengthening, lost or ill-fitting or undersized handles, and so on. Some winches have chain counters to measure the amount of cable that has run out, but some versions of these gadgets are much too delicate for their job and pieces break off in no time.

A serious fault is a gipsy that does not fit the anchor chain. If it is too big or small, the dangers are equal and frightening. The chain may slip or jam, or do both in turn. Either way, fingers get crushed or worse. The absence of any plug or cover for the chain hole is a minor fault in comparison, but during a long gale at sea it can contribute to sinking the boat by helping to fill her faster than she can be pumped out. The type of chain pipe that is set clear of the winch, or used when there is no winch, has its own set of problems. The covers break off easily, and the galvanised type seize at the pivot. Most of these pipes have tiny holes in the base flange, so they cannot be bolted down until the holes have been reamed out, and shipwrights succumb to the temptation to use toy screws. Some have loose covers with delicate safety chains that soon break, and some have no safety lines at all!

Powered anchor winches suffer more than most mechanical gadgets because they are located on the foredeck, and often get wet. The switches are fitted under the deck where there is a damp atmosphere and little ventilation. They corrode, especially if there is no thick layer of grease or a water-proofing on them.

When hauling in the anchor, the loads on the winch are high, and the lubrication may be salt water, so it is not surprising that bearings and seals wear fast. This lets water in, and then the damage accelerates. It helps if there is a waterproof cover, but these seldom keep all water away from the winch and they trap condensation. These winches are expensive and the price goes up in bounds as the size increases. There is a temptation to buy an undersized winch that has to struggle when getting in the anchor, and this further speeds up the deterioration.

Anchors that are stowed on deck or in an anchor locker under the forward part of the foredeck need lashing points. These are usually in the form of eye-plates and traditionally there were always three. Nowadays it is common to find only one or two, and few anchors are so well fixed down that they cannot slither slightly in a seaway. To make matters worse, the traditional practice of fitting three hard-wood chocks with grooves or recesses on top to take the anchor has died out. As a result, heavy anchors chip the deck gel coat and cause dents on wooden boats.

It's a good idea to have some sort of semi-soft lining at the bottom of an anchor locker to prevent this sort of damage. This padding can be a couple of thicknesses of PVC cloth or a neoprene sheet, and it should extend up the sides as well as cover the bottom. If the yacht is to go offshore, the anchor locker lid must be strongly fastened, especially where there is a lot of chain in the locker. One little turn-button and two screwed-on hinges will not retain a long length of heavy chain if the yacht is hove down till the crosstrees are getting washed.

Some arrangement for securing the bitter end of the chain or warp is needed. It can be an eye-plate bolted to the aft bulkhead of the anchor locker with a strong backing pad. If there is a cut-out slot in the lid for the mooring line, the strong point can be on deck, and may be one of the mooring cleats. Inside some of these bow lockers there are chain-pipes that lead below. These can take in tons of water in severe conditions, because the sea may come into the locker faster than the drain holes clear it. This is especially true if the locker lid blows open, or it breaks adrift. If the drain holes become blocked, the locker will stay full of water, so it has to be totally watertight. When the anchor is stowed without being fully cleaned, weed and mud from it can block quite large drainways.

Stemhead rollers and other bow fairleads are seldom made to stand up to severe weather. Many yachts are kept in marinas, so the stemhead roller is omitted on racing yachts and made small on production cruising craft. The side plates are of sharp-edged metal that cuts through mooring warps. They are sometimes so low that in wild conditions the mooring line is not kept in place. If it is of wire or chain, once it has jumped over a side plate it can cut through the deck-edge and work its way down to the topsides till the boat sinks.

All vessels should be able to stand up to force 12 in their home waters, and on their usual moorings. The side plates of stemhead rollers need some sort of locking arrangement to keep the mooring in. It is usually a 'keep-pin', which is like a bolt across the top. It will have some quick-release device such as a drop-nose, or a short threaded section that screws into one side plate. Even if there are just large holes in the side plates, at least a lashing can be put over the top of the mooring.

On perhaps one yacht in three hundred, the deck will have chafe marks at the first obstruction aft of the stemhead roller, where the mooring has come off the bow roller. The damage is normally by the forward leg of the pulpit, which sometimes also shows signs of being torn up. When this evidence is seen, it is not enough to repair the deck-edge. A new larger stemhead roller fitting is probably also needed. Stemhead rollers are now made so small that they wear out fast. Axles and rollers are 'lubricated' by sea water, sometimes mixed with the gritty mud that comes up on the anchor. Some axles are welded in place, which makes it hard to grease them, and some are so badly secured that they come out by accident in the first year. This leaves the mooring resting on the stemhead base plate, and a mooring chain has broken here in at least one instance.

The old style of roller, made of galvanised mild steel, has a habit of binding, seizing or rusting. On some traditional craft its axle is a bolt through the top of the stem. As the surrounding wood becomes slightly softened, this bolt tilts down under the load of the mooring in bad weather. The stem forms one 'ear' of the roller and the other is an angled plate, secured to the stem by one or two bolts. These do not always form an adequate support, and the outboard side plate gives all sorts of troubles. It gets wrenched forward, aft or outboard; it rusts, wears and jams the roller.

The strong point forward to take the mooring also has to be used when the vessel is towed. It needs to be enormously strong, but in recent years there has yet again been a tendency to reduce its size and strength. This in turn means it is held by flimsy fastenings. This presents the surveyor with a dilemma, because components that are now standard on many classes of boats must to some extent be considered generally acceptable. These small mooring cleats and bollards are found on perhaps 30% or maybe 60% of all the craft seen at a typical boat show. The surveyor can only point out the risk of depending on lightweight mooring components.

For long-range cruising it is obvious that the mooring facilities must be massive. A surveyor will probably suggest that the existing cleats should be left in place and an extra (much bigger) pair should be fitted, with better local structural strengthening all round. If there is a sampson post, it should have whelps on the edges. These are rounded metal plates

The side plates of a stem-head roller may have sharp edges which will chage through a mooring line in one stormy day. This fitting has a pair of fairleads welded to the base plate. These fairleads are made from light bent bar and may not be strong enough for rugged conditions.

that prevent wear. If there are none, it is usual to find that chain or wire has cut deeply into the wood, which may have lost half its strength. A post is only as good as the beams that hold it, and they should be bracketed together to give mutual support.

When looking at a boat in a marina, a glance at the warps may show that there is too much wear at the fairleads. This indicates that the edges of the fairleads are sharp and dangerous. Craft over 12 m (40 ft) and all ocean cruisers should have one fairlead on each side-deck amidships to take the mooring springs. It is a good idea to point it out if the mooring warps are in poor condition, so that the owner or buyer can fit replacements without delay. Because a surveyor's job is to protect life and property, regardless of who owns it now or in the future, it is sensible to tell marina staff immediately about damaged warps.

Stanchions and pulpits should be given a good shaking, to make sure they are strong enough and not coming loose at the deck. This raises the question: 'What is strong enough?' On fishing boats, pilot boats and yachts making long voyages, each item must be so strong that if anyone falls against it no destruction will occur. However, on boats under about 7 m (23 ft) stanchions and pulpits are seldom more than steadying handles. They flex even when given a gentle shove. They must be bolted down, like all deck fittings, but if anyone lunges heavily against them they will bend and may snap off. They mark the edge of the 'playground', but they are not a safety fence round it.

On many quite large, fast motor boats the pulpits are too delicate to stand up to moderate (let alone rough) treatment. They are styled with so many curves and bends that even if they were thick enough, and have rugged base plates, they will not keep anyone on board if he lurches awkwardly. This has become part of the accepted climate. Owners of craft that are equipped with this sort of delicate equipment are like people who buy fast cars or motorbikes – everyone knows there is a high level of danger, and they have to take adequate precautions.

Pulpits can be strengthened to some degree by welding on diagonal bars or tubes to form corner brackets. A pulpit that is unbolted and strengthened with 200 mm (8 ins) long, 6 mm ($\frac{1}{4}$ in) diameter bars, where each vertical tube meets each horizontal one, becomes surprisingly strong. Shorter bars of similar diameter welded from the base plates 100 mm (4 ins) up the vertical legs also make a substantial difference. For best effect, larger flange plates have to be fitted.

···················

CHAIN PLATES

There is a rough rule that says that the chain plates on one side should be strong enough to lift the entire boat fully loaded. Another rule says that each chain plate should be more than twice as strong as the shroud fitted to it. These two crude guides give the surveyor an idea of how much metal there should be at the weakest point in a chain plate, which is at the hole where the toggle is fitted.

In practice, chain plates are less liable to cause trouble than the structure on which they are fixed. Here again, a few basic rules help. These include:

- Whatever the chain plates are secured on to should be doubled in thickness. The doubling should extend well out all round.
- The minimum number of fastenings should be three, and on boats over 6 m (26 ft) there should be at least five.
- Chain plates on cabin coamings must be well away from windows.
- Inner forestay or baby-stay chain plates tend to distort and damage their supporting structure. This is especially so if there is a forehatch nearby.
- Old-fashioned chain plates secured to the outside of the hull should have rub rails over them to prevent damage when docking.

These useful dictums need adapting to circumstances. For instance, there is a handy type of chain plate that consists of a stainless steel rod bent in an upside-down U. It is secured on deck with the 'legs' sticking down into the hull, where there must be a thick under-deck doubler and, in addition, on craft over 10 m (33 ft), some bracketing or a bulkhead close by. On the end of each 'leg' there should be a nut and locking nut, though one of the reliable patent self-locking nuts can be used. This fitting, known as a 'hair-pin chain plate', clearly only has two fastenings, but it is acceptable. It must have a large under-deck washer plate.

The usual arrangement is to fit this type of plate fore and aft, and the part above deck, which is in the form of a hoop, should be tilted inwards to line up with its shroud. However, these chain plates are mass-produced and come with only two standard angles of 'tilt-in'. These angles may not exactly match the shroud angles, and in theory there should be a packing piece between the flange plate on the chain plate and the deck, with another wedge-shaped packing piece on the underside of the deck. When examining yachts, surveyors seldom find these inserts, but then it is rare to find that any chain plate top section precisely follows the line of its shroud. Except on highly stressed racing craft, few people will quibble over an angle difference of 5 degrees. Partly to cope with this misalignment, there should be a toggle between each chain plate and its rigging screw. Time was when these toggles were only called for on medium-sized and large yachts. However, things have become tougher for rigging over the past few years. It is made with smaller safety factors, and boats are sailed harder because of improved sails, so every rigging screw should ideally have its own toggle.

Toggles still need care, and should not be 'girt' any more than a rigging screw should. 'Girting' occurs when a toggle is fitted on a chain plate, but there is not enough space between the inside of the crotch and the top of the clevis pin. This lack of space prevents the toggle from aligning itself properly. It is thoroughly bad practice to enlarge the hole in the chain plate, as this reduces the amount of metal at the top, and seriously weakens the plate. Modern chain plates are made to fit the correct matching size of toggle with small tolerances. In the same way, toggles are made to fit their rigging screws, which in turn accurately fit the shroud end fitting. This level of precision in rigging parts is found throughout the boatbuilding world, and means that parts showing measurable wear have to be replaced. Repairs are seldom easy, and often cost more than fitting an entirely new part. It also means that in many instances a given shroud diameter is selected, and from that follows the size of the end fitting, rigging screw, toggle, and probably the chain plate.

Aluminium chain plates are 'soft' compared with the fittings attached to them, and either have to be oversized to allow for wear, or have to have stainless steel bushings. These are short lengths of tube that line the holes for the toggles. Allowing for wear in aluminium instead of fitting bushes is difficult, because the manufacturing tolerances are tight, and there is seldom much space above the hole for extra metal.

Brass chain plates are found on old boats and on some traditional types that have been rebuilt. Cheap common brass is not safe, even on quite small craft, but a suitable bronze has strength properties akin to steel. The surveyor's problem is to recognise the difference, since bronzes tend to look alike. It is best to draw attention to the material used and query the specification. Cheap brass wears swiftly, and cast brass sometimes has blow-holes on the outside. If they are visible, it is pretty certain there will be more hidden inside that will greatly reduce the strength of the fitting. It should be condemned comprehensively.

Galvanised chain plates rust at the top hole and then wear proceeds apace, especially if the shrouds are slack. Stainless steel ones may have crevice corrosion or be under-cut where there is a welded-on deck plate. A chain plate that is bent at the top to make it 'look' up the shroud may have fatigue cracks. These should not be welded over. This is a clear indication that replacement is essential, and a means should be found whereby the bend is eliminated, or at least substantially reduced, by changing the angle of the main length of the chain plate so that it lies roughly in line with the shroud. It is also a situation where the replacement should, if possible, be larger than the original. This can be difficult with matching sets of linked components, because each one is designed to take only the same size of the adjacent item.

Such is the pressure on modern boatbuilders to reduce the weight, thickness and size of every part, that surveyors find themselves constantly writing in reports something like the following: 'The replacement should be 25% stronger than the existing fitting.' If this seems to be a repeated theme in this

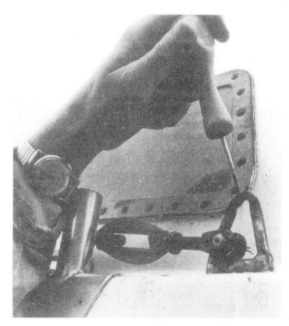

The rigging screw has worn away the top of this chain plate and careful inspection showed that there was corrosion here as well. It needs to be renewed or fully repaired.

book, it is worth remembering that one wholesale chandler has written: 'The majority of our business comes from owners taking off the standard fittings put on by boatbuilders and replacing them by slightly larger, stouter, more reliable replacements. This applies to deck fittings particularly.'

It is sometimes difficult to remove a set of worn chain plates because of corrosion, lack of access, or the method of fastening. In such a case, it may be best to leave the old ones in place and fit an entirely new set. Locating the replacements may be difficult, but as a general rule the aft one should be further aft, the forward one further forward, and all should be slightly further outboard – all to reduce the stresses. Naturally, not every owner wants redundant parts left in place, but it may be so hard to get them out that the only other economical alternative is to cut them off at deck level (or just below) and cover them over. Where a boat is used for heavy work, the chain plates should be spread well fore and aft. This applies on yachts used for world voyaging and on pilot boats that are often thrown about severely in the short steep seas found in tidal estuaries. Both these types of vessels work many days each year, and this causes increased problems.

Just as shrouds that are spread well athwartships reduce the loadings, so those spread fore and aft put

The two bolts on the right are both stainless steel. Crevice corrosion has attacked them so that the heads are honeycombed with holes and the thread ends are heavily corroded, in one case right through. In the middle of the photo there is a bronze coach-screw that has a hole down the centre. No survey could detect this type of flaw since it is totally hidden until the break occurs. The coach-screw on the left is a typical steel one that has corroded right away at the threads. This coach-screw was used to hold down a WC and the usual moisture round the base has ruined this fastening.

less stress on all the components. Aft shrouds that extend well back prevent the boom from swinging off square, but that is a small price to pay for lower stresses. There will be more chafe on the mainsail, and the boom may need doublers or chafing pieces where it touches the aft shrouds.

Where chain plates are bolted to a bulkhead or a plywood knee fitted down under the sidedeck, the best builders put a doubler piece on both sides of the supporting part. Lesser builders fit a single doubler on the side where the nuts are – and many production builders fit no doubler at all. It is common to find that the nuts of the chain plate bolts have been tightened up so much that the outer layer of ply is crushed. Sometimes the chain plate has caused a leak, and some enthusiast has gone round with a large spanner tightening all the nuts till the ply is crushed to half its original thickness. This makes it dangerously weak. It is good boatbuilding to fit a plate washer that extends over all the bolts, and is thick enough to prevent the bulkhead being compressed. Wood doublers should run up to the underside of the deck, and be three times wider than the chain plate. The thickness should be the same as the bulkhead. Where the doubler shows it must be of solid timber, because here ply will show its edges and this is a sign of low-quality building.

The most frequent trouble associated with chain plates is leaking through the deck. Where there is a screwed-down deck plate surrounding the chain plate, it is easy to lift the former, clean off the old bedding, apply a copious quantity of non-hardening

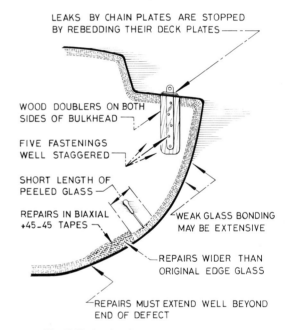

LEAKS BY CHAIN PLATES ARE STOPPED BY REBEDDING THEIR DECK PLATES

WOOD DOUBLERS ON BOTH SIDES OF BULKHEAD

FIVE FASTENINGS WELL STAGGERED

SHORT LENGTH OF PEELED GLASS

REPAIRS IN BIAXIAL +45-45 TAPES

WEAK GLASS BONDING MAY BE EXTENSIVE

REPAIRS WIDER THAN ORIGINAL EDGE GLASS

REPAIRS MUST EXTEND WELL BEYOND END OF DEFECT

Fig 46 Chain plate leaks and loose glassing

Leaks at chain plates are shown up by watermarks nearby. They are normally cured by rebedding the metal deck plates that surround the tops of the chain plates.

When a length of peeled glassing is discovered on a bulkhead or other structure, it must not be assumed that the defect only covers the obvious area. It may reach far beyond the easily seen trouble, and even if grinding off shows this is not so, the repairs should be extended well over the good areas. These repairs should be larger than the broken bonding in length and width. They should be made with tape that has the strands at 45 degrees each way (+45-45 is the specification) for maximum strength and effectiveness.

waterproof sealant, and resecure the deck plate. Larger screws may be needed to pull the plate down tight, and in special cases one might change to bolts. The bedding must ooze out all round, and not just nine-tenths of the way along the four sides of the deck plate. It must also squeeze up the tiny gap between the chain plate and the slot in the deck plate.

If no deck plates are fitted round the chain plates, it may be best to cure the leaks by using hard-wood half chocks that 'mate' either side of the chain plate. They save taking the rigging off to slide a metal deck plate over the chain plate. Wood also gives a little, being slightly flexible, and so retains the water-tightness when the rig is stressed.

· ·

HINGED HATCHES

Some boats, especially factory-built ones under 9 m (30 ft) long, have hatch tops that are badly secured. Some have no hinges, just a length of shock-cord hooked to the hull and to the hatch cover. Even the best shock-cord does not last long, and the hooks come adrift when someone rummages in the locker covered by the hatch. It is usual to have plastic-covered steel hooks at each end of the shock-cord, and these metal terminals rust, then break. All in all, these loose-lidded hatches are risky.

Surveyors find themselves with a dilemma when they see this sort of cost-cutting. The yacht broker or salesman says that the boat is cheap, and asks what one can expect for the money. Boat buyers nearly always go for craft that are 10% larger than they can afford. As it is a surveyor's job to protect life and property, he has to write in his report what he finds. A badly covered hole in the deck is an obvious danger. When the hatch top blows away, as it may in a strong breeze, the resulting opening can take in a lot of water, even in an estuary. Where the hatch covers the access to an aft locker that is watertight, the weight of water in the lazarette may load the boat down so much that she has too little freeboard aft. This makes it easy for waves to come aboard.

There's more. The load of water sloshing about in her may make her handle badly, and it can burst through a light watertight bulkhead. All in all, it can be seen that hatches without hinges should have two strong safety lines well secured at each end, and two (or, better still, four) clamps to keep the hatch in place. Almost as important is the seal round the inside of the cover. A boat used inshore can get away with a leaky hatch, though it will result in an uncomfortable cabin or a wet locker. However, offshore, when every wave sweeps along the deck, a poorly fitted hatch can let in more water than a dripping skin fitting.

Cracks in a hatch top may require more than a brief mention in a report, because repairs must put in additional strength, since the original structure has been proved inadequate. Fibreglass hatches fail near the metal fittings. There is seldom enough thickness where props or struts are bolted on, and the hinge bolts are hardly ever put through substantial glassed-in doublers. Hinges held by screws let go at the least provocation. Cracks are common at the edges and along the bottom of the turned-down flanges.

A wooden hatch top with drying-out cracks can be hard to seal up in such a way that it never lets in driblets. Simple stopping, even if of the not-hardening kind that adheres well to the edges of the slits, is seldom the answer. If the hatch is a lovely varnished teak one, it may be necessary to sacrifice the appearance and cover the top with a waterproof material that is not susceptible to the swelling and shrinking that causes the wood to crack and open up.

Aluminium-framed hatches are available in various makes and qualities. They have transparent tops, which may be tinted or clear. The former gives privacy for toilet compartments and sleeping cabins. It is often good sense for a surveyor to suggest that a troublesome fibreglass or wood hatch should be changed to one of these mass-produced alloy hatches. This may mean that the hatch opening has to be altered, but this is a small price to pay for watertightness and strength. If the hole is smaller than the hatch, it is not always necessary to enlarge the access. If the aperture through the deck is big, it may be best to get an extra large hatch – they are sold in a great variety of sizes.

Whatever the make and type of hatch, the hinges

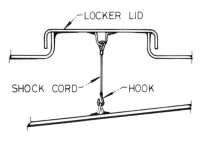

Fig 47

Production builders try all sorts of tricks to save money. Hatches that are only held in place by shock-cord can be dangerous in rough weather, and should at least have a back-up, preferably two metal clasps.

need checking. There should be at least three bolts for each hinge flap, and there should be a gap between each fastening equal to at least three times the bolt diameter. Bolts less than 5 mm ($\frac{3}{16}$ in) are too light, even for tiny craft. Hinges fail when the hatch top is thrown back too far. Chains or straps each side to limit the distance the hatch can fold back are a nuisance as they get in the way and are seldom strong enough to stand abuse. Some form of end-stop is what is needed, and it has to have a semi-soft cover to avoid damage to the hatch. Where a hatch comes down on to a sharp-edged anchor winch, it is probably best to recommend a flexible pad on both the winch and the hatch cover.

Transparent hatch tops become crazed after a few years, especially if they are bent to a curve either on purpose or by accident. Apart from the poor appearance, this crazing is a warning that the material is beginning to fail, so renewal is needed. Glass tops

get scratched, but this can normally only be criticised on the grounds of smartness. However, cracks and chips call for replacement.

To be effective, a hatch has to have a watertight rubbery sealing strip all round. The material these are made from has a limited life. If the hatch is kept closed for long periods, the seal becomes compressed permanently. It also perishes, the glue fails, especially at the corners so that lengths come adrift, and the endings become open enough to let in drips. A hatch only four years old may need a new seal; one eight years old is almost bound to need attention. Seals do not work unless there are at least two clamps or tightening screws. For serious offshore work, four clamps are preferred, but it is hard to get hatches with this level of sophistication. Some types of clamp are held in place by screws, and as the loads are high when crew become fed up with drips, the screws fail. When the hatch is badly bedded down on the deck or coaming, leaks appear, and anyone beneath assumes that it is the hatch seal that is to blame. They then turn the clamps down bar tight. This may distort the hatch frame and cause more leaking under the base flange.

To keep out burglars, there may be hasps on the outside of the hatch. These are only effective if they have concealed fastenings or bolts that have the nuts peened over. For the best effect, the hasps should be massive and on thick bars right across the top of the hatch. Thieves are by nature lazy, which is why they take up the profession, so anything that looks discouraging and hard to penetrate will encourage them to look at the next boat in the hope that she may be easier to enter.

MASTS, SAILS AND RIGGING

· · · · · · · · · ·

SPARS

Six identical masts may be found in a boatyard, with another dozen almost the same. The surveyor has to find the one belonging to the boat he is inspecting in this collection. He should check with the yard which mast belongs to the boat he is inspecting. He should also note the mast-maker's name and the spar numbers in his report, as a further confirmation that shows which mast, boom and spinnaker boom he has inspected. The maker's name-plate is usually on the front of the mast near the bottom. The boom name-plate is normally towards the fore end and on the bottom or side. Not all spars carry labels, because some have lost them, some never had them, and a few are made by amateurs. As a further confirmation that the correct mast is being inspected, its heel should be viewed to confirm that it matches the fitting on deck or down on the keel. Likewise, the gooseneck parts on the mast and boom must mate. All this seems rather elaborate, but there has been at least one instance of the wrong mast being surveyed – which might not have mattered had the yacht's

own mast not collapsed within a few weeks of commissioning.

Some alloy spars have the boat's name 'pop-marked' on the heel casting; others have the name chalked on. In the best-conducted yards, the name is written on using paint or indelible pen, near the bottom or top. It may be on the side of the tube or on the very end. Even this identification is not foolproof, for there may be two boats with the same name in one yard. However, the spars would have to be of the appropriate size and type. It might be thought that all the spars would have the same amount of weathering and the same colour anodising. This is not so, and one sees new masts with old booms as a result of a breakage, or a gold-coloured boom with a silver mast, because the yacht has been built by an amateur using secondhand spars. Spinnaker booms quite often are of a different colour, make and age to the other spars.

A yacht yard's mast store is seldom a satisfactory place for surveying. The spars are often jammed

Masts and spars are often stored so close together in racks that it is impossible to inspect them properly. The cost of lifting spars down, laying them on a proper spar bench, then putting them back afterwards discourages some boat buyers from ordering a full spar survey.

together tightly; they may be in the dark and high up out of reach, slung from the cross-beams of a shed. One spar shed that I know all too well clings uncertainly to a mountain slope that is steep and muddy. Another depends on a high lift crane to get the spars stored away, so the surveyor needs climbing kit to reach them. Often, the surveyor can only glimpse at short parts of the spar and long range.

The only way to inspect a mast is to have it set on a spar bench, row of aligned trestles, or some such. What we want is to see the spar with ample daylight, and be able to turn it over easily to see all sides. There should be space enough to stand back and look along the spar from both ends to see if it has any permanent bends, kinks or other defects. If there seems to be a bend in the spar, the surveyor wants to be able to turn it 90 degrees again and again to see if the twist comes out when the spar is inverted. For big spars, this means there must either be a team of helpers, or the spar needs to be on sets of well-lubricated rollers, as in a spar factory. Squinting along the track will show up bends and dents – and perhaps also crosstrees not properly angled.

A highly stressed racing mast is expected to be perfect in all respects, whereas a rugged cruising spar is designed to take a certain amount of harsh treatment, so it may be acceptable even if it shows signs of wear and tear. On craft used for long hard voyages, the spars have to be built with a large factor of safety, and in theory can be accepted with defects that would not be tolerated on an inshore racing boat. However, no vessel should set off on a major voyage with any defects that can be put right, and therefore even the toughest spar has to have all its faults listed, even quite minor ones. What conclusion the surveyor draws is another matter. He may be tempted to say that as the craft is about to make a major voyage the spar should be totally renewed, because a breakage deprives her of her main motive power. This is a typical surveyor's dilemma: does he let through some faults, or insist on perfection that is often impossible to achieve for various reasons? In practice, it is best to set before the owner all the facts, give him what practical guidance is possible, and let him make up his own mind. Some surveyors are prepared to make verbal suggestions that they will not commit to paper; the most experienced take care that their suggestions are not witnessed or recorded in one of these borderline situations.

Whatever the type of spar, all fittings should be rigidly secured. This applies not just to metal tangs and cleats, to winches and the gooseneck. It also applies to the lock or gate at the bottom of the track that prevents the slides from coming off when the mainsail is dropped. It is important that the mainsail tack fitting, the nuts on the ends of the gooseneck pivot bolts, the boom end plugs on alloy spars, and so on, are all firmly fixed.

Except perhaps on lightweight racing machines, there should also be adequate factors of safety: the gooseneck should be able to wear for a couple more seasons without risk of fracture, there should be more cleats than halyards, and the arrangement for holding the aft end of the mainsail foot should look outsize. This is a notorious weak spot, and the surveyor should feel that all the spars on the boat he is inspecting will withstand the yacht being hove down with mast horizontal, if not actually inverted.

· · · · · · · · · · · · · · · · · ·

ALLOY SPARS

Few things on a boat are so reliable, or so well able to stand up to the wind and weather, as alloy masts and booms on cruising craft. Racing spars, especially technically advanced masts, cause lots of trouble and fall down more often than insurance companies can stomach.

The materials used for spar-making are strong and stable. Spars are manufactured under controlled conditions and, compared with many other parts, spars are fabricated to high standards. Masts and booms can be designated as reliable, and this puts them at the opposite end of the spectrum to rudders, which so often have defects. The things to look for are corrosion, cracks, dents and bends. Cracks are rare but frightening, and serious corrosion seems to be common, mainly in old spars. It is seldom found to a serious degree in spars under eight years old.

Bends in spars are rare. A small smooth even bend,

say up to 5 degrees over a long length, can sometimes be taken out by bending the spar back in the opposite direction. It is sometimes done by an expert who may use the technique of bouncing the spar on two padded trestles until it is straight. The job is done with that subtle assured firmness that is the mark of an expert at work. This is not something that is lightly done, and it can only be risked when the mast is off a dinghy or smallish boat. In general, a spar with a bend in it has to be condemned or mended with a new length that extends well beyond the bend, held in place by sleeves at each new join. If an entirely new spar is needed, the fittings may be taken off the old one to save money.

Where a spar is made up of two lengths with a sleeve inside, usually the butt will be riveted without any welding. Ideally, the butt should be perfect, with the ends of the two adjoining tubes mating exactly. In practice, discrepancies that by fine engineering standards are serious, seem to be tolerable. However, on heavily stressed racing spars or ones used for extended deep-sea cruising, the join should be as near perfect as possible. One place that should be checked for trouble, especially corrosion, is under the coat of a mast that goes through the deck. Here water can be trapped for long periods and plenty of owners leave mast coats on far too long. A few even leave on old ones that have become weathered or perished, and simply add a new one on top, without first lifting the mast out or scrutinising it at deck level.

Two of the worst cases of alloy mast corrosion I have seen were both at deck level in wooden yachts. In both cases, there were copper and brass fastenings adjacent, and also stagnant salt water. In both cases, a very full repair was needed. One had corrosion only partly round the spar, and not too far up or down, nor was it right through anywhere. To make a strong repair, a sleeve was slid up from the bottom, inside the spar, with glue and rivets to hold it in place. Such a sleeving needs to be tough, as a spar is heavily stressed by the deck. The second mast was found to have deteriorated badly when the rubber coat was peeled off. Big areas of white powder circled the tube and, where the pitting seemed deep, quite a gentle push with a spike made a hole right through. The massive corrosion might have been visible from below in the cabin if anyone had taken the trouble to force aside the semi-hard rubber chocks at deck level.

There is a malady called 'poultice corrosion' that attacks spars when the anodising is destroyed and they are touched by wet wood. This trouble can be expected under mast coats where there are wood wedges, or the spar touches the deck. Poultice problems are relatively rare, but can be sensational because a sticky white product is formed in large quantities. The usual places to find ordinary white powder corrosion is at the base of a mast and at both ends of a boom. If the mast foot is in the bilge, it is usual to find at least a little local crumbling at the bottom, especially by the adjacent rivets or self-tapping screws. Where any fitting is secured to a mast, the characteristic white powder may be found, but it seldom goes deep. A probe with a spike will soon show if much of the alloy has wasted away. Factors of safety are not high, so wastage calls for repairs that put back all the lost strength and a little more for safety.

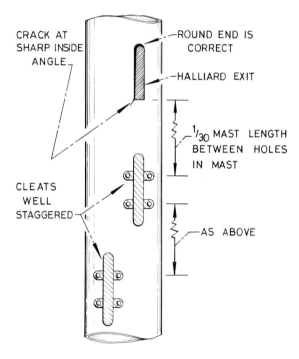

Fig 48

All masts need fittings secured to them. However, any interruption to the strength of the material weakens the spar. A screw holding a cleat, or a rivet holding a gooseneck plate may be the final straw that reduces the strength and causes the mast to collapse.

Regardless of what material the mast is made of, all fastenings and slots should be well spread out and staggered. For instance a mast winch or cleat should not be secured at the same vertical level as the gooseneck plate. No hole in a metal mast should have a sharp angle in it, as this is likely to cause a crack.

Where the drain hole at the bottom of a mast has been forgotten, or made too high, or become blocked with debris, water accumulates and starts causing trouble. Some mast heel castings have two or more pockets on top, but only one drain hole. This results in erosion around the area where the water cannot drain away, especially if salt water lies for long periods in the hollow.

Wherever a dissimilar metal touches an alloy spar, there is a good chance that corrosion will eventually start. The end plugs of masts and booms may be of light alloy, but are likely to be cast and therefore of a different aluminium alloy to the metal tubes. This is enough to start electrolytic action with pitting and the production of that white powder that are such handy indicators. Where there are stainless steel fittings, corrosion is likely after a few years, or a few thousand miles at sea. The corrosion will often start by the fastenings.

Denting is common because most spars have thin 'walls', as the metal tube thickness is called. Very minor dents can be ignored, except on highly stressed racing masts. It is not easy to define what is a 'minor dent', but it is certainly not one near a halyard exit, or one with a crack adjacent. It is perhaps best described as so slight that it is hard to notice, and so limited in area or depth that an experienced surveyor will confidently put to sea with it as shipmate in a gale. Dents located in way of crosstrees or jumper struts, or in way of the boom, or where the mast goes through the deck, are all serious. Dents that are deep but small in area, or shallow but extensive, are also considered serious. The mast may need a new section or an internal sleeve. However, serious dents may prevent a sleeve from being slid up inside the tube. Sometimes dents can be taken out by 'dressing', and on occasions a piece of doubler material can be secured with rivets on the outside, extending well beyond the damage in all directions. This action is not popular with owners, as it takes away from the good appearance of the spar. An external patch is not often used, partly because the material must fit accurately round the curve of the spar, and partly because unless the job is expertly done, it is hard to be confident that the lost strength has been entirely restored.

Slight regular undulations across the length of the tube are due to a mild defect during the rolling process that makes a round tube oval. This irregularity is quite subtle and, though it might be noted, it is generally not considered more than unsightly. It does not appear to affect the strength of the spar.

Cracks are found most often:

- at slots in the mast where halyards emerge;
- at fastenings;
- at the ends of spars;
- at the ends of welds.

Any hole in the tube that makes up a spar is a weak point, especially if it is a long one, such as those that lead ropes into or out of the spar. Cracks occur at the ends of these slots, especially if there is a sharp internal angle. A bulge at the end of a slot or by internal sheaves for the spinnaker boom lift is a real danger sign and indicates that the mast is contemplating collapse next time it is out in a fresh breeze. The same outward or inward distortion of the mast wall by the headsail halyard sheaves on a three-quarter rig mast is a clear danger sign.

It is essential that halyard slots, and indeed any hole in a spar, should be isolated. That is to say, there should be no other hole for some distance above or below. It is hard to give exact distances, but as a rough rule the bottom of one hole should not be within one-thirtieth of the length of the mast from the top of an adjacent hole. A gap of 1 ft on a 30 ft mast ensures that there is no serious weakening at any level. The only exception to this is that deck-stepped masts can have several exits near the bottom where the bending moment is small, but even here the holes should not be near the gooseneck or the fitting that takes the bottom of the boom vang (or 'kicking strap', as it is sometimes called).

If the anodising has become chafed or scratched off, this should be noted, because it means that the mast's protective coating is missing. Weathering and corrosion will soon follow, especially if the spar is treated roughly, or wire halyards continue to assault it. The white gritty corrosion products are often relatively unimportant, but pock-marks mean trouble, and a critical loss of strength.

All fittings on spars should be fixed so that there is no movement. Loose rivets allow a fitting to 'work', so that the sloppiness increases and in time the end rivet fails, then the next, and the next, till the part comes adrift. When carrying out repairs at fastenings, it is a good idea to fit the next size up, because the original ones have been shown to be inadequate. Wear on rivet ends is serious. There have been cases of wire halyards chafing rivet heads right away. This happened on a crosstree end fitting, which resulted in the mast coming down. On gooseneck fittings the jolting caused by major gybes may tear rivets loose.

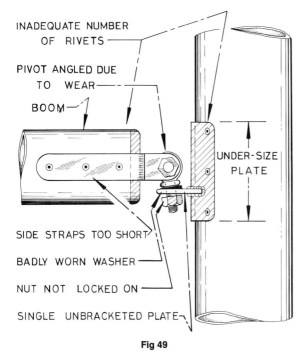

INADEQUATE NUMBER
OF RIVETS

PIVOT ANGLED DUE
TO WEAR

BOOM

UNDER-SIZE
PLATE

SIDE STRAPS TOO SHORT

BADLY WORN WASHER

NUT NOT LOCKED ON

SINGLE UNBRACKETED PLATE

Fig 49

It is usual to find at least a little wear on the moving parts of a gooseneck, especially if some of the components are of cast aluminium. This diagram shows three types of defect: poor design, inadequate fastenings, and the results of wear.

Small boats and cheap old boats often have at least two of these defects, but these problems are not so easy to spot when the spars are laid up off the boat. Worn pivot pins, oval holes and tapered washers are signs of trouble.

Wear at gooseneck parts is common, especially when the parts are not lubricated and made of light alloy. In three seasons of intensive sailing, a toggle can wear so badly that replacement is needed. The type of gooseneck that imposes an overhung load is particularly susceptible to wear. No engineer ever likes to see loads that are not neatly balanced by twin supports. The pivot on a well-made gooseneck or vang has a support above and below it.

Stainless steel tangs sometimes get cracks, especially at bends, joins and welds. I once came across a sensational case of this. Every single tang on a large ketch was cracked badly. Most had these fractures on both sides. I made the mistake of being hoisted to the top of the mainmast and admiring the surrounding view as I went up, instead of looking for mast defects. It was a little worrying coming down, because close to the three sets of crosstrees there were serious cracks port and starboard. The yacht had done many miles under power with all the rigging vibrating, and this was responsible for all this fatigue failure. Certain

types of tang are supported by a single bolt that allows the fitting to pivot. It is important to make sure that nothing is sloppy or worn, and that the mast adjacent does not bulge inwards or outwards, or show signs of wear. Mast track should be checked to ensure it is well secured and straight. Rivets should be staggered, and typically about 75 mm (3 in) apart. Endstops or gates or pins at the top and bottom of mast tracks are needed to keep the slides on.

A good motto when in doubt about any surveying problem is 'Consult the makers'. This is especially true so far as spars are concerned, because there are not many manufacturers. Each one probably supplies 50 boatbuilders, so the spar fabricators have an annual production of say 50 times the number of boats produced by the average boatbuilder. This shows who is gaining experience fastest, and applies to other equipment makers.

It is common to find cleats that are too small. Racing boats are a law unto themselves and have everything as light as possible, but for cruisers, the normal cleats should not be less than 125 mm (5 in) for a 6 m (20 ft) boat. For every increase in the boat's length of 6 m, there should be an additional 50 mm (2 in) at least on the length of cleat.

Some people feel a loose heel casting is not important, but it introduces a weakness in the mast, and in severe weather could allow the heel to move slightly – then more extensively. Where there is any risk that the mast can move on its support, there has to be some restraint. This may take the form of chocks ahead and aft of the mast heel, or bolts through the heel and the step. One bolt alone is sometimes used, for instance on a mast that can be lowered by pivoting it down on the single bolt. However, once the mast is upright, a second bolt should be fitted through the heel fitting and the step. Parts such as lights, radar reflectors and brackets for instruments all need checking to see that they are tightly held, are free from faults, and are not likely to tear sails. Radar scanners are so cumbersome and bulky that they put a lot of stress on their support brackets. After an ocean voyage, the fastenings may have started to ovalise their holes in the mast, or the bracket may have become distorted.

Most masts now have alloy sheaves, because plastic ones wear so easily. The sheave should be a firm fit on its axle, and between its side plates. The trick is to grip the sheave in the fingers and ensure it cannot be rattled sideways or endways.

WOODEN SPARS

Most yacht spars these days are made of aluminium. This has been the case for many years, so when a boat is found to have wooden spars, it is likely that they are old – maybe very old. As a rough guide, a wooden spar will last 40 years if well kept, and it should last 25 years even with a little neglect. If a spar is left out in the open and seldom varnished, it can easily become dangerous in 15 years, and if it has been badly made with poorly glued joins, or water has been trapped inside, it can fail in five years or less.

The most dangerous condition, rot, is the least common. It is found at the bottom, especially if there has been deep bilge-water, or a puddle has been trapped in the mast step. Sometimes it is found at the top, particularly if moisture has been able to enter end grain or a fissure where a glue line has opened. At deck level it is found in keel-stepped masts, often where there is a row of nails holding a collar round a mast coat. This circle of nails is inexcusable, as they weaken the mast where it is in any case most likely to break. Rot is also found by mast bands, at drying-out cracks, and at openings of any sort. It is detected by tapping and with a spike, but when examining a hollow spruce spar of immaculate appearance, the spike should only be used with great care.

Open glued seams are a real danger and not easy to repair reliably. Running thin liquid glue may work, but it is hard to know how far the glue penetrates. It is often better to open the seam fully, clean it and dry it out, then reassemble the spar as if building a new one. This is another of those situations where a surveyor has to coax the shipwright to do a comprehensive job, rather than a quick, easy repair.

When examining any mast that is standing, it is important to start work from the bottom. If serious trouble is found low down, the upper parts are left until the mast has been lowered. When younger and rasher I have gone right up masts that looked fine from below, and come down rather hurriedly, feeling a pale shade of white. It is frightening to discover massive troubles at crosstrees that one has been working above for half an hour. Some otherwise well-kept boats have galloping rot in the masts, especially when the spars have been left standing year after year. A sensible precaution to take when going aloft is to secure two halyards to the ring on top of the bosun's chair. One halyard is used for hauling the man up, the other is a safety line that is tightened up steadily as he goes aloft. On two occasions, both times on boats that looked well maintained, I have been hauled up on winches that have suddenly snapped apart.

The most common fault on any wood spar is weathering. This shows up by discoloration and failing varnish. Full weathering with blackening and signs of mildew growth suggest that the spar has been badly neglected. The wood begins to soften then weaken when wet and unprotected. The practice of varnishing masts is an excellent one, as it allows the owner and crew to see troubles early. However, for sailing in tropical climates, a white or pale-coloured paint lasts longer and seems to protect the wood better. Even so, annual repainting is needed most years.

It is not unusual to find widespread bruising on wood spars. If this is near the gooseneck on the front, it is probably where the butt of the spinnaker pole has thumped into the mast. Farther up it may be due to the way the spar has been stored in a jumble with too many others over-close. Provided the bruising is not deep and that it is kept well varnished over, masts seem to be able to stand up to this sort of damage. It gets worrying if it is over 3 mm ($\frac{1}{8}$ in) deep, or half that depth on a boat under about 8 m (26 ft) long. Any deep or extensive damage to the surface is serious, and a new length of wood has to be glued in, or a new length of spar grafted on.

Sometimes there are signs of alterations that are hard to understand; they may be changes when the rig has been altered from three-quarter to masthead forestay, or from a keel-stepped mast to a deck-stepped one. There was a fashion for making three-quarter rigged keel-stepped masts into masthead rigs stepped on deck. This was done quite simply by lifting the original heel up to deck level, cutting the thin top part off the mast, fitting a new masthead fitting, and lowering the boom. This gave improved performance, prevented water getting into the cabin via the mast hole, and cost a lot less than a complete re-rig.

A surveyor looks for broken runs of grain, especially near mast bands. If in doubt, the mast bands have to be taken right off to make sure there is no crushing beneath, or the screws and bolts have not pulled down through the grain. Crushing by a band right round the mast is particularly serious. Not only is the grain broken round so much of the circumference, but the defect extends inwards. The outer layers are forced inwards and bend or fracture the next growth ring, which in turn distorts the next inward run of grain, and so on, almost to the middle. This means that in the vertical plane the lines of growth have double joggles: one kink at the top and one kink at the bottom of the mast band. This is a thoroughly dangerous condition that condemns a mast if it is serious.

Compression shakes can be the most difficult defects to discover. In a bad light where the shakes are subtle, it can be almost impossible to find them unless the surveyor knows exactly what to look for and where. This is one reason why a surveyor tries to keep in touch with local happenings, and hear about every case of dismasting. He wants to know as many details of the accident as possible: what failed, was the wind on the port or starboard side, how tight were the shrouds, and were all the rigging screws properly wired up?

A compression shake is seen on a spar as a joggle in the grain. It can be tiny, perhaps only 3 mm ($\frac{1}{8}$ in), but it is critical because it is a cessation of the line of strength. It occurs on the inside of a bend when an excessive strain comes on the spar. It will be found on the starboard side when a port shroud fails. It can happen when a squall hits a yacht and her mast bends like a bow. The crew may be thrilled to see the mast straighten as the wind lightens, or they get the sails down. They may congratulate themselves on a lucky escape, but the damage may be there in the form of one or more shakes. Next time the mast is well loaded, but not necessarily very severely, it may collapse. The defect is caused by the stretching of the windward side and the compression of the lee side. The wood has better stretch properties than compression ones, and this causes these compression shakes while the opposite side of the mast may remain strong. Sometimes a slight permanent bend gives warning of these shakes. They will be on the inside of the bend and roughly in the middle of it. There may be more than one, and possibly more than one group.

Another cause of bends in wood spars is bad stor-age. Wood remains in a given shape if it is set and held in that position for long. Four months is ample time for a bend to become permanent. If, for instance, a mast is laid along a straight bench with a chock in its middle 2 cm ($\frac{3}{4}$ in) high so that the mast lies with a 2 cm bow upwards, when the chock is taken away the mast may be found to have a permanent bend. The set may be only 1 cm and not the full 2 cm, but a bend there may well be. Admittedly, the kink has normally to be much larger to ensure that it stays, but this characteristic of wood is so marked that shipwrights sometimes use it to their advantage. For instance, when they want to make a pair of curved cockpit coamings they strap the pieces of wood into a constrained bend and increase this a little every week, till they have more than enough curvature. On releasing the boards, some of the shape springs back, but a nicely curved pair of coamings is obtained.

If the mainsail fits in grooves on the mast or boom, there may be wear at the ends. At the bottom of the mast groove or fore end of the boom groove, it may be necessary to put hard-wood inserts to replace the parts that have chafed away. Sometimes the sides of the groove crack, and need very careful gluing, perhaps with screws to reinforce the repair. At the aft end of the boom the pull upwards of the

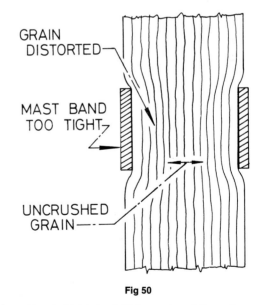

Fig 50

A mast band which is too tight does not crush the surface grain only. The outer layers press in against the next layers, almost to the centre. Because the outer grain contributes most of the strength, this type of crushing is serious and often means the spar must be condemned.

mainsail leech causes the groove to split or wear and then the foot pulls out of the groove. This is a notoriously vulnerable area. There should be some arrangement to hold the aft end of the sail foot firmly down, such as a pair of long brass plates well fastened, to strengthen the aft end of the groove. A lashing round the boom can be used, but it prevents the sail foot from being easily adjusted to suit different wind strengths and directions.

Sail tracks should have screws at no more than 75 mm (3 in) intervals. This applies to masts and booms, on both small and large craft. Plenty of screws are tested for tightness, especially those at the ends of the tracks. If available, a slide may be pushed along the tracks to ensure that no screws stand up, and that the joins in the tracks are exactly aligned and fair. Fittings should be tested to make sure they have plenty of fastenings. It is far more common to find loose cleats on wood spars than alloy ones. Even a tiny amount of slackness is unacceptable. The base of the cleat should be hollowed to fit round the curve of the mast. It is worth gluing as well as screwing each cleat.

Winches and mast bands sometimes have screws that are too short, too thin, or too few. Even if the screws are holding, they may have become angled sideways along the grain by the tension on the cleat or fitting. A winch should, if anything, be angled with its head downwards just a little to give a good lead of the halyard on to the barrel. Tangs for shrouds are normally fixed with one bolt and a number of screws. The latter need to be very numerous if there is no bolt. Each tang or similar fitting must extend exactly in line with the shroud it holds. At the first signs of rust, a fitting needs taking off for shot blasting and regalvanising. If this is not done, the rust will damage the adjacent wood, and in any case mast fittings are lightly made with little reserve strength to allow for corrosion.

Sheaves and their axles in the mast seldom get lubricated, and because the loadings are high they wear fast. Each sheave should be grasped and moved vertically to see how much wear there is, and how much the sheave can tilt. A sheave can be rebushed, but a worn axle must be replaced. The sides of the casing must lie snug against the sheave, otherwise the halyard may get between the two and jam. This is a hard fault to cure at sea, as a man must go aloft to deal with it. The wire or rope may wedge itself so tightly down beside the sheave that only a lot of force will shift it; and once the rope is back on top of the sheave, what is there to stop it quickly coming off again? A sheave cage that is less than perfect is clearly something to condemn.

A badly leading halyard can be cured in various ways, such as fitting a new block or relocating a block. It is worth remembering that an old-fashioned bull's eye fairlead has many advantages for leading halyards. It is easy to fit, and though it may wear fast it is cheap to replace.

Crosstrees are vulnerable and suffer from thoughtless crew who stand on them. For offshore cruisers, we have several times recommended wood crosstrees be replaced by tubular steel ones for extra strength, and because the metal ones do not suffer from drying-out shakes, splitting and weathering.

As they cost little, it makes sense to recommend that even slightly damaged crosstrees are replaced because they are so important. They should be of a reliable hardwood such as oak or ash, with some arrangements at each end to prevent splitting, and something to hold each shroud tightly in its end fork.

· · · · · · · · · · · · · · · · ·

STEEL SPARS

Commercial craft and fishing boats have steel masts and spars, and very occasionally they are used on large yachts for cheapness and perhaps for extra strength. They are not used on performance craft, because aluminium weighs about one-third as much as steel and has about two-thirds the strength for a given size of spar. Steel tubes should be tested ultrasonically, because on the whole this technique is quick and reliable. Failing ultrasonics, drill testing is advisable, followed by welding to restore the lost strength.

The ends and hidden areas such as round a mast

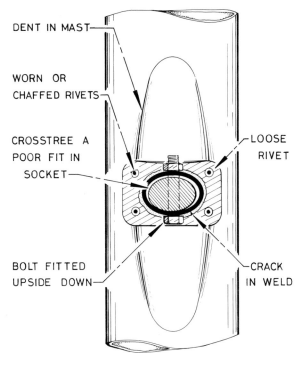

DENT IN MAST

WORN OR
CHAFFED RIVETS

CROSSTREE A
POOR FIT IN
SOCKET

LOOSE
RIVET

BOLT FITTED
UPSIDE DOWN

CRACK
IN WELD

Fig 51

Damage near crosstree sockets is common because masts are stored close to each other in crowded racks. If a mast is dropped so that the socket lands on a hard surface, the wall of the mast may get dented, and this is serious.

When a crosstree is wrenched down or up, the flange plate of the socket that is secured to the mast may be distorted. This is often found on small old boats. Cracks in welds are rare, but loose, bent and corroded rivets are seen fairly often. So are crosstree end bolts that are put in with the nut on top, and this is a needless risk.

coat are trouble spots. Places where water can lie should be tested. For instance, above a mast band there may be a fine gap between the spar and the strap. Moisture that seeps in will corrode the spar just where the stresses are likely to be high. A fillet or ridge above or below a mast band may look like a line of welding securing the band to the tube. Hammer the paint away to discover the truth. What looks like a weld painted over may be layers of rust held together by frequent applications of the best ship's enamel. An uneven surface or undulations beneath the paint are indications of corrosion, as are

red rust smears running down from pin-holes or cracks in the paint.

The lifting gear on commercial craft sometimes has test certificates that are likely to be kept with other ship's papers. These may save the surveyor a lot of time, provided they are up to date and show that the equipment has been recently tested. Incidentally, a browse through the various certificates relating to the liferafts, radio, anchor chains and so on may reveal a lot about the ship, showing whether the gear has been examined regularly and recently. It will also show what has been done about defects, and give an indication of how well the owners care for their vessel.

Steel masts are vulnerable when they are in enclosed steps. This is true whether the heel of the mast is on deck or down in the bilge. Hearty work with a hammer gives a lot of information, but for a comprehensive examination the mast has to be lifted out and laid horizontal. Very occasionally, a steel mast is fitted with a wood topmast socketed down into the top of the steel tube. This is bad practice, and the wood may have rot in it after only a few months. Tubular metal stiffeners on wooden spars, are just as likely to cause trouble.

Steel goosenecks and other moving parts wear fast. Paint or galvanising is ground off when they move, even under no load. Rust starts right away, and it is chafed off whenever further movement takes place. For instance, a derrick may seem well secured, but can still swing a few degrees each way as the boat rolls on moorings or out at sea. The motion is sometimes continuous for weeks on end, so the wear goes on all that time, abetted by rust.

The speed with which an unlubricated metal-to-metal contact grinds itself away is astonishing. I have seen the 20 mm ($\frac{3}{4}$ in) thick steel eye at the bottom of a fishing boat's forestay worn away to little more than 3 mm ($\frac{1}{8}$ in). The shackle through the eye was in a similar condition, and these parts had chafed each other away between surveys. This forestay supported the mast, which was used both for fishing and for offloading the catch. The crew, as is usual, worked in a close group on deck, so the falling mast could have wiped out all of them apart from the helmsman if it had been left just a few weeks longer.

STANDING RIGGING AND RIGGING SCREWS (TURNBUCKLES)

(For information on rigging sizes, strengths etc, see my *Boat Data Book*, published by Adlard Coles Nautical in the UK and Sheridan House Inc. in the USA.)

When looking at standing rigging, the type of craft being inspected has to be taken into consideration. On fishing boats and commercial craft, everything tends to be made heavy and thick with a large factor of safety. Moderate wear here may be acceptable, and lower standards of maintenance may be tolerated, within limits. Cruising yachts used to be rigged with factors of safety around 6 or even more. Some old-style naval architects worked on the basis that any one piece of rigging could fail without causing serious anxiety on board. This attitude has long since gone. Modern yachts are built in factories where every item is selected for its cheapness. As a result, the factors of safety of the rig are now down to 2.5 and sometimes lower. Some little cruisers, turned out in large batches, have rigs that are not fit for use offshore in severe conditions.

Racing craft are obviously built with the smallest factor of safety that the designer feels he can get away with. As a result, even quite tiny defects on these boats mean that the damaged component has to be replaced. A widely accepted general guide is:

- The stainless steel standing rigging on cruisers should be replaced every ten years.
- The stainless steel standing rigging should be renewed on an ocean cruiser every five years. When there is the least doubt, it should be renewed before a major voyage. It will normally be one or two sizes larger than on the same length of coastal cruiser.
- The standing rigging on a typical well-used cruiser/racer should be renewed every five years, but if she does not work hard each season, this might be stretched to seven or eight years.
- Light inshore racing yachts should have new standing rigging every five years, and any item that shows a fault needs instant replacement.
- Extreme racing craft, built for 'ultimate' performance, should have new standing rigging every year or every other year.
- When replacing the standing rigging, the guardrail wires should be replaced at the same time.

The old-timer's 'rule of thumb' when assessing the rigging on any yacht was: 'The strength of the shrouds on one side should be ample to support the entire weight of the yacht, and the forestay is always one size bigger than the rest of the rigging.' If in doubt, a surveyor is safe to call for rigging up to the recommendations of one of the well-known long-established rigging specialists such as Norseman-Gibb Ltd of Ollerton Road, Ordsall, Retford, Notts, England DN22 7TG (Fax 0777 860346, International + 44 777 860346). Their address in the USA is SECO South, PO Box 1158, 2050 34th Way, Largo, FL 34541 (Fax 813 536 6314, International + 1 813 539 6314).

A brown stain may be found on stainless steel rigging. In general, this is probably not important, as it is either preservation oil or a mild surface corrosion. Real corrosion, with definite pitting that may be quite shallow, is entirely different. It is so serious that total renewal is essential without delay. Stainless steel also develops hairline cracks that are difficult to see without a magnifying glass or crack-detecting fluids. These fissures are as serious as corrosion. The place to look for trouble is at the crosstrees, and at the end terminals. Water may lie for long periods at the top of a swaged terminal and cause erosion. This is also where broken wires are found. One broken strand, even in a thick over-strength shroud, is a firm warning that all the rigging needs renewing.

Galvanised wire has the agreeable habit of giving everyone due warning when it is coming to the end of its useful life. It displays ever-increasing signs of rust, which work up from the bottom. When the rust is just detectable, the wire almost always has another year's use in it. A widespread practice is to turn the wire end-for-end to get an extra season or two from it. It may be my imagination, but I believe I detect a slight shift back to galvanised wire, though stainless on yachts is almost universally fitted when boats are new. Galvanised wire is cheaper and often considered safer than stainless, which is regularly accused of breaking without warning. One does wonder if these sudden fractures, which are reported to come 'out of the blue', are on craft that are meticulously inspected all over and painstakingly refitted each winter. In practice, it is getting hard to find suppliers of galvanised standing rigging, which explains partly why this cost-saving material is not widely used.

When any piece of rigging starts to put out 'gashers' it is time to renew it. A 'gasher', called a 'whisker' in the United States, is a single strand of wire that has parted and stands out from the surface. Anyone sliding a hand along the rigging gets sliced painfully through the flesh. A single parted strand may not seem serious, except to the person sucking a bloodied finger, but, having found *one*, careful examination will show others exist. This is a sure sign that the wire is due for renewal.

Kinks in wire are bad. If they are 'turned right over' where a wire has got into a small loop then been pulled tight, the wire will sweep sideways then come to a sudden change of direction, before bending back to the main line of the cable. This is a disastrous condition, and no wire with this fault can be trusted. A more common kink is a permanent change of direction a few degrees, in a moderate radius. The wire may be weakened, but it will go on doing its job on a conservatively rigged cruiser or commercial craft with good factors of safety. This assumes there are no parted strands at the kink. Even if there is no single failed piece of wire in the bundle, if the rigging is stainless, the item that is kinked should be condemned.

There are exceptions. If the vessel works in sheltered waters, and if the kink is a gentle bend at a crosstree that is properly radiused, and if there is a good factor of safety, then the shroud might be retained. Even the mildest kink in rod rigging is not safe and calls for renewal. The fittings on the ends of shrouds, forestays, backstays and so on come in four forms: swaged terminals, swageless terminals, pressed collars (called Talurits, or Nicopress fittings) and splices. Cable clamps, or bull-dog clips, are like dumpy shackles with plates that are forced down on to the doubled-over wire. They are risky, especially when used singly, and should only be used in emergencies to get a boat home after a wire has parted.

A swaged terminal, which is in the form of a tube over the end of a wire, will be seen to be tapered either over their whole length or at the end remote from the eye or fork. To secure one of these fittings it is slid on to the end of the shroud, then forced tight on to the wire by pressing extremely hard on the outside. This metal squeezing is done by a special swaging machine. Like so many simple devices, there is skill in using it, and the finished job should look neat. The terminal should be straight, though a little bend may be acceptable. What no one wants is a 'banana', a well-curved end fitting. These are best condemned, and any terminal that has splits, cracks or serious distortion should be thrown away without delay.

Swageless terminals come in several forms, of which perhaps the Norseman type is the best known – almost certainly because it was the first on the market. It comes with an eye or fork or rigging screw threaded part on the end, and it is shorter than a swaged fitting. It can be fitted by an amateur without any special tools. The job is so simple that an intelligent ten-year-old dinghy owner will have no difficulty in making up a set-up, provided the instructions are followed and the job is not rushed.

To fit one of these ends, the tapered tubular part is slid on to the wire, the wire end is opened up, and a cone is lodged down among the strands. Next the tubular part is slid towards the end of the wire and the head part that has the fork or eye on it is screwed into the tube unit. There is little to go wrong, though of course ten-thumbed people are found wherever there is critical work, and some riggers manage to distort the wires, or put on the wrong size of eye for the adjacent toggle.

The things to look for are:

- Is everything the correct mating size? It is a feature of modern rigging that each part fits exactly with the next. The chain plate must match the toggle that in turn must fit the rigging screw and this must link on to the same size of Norseman or swaged terminal.
- The wire where it goes into the terminal must be free from kinks or corrosion.
- There must be only a little thread showing where the head of the fitting has been screwed into the tapered tubular part.
- The body of the fitting must not be damaged, and it is bad news if the flats for the spanner are chewed up, because it suggests that someone inept has been around.

Surveyors do not open up Norsemen end fittings to check the inside, but may recommend that a rigger is told to do this. Before going off on a long journey, any careful owner will organise this inspection. Pressed collars are made by the Talurit process or by using a Nicopress clamp. This again is basically a simple process, but there are people who cannot even eat an ice cream on the South Pole without making a mess, and so we are not astonished to find distortions and other damage here too.

The eye in the wire is made by:

- Sliding a short thick-walled flattened length of tube on to the wire.
- The wire is passed round a thimble.
- The end of the wire is poked back into the short thick tube.
- The short fat tube is squeezed on to the two parts of the wire extremely tightly. This is done by a hand-operated hydraulic press or a special pair of giant pliers. These look like wire cutters, and often double as croppers.

Defects include loose thimbles, distorted Talurit clamps, signs of uneven squeezing, signs that all the squeezes have been done one way resulting in a curved clamp, corrosion near the fitting, broken wires at either end of the fitting, and general signs of metal butchery. A good workman, here as elsewhere, leaves the job looking neat, clean, natural and elegant. Talurits are mostly found on running rigging and, as a broad generalisation, are not found on standing rigging except on cruisers under 8 m (26 ft). The short thick-walled tubes sometimes corrode, especially if the rigger has selected the wrong metal tube unit for the job.

Splicing is seen less and less because it is a dying art, and is the sort of job that takes time, skill and a pride of workmanship. It is also generally unsuited to many types of wire, especially the 1×19 lay-up used for most yachts' standing rigging. If the shrouds are spliced, they will almost certainly be made up of 7×7 wires. It is not part of a surveyor's job to strip the serving off the outside of the splices for inspection. He can detect a very lumpy splice through the outer protection, but unevenness does not necessarily mean the splice is weak. A safe splice consists of at least three full sets of tucks followed by tapering out by missing alternate strands, and then the remaining strands are tucked over two and under one. Anything less than this is suspect.

Any fork end fitting that goes on to a chain plate

or stemhead fitting plate must align accurately with it. If the chain plate is nearly vertical, and the shroud is a lower one angling inwards at typically 14 degrees, the fork is liable to be tortured. Its two legs will be forced apart or bent. This is a thoroughly dangerous situation, especially on yachts over 12 m (40 ft). The fork may be a toggle, a Norseman end fitting, or a rigging screw – it does not matter which. The danger is real and the loss of the mast entirely possible. The failure may occur where the wire emerges from the Norseman terminal, because it will be sharply bent there.

Renewing standing rigging is not expensive when compared with many other jobs that form part of the winter refit every few years. This is a minor reason why many surveyors condemn a whole gang of rigging if they find one or two fairly small defects. The principal reason that surveyors make exclamation marks all over their note-books when they find rigging defects is the consequences of a breakage. If one shroud fails, the whole rig goes overboard. This only happens in bad weather. Sometimes the mast lies alongside and batters a hole in the hull near the waterline. On other occasions the whole rig has to be cut free and so it is lost, complete with mainsail and headsail. Even when the hull is not damaged, the result of one wire breaking can be a repair that costs 15% of the value of the whole yacht, because electronic equipment may go with the mast.

It is good practice to call for renewal whenever there are signs of patching and makeshift work. Sometimes there are two shrouds bunched on to one eye of a chain plate, so that the rigging screws interfere with each other; or there may be short lengths of chain at the bottom of shrouds. Occasionally one sees flexible wire rope used for standing rigging. This is only permissible when a runner has to pass round a sheave, and here it is essential to use the easily bent type of wire.

Rigging screws or turnbuckles

For every shroud that parts I would guess there are five, or maybe ten rigging screw or end fitting failures. A bent rigging screw has to be replaced right away. It must never be straightened out.

It used to be the practice to fit rigging screws one size larger than the adjacent wire to compensate for this relative weakness, but this is seldom possible now that all fittings are made to fit exactly into each other. Owners who want to make long deep-water voyages have to go for a complete gang of rigging

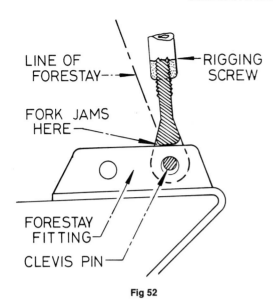

LINE OF FORESTAY

RIGGING SCREW

FORK JAMS HERE

FORESTAY FITTING

CLEVIS PIN

Fig 52

If the distance from the top of the clevis pin to the underside of the rigging screw fork is too small, girting occurs. The rigging screw cannot lie back at the correct angle, so it bends, or distorts the clevis pin, or gouges the forestay fitting.

one size (or occasionally, two sizes) bigger than the sail plan would normally have. Rigging screws should always have toggles below them, even though the chain plate is correctly aligned with the wire. On small cruisers it is usual to find that no toggles are fitted in order to save money. On some racing boats extra toggles may have been introduced to allow the crew to change the mast rake and bend between races.

All the parts of each rigging screw should be in perfect condition, free from rust, wear, bends, cracks, or signs of fatigue. Clevis pins get worn, especially if the chain plate is thin. Split pins should be as thick as possible and only just fit in their holes. Lots of stainless steel rigging screws have locking nuts on the threaded sections. The nuts are supposed to be tightened up against the middle barrel, to prevent it from unwinding at sea. These nuts are a failure either because they are tight enough to work and then they overstress the threaded sections of the turnbuckle, or they are not fiercely tight and when the load comes

on they no longer jam tight against the barrel. There is just enough of a gap between the nuts and the barrel to allow the latter to start unwinding, so that in time the screws come unthreaded and down comes the mast.

All this means that the rigging screw barrels must either be the kind that are locked with split pins or there must be proper wiring up. This is done by passing two complete turns of a good-tempered easily worked wire through each end fork and through the middle of the barrel, in such a way that the rigging screw cannot unwind itself when highly tensioned. Some rigging screws such as the Riggarna CR4 have metal threads or mini-bolts that prevent unwinding.

Girting

There is one subtle fault occasionally found in rigging screws and toggles that can have catastrophic consequences, because it may cause repeated failures before it is detected. This defect can be summed up in the phrase 'inadequate swallow', also known as 'girting'. I have found it in mass-produced boats and believe that at least one whole class had it. This defect comes about when the legs of a fork or toggle are too short to allow the end fitting to rotate back so that it lies in line with the wire. In theory, all that has to be done is to file the hole for the clevis pin downwards towards the end of the fork. This lengthens the distance between the crotch of the fork and the clevis pin, and prevents the 'girting'. However, this filing is dangerous as it leaves insufficient metal round the holes for the clevis pin, and thus a break will occur. The cure is to fit a long-jawed toggle; this may be hard to find and may have to be specially made up.

This serious defect is hard to detect if the mast is not standing. If the mast is up, a bent rigging screw is often the first inkling that something is seriously wrong. If the mast is down, signs of metal crushing or flattening may be seen, with the inside of the jaws and the chain plate pressed into shards or flakes of metal. Even a polished or worn area may alert a sharp-eyed surveyor, and warn him that this worrying problem is present.

RUNNING RIGGING

(Suitable dimensions for running rigging are given in my *Boat Data Book*, published by Adlard Coles Nautical in the UK and Sheridan House Inc. in the USA.)

Running rigging consists of halyards and sheets, outhauls and topping lifts, barber haulers and reefing lines, downhauls and flag halyards. This has become a specialised field within the last few years, as different types of rope have been introduced, accompanied by new racing techniques and a new enthusiasm for minimum weight aloft and alow. At the same time, owners of all types of craft want to spend less time and money on maintenance, and this puts greater demands on rigging.

When doing a survey before a yacht changes hands, it is common to find that the boat has been laid up in the open with much of the rigging left on the mast and on deck. A winter out in the weather leaves the ropes chafing where they have worked just a little loose and have been flapping in the wind. Rain and wind have carried muck from the nearest town to darken the cordage, and the sun has hardened the manmade fibres. There may not be much wrong with the rigging that can be pointed to specifically, but the sensible course is to recommend a complete renewal.

Even if the surveyor goes up the mast, he will not be able to see every inch of every halyard. Rope can wear unseen inside a mast against sharp edges. There may be no signs of serious chafe on any of the cordage, but the consequences of a broken rope have to be considered. It is good seamanship to renew all the running rigging when a boat is taken over by a new owner, even if no one can point a finger at a particular bit of rope that has become seriously weakened. A complete replacement, possibly one or two sizes up throughout, is essential before a major voyage.

Reasons for calling for renewal include:

- Running rigging is relatively cheap.
- It is not renewed often enough by the great majority of owners.
- It is good sense to avoid the risk of accidents, and keep the insurance premiums down.
- At least part of the old rigging can be kept for spares.

The majority of running rigging is of Terylene or Dacron. This wears well and lasts for years. If a rope is taken off the deck and stowed below when not in use, and if the halyards are taken down every winter, a set of running rigging often lasts eight years of not-too-strenuous use. Of course if the boat is cruised round the world, the rigging will need replacing halfway round, and if she is raced that distance it will need at least partial renewing at each stopover.

For racing, many boats now have Kevlar ropes that consist of strong aramid fibres held together by a plaited sheathing of polyester. These ropes are used because they can be thinner as well as lighter for a given strength. As a further means of weight saving, keen racing owners strip off the outer braided skin, leaving a rope that at first sight looks as if it has been damaged. Of course, if the rope looks a mess, maybe it *has* been damaged! Kevlar ropes are usually colour-coded so that the crew can quickly recognise which rope they want to grab in the hurly-burly of a race. A meticulous surveyor looking over a racing machine might draw attention to a lack of colour-coding, because this might lose a race.

Ropes made of Spectra are even stronger than Kevlar and stretch less. They are used for halyards, among other things, as they reduce top weight so much as compared with flexible wire with rope tails. The latter type are notorious for failing at the wire-to-rope splice, especially if it has to go over sheaves. If the splice is served, it is often worth recommending that this covering should be stripped off for inspection underneath.

On ocean cruisers there should be at least one spare halyard to the masthead, with at least one more to the top of the forestay on craft over 11 m (36 ft). Halyards made of wire throughout the whole length are led to special reel winches. These have drums designed to take the entire down-haul part as it is wound in. The bitter end of the halyard is often poorly secured to the winch drum because of bad design or fabrication. A single metal-thread screw tapped into a flimsy thin-skinned barrel is asking for trouble, and should receive it in the form of a few damning phrases in the surveyor's report. Nothing libellous, just a keen line in innuendo.

A small-diameter rope of any sort can be a nuisance because the rope may be awkward or nearly impossible to grip. Racing crews have to put up with this sort of problem and do not need our sympathy – added to which, they have special gloves that reduce the problem. For a cruising yacht, any rope less than 8 mm ($\frac{5}{16}$ in) diameter is too thin to grasp, except for jobs like flag halyards and reef points. On ocean cruisers a good case could be made for having virtually all lines at least 10 mm ($\frac{3}{8}$ in) thick. These extra thicknesses over and above what is needed for adequate strength add an additional factor of safety. Long-range cruisers that are properly rigged tend to have factors of safety between 20% and 50% above cruisers operating in narrow seas.

Chafes and cuts are the main enemies of ropes. They not only reduce its strength, but can jam in blocks. Even a chafe just 5% into a rope condemns it, but the fluff that appears on the surface of Terylene and Dacron ropes is not a worry. It is due to mild rubbing and seems to slow down further wear. Occasionally, three-strand rope will be seen to have a 'long' look, because the strands slope too much along the line of rope. This is the result of a bad lay-up during fabrication or possible over-stretching. In either case, this rope is too soft and floppy as well as unreliable, so it has to be written off.

Another fault found in three-strand cordage is a reverse twist, producing a 'crow's foot', which are miniature loops in the three individual strands. This reduces the strength by half and this rope has to be thrown away, unless it is long enough to be cut at the defect, leaving two shorter lines that are useful. Sometimes the 'crow's feet' have been carefully untwisted, but there will still be a short length that is sloppy and soft to show where the weakness is.

Manmade cordage is fabricated from oil products, so it is easily burned. This is why the ends are so often sealed using a match. Unsealed or unwhipped ends unravel and ruin the rope progressively as the unwinding works along the cordage. Ropes that have been subject to excessive heat melt and the fibres become damaged so that there is a significant loss of strength from a limited burn. This can occur when a rope is stored near a hot exhaust or passed quickly over metal so that friction heating results. Accidents like this have happened on winch drums. Polypropylene ropes are used for securing alongside in harbour. They weather and deteriorate, so that when the surface is scratched little pieces come away and the rope has to be ditched. Ropes that become heavily soiled, for instance by dipping in oily harbour waters, are unacceptable on any vessel. However, warps on commercial craft often get filthy the first week they are used and then stay that way for the rest of their life.

Long splices are no longer found on yachts, partly because they were always a sign of 'making do' instead of replacing a damaged rope, and partly because there are few of us left who can tuck this sort of splice. Eye splices are different, and all competent sailors can make one, but they do not always do so safely. There should be three full tucks of each strand including the mating tuck, followed by the usual tapering out, which should in effect extend the splice a further 25% in length. It may be necessary to cut back the serving to examine a splice, but this is not done by the surveyor. An eye splice is almost always made round a thimble, otherwise the eye turns too sharply and the rope loses significant strength as a result. The thimble must be tightly held by the splice or by servings or both. If it falls out, the rope suddenly loses the protection of the thimble and becomes in effect badly weakened because it has to bend round a sharp curve at a shackle pin or anchor ring or some such.

Halyards may be of flexible galvanised wire or flexible stainless steel wire rope. The former tends to rust, which gives warning of failure, and the latter work hardens more quickly. If a hand is run along the wire and comes away blood-stained, it is a sign that strands have broken and 'gashers' are standing up from the surface, even though they may be too small to see. This wire needs replacing.

The Talurit or Nicopress collars at eye splices have to be checked for corrosion, distortion and loose thimbles. There should be no broken wires near the metal closures. If the halyard is in good order apart from by the eye, it is often possible to cut away the end of the halyard and make a fresh eye. Thin halyards, typically those under $\frac{5}{16}$ in, are very cheap; however, they are prone to fail without warning, therefore it is good sense to replace them when there is any sign of trouble. Where there is no equipment to make a pressed-on eye, it is not difficult to tuck a traditional splice in a wire halyard that is made from the usual 7 × 19 flexible wire rope.

Natural fibres, which include sisal, manilla, hemp and cotton, are no longer used on small craft because they are so much weaker and less reliable than manmade rope. If they are found aboard, the surveyor assumes that the boat is being run on a worn-out shoestring – one made of old sisal.

SAILS AND CANVAS WORK

Comments in this section on sails also apply largely to awnings, cockpit tents, fender cloths, dodgers on guardrails and other items made of Terylene, Dacron, canvas and PVC.

A large clean space is needed for examining sails. If the weather is fine, there is sometimes a handy pier that is free of dirt on the top surface, or there may be a dry lawn. A spacious clear deck is sometimes a good place to survey sails. The deck need not belong to the same person as the sails! A mould loft can be good, but it usually needs a good sweeping before use. I have examined sails spread out in a large office after everyone had gone home. Church halls are good too, and in my experience they are well kept and clean. Of course, by far the best place is a sail loft. The job can be done with the assistance of a sail-maker, who in any case almost always knows more about sails than even the most experienced surveyor. In practice, most surveyors do the best they can under adverse conditions. This involves hauling each sail out of its bag in the cabin and examining the corners. Most of the wear and other troubles occur at the head, tack and clew, so this technique gives a good idea of the general condition.

When judging sails it is necessary to temper the opinion according to the future use of the boat. A racing boat at the top of the points list needs sails that are no more than half a season old, and without any blemishes. A retired couple who cruise gently when the weather is fine can get away with using sails that are aged and much repaired.

Headboards suffer from slack and corroded rivets, elongated shackle holes and sometimes partial disin-tegration − usually due to corrosion. The cloth occasionally wears at the corners of a headboard. Where there is a luff tape, wear, chafe and tears are common on both mainsails and headsails, almost always right at the top. The other worrying part of a mainsail is the clew. If there is a foot rope, its aft end often gets torn. The pull upwards of the leech does all sorts of damage, including tearing the foot rope out of its tape, chafing the stitching near the foot rope, tearing the corner eye right out, and tearing the foot ahead of the corner.

With age, Terylene and Dacron harden and become brittle, though in a way that is easy to detect at first. At the same time, the cloth normally darkens and looks dirty. Incidentally, oil-stained sails are extremely hard to clean, though the oil may not cause any serious troubles. Headsail hanks seize up, but are easy enough to free off. However, the bronze type wear if used a lot. The top ones have by far the most wear as they travel furthest up and down the rough surface of the forestay, so it is not unusual to find that the top batch need replacing, but that the rest are fine. The modern type of hank has a metal arm that engages through the eye in the sail, and is hammered closed. This arrangement rarely gives trouble, but there must be a plastic protector between the hank and the sail, otherwise wear on the cloth of the luff occurs. It is serious as it weakens a part of the sail that is highly stressed and is liable to be seen at almost every single hank.

Headsails that have luff wires suffer from metal corrosion and rust. A new wire has to be fitted if this form of deterioration exists, but this repair is not that expensive and is no reason to condemn the sail. On old headsails the eyes for the hanks corrode and work loose, so they have to be replaced by the next size up. If the hanks are held with tape or stitching, in the old-fashioned way, wear here must be expected.

The main eyes at the corners and at reefs are nowadays made of stainless steel hydraulically pressed in place, so they give much less trouble than formerly, though some types do corrode. When this starts, it shows as crystals and rough edges. The metal eye needs prompt replacement as the loadings on sails are very high these days. The old-fashioned bronze ring-and-turnover eyes suffer from ovalising, chafed stitching and corrosion. Replacement with a modern stainless eye is the usual cure.

Batten pockets are so vulnerable that some ocean-cruising yachts have mainsails with straight or hollow leeches and no battens. To test a batten pocket, a finger is put in its end and an attempt is made to break the pocket upwards and downwards. Where there are full-length battens there is often trouble at the front and aft end of each pocket. Special slides at the fore end of full-width battens wear and need regular inspection and lubrication.

Surveyors soon get to know which companies make good sails, and which ones cut corners, metaphorically speaking. Of course, companies change managers and craftsmen are tempted away by rival firms, so this year's excellent firm can be next year's dud, and vice versa. On the whole, though, a good firm has momentum, and if it is producing good sails this year, it probably will be next year, and perhaps the year after. It is important to remember that just because a sailmaker (or a boatbuilder for that matter) has lovely coloured glossy advertisements, it does not mean that the products are as good as the pictures suggest.

Fifty per cent of a sail's cost is in the material. Most of this is in the sail cloth, so a less than scrupulous sailmaker puts sails together using a cloth that is one or two weights below what is best for a job. He secures orders in this highly competitive industry by supplying sails that lack basic strength and a potential for a long life. Such sails stretch badly when used in strong winds, and in time the corners get tension lines or creases.

With use, sails inevitably become chafed, principally at the corners and where the roach of the mainsail touches the backstay. On yachts with runners, the mainsail stitching is chafed where the rigging rubs, and genoas get chafed on crosstrees as well as on the shrouds. The stitching should be able to stand up to a thumbnail rubbed energetically over it. If the stitching looks fresher than the sail or it is a different colour, this shows repairs have been carried out. All sails should be sent to a sailmaker every winter, but in practice less than one owner in three carries out this precaution, so few sets of sails stand up to a thorough inspection.

If the yacht is larger than 15 m (50 ft), handling the sails can be hard work. On boats appreciably bigger than this, one person will struggle to get a sail moved about, or out of its bag and back again after an inspection. In this situation the surveyor may well hand the whole job over to a sail loft, who will charge separately for the work done.

In theory, it is useful to know how old a sail is, since, other things being equal, the residual life left in a sail depends on how old it is. However, in the world of small craft few things fit into such a neat pattern. A sail may have its date stamped on it by the maker or by a measurer, but in practice this is not much of a guide to the condition of the sail. Some owners have favourite sails that they use often, leaving other perfectly good ones in the bag year after year. Many owners never set storm jibs, and it is common to find one of these of great antiquity with no sign of use at all. On the other hand, a storm jib that has to survive a force 11 for a long period may be due for replacement even if it is only weeks old.

Roller headsails must not be unrolled when the yacht is in a marina or ashore, because there is a good chance that damage will occur. Admittedly it is quite common to see all sorts of sails set on boats in marinas and laid up ashore. This is great for surveyors and sailmakers, as they get the damage survey work and end up with the sail repairs. However, for the owners of the torn sails and dented boats, it is an expensive exercise. A roller headsail that is left on the forestay all winter, out in the open, subject to the worst the wind and wet can do, suffers from chafe, ageing and discoloration. The clew, which is the hardest worked part of the sail, becomes weakened and may become chafed. If there is a strip of ultraviolet protection cloth, its stitching becomes worn. One does not have to be the most brilliant surveyor to spot all this, and the fact that the owner cares so little about his yacht that he leaves an important sail out in the weather during the bad months tells us a lot about him. We know what to expect when delving into the bilge, checking the safety gear, and looking for trouble in the dark lockers.

Occasionally, a sail is found to be weak at the corners. A lack of multiple doubling must make the surveyor suspicious. I once surveyed a yacht with a whole batch of almost new headsails that were unsafe. The head eyes were put in at a point where the sail was too narrow, so there was an inadequate amount of cloth each side of the eye. When going through a batch of sails, it is rare to find a perfect sail that needs no attention. On well-used boats it is fairly common to find some sails that can only be used in light airs, and even then the crew will have the feeling that the sail will not come down all in one piece. Because not enough sails are sent for annual repairs, it is inevitable that during the majority of surveys the sails will be found to be in need of repairs.

Testing sails afloat

An excellent way to test sails is to go sailing, putting up each sail in turn. Moderate conditions are needed, and ideally the sailmaker who is going to do the repairs should be on board. To make a real job of it, someone should go off in a powerboat and photograph each sail from three different angles.

Testing afloat is unusual, because it takes so much time and is expensive – though a sailmaker may not charge a fee if he is to get plenty of renewals and repairs. When a yacht is being sold the broker may offer the potential buyer a trial sail, and this is a good time to try out the whole wardrobe in the sail locker. However, the surveyor is seldom present at this stage. On a few occasions I have been called in by thoughtful owners who have asked for help right through the whole set of events leading up to the purchase.

If the yacht is to be used for serious racing, the sails are such an important part of the equipment – the driving power – that a full test makes sense. The sails can also form such a high proportion of the total value that a comprehensive trial is good economics. Admittedly, some sail lofts have test rigs ashore, but these are seldom as good as trials on the boat. When testing a sail afloat it should be examined as it comes out of the bag, and progressively as it is hoisted, then all over when it is up. The boat has to be out of the marina and clear of the moorings, so that the job can be done safely and at leisure.

Experience teaches subtle ways to tell if a sail has had a lot of use. Modern sail numbers are stuck on, and after a lot of use the numbers start to peel off at the corners. If the numbers have been stuck on then sewn round the edge, this probably means the sail is well advanced in age. A good sail can be given an extra lease of life by being sewn down the middle of each seam. Often this extra line of stitching done during the sail's middle age is easy to detect, because the thread in the middle of the other two runs is fresher and may be of a different colour or spacing.

MACHINERY AND SERVICES

ENGINE AND STERN GEAR INSTALLATIONS

Marine engineers survey engines, stern gear, auxiliary generators and all things mechanical. At least, that is what is supposed to happen. It is almost always the case that craft under about 22 m (72 ft) do not have special engine surveys, but the hull surveyor makes an external inspection of the machinery.

Experience varies with surveyors, but I find that less than 2% of the craft we inspect have a full separate engine inspection by a marine engineer. The job is usually done after the rest of the check-over. No one wants to spend additional money having the machinery stripped down for inspection if a massive amount is needed on the structure and the sale is aborted.

Different hull surveyors look at engines in various ways. A practical approach is something like this:

• The engine is seen to be smart, clean and free from visible signs of wear, corrosion or abuse. Nothing is rusty, blackened, dripping, oily, smelly, cracked, split, leaking, burned or damaged. In short, the engine looks as if it was taken new from the factory a short time ago and installed by craftsmen. The conclusion must be that this machinery is likely to be as good inside as out, and a buyer would be unlucky to have any trouble for a few years provided he looks after the engine and keeps it as it is. No one can guarantee the hidden parts are as excellent as the outside, but the odds must be that it is.

• At times we see exactly the opposite. The engine is so bad that no one can find anything good to write about it. The leaks of oil vie with those of water to see which can dribble most profusely. The smell is a mixture of fuel puddles, smoke and mildew. The hoses have perished and their clamps have rusted right through. All the bolt heads are rounded with abuse, nuts are missing, fastenings are loose or broken, and the thick layer of rust

over all conceals untold horrors. The electric cables are festooned like creepers in a jungle, weaving through sagging, kinked piping. The drive belts are so worn that they no longer grip, and the filters are so old they practically have 'Made by Noah' stamped on them. This engine may work, but it would be a stupid owner who trusted it even to cross a marina. It may be possible to make a good job of repairing this machinery, but the evidence available (without opening it up) suggests that a new engine is needed, together with new components such as the piping, wiring, exhaust, and so on. At least a buyer feels he knows where he stands here – at the bank manager's door, asking for a loan to buy a new engine!

• The great majority of engines fall somewhere between the above two extremes. It is usual to find that at least 10% of the surface is rusty. There are the suspicions of an oil weep, which might be where someone was careless when checking the dipstick. Most hoses look fine, but one or two have those subtle short cracks that suggest that perishing has started. Some of the hose-clamps are stainless steel, but there are a few that have been painted over fairly recently, and there seems to be a rough surface beneath the enamel that is probably rust – perhaps still eating away at the metal under the paint. The alternator drive belt does not look new, but the filters do – though they do not have that ultimate mark of a good marine engineer who writes the date of renewal on the filters. There are fresh spanner marks on the nut that holds the internal sacrificial anode, suggesting it has been renewed, and the sump oil is not too black or thick. This is the sort of moderate neglect and wear that so often comes in sight when the surveyor opens up the engine compartment. Without doing fairly comprehensive dis-mantling, no one can tell if this engine is going to go on working for a month or a decade. However, marine diesels are reliable when properly main-tained. If the seller can show that each year the correct laying-up procedure was followed, and the engine was not allowed to freeze with water in it, the chances are that everything will be fine until the engine is about 12 or more years old. If the engine is already ten years old, it is in good order for her age; if it is three years old, it is disappointing.

Of course not every engine lasts 12 years. Those that get left out in the open, are never cleaned and checked, never have new filters, anodes, pump impellers and drive belts give trouble sooner than those that are pampered. The 12-year prediction is just a handy 'rule of thumb' that indicates approxi-mately how often most boats need an engine replacement. Petrol engines tend to last about ten years, but these are only the vaguest indicators. Every surveyor can tell you about seeing what looks like a new engine; as it gleams in front of him, he is puzzled because he does not recognise the model. It turns out that this elegant prime mover was made five years before he was born and has been out of production 25 years.

So, summing up, looking at the outside of engines is seldom conclusive and, as always, the first thing is to gather as much evidence as possible. It may be necessary to call in a marine engineer later, or leave the buyer to make the best of incomplete informa-tion. Helpful surveyors give what verbal guidance they can, based on experience with engines of the same make and age.

Wear and tear

Rust on the surface is seldom serious, but it often indicates where the water leaks are. These come from the cooling system, the water pump, and from the point where the water runs into the hot exhaust. At this particular point there are big changes of temper-ature, and hence big demands on the joints. Exhaust manifolds cannot be kept painted, so they rust a lot. Here as elsewhere, tapping to see if the rust is peeling gives an idea of how much metal may be left. It is important to renew all parts of the exhaust in good time because people who breathe in engine smoke die quickly.

Tapping on nuts and bolts may show looseness or

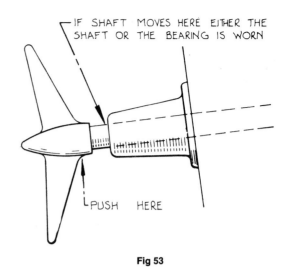

Fig 53

A propeller should always be heaved upwards to see if there is wear at the point where the shaft enters the hull. The wear may be in the shaft or the bearing, so the shaft is withdrawn for examination. This is a good time to check the engine line-up, though final lining up must be done afloat.

even advanced corrosion if the hammer knocks off a head. The propeller shaft should be gripped and moved energetically vertically and sideways to detect wear at the stern gland or gearbox bearings. No propeller shaft should be unsupported for long lengths. As a rough guide there should be a bearing every 2 m (6 ft). A bearing may be in the form of the stern gland or a plumber block (which in the United States is called a pillow block). Alternatively, it may be a thrust block at a universal joint. These are becoming more popular, as they deal so effectively with misalignment problems, ease the installation of an engine, cope with flexible hulls that bend when the rigging is twanged up tight, and so on.

The support plates of universal joints have to be on substantial scantlings because they have to take reversing and pulsating loads equal to the thrust of the engine. It helps to think of a 30 horsepower engine as 30 enormous stallions sweating hard – and then imagine what they would do to the structure. If the base plates are glassed in, expect peeling of the fibreglass here. I like the plates to be drilled with a few thumb-sized holes and the glassing fed through these holes from both directions, so that it bonds well. The glassing should cover the whole of the port and starboard plates, and be thick along the top, bottom, forward and aft edges.

Shaft wear is common at plumber blocks and other places that are hard to reach and therefore awk-

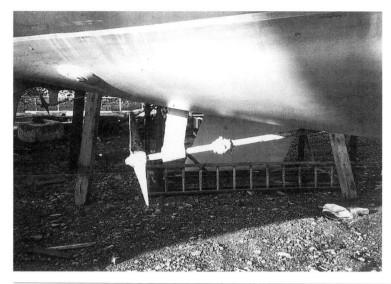

This propeller shaft is too long, because the length between the aft end of the P-bracket bearing and the propeller should not be greater than 1.5 times the shaft diameter. That sacrificial plate on the shaft is due for renewal.

ward to lubricate. The greasing arrangements should be checked throughout the length of the shaft, even if there are remote grease reservoirs. Even professional crews forget to screw these down or refill them. Grease cups that are tight down make one suspect they have been that way for a long time. These cups are fitted in awkward recesses, so they should be tested for security by giving them a sharp twist fore and aft and athwartships. The piping of a remote greaser needs clips at 200 mm (8 in) intervals and must have no kinks or sharp turns. If it is cracked or badly joined at the ends, the grease spews out here instead of feeding the bearing.

Plumber blocks should not be secured with coach-screws, because these depend on the grip of the thread in the timber. However, it can be difficult to get in a standard bolt with a nut on the bottom. Where coach-screws have to be used, it is best if they are doubled or quadrupled by securing the base flange on each side of the plumber block to a bolt welded to a thick steel plate. This plate is then held down by two or four coach-screws. The same treatment is needed where these outsize wood screws are used on engine feet. In theory, they should not be asked to hold down engines, but often there is no alternative – especially of the boat is cramped.

Propeller shafts sometimes look rather thin. This may be because the engine size has been increased, but the sterntube cannot take a larger shaft. If in doubt, it is best to consult the engine maker about the diameter of shaft, remembering to tell him the material used for the shaft, the engine and gearbox specifications, and also the propeller dimensions.

Coupling bolts, keys in keyways and holding-down bolts can all be gently but firmly tapped with a light hammer to check for tightness. Bolts through all couplings need some sort of locking device; this can be a patent washer, or nylon inserts in the nuts, or split pins.

Drive belts working alternators and pumps suffer a lot of wear, especially when the driving and driven wheel are not exactly in line. A straight edge across the face of one wheel should extend across the front of the other and show that:

- The two wheels are at exactly the same angle, that is, their axles are parallel.
- The fronts of the two wheels are level so that the straight edge touches them both on each side.

If both these conditions are *not* fulfilled, there will be excessive belt wear. It may be possible to align the driving and driven wheels by using washers or packing pieces to adjust the precise location and angle of pump or alternator. Worn belts should be renewed without question – they are cheap, but if one breaks the engine is out of action until it is replaced. No one witnesses these breaks happening, so no one knows when trouble is brewing fast.

Water pump impellers must not be run when dry. The impeller, which is easy to take out unless the pump is tucked away inaccessibly, looks like a baby rubber octopus. It has flexible 'arms' with round pads on the end, almost like hands with no fingers. These hands press against the inside of the pump as it whirls round, and the water running through supplies the lubrication. If there is no water, the arms wear away

Has this yacht been put together without proper attention to basic engineering? Stopping has been applied round the top of the P-bracket, suggesting that there is at least subtle movement here, and perhaps slow leaking. The metal heel fitting at the bottom of the skeg has a 'start' line along the top where it joins the fibreglass. This is an indication of a poor join, perhaps due to undersize or too few fastenings.

and the pump rapidly loses efficiency. Even a little wear calls for replacement – again because spares are inexpensive, but a failure here can be very costly.

Electrical components on the engine are checked for corrosion, broken insulation, looseness and signs of damage. Drips through a hatch or from a water connection cause endless troubles. 'Skirts', which are waterproof covers open at the bottom, are sometimes fitted to deal with water coming down from above. They are better than watertight containers in that they should allow air to circulate and cure condensation. However, they do not prevent trouble from water splashing up from below. The tray or sealed catchment area under well-installed engines, sometimes called a sump tray or drip tray, collects oil and water and should be kept empty. If it is very full of seawater, there may be corrosion on the bottom of the engine sump.

Where there is a starting handle, the surveyor may turn the engine over by hand. On racing craft, heavy gear such as the starting handle is left ashore to save weight – so it may not be found on board. A diesel can only be turned over by hand if the decompression levers are down – or unless the engine is a small one in bad condition, with seriously low compression. A small petrol engine can be turned over even though it will have no decompression lever. If the job is easy, compression has been lost and the engine needs repairing. A lot can be told about the condition of an engine by testing the compression on each cylinder, and this is a quick job for a marine engineer.

The amount of space needed to use a starting handle is critical. Small craft are often narrow and cramped just ahead of the engine. The space is also limited by adjacent furniture, the cabin steps, or sections of the engine casing. The best people for turning over an engine are big burly fellows – however, such people usually have large hands, so there must be 75 mm (3 in) or more clear space outside the starting handle right round the swinging circumference.

Fuel systems

Provided there is a steady supply of clean fuel, free from air bubbles, a diesel engine will almost always start promptly and run steadily. A surveyor runs his eye along the whole pipeline, making sure it is clipped up securely, with no 'hills' or upward pinnacles in the run of piping that might trap air bubbles.

There must be a flexible section of piping adjacent to the engine to deal with vibration, and a minimum of two filters. One is customarily on the engine and one secured on a bulkhead nearby. If the filter has a glass or plastic bowl, it may be vulnerable to cracking or fire, so there is a trend towards metal bowls. Bleed screws on the filters and elsewhere in the system allow the crew to take air out of the supply line. However, if there has been trouble here, the bleed screws may be chewed up because they are small and not designed for daily use over a period of months.

Drips of fuel under filters and at the low points along pipes tell of leaks. Oily puddles in the drip tray or bilge confirm that fuel is getting out somewhere. Leaks cause smells that bring on seasickness, and little weeps become bigger leaks. In time, a serious amount of fuel gets into the bilge, then travels

The damage to this propeller occurred in one summer. It was due to an electric current leakage that would have been halted if the batteries had all been turned off when they were not in use. The propeller must be badly out of balance as a result of this erosion, and the shaft bearings should therefore be checked for wear.

around soiling furniture and bedding, shoes and clothes, charts and food.

Everything about the engine should be well fixed down. This includes the batteries, the exhaust (though this needs a flexible section near the engine) and the fuel tank. If in doubt, place a foot against the object that appears to be insecure, and shove hard. Nothing should give or bend, except within the correct limits of flexible mountings and couplings.

Engine bearers and holding-down bolts

On two occasions I have moved a rigidly mounted engine by pressing sideways rather hard with my foot. I've come across broken holding-down bolts, loose ones, bolts from which the nuts have fallen off, broken engine feet, and also sheered and missing bolts holding the engine feet to the engine block. I once inspected an engine held in place only by a single foot bolt and the shaft coupling. The holding-down bolts should fit very snugly into the holes in the feet, otherwise the engine can shift even if the bolts are fairly tight. All bolts should have half-nuts to lock on the main nuts, or the type of nut that is self-locking. Tab washers that have turn-up sides intended to lock a nut in position do not seem to be as reliable as their makers and users would wish – or perhaps they are subject to inept fitting. Either way, it is advisable not to trust them. As boats sometimes roll right over, the engine should be held down firmly enough to put up with this sort of treatment.

The bearers must absorb the vibration and take the thrust of the engine, even when it is rapidly taken from full ahead to full astern. Technical books say that the engine bearers should be at least twice the length of the engine, and three times on high-speed power craft. This is true, but these recommendations are seldom followed. It is common to see bearers only a little longer than the engine, and sometimes the length does not even extend from the aft end of the gearbox to the fore end of the engine. This is bad practice, but of course it saves the builder money.

Each end of each bearer should taper out, so that there is no sudden drop down to the hull. This may well be found at the aft end. Here the slope of the top of the bearer runs down to the hull shell, which is curving up towards the stern. At the fore end the engine casing is kept as far aft as possible, often to make room for the cabin steps. This means that the bearers have to terminate where the engine does, because they cannot conveniently be continued on through the casing. Vertical-ended bearers are a sign of bad engineering, and this is where there may be cracks in the inside gel. Along the sides of the bearers cracks appear if the radiusing on to the hull is too abrupt. Part of the cure may be to add side brackets up the bearers and on to the hull shell. A structural floor or full athwartships bracket that links both bearers and extends out to the hull is a sign of good design engineering. It is also a good way to cure weak bearers, and compensate for their lack of length.

Even a small diesel has a considerable punch, and it vibrates ferociously, especially if carelessly installed or misaligned. It can tear itself free or weaken a pair of bearers in an hour. If the original

The blade sheered off this propeller in normal service. If the intact blade is examined carefully, lines in the metal can be seen exactly opposite the break, suggesting that the other blade is also weak.

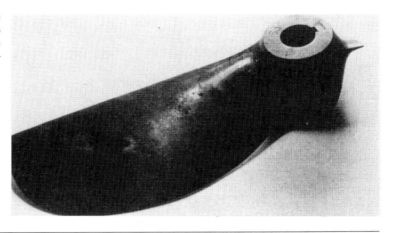

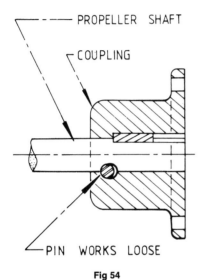

PROPELLER SHAFT

COUPLING

PIN WORKS LOOSE

Fig 54

Propeller shafts should be properly secured to couplings with a taper on the end of the shaft and a locked nut inside the coupling. The cheap substitute which depends on a pin driven into a hole bored half into the propeller shaft and half in the coupling is dangerous because the pin works loose.

installation was a petrol engine, and this has been changed to diesel without some beefing up of the bearers, then expect trouble.

It is not the best practice to set steel engine feet down on fibreglass bearers, though it is done often enough. The metal will not lie flat on the GRP, but perch on a high spot. This causes excessive local loadings and is an invitation to cracking. Builders will say that as they are using flexible mounts, they are not really putting harsh steel directly on to vulnerable fibreglass.

A better practice is to put the engine feet on long steel angle-bars port and starboard and bolt the latter to the fibreglass bearers. Sometimes these angle-bars are located on the inboard sides of the fibreglass upstanding strength members, with the vertical flanges of the steel bolted athwartships. There should be a minimum of four bolts each side up to 8 hp and sometime like one more for every 6 hp added. Setting the steel angle-bars inside the main bearers allows the latter to be higher than the bottom of the engine feet, and therefore they are stronger than usual.

Where engine feet have dug into the tops of the bearers, as happens sometimes with fibreglass and wood, it has to be assumed that the engine is no longer properly aligned. Checking this can only be done afloat, because boats change shape slightly as they are launched. The alignment is verified by undoing the coupling bolts; each one should slide out effortlessly with just a slight 'drag' caused by the snug fit. Couplings are tested with feeler gauges at top, bottom and each side to make sure the two mating faces are exactly parallel. In the same way, a straight edge laid at the top, bottom and sides should confirm that the edges of the two halves of the coupling are precisely in line, as they must be if the bolts are to slide easily into their holes.

Testing the alignment is normally done by a marine engineer and not by hull surveyors. Sometimes we are asked to confirm the findings. Some fitters say that a precise alignment is not necessary because there are flexible mountings under the feet, and because the coupling as well as the stern gland are flexible. However, the best marine engineers insist on lining up engines as accurately as possible to reduce noise and vibration, and also wear and future problems. Even when there is a form of universal joint that allows for misalignment, it is best to make the minimum demands on this – not least to save fuel and unnecessary stressing.

Running tests

There was a time when surveyors quite often tested engines without outside help. This job would only be done when the boat was afloat, because of the problem of setting up a flow of cooling water through the engine when the craft was ashore. With a freshwater cooled engine there is a point of view that the engine can at least be started and briefly run even when there is no salt water running through the heat exchangers. Against this, a short run is not a lot of use – a trial should run for two hours or more.

There is no doubt that even a short run does give some information, especially about how eager the machinery is to start, and it is tempting for a surveyor to press the starter to see what happens. However, there is a critical consideration here. We live in a litigious age, when too many people rush to a lawyer when they have some real or imagined or trumped-up grievance, so surveyors have to be ultra cautious. Engine-running trials are now done either by the owner while the surveyor looks on, or by a boatyard mechanic – or by anyone who can take the blame if it goes wrong, or the owner *claims* that it has gone wrong. The engine may have been defective before the test, but a few owners try to gain financially by claiming the tester has caused the problem.

A good engine test run lasts two or more hours because this gives time for the whole unit to get hot right through and any overheating problems to develop. It gives a chance for a poor fuel supply to make itself felt, and for the surveyor to crawl around the vibrating engine and take notes.

The things to look for are:

- Reluctant starting. The use of 'squirt' cans into the air intake tells a tale. Of course, the batteries must be fully charged for a fair test.
- Loose components and bolts, especially holding-down bolts.
- Leaks – which may only show up when the engine is running because the owner has been around the day before the surveyor arrives to clean off oil weeps and water dribbles.
- Exhaust leaks that can be smelt or felt or, in horrifying cases, seen.
- Too much vibration, or indeed any juddering of a rubber exhaust against a solid object, as this will cause chafing and, in time, asphyxiation.
- Overheating.
- Uneven running.
- Excessive noise.
- Lack of charging.
- Smoky exhaust discharges.
- Lack of ample cooling water at the outlet.
- And anything else that looks worrying!

· ·

ELECTRICAL EQUIPMENT

Of all the equipment on a boat, the electrical items are among the most worrying from the surveyor's point of view. An electrical 'box of tricks' that works on Monday may be out of action on Wednesday (as a result perhaps of a drop in voltage), back in action on Thursday when the batteries have been recharged, and defective by Saturday due to drips through a hatch or a corroding component.

Marine electronics and electrical equipment is not just a specialised business – it is also changing at a rate that even experts admit is disconcerting. Equipment that is too bulky and costly for most owners this year will be reduced in size as well as price and

connected on medium-sized racing yachts next year. Some three years later, it will be fitted on quite tiny cruisers.

There are so many aspects and complications in this matter that some surveyors simply ignore all the instruments, radios and navigation aids, while others list the type and name (also, where possible, the serial number) of the gadgets, but make no further comments. Part of the problem is that this gear cannot always be tested during an inspection, even if the surveyor knows how to operate the equipment and what defects to expect.

For instance, if the boat is ashore, the echo

sounder cannot be tested. In harbours and ashore it is illegal under some circumstanes to use radio transmitters. Many surveyors do not have all the necessary radio licences that allow them to transmit on all the equipment they come across. Radar cannot be used if there is a risk of anyone looking closely into the scanner, or if the scanner has no enveloping cover and might foul a loose halyard as it rotates. Instruments like radios and position finders that depend on satellites will not work if the vessel is ashore in a steel shed; and of course everything depends on a power supply, so if the batteries are not on board, or not properly charged, little testing can be carried out.

On any well-conducted boat the electrical equipment is serviced by an electronics specialist each year. Even so, some items will not run continuously and without trouble for 12 months, especially if the boat is out in all weathers and is hard driven. I have heard of naval vessels fully manned with skilled technicians that have had 20% of the electrical equipment out of action even though the ship was in full commission. Sea water and electricity do not get on well together, and it is the water that wins. Some items like radar and Decca may be rented, and the annual fee includes servicing. Under these circumstances the owner of the vessel will get reports from the firm hiring out the electronic equipment, and the surveyor is seldom involved, except perhaps to note the name, type and number of each item on board.

In general, most surveyors approach electrical gear in the same way as they do the engine. They look at it without opening up anything, or doing any dismantling. If there are signs of external corrosion and ageing, they will warn of probable troubles. They may indicate that valuers quite often depreciate electronic instruments over five or seven years in a straight line. This means that every year each item drops in value by a fifth or a seventh, so after four or six years the equipment will have a very low value. Admittedly, well-made instruments that are reliable often last for ten and sometimes 20 years, but few sailors rely on this. In general, good-quality VHF radios and echo sounders seem to run and run, although even here they must be protected from the weather and salt spray.

Signs of neat wiring and tidy installation are encouraging. Good installations have no festoons of cables hanging slackly, and the wiring is kept out of the bilge, away from machinery, and is not run along inside lockers where heavy gear is stowed. On well-wired craft there are clips every 15 to 20 cm (6 to 8 in) made of non-ferrous material with non-rusting fastenings. Groups of wire running in the same direction are tidily bundled together with plastic ties. There is at least partial colour-coding, and on the switchboard all switches are labelled. Joins are made at junction boxes and not just twisted together under a rough wrapping of plastic tape. Switches look as if they belong on a boat and not in a house, and there are no signs of rust or corrosion at the lights, motors, pumps, instruments and sockets.

In practice, it is quite common to find that the electrical installation is a mixture of good, so-so and horrible. If the boat is a typical mass-produced cruiser, many original components will be light in weight and rather delicate for ocean-going work. The wire may be undersized for the longest runs through the length of the boat if there is to be no voltage drop, but on the whole owners today are aware that batteries must be kept well charged, due to the heavy loads put on the electrical system.

If the original installation is about average, the surveyor cannot make many complaints, though he should warn of existing or impending troubles. In practice, a great many craft have additions to the original wiring system. Sometimes the old circuits have been abandoned but not taken right out, and this is risky.

Typical trouble spots to expect are:

- Fittings intended for motor cars used afloat. This equipment cannot stand up to a salt-laden damp atmosphere, and much of it lacks ruggedness or corrosion-proofing.
- Signs of corrosion at junction boxes, lights, motors, etc — especially where there is a hatch nearby to let in drips, or where the fitting is low down and can get splashed by bilge-water in rough weather.
- Signs of perishing. This used to be seen in the insulation on the cables, but now it is more common on grommets, where cables go into alloy masts or through bulkheads, or into pulpit tubes.
- Electronic equipment adjacent to equipment like electric motors, which cause unacceptable current surges.
- More than one item that uses heavy current on one 'thin-wired' circuit. Windscreen wipers and anchor winches take a lot of power. The latter must have their own private circuit.

- Two important items on the same circuit, so that both will fail at once if a fuse goes. It is clearly absurd to have two electric bilge pumps wired into the same line. The same applies to the principal and secondary navigation lights, both windscreen wipers and, on a big vessel, all the power winches on deck.
- Cables and bunches of cables that 'jump a gap'. This fault consists of running wires across an open space with no support. If anyone falls against them, or a heavy item rolls across the surrounding space, the wires take the thump. They pull out of the adjacent junction box or tear off the gadget they are supplying. It is a common defect even on well-wired craft and is found in the bilge and by engines, and also on deck near the watertight glands and the foot of the mast.

  In severe cases these loops of wire can move as the boat rolls, and in time the metal fatigues and the wire breaks. This can happen inside the insulation, so no one knows about it, and this can be the most difficult fault to trace, especially if the ends of the broken wire touch intermittently – so that one minute the fault is there, then it's gone, then it's back again.
- Electric cables near fuel tanks and bottled gas containers. This is asking for trouble. Where there is no alternative, the cables should be in metal conduit that is earthed.

When carrying out a comprehensive inspection on a large vessel or prior to a major voyage on a smaller one, a good case can be made for having specialists working alongside the hull surveyor. There may be an engineer working on the machinery, a fridge specialist checking the cooling equipment, and an electronics man working in his field. If the purpose of the inspection is to inform a buyer about the condition of the vessel before he parts with his money, a more logical approach is to have the hull survey first. This may reveal so much trouble that the secondary surveys are not worth starting.

Whoever does the electrical survey should spend time on the navigation lights, especially if the boat is old or under 9 m (30 ft), because these craft so often have problems. It is common to find that the lights are not rigidly fixed, so there may be fatigue cracks on the brackets or chafed wiring. Starboard lights that show to port and vice versa are found in something like one boat out of eight or ten. Stern lights that do not show over the required arc because of nearby obstructions like lifebuoys, ensign staffs and pulpit stanchions are found in perhaps five boats for every hundred examined. Naturally, the glasses must not be cracked or loose and the reflectors should be shiny all over, free from corrosion and securely held in place.

Cables should run upwards into all electrical items, but especially navigation lights, to minimise the risk that water will find its way into the casing. Where the cables enter any fitting there must be a tight seal, and the bedding compound round light glasses and access covers must be fresh, flexible and intact.

. . . .

BATTERIES

The batteries on any craft have steadily increased in importance, as more and more electrical equipment is fitted. It is widely agreed that fishing boats, pilot boats, yachts over 8 m (26 ft) long, and even the smallest commercial craft, need at least two principal batteries. One is for starting the engine, and the other for general services. These batteries are on separate circuits, so that the failure of one does not endanger the ship. On craft over 12 m (40 ft) the trend is to have at least three batteries, though two may be on one circuit, which usually deals with lighting and electronics, etc, with the single one reserved for engine starting. It is the general practice to have changeover switches so that both banks of batteries can be used for both main purposes, but only when the crew make a deliberate changeover.

Just where a surveyor starts to make recommendations and condemnations is a matter of experience, local conditions, the use to which the craft is going to be put, and the requests made by the person commissioning the survey. My own procedure is to look at the electrical system as a whole, and encourage owners to go for more than basic safety. In bad weather offshore, one wants extra safety features, reliable equipment and secondary sources of power. For instance, on craft over 14 m (46 ft) used for extended cruising, I suggest that there should be a spare stand-by battery (located high up above potential flooding), which can be used for radio transmissions, etc if the main banks of batteries are swamped. They have to be stowed low down because they are heavy, so they are vulnerable to early drowning if water starts to get into the hull in large quantities.

Battery stowage is poor on about half the vessels afloat. Each battery should be in an acid-tight container, located so that the gases given off during recharging are taken away effectively. No battery should shift even slightly when the vessel turns keel upwards, or runs aground at full speed. On fishing vessels it is common to find that the batteries are not secured tightly, unprotected from spray, and not positioned so that it is easy to check their condition.

Even if the batteries cannot be given any electrical tests, they should be inspected to see when they were made, their capacity and voltage, and also their external condition. There should be ample grease at each post, and the cable end fitting should be clean, greased all over and well secured. There should be no sign of corrosion or salt deposits. The top should be free from cracks, level and even. Each battery casing

should be checked for damage, leaks and signs of abuse. In some countries there are regulations covering the way batteries are installed, and freed from gases. Many yacht racing rules have special requirements about the securing of batteries, and surveyors have to know about these.

Quite often when a vessel is laid up, the batteries are taken off and put on trickle charge in the boatyard's engine shop or in a special battery store. This is good practice and indicates that someone cares about the boat. When the batteries are on board, a few surveyors test their condition. If the main switchboard has a voltage tester, it is worth seeing what this gives as the condition of the batteries, though the cheaper versions of these gadgets are not 100% reliable and accurate. When fully charged, a 12 volt battery should give nearly 13 volts, and the hydrometer reading should be about 1.212. The plates should be covered by the fluid electrolyte, and this is something many surveyors confirm. This check cannot be made with sealed 'maintenance-free' batteries, but this type should be looked over for external signs of over-heating.

In general, batteries that *look* as if they should be on the scrap heap probably should be. They have a life of about five years, and they are too important to ignore or treat leniently. If in doubt, new batteries should be recommended. It is almost certainly true to say that battery failure is one of the seven most common sources of trouble afloat.

· · · · · · · · · ·

TANKS

As a surveyor travels to look at a boat, he knows he is going to find defects in one out of three tanks. He knows that fishing boat tanks tend to be rusty inside and out, with no sign that the inspection door has been taken off in recent years. Proof of this is the unblemished paint on all the bolts. As he drives along, he recalls that many cheap yachts have flexible plastic tanks just laid inside rough fibreglass hulls, so the tanks get chafed as the boat rolls. These floppy low-cost tanks are not firmly secured, so if the boat inverts the tank will come adrift. There should be some form of semi-soft padding or at least a PVC

cloth between the hull and the tank to prevent abrasion.

Big motor-cruisers have tanks that are so well built in that it is impossible to replace them without a massive amount of extra work, removing piping and wiring, as well as a generator or two. Such tanks must be suspect, because no one wants to go to the expense and trouble of doing all the dismantling and reassembly work, just for boring old tanks.

It is daunting to realise that a mild steel tank can rust at about 0.125 mm per year *on each side*. This means that a tank made of 3 mm ($\frac{1}{8}$ in) plating will last 12

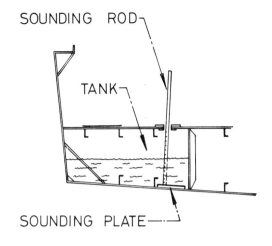

SOUNDING ROD

TANK

SOUNDING PLATE

Fig 55

If no sounding plate is fitted in a steel tank it is likely that there will be a lot of corrosion where the sounding rod strikes the bottom of the tank. It is important to examine this area as well as any bottom corners of tanks because this is where corrosion is most likely.

years. If there are outside effects, such as bacteria or galvanic action, the erosion rate can be more than three times as fast. The outside of a tank is often wetted then dried, which speeds up the process of erosion. Inside, the growth of bacteria is unseen – and thus unsuspected. Few owners believe that their mild steel fuel tanks can become useless within four years, but it does happen. The signs are drips round the bottom. If fuel is weeping out, it darkens the tank and a finger rubbed over the stain becomes oily and smells of diesel. Rust on the outside is indicative of the same inside. Water lies at the bottom of all fuel tanks, and though it may only be a tiny puddle, it is enough to cause constant corrosion. It gets there by condensation and from the fuel, which contains a little water accumulated from the storage tanks and delivery vehicles.

Large steel tanks, in big well-built motor-cruisers, have drip trays beneath and drip channels along the bottom of inspection doors. These drip-catchers should be dry, so if there is any fuel in them the surveyor starts searching for tiny holes in the plating (often too tiny to see without a magnifying glass) and defects in the access door seals. Some tanks have sight gauges down one side and the cocks on these should be tested, as they tend to seize up with monotonous frequency. Every fuel tank should have a cock right at the beginning of the fuel supply pipe, as well as on the engine. Incidentally, sight gauges have

the advantage of reliability, whereas more modern fuel level indicators are not consistently good.

On small craft such as yachts and motor-cruisers, it is rare to find two shut-off cocks in the fuel line. The one that is fitted has often seized, and is accessible only to an emaciated pygmy. It is also cunningly hidden. A surveyor might help everyone by suggesting how it could be made more accessible, then it would be used more and work longer.

All tanks, whatever they are for, must be firmly fixed down, so that they do not move even slightly. If a tank is full it can be heavier than the engine, so it needs to be as well secured. If it is three-quarters full, it can build up momentum when the boat rolls, and start to try and batter its way out. If it wriggles enough to get a little bit free, it will enlarge the movement by constant jolting. Even before this becomes dangerous, it can sever pipes leading from the tank, emptying the contents into the bilge. These pipes should never be part of the securing arrangements, unless the tank is less than 5 gallons capacity when the filler may act as a secondary support. All medium and large tanks need chocks or a strong bulkhead or pillars at the fore end to prevent the tank slithering forward when the boat grounds or is in a collision.

Even if the vessel does not go to sea and the tank is so heavy that it seems safe, it still needs to be well fastened in place. Inshore craft often go aground, and then may heel steeply. They also bump into solid objects and stop with a jolt. The tank should not move under these conditions. Where a tank is fastened to the hull by flanges, there should be at least three and, better still, a minimum of five bolts in each flange. Screws are only acceptable where it is impossible to reach in and put nuts on bolts. These screws have to be heavy ones – at least 12 gauge even on a small vessel. The flanges should run right along the side of the tank, though in some cases it is acceptable for them to extend three-quarters this distance. Short flanges sheer off, especially if they are thin or not welded 'round the end'.

Solid plastic tanks, especially the sensible type that are transparent so that the contents can be seen, are often held in place by straps. The rules here are:

● There should be at least two straps.
● The straps should ideally be made so that they can be tightened, though this is rare.
● Each end of each strap needs at least two bolts in sheer. If screws have to be used, there should be

three each end, always in sheer – never in tension, because they might pull out.

- As each strap has to be strong enough to support four times the weight of the full tank, it is usual to use metal straps.
- There must be some form of padding between a metal strap and a tank, even if the tank is metal. This padding may be wood, felt or plastic, and it needs securing so that it cannot slide out sideways when the straps stretch a little.
- Straps on their own are not enough. There must be chocks, pillars or strong bulkheads as further restraints. If a strap has been rubbing on a tank, look for weld fractures and denting if the tank is metal, and for chafing if the tank is plastic.

The importance of holding tanks down properly was emphasised in one light GRP hull I was inspecting. The stainless tank edge was against the inside of the fibreglass shell and able to move slightly; it had ground through a substantial depth, and was literally working its way out to the sea. Of course, metal tanks need padding between them and any fibreglass structure.

There is evidence that rigid plastic tanks age harden, and should be kept out of direct sunlight. This may involve fitting a PVC cover over, or some such. Their edges are sometimes well rounded, which means chocks at the base have to be high and reach above the radiused part. Flexible plastic tanks need clever strapping in place to prevent them from shifting when almost empty, yet they must be able to fill fully. There is seldom a shut-off cock on each one, but there should be, bearing in mind that the cheap versions of these containers have a reputation for lasting about four years. If one leaks, this should not result in all the water escaping into the bilge. It is double common sense to fit each one with its own isolating cock where these tanks are used on long-range cruisers to supplement the tanks originally fitted. Whatever tanks are fitted on ocean-crossing yachts, there should be some simple way of getting a supply of drinking water if the galley pump fails. Incidentally there is a vast difference between the common and the expensive versions of these rubbery tanks. The best versions are made by firms that supply the aircraft industry, and cost maybe three times as much as the cheap type – but seem to outlast them by a large factor.

Diesel fuel cannot be stowed in copper or galvanised tanks because chemical reactions occur. Fuel tanks made of fibreglass must contain a self-

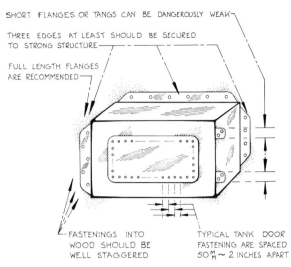

SHORT FLANGES OR TANGS CAN BE DANGEROUSLY WEAK

THREE EDGES AT LEAST SHOULD BE SECURED TO STRONG STRUCTURE

FULL LENGTH FLANGES ARE RECOMMENDED

FASTENINGS INTO WOOD SHOULD BE WELL STAGGERED

TYPICAL TANK DOOR FASTENING ARE SPACED 50 M/M ~ 2 INCHES APART

Fig 56

Tanks made of metal or fibreglass need to be secured in place so firmly that they will not wiggle when the boat turns over. Some tanks are made with flanges along the edges to take bolts. Provided these flanges extend almost the full length they work well, but short ones fail where they join the tank. Tank doors need close spaced bolts to prevent leaking, especially when diesel is carried. The gaskets under tank lids need renewing every few years.

quenching resin. Just looking at the tank will not tell anyone just what material has been used, so a certificate from the manufacturer is needed. Diesel destroys ferro-cement, and fuel tanks in craft built of this material need double protection, such as extra-strong thick-walled tanks plus drip trays.

A surveyor has to be familiar with his country's government regulations concerning tanks. It is a pity that such rules, which are laid down as minimum standards, promptly become the maximum any builder is prepared to go to. This is seen for instance in regulations laid down concerning baffles. These internal walls are principally fitted to prevent the fluid sloshing about too much. However, they serve a secondary purpose, in that they substantially strengthen a tank.

One set of regulations lays down that baffles should be 70% of the height and width of the tank. Anyone determined to save money can see that the easy way out is to carry the baffle up from the base for just 70% of the height. This, though, gives no support to the top of the tank, which is always walked over when sole boards are taken up. A good baffle extends to the top, bottom and out to the sides of a tank, with a hole in the middle to allow anyone peering in the access door to see to the end of the tank, and reach in to clean the full length. It also needs so-called 'mouse-holes' at each bottom and top corner to allow fuel to flow freely along the tank.

When surveying, it is hard to tell if a tank has got proper baffles without taking the door off, though tapping along the tank may give some clues, as the sound will change at a baffle. There may be weld dimples on the outside, but unscrupulous fabricators just fit angle-bars inside tanks instead of proper baffles. When checking through one 80 ft motor-cruiser I came across a sensational problem caused by fitting too few baffles in a stainless steel tank made with plating that was too thin. This water tank was filled up in a commercial harbour with a hose that delivered a lot of water in a short time. The tank bulged so that the sides bellied out, and the top curved up. The result was:

- A cabin bulkhead was pushed up at the bottom and forced sideways.
- The cabin sole lifted and refused to go back in place.
- The sole bearers were torn up at the ends.
- Two cabin doors refused to shut.

Stainless steel tanks are now widely used, but the welds are not always made with the right material, so rusting occurs along the edges. The best tanks have folded edges at the bottom, as this saves a lot of welding. Stainless steel tanks in the bilge of a steel vessel should be painted on the outside, though this is rarely seen.

Tanks must be seen to have a strength and wall thickness consistent with the size of vessel. A surveyor's second-best weapon, after his eyes, is a heavy foot. This is placed against a tank edge and top, to see if there is any movement, and check whether the tank is made of paper-thin material. Stainless plate down to 1 mm ($\frac{1}{32}$ in) is only acceptable on small racing craft. The least one can accept for sea-going vessels is 2 mm ($\frac{1}{16}$ in), and this requires proper supporting on the underside, and three tank edges secured. The consequences of a tiny failure in a tank are large. Races are lost and cruises are ruined. Getting rid of the smell of diesel or sewage from the bilge after a tank has dumped its contents is a long unpleasant business.

It is not usual to open up tanks during a normal survey, unless the boat is going off on a round-the-world trip. However, if the engine is to be taken apart, this is a sensible opportunity to look inside all the tanks. A large steel tank that has no access hatch should be treated with suspicion. It might be tested ultrasonically, but the part most likely to be corroded is the bottom, and this will be hard to reach on many craft. A good rule is that all tanks should be inspected internally and cleaned out at least once every four years.

Surveyors spend a lot of time being told by owners that there is not enough money for a particular repair job. However, a good surveyor can earn his fee (and some acclaim) by suggesting that a rusty galvanised water tank can sometimes be repaired very cheaply. This idea is beautifully simple. The bottom is cut off and perhaps 25 mm (1 in) of the sides at the bottom. It is easy enough to weld on a new bottom and the tank loses very little capacity. It would have needed regalvanising even if it had been in fairly good condition, and the cost of repairs is far less than the cost of a new tank. Little if any of the piping will need altering, and the tank will fit in place with just a few adjustments to the top chocks and straps.

Fuel tanks should in theory never be sited so that they feed to the engine by gravity. On small craft one has to put the tank where there is available space, and ensure that leaks are unlikely. Some small power plants do not have fuel suction pipes, so they have to have a gravity feed. In this case, the tanks should not be larger than 2 gallons capacity.

If there are signs of fuel in the bilge, the surveyor should make a fuss about this in his report. Under what are admittedly rather unusual circumstances, even diesel fuel can catch fire. Petrol in the bilge is so serious that the boat must be put out of action until the source of the leak has been found and cured. Also, the spillage in the bilge has to be scrupulously removed. By running a hand all round the bottom of a fuel tank, it is possible to discover if there are drips here. As fluids run downhill, the drips will be at the lowest corner of the tank, but the hole may be at the opposite side or at a pipe connection. Pipe ends are a weakness, which is why the best builders put the fuel suction line out through the top of the tank, with the pipe extending down inside the tank.

Fresh water tanks must not be adjacent to fuel or sewage tanks. There must be at least two oil-tight barriers between them. In theory, water tanks should not be next to areas that can contain oily bilge-water, but this is seldom achieved. No tank should be close to an exhaust pipe or other major heat source.

TANK PIPING

After I have refuelled my boat, I stick duct tape over the filler on the sidedeck to prevent water getting into the tank. This says a lot about the widely used flush-deck tank fillers. They have screw-caps that depend for their watertightness on a thin washer under the screw-down cap that does not last long. It soon becomes compressed hard, perishes or breaks, or even gets lost overboard when the cap is off because it does not fit tightly.

In our office, when we are designing anything over 14 m (46 ft), we like to work in special fillers that are located well above deck, with bronze screw-on cover caps. These are made in the form of inverted bowls with plenty of thread length up the inside of the 'skirt'. Water has to find its way through this ample threaded section before it can get into the tank, and as a further line of defence there is a thick, flat, full-width washer beneath the top of the cap. Now *that's* what I call a safe sensible filler — but unfortunately the surveyor rarely discovers anything so reliable (except perhaps on large craft).

What he does sometimes find is a horrible arrangement whereby the deck filler cap is taken off and underneath there is a second cap. When refuelling, spillage goes into the bilge because there is a gap between the deck and the inner filler. This makes for smells if the fuel is diesel, and explosions if it is petrol. Even when this inlet is for the water tank, it is a nuisance having the inside of the boat made wet unnecessarily (See Fig 57.).

For these reasons, it is universally agreed that any filler should be connected directly to its tank, usually by a plastic pipe that slides on to the deck fitting and on to a short length of piping welded to the top of the tank. There should be two hose clamps on each end of this plastic pipe. The deck filler is made of metal, and it should be electrically bonded to the tank. This is seen on expensive boats, but not all of them. It is important that all fillers are labelled, but I have seen the inlet for a diesel tank marked with the word 'Gasoline', which means petrol in most languages. I have also seen water and fuel tank fillers close together; this is risky, and something a surveyor should condemn.

In theory, a *small* tank does not need an air pipe, merely a small hole at the top of the filler. There are even official organisations that accept this, though they do not encourage it. The practice is probably tolerable on a low-speed power-driven estuary boat used for fishing, where the tank is inside the undecked hull. However, even here it seems unsatisfactory since water can get in, and the hole may get blocked with dirt because it has to be small. A good air pipe is twice the diameter of the fuel supply line or, better still, half the diameter of the filler. What one finds in practice is that on well-built craft up to about 11 m (36 ft), the air pipe is 12 mm ($\frac{1}{2}$ in) and works satisfactorily, except perhaps when filling the tank very fast. Air pipes much smaller than that seem to be unreliable, and I've come across blockages in 6 mm ($\frac{1}{4}$ in) air pipes caused by overflowing fuel or water that seem hard to get out of the pipe.

Air pipes on fuel tanks have to be led up on deck to a sheltered spot, and terminated by a gauze cover or flame screen. Water tank breathers may be carried up to a high point inside the hull, but should be located where no damage can be done if there is an accidental overflow. This means somewhere in the galley or toilet compartment, and not in a clothes cupboard. The top of all air pipes should turn through 180 degrees, so that the end points downwards and dirt cannot get in. They have to be high above the top of the tank, even when the boat is heeling well over, in order to prevent spillage.

Fuel supply and return pipes are generally of seamless drawn copper, except on cheap boats where they are made of plastic from tank to engine. The latter is becoming accepted on small cruisers with diesel engines on the basis that the run of piping is short, and that a length of flexible tube is needed in any case by the engine to cope with its vibration. However, surveyors do worry about using piping that is not fireproof, and on petrol engines this is entirely unacceptable.

A dreadful practice, found on botched-up boats, is a fuel return pipe that does not lead back to the tank. Sometimes they go to a portable can, and I've even seen one led to an old milk bottle that had to be frequently emptied into the fuel tank. Modern diesels are designed to pump through a great deal more fuel

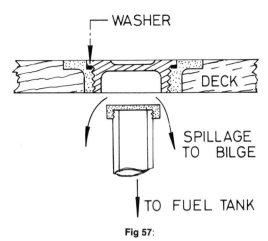

WASHER

DECK

SPILLAGE TO BILGE

TO FUEL TANK

Fig 57:

A common cause of petrol explosions in the bilge is spilt fuel. When filling the tanks it is easy to let some dribble down the side of the filler pipe if there is a gap below the deck. Overfilling the tank is even more serious with this type of installation. The cure is to have a filler pipe which extends right to the deck, so that the pipe cap and deck plate are all one.

than the engine needs, so the return pipe carries a lot of fuel in an hour. It should be led in through the top and down inside to the bottom of the main fuel container to prevent it causing bubbling in the tank, because this results in air trapped in the fuel supply line. It is logical to use aluminium piping on aluminium craft for all the pipes, though there will normally be short lengths of plastic to make the fitting of tanks easy.

When checking pipes for leaks and security, it is important to peer closest at any that 'jump across gaps' with no supporting structure. Unsupported pipes are vulnerable to heavy-footed people who tread without looking and break or bend things. Pipes should be clipped up at close intervals. On cheap boats they are looped through lockers, totally unsecured so that gear drops on them, and they get squeezed or kinked and choked. When there is time and opportunity, it is a good idea to look inside filters. Tanks made of fibreglass give off fluff, if badly made, and this clogs pipes and filters. Where any two tanks serve one supply line there should be shut-off cocks, so that each tank can be isolated, and when the tanks are fitted port and starboard there should be a balancing pipe with a cock in the middle. Without this shut-off valve, the tank contents will always flow to the 'downhill' side; this is bad for stability and may result in difficulty getting the contents out of the tank if the suction point is on the 'uphill' side.

· · · · · · · · · · · · · ·

PLUMBING

As with so many parts of a boat, an enthusiastic surveyor is tempted to dismantle all the plumbing. In theory, he would like to disconnect every pipe, heave out all the tanks, strip all the pumps, and (ideally) slice up lots of parts to see what they were like inside. In practice, he does the best he can within the limited access inside all craft and within the time he can reasonably allocate to each part.

Prior to a major voyage, a good case can be made for a massive programme of dismantling. This might enable the total number of seacocks to be reduced, and this always makes for extra safety. Seacocks are one of the vulnerable parts on all craft and are probably responsible for one in two or three of all sinkings not caused by bad weather. A good basic rule is that every four years all seacocks should be taken right off the vessel, fully stripped down, examined, serviced, greased and reassembled, then refitted with ample bedding. Some surveyors recommend that one-quarter of the seacocks are taken out every year, but this seems to me to be less than clever. On plenty of small craft there are only eight seacocks, so if any are being taken out it's sensible to do the lot at once. If the work is being given to a boatyard, it will certainly be cheaper that way.

When a boat is being bought, unless there is clear evidence that all the seacocks have been recently stripped down, the buyer automatically has them all out for a full inspection. The surveyor does not need to mention this, just as he seldom mentions that the boat needs anti-fouling. What most surveyors do is turn on each seacock then close it, to see how much wear is apparent. He may tap each one with a light hammer to see if there is massive corrosion, but this cannot be done when afloat in case the answer is 'Yes' and the boat promptly starts to sink! Only once have

I broken a seacock on a yacht that was afloat, and that was by accident when I slipped against it. The cock was a new-fangled one made of plastic. I had one of my sons with me, and we both agreed that the seacock looked unseaworthy, so we were both taking care not to bash it even lightly with a hammer. The sole boards were up and I was manoeuvring cautiously past the seacock. I then stood on some grease, slid spectacularly, and confirmed our suspicions. I held my thumb over the hole, while my son sharpened a brush handle and stuck it in the hole, before making notes about flimsy plastic seacocks.

Good plumbing, like all boatbuilding, *looks* good. It is neat and uniform. That is to say, the seacocks are not a motley collection, but all are alike – or at least are in batches that are all the same. It is suspicious if no two seacocks match and the piping is part steel, part copper and three sorts of different plastic, because this suggests amateur botching and bad professional repair work. Well-built fibreglass and wooden yachts have doublers on the hull in way of the seacocks, and the very finest steel and aluminium hulls have extra-thick plates in the way of the cocks, though this is rare. The very best doublers taper out

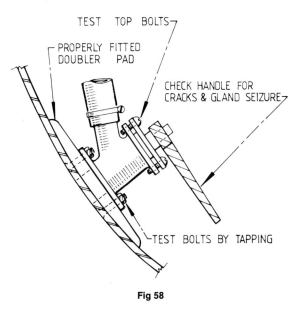

Fig 58

All seacocks should be stripped off and examined when possible. Sometimes this work is left until after the survey, so the surveyor just taps the securing bolts, taps the gland all over and checks that the handle is in position. If the handle has a crack it suggests that the gland has been very tight and seized at some time. A seized gland needs taking apart for full maintenance and if the handle is missing it must be replaced because it will certainly be needed in a hurry one day.

at the edges. Thin hulls with no doublers receive a curt note on the surveyor's clipboard.

If a seacock is inaccessible, it may be many years since it was last checked. A buyer will appreciate a suggestion or two to show how the adjacent furniture can be altered or perhaps a better access hole jigsawed. Much of the piping will be hidden, so the general condition of what is visible has to be assessed. Boats that are kept in freezing climates must have no dips in the runs of metal piping unless there are drain-cocks at the bottom of each loop, otherwise the pipes cannot be entirely emptied and they will burst in the coldest weather. Standard fibreglass boats are not fitted with drain-cocks in the water systems, because all the piping is of cheap easily-run transparent plastic.

Some soft plastic piping is unsuitable for hot water as it becomes too soft when it heats up. Clear plastic pipe used for fresh water should be of 'food' quality; however, it is often just the ordinary sort. Not many sailors seem to die from this, doubtless because they drink so little water. The correct quality of piping often has a faint mauve tinge to distinguish it from the commercial type. There is a fallacy that plastic piping can be taken round almost any bend. On the contrary, one of the common plumbing faults is a kinked plastic pipe that is throttling the flow of liquid. Where a plastic pipe has to go round a sharp bend, it is necessary to fit a metal angle pipe section or, better still, an 'elbow' that sweeps round the curve gently and does not impede the flow the way that a sharp bend does. At each end of every plastic pipe there should be a stainless steel hose clamp. The best-built boats have twin clamps at each junction, but this is rare. Clamps that are not stainless steel rust quickly; many of these low-price substitutes have a thin layer of electroplating or a sprayed-on compound to keep away the rust. I have seen new boats in boat shows that already have rust on this type of hose clamp.

It is quite common to find many seacocks seized solid, especially those under the cockpit that are usually hard to reach. Even if only one or two are seized, it is sensible to recommend that they are all taken out for a full service. If no amount of hole-cutting in quarter-berth sides or ends or bases makes these cocks accessible, it is probable that the answer is an extension on each handle. These long rods are often secured to the seacock with a universal joint, so that the handle can be angled to some convenient point where the crew can easily reach it without being contortionists. The drains from the cockpit should be crossed, so that the port one goes out of the starboard seacock and vice versa. Only if the cockpit well is high above sea level can this precaution be ignored. On cheap boats, outlets that are above the waterline have no seacocks. This applies to important drains, large ones, ones very close to the waterline, and ones immersed the moment the boat heels a little. This has become the widespread and presumably acceptable practice used by a large section of the industry. It is perhaps justified by the relatively few craft that sink as a result. It does confirm the recommendation that all boats should have in their safety kit a set of suitable soft-wood plugs for bunging up these holes.

Many years ago it was the practice to fit lead piping. Among the techniques used was one whereby the end of the pipe was belled out, and the flange made in this way was nailed directly on to the inside of the hull. It is a miracle that this arrangement survived even a week. It looks risky – and it is. The fastenings do not grip tightly, the lead corrodes, and it is so soft that it can easily be pierced by a small accident. Lead piping is no longer acceptable afloat.

Basins and sinks need checking to confirm that they are firmly secured in place. They may flood back when the boat heels, so it may be necessary to fit a pump to ensure that they can be emptied at sea. WCs need checking for cracking, particularly round the base flanges. If a bolt is over tightened or is not square in its hole, or the semi-soft washer under its head or nut has been forgotten, cracking is likely. Holding-down bolts are hard to fit, so that some of them get forgotten, or become loose, or they are so badly put in that they are ineffective. They live in a damp climate and they rust unless they are of good-quality stainless steel or bronze. The base plinth is often wet and stressed, so it may become loose or its fastenings may fail. There is nothing so disconcerting as sitting on a WC that breaks free in a rough sea, so a surveyor needs to spend time with his head down in this area to decide what fitting might come adrift.

The pumping on WC falls into two classes:

1 Modern, lightweight, fairly cheap to replace, but prone to cracking, especially at flanges and bolts. Also, they wear after a few short years at the top pump glands, where there is no method of tightening the seal. Rough handling, which can be inevitable in heavy weather offshore, causes bent and broken pump handles and sometimes broken pumps. Renewal of parts, not repairs, is the cure.

2 Traditional, heavier, but more reliable. The components are made of metal, or at least the vulnerable ones are. Repairs are usually possible and there is a gland that can be tightened where the handle rod (or rods) emerges from the pump(s). These glands can be repacked, and this should be done every few years – or more frequently if the crew live aboard.

Toilet seats and covers work loose because they are badly made or secured. Some are held by plastic bolts that stretch easily and break if well tightened. The answer is often metal bolts with semi-soft washers under the metal washers at the heads and nuts. Pump clevis pins and other linkages wear, so bushing or other repair work is needed here. However, repairing a toilet has become expensive, and quotes should be obtained for fitting a new one if there are many defects. To keep down the cost of replacement, it is best to fit a new version of the current model, provided it is well made. Rust, corrosion, cracks and leaks are found on all old WCs. No one likes the resulting smells and problems, so this is one area where perfection is universally sought.

There is one make of WC that is flushed by dropping the lid and sucking the contents out with a diaphragm pump. The lid seal must be renewed if it becomes loose or perished. Here, as with all diaphragm pumps, the flap valves need replacing every so often, though they can be turned upside down if they have become set with a permanent bend. This type of pump must be bolted in place, never screwed. There have been reports of small children working the pump while sitting on the lavatory and this could be dangerous. The pump handle should be well away from the WC, so that children cannot reach it while sitting on the pan.

VENTILATION

There are people who feel that ventilation is hardly the concern of a surveyor. The argument is that it is a minor matter, and that one might as well comment about the colour of a boat. However, it just so happens that colour does matter: dark colours make a boat hot in the tropics, and increase the need for effective ventilation.

Incidentally, dark colours fade faster than light ones, and blue fades quickest of all. Dark colours, though, make a boat look smaller, so if a boat has just been changed from a light colour, and the owner has put her on the market at the same time, maybe he is trying to hide more than most owners who are trying to find a buyer.

Two types of ventilation are needed: the first is to ensure that the crew do not get headaches, or even die; the second is to keep the inside of the boat dry and free from mildew, corrosion, rot and other problems related to dampness. In practice, on most boats the crew are supplied with some air, but seldom enough, and the hull has to do the best it can with what little flow of air there is.

Most small craft are built down to a minimum price, and not up to any particular standard of excellence, so ventilators are kept to a minimum or left off entirely. Even when provision is made to get air flowing through the deck, little effort is made to circulate it round inside the whole hull. Even a beginner in the surveying profession knows that the majority of boats more than three years old have puddles in low-level lockers. He knows that water in the bilge seldom evaporates because air cannot flow under the sole. He appreciates that carpeting glued to the hull at bunk-sides gets dark mildew stains because moisture is not dried up promptly. He soon appreciates that almost every locker afloat lacks the necessary holes or inlets to let air flow in and out again, to ensure dryness. Some high-quality builders put wickerwork or woven straw fronts to the lockers and this lets a little air through. Others cut decorative shapes out of locker doors, in the form of anchors or flowers. This is a small step in the right direction, but it is far from adequate. What is needed are big unblocked holes, large enough to put a hand through, so that air flows at all times, unimpeded,

helped by the smallest changes in the local pressure and temperature. Good ventilation is non-stop ventilation.

Louvres in doors do work quite well, but not as effectively as large rectangular slots. In the same way, a row of 25 mm (1 in) diameter holes in the door of a locker do not guarantee that air will flow through. What is needed are two holes at least 150 × 50 mm (6 × 2 ins) located at diagonal corners of each enclosed space to make sure plenty of air can get in and out, carrying away moisture with no effort. One of the best ways to ensure air flow is to cut away part of the tops and bottoms of doors into compartments and lockers. This can be done in an attractive way, leaving the door-posts intact, and scalloping out neat ovals. The rising warm air goes in the bottom and out the top, taking droplets of moisture with it. When the weather is getting colder, chilled air filters in the reverse direction.

Lack of ventilation accelerates metal corrosion, and is seen at light fittings and cheaply made door furniture. Under berth cushions there are sometimes extensive puddles, but of course these may be caused by leaks. It is a good sign to see hand-sized slots in berth bases to ventilate the undersides of cushions and the insides of the lockers.

Electric fans are seldom a comprehensive cure for ventilation problems, because they only work when there is plenty of electrical capacity. This means that they are on for perhaps a third of the time the crew are on board, and hardly at all on long voyages. Gadgets like wind-generators can be linked to power-driven vents, so that once the batteries are topped right up the fans start to work. Solar panels can be linked the same way, and one special type of flat vent has its own solar panel. Fan vents are principally found in toilet compartments and over the galley. They will not work well in either location if air cannot easily flow to them. This confirms the need for large slots in doors.

The boat's own fans are silent during the winter period when the boat is ashore. This is why careful owners put heaters or fans (or both) low down on board in the off season, to circulate warm air and lift moisture out. It is essential to have capacious inlets and outlets to encourage air to flow freely, which explains why experienced owners lock the main and forward hatches, so that they are burglar-proof but slightly open. Built-in fans should be flameproof or sparkproof, a fact that is noted on the fan's motor. This is seldom important if the fan is over the toilet, but all fans should be interchangeable so that one set of spares suits them all. As the fans in the engine compartment must be safe and spark-proof, it is logical to have them all like this.

Forced and natural ventilation in the engine space should be ducted to a low point. In an ideal world there should be an inlet and outlet for the air that passes through the machine compartment, but it is surprisingly difficult to achieve this all the time. A popular approach is to acknowledge that the engine will suck in a vast amount of air when it is working, so there is less need to force *air* into the engine bay. The logical thing is to blow it out, and this is the way a single engine room fan should work. It must not discharge into the crew's face when they are sitting in the cockpit or wheelhouse. Its job is to get rid of fumes, fuel vapour and smells. A good arrangement is to have the engine fan linked to the engine switch, so that starting one gets the other going at the same time.

Bottled gas compartments almost always rely on the fact that this gas flows downhill, being heavier than air. Thus its vent piping is taken from the bottom of the locker, and led in a gentle slope (always downwards) to the outside atmosphere in such a way that no puddles can block the free flow. Gas trying to go down a pipe that has a dip below the horizontal will often find a puddle of condensation blocking the exit.

Lack of ventilation is normally easy to cure, but time and money are needed for the job. It is always tempting to go for the cheap way out, but before plastic mushroom vents are fitted it should be remembered that these are delicate. If a child stands on one it is likely to fracture across the middle bar that supports the threaded vertical rod. Owners like to sit the broken vent neatly in place and hope that the surveyor misses the break. The cure is either a metal mushroom vent, or a new plastic one with a metal guard over the top. If only one side of this cross-bar is broken, the trouble can only be seen from below. Repairs normally cost as much as fitting a replacement. Mushroom vents fitted right at the bow and right at the stern of wooden vessels are well worth having, even if they have to be closed down tight before leaving harbour. They circulate air in those vulnerable regions that always rot first: right up in the bow at the breast-hook, and round the transom, together with its framing, and at the quarter knees. Deck leaks at the extreme ends of many wooden boats are out of sight and thus out of mind, and this is why these mushroom vents are such a sensible precaution.

Metal cowl vents should be checked for cracks, corrosion and crude repairs. If a steel cowl has rusted round the bottom, it is sometimes cheaper to cut off the lower part rather than go for total renewal, provided there is enough length of upstanding tube.

Bronze cowl vents are expensive, and few owners have the time or the paid crew to polish them. Also, they do tend to dent easily unless they are cast – and these are as rare as fisherman topsails. However, when a surveyor comes across them, he knows that he is usually looking at a very well-built vessel.

Steel cowl vents should be galvanised and painted. Even then, they have a propensity to rust round the base, often from the inside. All cowls should be designed so that they can be swivelled into or away from the wind. Metal ones tend to seize, or become so loose that they can be swept off by a breaking wave.

Plastic cowls weather and harden with age. They need safety lines, as they get knocked off by careless deck-hands or by headsails if they are located forward of the mast. Like all cowls, the best versions come with deck plates or covers, which means that the crew can seal the hole through the deck at the onset of severe weather.

Boats going far offshore should be able to seal all vents tightly, to make the hull as much like a submarine as possible. Where there is a proper engine room, complete with a CO_2 system to douse fires, it must be possible to shut all vents to this space from outside. What is more, the vents have to be able to be closed instantly by the dumbest, weakest person on board. This means the closures have to have simple knobs to turn or levers to pull, with clear instructions as to which way the turning goes.

There is disagreement about how much ventilation is needed on any vessel. There are two main sides to this argument: one is that few people specify the operating conditions before laying down what air intake and discharge should be fitted. The other is that some people think that only an inlet is needed because the discharge can be through a partly opened hatch. It must be clear that a boat working in bad Arctic conditions does not need the same throughput of air as one in the Tropics; and it is obvious that a vessel running before a breaking sea cannot have any hatches open.

Though it is possible to buy vents smaller than 100 mm (4 in) diameter, it is best to avoid them as they do not encourage a flow of air in light winds. A 100 mm vent will pass about 12 cubic ft of air per minute in a 4 knot breeze. As the average person needs between 10 to 15 cubic ft per minute, one vent this size is needed per person, and a second to get rid of the air if the hatch cannot be open. In northern European waters, a lot of designers opt for a single 100 mm (4 in) diameter cowl for every two people on board, but this is probably the influences of cost accounting and cold weather working together. A 150 mm (6 in) vent gives 35 cubic ft per minute throughout in 4 knots of breeze, and though it costs more, its fitting costs are about the same. Also, this size of vent stands higher, so it works better in light airs when the wind is almost stationary close to the deck. For hot weather, large vents are essential.

Low-profile vents, also known as 'inverted soup plates', are inefficient – especially in gentle breezes. They lack big gaping holes and lie close to the deck, where the air flow is in any case slowed down. Some have built-in fans, and these are effective until the fan gulps in water – which seems to happen sooner rather than later.

The ventilation system on any vessel is not something that makes or breaks a sale, but it can tell the surveyor a lot about the design and construction. If he suspects the boat has been built by super-profit-grabbers and designed by stylists who have never been far offshore, a study of the vents may confirm his fears.

SAFETY GEAR AND FURNITURE

. . . .

ANCHORS AND GROUND TACKLE

(For recommended sizes of anchors, warps, etc, see my *Boat Data Book*, published by Adlard Coles Nautical in the UK and Sheridan House Inc. in the USA.)

Anchors

One way boatbuilding factories keep down prices is to sell their products with the minimum of ground tackle. Even well-known firms with good reputations for high quality only put a small anchor and short warp on board as the boat leaves the factory. Plenty of owners never add to this wholly inadequate set of ground tackle. In a way this makes life easy for a surveyor, because he knows it is a fact of life that the great majority of craft are improperly equipped.

Fishing boats and contractors' craft are just as bad. They are regularly found to have just a single anchor, joined with a deeply corroded shackle to worn rusty chain too short to anchor the boat in local waters. If the link between boat and anchor is chain, it has to have, at the very least, a length equal to three times the depth of water at high tide. Four times the depth is a much better minimum length. If rope is used, the length should be at least six times the depth of the harbours where the boat is likely to stay. For year-long use, eight times the depth is a better working figure. With a rope, there should be a piece of chain between the anchor and the warp that is the same length as the boat. The only craft that can get away with a single anchor are dinghies and inshore racing boats. For ocean cruising, the smallest yacht needs three anchors and on craft 12 m (40 ft) long, owned by experienced people, there will be five anchors.

As the sea-bed varies from rock to shale, from sand to thin mud, different anchors are needed to suit the terrains. For weed and kelp, a heavy fisherman anchor is hard to beat. A Delta is good for all sorts of sea-beds and, having no moving parts, it does not wear at the pivot pin as do CQRs. However, it has sharp edges and one has to check for rust here. It is easy to regalvanise, unlike anchors with moving components. Danforths are reported to work poorly in clay or hard mud, especially if they weigh less than about 14 kg (35 lb), because they are slow to dig in. Also, their shanks bend more easily than most. Against this, they stow flat, so they are handy on a foredeck, and they seem to rust slowly except at the points. At least they have sharp points which, on the whole, dig in well – in contrast to the so-called Admiralty pattern, which is only suitable for big ships and has no place on small craft.

It will be found that there are big differences between the weight of anchor recommended for a particular size of yacht in my *Boat Data Book* and in the makers' catalogues. This is because the manufacturers are trying to coax people to buy their products, so they claim, for instance, that their 30 lb hook will do for a 12 m (40 ft) craft. Personally, I feel this is too light, except for a brief stop to have lunch in a quiet bay. It seems that the makers want to give the impression that they make anchors so effective that a small (and therefore cheap) one will be adequate in bad weather on big craft. This salesmanship is found all over the world, but especially in the United States. One result of this is that every time there is a lot of wind, plenty of boats drag ashore. The anchor-makers wring their hands and say it was blowing a hurricane, and no anchor can be expected to hold in such conditions. This is equivalent to saying that car brakes cannot be expected to work in wet weather, or a mast stand up to anything over Force 10.

The plain truth is that an anchor is a sailor's first and last security. It's the symbol of hope worldwide. When the engine fails, when there is no wind and the boat is being taken by the tide towards rocks, when the crew are exhausted and the fuel tank is empty, when the rudder has broken and the wind is onshore, it is then that lumpy well-made anchors with thick warps and heavy chain save the crew and the boat.

A surveyor's job is to protect life and property. He knows that in any ten-year period there are at least two severe gales in most areas, and only properly anchored craft survive these. Because anything that is immersed in water seems to lose weight, and because anchors have to dig themselves in if they are to work, a good case can be made for always having anchors above a 'minimum effective weight'. This seems to be about 14 kg (35 lb). Just as important, the pointed end of an anchor will not fidget its way into the sea-bed unless it is sharp, and forms a narrow taper; this applies to all makes and sizes. Some old salts sharpen their anchor flukes. A sharp-eyed surveyor will condemn an anchor that is unlikely to penetrate the sea-bed because of poor proportions and design.

It is quite common to find that anchors have been damaged or have poor repairs. One of these imperfect 'ground hooks' may be carried as a spare. However, it is best to condemn them, because in the middle of a wild and dangerous night the crew may not be able to distinguish between the best anchor and the reserve one.

The arms of fisherman anchors bend or break at the root, especially if not thickened out where they meet the shank. CQR anchors and some of their cousins have a tendency to crack across the broad ends of the blades. They also have lead inserts at the cleavage, which means they cannot be regalvanised without removing, and later refitting, this ballast. Regalvanising should be recommended as soon as rust shows, otherwise the anchor will lose weight and strength; also, the sharp ends will become blunt, and the ring or eye will wear fast. Besides, no proud owner wants rusty equipment on board; it has a poor appearance and it makes a mess.

Chain

To survey a chain it should be hauled out of its locker and laid on the ground, on a tarpaulin or duckboards. It is ranged in zigzags of one metre or one fathom in extent, so that the total length can be quickly seen. When checking that there is enough chain, an allowance has to be made for the distance from the waterline up to the stemhead roller and aft along the deck, then down to the clench plate where the end of the chain is secured in its locker.

Incidentally, chain should be ranged out well back beneath the bow of a boat, and not out ahead of her to avoid the risk that a vehicle will be driven over the chain. It might seem unimportant if the chain is lying flat on the ground, as the chain looks quite strong enough to withstand the load of a tyre running over it. However, where a zigzagged chain turns round, one link is sometimes laid on top of another. If a heavy weight such as a vehicle tyre presses hard down here, the chain may suffer damage. It can be impossible to spot this weakness.

On one boat in three the clench plate is badly fitted, too flimsy, half corroded through, or consists of a piece of worn rope that is too weak for tying up a lap-dog. There is a fashion for drilling a small hole through the bulkhead at the aft end of the chain locker and knotting a line through this to take the chain end. If the bulkhead *has* to be used, it should be doubled or trebled in thickness, and two sensible holes drilled through with a strong thick line led through. A clench plate should be high in the locker,

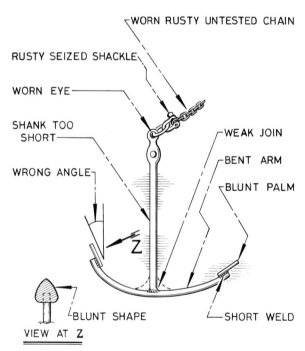

WORN RUSTY UNTESTED CHAIN

RUSTY SEIZED SHACKLE

WORN EYE

SHANK TOO SHORT

WRONG ANGLE

WEAK JOIN

BENT ARM

BLUNT PALM

Z

BLUNT SHAPE

SHORT WELD

VIEW AT Z

Fig 59

Surveyors often inspect ground tackle extra carefully because they realise that if it is not of good quality the finest vessel may be wrecked. The defects shown here apply to all types of anchor, and not just to the folding fisherman type illustrated.

No anchor that has blunt ends at the point where it has to dig in will be effective if the seabed is thick clay or gravel or hard sand. Some old seamen used to file the anchor blades sharp to ensure they worked regardless of what the seabed was made of. Poor joins, bent sections, worn pivots, corroded parts and defective shackles are all common faults.

so that the bitter end can be freed even when the whole of the chain is in its locker.

Chain link diameter is measured to make sure it is adequate. Galvanising adds about 1 mm ($\frac{1}{16}$ in), so that chain that seems to be 8 mm ($\frac{3}{8}$ in) is actually 7 mm ($\frac{5}{16}$ in). Measurements are taken near the anchor end as this gets most wear. However, chains get reversed to even out the wear, so it is advisable to measure both ends. End shackles are notoriously weak links, so they should be inspected for wear, bent pins, and lack of mousing to keep the pins secure.

Rusty chain wears fast, and it makes a mess in its locker – which in time dribbles through to the rest of the bilge. It is therefore advisable to have rusty chain regalvanised without delay. However, it ought to be inspected link by link before being recoated, but this is not the surveyor's job. Ideally it should also be retested for tensile strength before being regalvanised. This is done by a firm specialising in engineering testing, and is rarely undertaken unless the vessel is large and is kept up to a standard such as Lloyd's 100A1.

Anchor gear

On deck, anchors should lie in specially shaped chocks that have recesses to take the top of the shank, the fluke(s), and so on. Anchors are heavy, so they need two or three strong lashings to ensure they stay in their chocks. These lashings may require eye-plates or some such bolted through the deck. On large craft the lashings are replaced by metal hasps, or similar locking devices. A runaway anchor and chain can produce a spectacular disaster. If the anchor slides sideways and then overboard, hauling the chain after it, the effect can be like a saw working on the gunwale and then the deck-edge. Each link, dragged at an ever-increasing speed, acts like the teeth of a saw, cutting through the structure. Even if the hull withstands the ferocious rasping of the anchor chain as it runs out, it may be impossible to lift the whole weight of the chain and anchor on to the winch gipsey, so that the chain can then be hauled back on board.

On craft over about 18 m (60 ft), there ought to be chain brakes or chain compressors or both to control the anchor chains. This gear went out of fashion except on the largest craft, but is now coming back into use as people realise that good equipment properly maintained is the way to avoid anchoring accidents. Chain brakes and compressors wear fast and

can be sorely tested in use, so they need careful checking. They also have to fit the chain exactly, as must the gipsey(s) on the anchor winch.

Where an anchor is pulled up into a hawse pipe there should be a locking device to tighten in the chain the last short distance and then secure it immovably. If there is no such device, the anchor may bump when the boat pounds to windward or rolls downwind. It is bad practice to expect the winch to pull the chain extremely tight, when the last few links come in, and then hold the anchor right up. If anyone makes a mistake when the winch is holding the chain, the whole lot may run out unchecked while the boat is moving along at speed. Where a heavy anchor is stowed on deck, there must be equipment to lift it in over the guardrails and lower it gently on to its chocks. Traditionally, cat davits are used. Typical defects include:

- Lack of reserve strength, shown by bent parts and even a bent main stem.
- Rust and corrosion of working parts, especially where the davit fits in the deck socket, and at the top swivel.
- Lack of gear, especially pairs of guys to secure the davit when swung inboard or outboard. Also, lack of arrangements for clipping the anchor on when it comes up above the sea surface. Likewise, lack of a reliable quick release hook to drop it safely.
- Worn gear, especially lifting and securing tackle and patent release clips.
- Lack of safe stowage facilities for when the boat is at sea and the davit has been lifted out of its socket, and secured on deck or down below.

This list is a handy one, as it applies to other gear such as dinghy davits and side companion ladders.

Warps and fenders

(Typical lengths and thicknesses of warps are given in my *Designer's Notebook*, published by Adlard Coles Nautical in the UK and W W Norton and Co in the USA.)

As a rule, surveyors do not range out the warps or comment on them, as they are considered part of the consumable stores that need regular replacement. A warp hung up for a long period may be worn by the lashing or chafed as it swings against a bulkhead that is not perfectly smooth.

The number and type of fenders depends on the home port of the yacht, as well as her use. If she is almost always on moorings, she will need only one fender for every 1.2 to 1.5 m (4 to 5 ft) of length over all. However, if she is permanently alongside a wall, she will need a fender every 1 m (3 ft) and half that number on the offshore side. The fender diameter should be about 100 mm per 6 m of length (4 in per 20 ft). Commercial craft and fishing boats need a profusion of outsize fenders, as they are heavy and wear their gear rapidly. Fender lines take a lot of punishment and should be about two-thirds the diameter of the warps. They need checking for chafe and unsealed ends.

. . . .

Firefighting Gear

Apart from sailing dinghies, almost everything afloat needs at least one fire extinguisher. In different countries there are regulations that local surveyors learn, but rules by themselves do not make a vessel safe. For instance, there was a large motor cruiser that had a new CO_2 system fitted in her engine room by a reputable manufacturer. The crew checked the installation, as did the local government inspector, the supervisor of the installation firm, and the boatbuilding company involved. It was a pity no one peered closely at the first join in the piping, where the CO_2 bottles were connected to the distribution tubing. This pipe join was never completed. When a generator caught fire, the captain on the bridge pulled the extinguisher control handle and all the CO_2 gas was discharged into the atmosphere instead of into the engine room.

Small engine compartments are often fitted with self-actuating extinguishers that go off when they reach a certain temperature. Some of these gadgets will burst into action by accident in a hot climate when the engine heat combines with the high ambient temperature. So this type of extinguisher must not be mounted too near an exhaust manifold, for instance. On the other hand, it must be fixed above the engine and should be near the most likely sources of conflagration. These are the alternator, starter and other electrical equipment.

Twice I have surveyed boats that have had engine fires that should have been put out automatically by these self-operating extinguishers. On each occasion I found the extinguisher was well off to one side of the engine, and near an air intake. When the fire had started, the heat rising from the flames drew cold air through the vent trunking and over the extinguisher, which was kept cool at the one time when it should have heated up rapidly and set itself off.

Over the years, the recommended type of extinguisher has varied as science discovers a new chemical that works well. Then more science shows that the latest invention kills off more people than fires. As a result, last year's miracle extinguisher may be banned in a couple of years' time. Surveyors have to try and keep up with changing demands and recommendations in this as in other branches of small-craft technology. There is one type of extinguisher, though, that continues to be popular: the fire blanket. It does not become out of date, or need replacing because its container is rusty, and is not dependent on high or even medium technology. Boatowners love a gadget that costs little and gives them such a glow of virtue. What a pity that many of them secure the blanket in its container right above the galley, so that when the cooker catches fire, the flames lick round the blanket, and no one can grab it safely.

Just as stupid is the skipper who keeps an extinguisher where an engine fire will send flames up to caress it. It is also wrong to screw up a holding bracket with the 'jaws' pointing athwartships, because when the vessel rolls heavily the extinguisher is thrown out of its holder. Extinguishers made principally for the household market have brackets that are not reliable at sea, and that rust within days of being brought on to a boat. It is quite usual to find extinguishers badly located, such as under a hatch where drips corrode the casing, or under a cockpit locker lid where rust breeds like mice in a blanket. Many extinguishers carry a date of manufacture, and a typical life expectancy is about ten years – or less for the small, cheap kind. The best manufacturers put the replacement date on extinguishers. However, as many owners never look at their safety gear, it is not uncommon to find that otherwise well-maintained craft have senile extinguishers.

One type of extinguisher has a small gauge on, showing the state of the pressure. If the needle of the dial is in the danger zone, the extinguisher has to be condemned. In practice, it is frequently found that the gauge tells the world that all is well, but the outer casing of the extinguisher is deeply corroded and can no longer be trusted.

Rust is a havoc-maker, and causes endless problems, including the following:

- Instructions that cannot be read.
- Seized casing tops, so that opening up and recharging are difficult or impossible.
- The whole extinguisher is seized on to its bracket.
- The contents are leaking out.

Because the boat industry is an international one, and craft of all sorts move about the globe, one may find that the instructions on extinguishers are written in languages that no one on board can understand. This applies also to the information given on liferafts, names on seacocks, and engine manuals.

Few small craft have what can be called a totally comprehensive set of firefighting equipment on board. A useful guide is:

- There should be two extinguishers on a 7 m (26 ft) vessel, and one more for every 3 m (10 ft) of additional length. All craft should carry a fire blanket as well.
- The seriousness of a fire increases as the size of the vessel decreases, so small craft should not have small extinguishers.
- The smallest sensible size of extinguisher afloat is 1 kg (2 lb). For craft over 12 m (40 ft), the extinguishers should be the 2 kg (4 lb) size.

The majority of craft do not have sensible fire-extinguishing equipment and, even when the quantity is right, the quality is usually poor; this applies both to commercial and pleasure craft. Also, the standard of maintenance of this equipment is consistently disgraceful. Where there are government or other official regulations, these are often interpreted as the *maximum* needed, never as a guide to what is barely adequate.

. . . .

FURNITURE

(For minimum sizes of berths, seats, etc, see my *Boat Data Book*, published by Adlard Coles Nautical in the UK and Sheridan House Inc. in the USA.)

For the most part, internal furniture is the least of a surveyor's worries, because repairs are normally easy and cheap. More important, defects in the furniture seldom affect the safety of the ship or crew, though there are exceptions to this. Some craft are built with such flimsy lockers and drawers that they shatter if anyone falls against them in rough weather, and no one enjoys being impaled on splinters. Lightweight interiors are accepted in racing machines, but craft intended for serious cruising or for commercial work need rugged components throughout.

The level of wear and tear inside the cabins affects the value of a yacht or a prestige vessel such as a directors' launch. Anyone buying a yacht that is reported to have signs of heavy use for her age must suspect that she has been used for chartering. This leads on to the thought that she has probably been battered about by incompetent crews, and there may be lots of hidden troubles that have been plastered over and concealed by careful cosmetic work. Cushions that are well worn can easily and cheaply be recovered, but cotton bottom parts to the leather-cloth or tweed coverings on cushions and mattresses are doubly bad news:

- The cotton rots when the rest of the covering is still in good condition. Cotton stitching also tends to rot sooner than the rest of a cushion's cover.
- If the top gets damaged, the cushion cannot be turned upside down to hide the trouble till repairs can be made in the off season.

Cushions and mattresses need checking for fit, quality, rotten stitching, seized zips, burn marks, tears, and crumbling foam plastic interiors. The head-room over seats needs checking, so does the length, width and space above each berth. In one Folkboat I surveyed, the longest bunk was under 1.88 m (6 ft

2 in). Two were under 1.80 (5 ft 11 in) and one was under 1.77 m (5 ft 10 in). As the average height of human beings increases every year, this boat needs altering, or she will certainly be difficult to sell.

Cockpit comfort is not something most surveyors make comments about, because it does depend in part on the size of the crew and their heights; also, it is something people have different views about, based on their past experience or lack of it. However, the view forward from the steering position can be so bad that accidents are likely, and this does interest the surveyor. Coming into a marina berth, or racing in a big fleet, are just two occasions when the helmsman needs to be able to see all round. Sometimes poor visibility can be improved by adding a thick grating or set of duckboards or other plinth for standing on at the steering position. Sometimes all that is needed is a raised seat, or just a thick cushion on each sidedeck. If the cushions are filled with flotation material and have grab-lines all round, they will double as lifebuoys.

Doors and drawers that do not fit well may have been made badly, or the hull may have been strained, perhaps by grounding and bumping on a hard

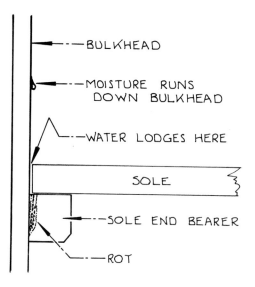

Fig 60

A wood sole bearer made fast to a bulkhead is likely to rot because moisture runs down bulkheads. The small crack at the end of the sole gets dirt in it and tends to hold moisture for long periods. This type of rot is found in fibreglass and steel boats as well as wood ones, when the bearer is wood. If the bulkhead is of a material that is likely to sweat, there is a particular chance of rot in the bearer.

bottom. On Sigma 33s that have been set up with taut rigging for racing, the door at the fore end of the saloon will not shut, unless the owner has faired away something like 5 mm ($\frac{3}{16}$ in) at the top. On other racing classes the amount that has to be sliced off is greater. These boats seem to go on racing without falling apart, but this is an indication of their stiffness in way of the mast.

Cabin soles are prone to a host of troubles. Some builders screw them down so much that, if the boat is holed, no one can reach the problem without spending ages frantically unscrewing the sole. Other boards have no fastenings and may come loose in a gale. Some have no supports under the ends, so if someone treads on them in this part the opposite end pivots up and smacks him in the face, just as if he had put his foot on the tines of a garden rake.

Rotten floorboards are much rarer than rotten sole bearers. Rot occurs in bearers regardless of what the hull is made of. Fibreglass and metal hulls usually have timber soles and bearers. Condensation or drips from an adjacent hatch run down the bulkhead and cause rot on the mating face of the end bearer, especially when it is not secured to the bulkhead with plenty of waterproof bedding. Even more common are bearers that have torn or loose fibreglass on the ends, so that they are sloppy and insecure. Soles and their bearers cause a variety of problems by sagging down on to piping and wiring, tanks and steering cables. In extreme cases, one finds pipes broken right through, electric cables with the insulation chafed away, tanks dinged down on top, and the sheathing on steering cables worn away.

On poorly built boats, steel minor parts are used in the furniture. Sometimes the steel is totally untreated, so it rusts in the first few months; on other occasions, various forms of electroplating are put on in a vain attempt to slow down the corrosion. Screws and hooks treated in this way wait till the second season before starting to corrode away. Steel screws in furniture, steel pins in brass hinges, steel hinges and steel coathooks are all inventions of the devil. He is abetted by accountants who think it is more important to build a cheap boat than a good one.

Good builders put large hinges everywhere, because these fittings have a rough time out at sea. Loose hinges are a common defect even on well-built craft, especially when they are over 20 years old. All hinges should have 6 gauge screws or larger. This establishes the minimum size of hinges that are reliable. This handy dictum applies to everything that floats, even the smallest cruiser. In some ways, such vessels are the worst when it comes to destroying their own furniture, because they jump about so much when banging to windward in a lumpy sea.

A competent builder puts good door furniture on even the smallest locker. There are all sorts of clever catches and latches, locks and clicks to keep doors closed. They all seem to have faults, and few are tough enough to be reliable. Magnetic catches are useless: when the boat rolls, the contents of the locker fall against the door, which bursts open at the very worst time – ensuring that the contents tumble all over the cabin sole. For ocean cruising, there should be an ordinary catch or securing device on each locker door and drawer as well as an extra turn-button or some such for use in severe conditions. Good builders also round off all protruding corners of lockers, sideboards and tables to save the crew from bad bruising. Many interior decorators of large yachts seem to think they have risen above the laws of the sea, and design furniture with sharp edges and protuberances that can cause nasty injuries.

Horizontal surfaces in all compartments need adequate fiddles. These have to be at least 75 mm (3 ins) high, even on steady stolid craft. Modern light-weight boats are so lively that experienced offshore crews want much higher fiddles. A tour round any boat show is instructive, because the vast majority of craft have fiddles well under 50 mm (2 in). Even craft on inland waterways need good fiddles throughout the furniture, because another vessel passing at speed will cause rolling. Crockery that slides off the cabin table every time another boat goes past is an expensive nuisance.

In the galley and toilet compartment, and sometimes in other areas as well, the furniture and bulkheads are covered with a thin plastic laminate. Formica and Wearite are two well-known makes.

They are widely popular because they are easy to keep clean, though thoughtless rubbing with the wrong compound, or the accidental application of a lit cigarette, will cause damage. The surveyor has to report this, because it lowers the value of the vessel and repairs are not always cheap.

A very hot pan laid on one of these plastic surfaces causes it to swell up from the wood beneath. Formica and such like should be glued to wood that has had a pattern of thumb-sized holes drilled in it to allow air to escape. To be safe, panels of plastic should be made about 600 mm (2 ft) wide or less, with small expansion gaps between. On bulkheads, these slits would be covered with something like strips of a decorative hardwood. A plastic laminate that has peeled off should not be neglected, because water can lodge underneath and start rotting the furniture. Also, the edges of this plastic are thin, sharp and dangerous.

Blockboard is used for some furniture. Its edges should be carefully scrutinised, because when this material gets wet it holds moisture for long periods and rots easily. Delamination and discoloration occur even when the board is in a damp atmosphere. Any blockboard that is mottled with dark stains, or near the bilge, should be probed with a spike.

Quite a few furniture features are a matter of differing opinions. Some surveyors make a great fuss about these details; some just give them a mention; and others consider them trivia or the owner's personal concern. Typical of these things are the absence or small size of the oilskin locker, or the presence of carpeting glued up alongside quarter berths, or the absence of a safe seat for the navigator. To sum up, a surveyor is acting in his client's interests, so it cannot do any harm to mention what is felt to be a defect, though presumably the buyer has noticed the absence of leecloths on the berths (to take another example) and accepts the boat as she is.

POWER CRAFT AND OPEN BOATS

. . . .

MOTOR YACHTS

The remarks made in earlier sections about structure and components apply equally to motor yachts, but these craft have special problems that surveyors need to recognise. For a start, it is broadly true to say that power yachts are less strongly built than sailing craft, because they do not have to cope with the 'terrible twins' that afflict wind-driven yachts: the tall rig, which causes serious wringing strains, and the ballast keel, which spends its life trying to tear the hull apart.

Builders of motor yachts assume that their products will not be banged and bashed into high waves for long periods. The crew find such a process noisy, often frightening, and not to be tolerated. Few power yachts spend many hours offshore in bad weather. This is partly because their speed and modern weather forecasting make it possible to get into port before bad conditions arrive, and partly because they are seldom suited to rough seas. Once in harbour, there is little temptation to go out again until the weather is tolerable. Only a small number of specialised power yachts are used for racing, whereas a vast number of sailing craft take part in at least two races each year.

Some motor yacht builders clearly believe that as their craft are not going to be highly stressed, the hulls can be lighter, thinner and less reinforced than comparable sailing craft. It is common to find topsides that do not stay still when a firm shoulder is pushed against them. Large transoms sometimes have little or no internal stiffening. Some will 'ping' in and out when the stern ladder is given a strenuous jolt; others have no local reinforcing where the ladder is secured, so that cracks soon appear at the fastenings.

Few of these craft have special internal stiffening to take dinghy davits on the stern. Such davits are popular, because the dinghy is out of the way and not taking up deck space that could be put to better use. The doubler pads fitted inside the transom for these davits are often too small, not glassed in, not thick enough, and not properly bedded down in a waterproof mastic. As a rough rule, the doubler pads in way of stern davits should be 25 mm (1 in) thick for every 9 m (30 ft) of boat length. Assuming these pads are square, the length of each side should be 300 mm (12 in) for every 9 m (30 ft) of boat length. Ideally, the pads should be tied in with stiffeners that extend the full depth of the transom.

It is fairly common to find local hollows near the surface along chines and spray rails because of the difficulty of getting glass cloth to go right into sharp angles when making a moulding. When popped, these bubbles look like cavities, typically 10 mm ($\frac{3}{8}$ in) in diameter, but they can be far larger. Sometimes they are quite narrow, but extend intermittently along the sharp edge. They are also found along the edges of moulded-in toerails that form part of the deck moulding. The deck-edges of motor yachts frequently extend outwards to form a bold flair forwards. This is seldom well protected, and is vulnerable when coming into harbour. Once moored up, the fairleads do not always protect the deck-edges properly, and the surveyor may have to suggest that metal chafing strips are fitted by the fairleads and perhaps by the mooring cleats or bollards.

Fast powerboats do a lot of damage to themselves when they hit flotsam, because any destruction is proportional to the square of the speed. Therefore one looks for cracks and scratches on the underside of the bottom in the 'target zone'. Another area to check extra carefully is by the propeller. There may be chafe or deep gouging here where the prop has hurled something solid against the hull.

If the shell is of metal, the structure inside and outside near the propellers should be very carefully scrutinised for vibration troubles such as weld fractures. Sometimes the plating pulsates every time a propeller blade passes over the top of its arc, and this fatigues the welds with wonderful swiftness and efficiency. The cure is thicker local plating and more stiffeners made of extra-thick material, all fully and continuously welded.

This type of craft usually has a long straight keel, or what passes for a keel. When laid up ashore, the keel support chocks should be exactly aligned, otherwise the hull weight is all taken on one or two blocks and the keel may hog or sag. This results in bulkheads, frames, stringers and engine bearings coming adrift or cracking.

Engine bearers

When the boat is put afloat, she is fairly evenly supported along her full length by the water. Ashore, or when pounding into a steep head sea, the support may be very local. The engine weight forms a high percentage of the total, and the engine bearers need to be deep, strong, well bonded in and free from sudden changes of section.

Bearers sometimes crack right through where they have a sharp change in width or depth, or where the engine feet rest. A thick bolt through a bearer takes away a lot of the strength just where it is most needed. Bearers also peel off bulkheads and off the inside of the hull. Few bearers have limber holes, which means that water gets trapped outboard of them in areas that are not reached by bilge pump suction pipes. To be effective, engine bearers need to be long and deep. There used to be a handy rule that said that all bearers should be at least three times the combined length of the engine and gearbox, but that rule is seldom quoted these days. In practice, engine compartments are now short because engines have become so compact. The bearers often extend only from one end of the engine space to the other, and sometimes the bonding on to the bulkheads is weak or discontinuous.

Large engines should not only have bearers that are massively glassed at each end, but the bulkheads should be stiffened to prevent flexing. It helps, when surveying a vessel with a 200 hp engine, to pause a minute, and think about 200 big muscular horses. Imagine the amount of pull they can generate – can the structure stand such a force? Think about the damage all these horses can cause if something goes awry for a brief instant.

Couplings

I once surveyed a 14 m (46 ft) medium-speed power cruiser that had a pair of 250 hp diesels. The coupling bolts were taken out to check the engine alignment by the paid hand, who knew all about the troubles that ensue if engines are not carefully lined up. He put back the old Nyloc nuts, whereas he should have used new ones, carefully tightened with a torque wrench. When this craft next went to sea, one by one the nuts loosened and fell off, so the bolts holding the two halves of the coupling dropped out. As the second to last bolt slid free and dropped into the bilge, the engine whipped the shaft sideways, putting a bend in that 50 mm (2 in) diameter steel bar as if it were rubber tubing. The sterntube wrenched sideways and water quickly poured in. There is no way such an inrush can be controlled. By luck and swift action, the crew managed to beach the boat before she sank.

This brings up another common fault in power yachts: they seldom have a bilge pump capacity to deal with a moderate leak, let alone a severe one. In theory, the engine cooling water pump can be used to suck water out of the bilge and discharge it through the exhaust, but facilities for this are rarely seen. It is unusual to find two good hand bilge pumps properly bolted down and plumbed in on motorcruisers. Electric bilge pumps should be considered secondary to manual ones. A rough guide reads something like this: there should be one hand bilge pump and one bucket for power cruisers up to 9 m (30 ft) and one extra pump as well as an extra bucket for each additional 3 m (10 ft).

Deck fittings

These components are sometimes designed to look fashionable. The more modish they are, the weaker and more impractical they tend to be. Pulpits are made with too few legs, and long unsupported top bars. They seldom have corner brackets, or stiffening struts or proper broad base plates. Some even extend so far forward that the crew are liable to fall between them and the deck-edge when handling the anchor or coming alongside.

Through-deck ventilators are in short supply, and lockers both on deck and below are seldom given proper slots to ensure that a drying flow of air passes through all the time. Where there are vents, they are too often of the shell or clam type that let water in if the vessel is moored in a marina, harbour or river stern to the wind. It is often worth hose testing these craft, to see where water gets in. Because deck fittings are seldom made accident-proof, it is common to find they are damaged or inadequate in bad weather. I once surveyed a craft that had an anchor windlass made without a pawl, and no gear to shift the load of the anchor warp and chain to the mooring cleat. The casing of the windlass was made of thin weak aluminium. The stemhead roller had side plates so thin that they could be flexed with the foot, and these plates were razor sharp on the front. This ensures that they will chip the galvanising off the anchor chain and sever a mooring warp in a hour if the bow pitches up and down in a moderate sea.

Engines

The engine of a power yacht is more important than in a sailing vessel, which should be able to get home using the wind if the machinery breaks down. This means that the surveyor's report has to dwell with more urgency on mechanical defects and potential failures.

It is common to find that in twin screw craft there are two fuel tanks, one serving each engine. However, for convenience when filling the tanks, there is usually a balancing pipe that links the tanks at the bottom. This may or may not have a shut-off cock. If there is one, it is normally kept open all the time, whereas it should normally be kept shut or a leak in one tank will empty both of them into the bilge.

Safety in motor-cruisers gets mixed attention from designers, builders and owners. It is common to find that there is no way to see into the engine without lifting a heavy hatch, or going through a tiny door, and sometimes access can only be achieved after lifting aside a set of steps or other furniture.

On the best-designed craft there is a window into the engine room and good lighting, so that the machinery can easily be checked visually. Very seldom are there any grabrails in the engine space. If there are turbo-chargers that get hot or an unprotected exhaust that is not water cooled, the crew can get badly burned during a visit to the engine space. Turbo-chargers that get hot do not restrain themselves. I have seen them glowing red in a dark engine compartment – an awesome sight when far offshore in a rising wind. The heat from these units has to be dealt with properly with fans to dissipate the heat and fireproof barriers on nearby structures. Ideally, there should be nothing near, but engines are seldom given enough space and it is quite usual to see the deck-head only a few inches above a hot engine.

Hand-operated engine shut-down controls are needed as a precaution if the normal ones are dependent on electricity. Corrosion or lack of current can so easily make the electrical stop controls fail. Where the engine is linked to a Z-drive or stern drive, special care is needed. Extra gear loaded into the aft end of a boat puts her down by the stern, so that the drive unit becomes too deeply immersed. On some versions the seal on the gearbox oil replenishment cap is unreliable, so if this cover is permanently or frequently immersed, water finds its way into the gear casing.

A rare but disconcerting fault may only come to the surveyor's notice when an owner complains that his boat is slow. It may be found that the Z-drive leg is too high, so that the water flow to the propeller is partly cut off by the bottom of the transom. If the stern drive has a lifting arrangement, this sometimes prevents the propeller from going right down, and a loss of speed results.

Another common trouble (which is also found on 'Sail-drive' legs) is blocked water inlet slots. At first sight, these side slits in the vertical casing, which take in cooling water, seem quite clear. The owner has brushed off the accumulation of small barnacles that gathered at the end of the summer when the anti-fouling paint was beginning to lose its effectiveness. What he has *not* done is to poke a hooked wire into each slot, and rake out all the growth inside the casing. By next season the growth will have increased, but it may take three or more summers for the deep-seated blockage to become so solid that cooling water cannot flow in sufficient quantity. It is sometimes necessary to dismantle the casing to get out the blockage caused by crustacea. Any growth inside the slots should therefore be reported.

Hydraulic equipment needs specialist attention and is outside the range of most surveyors. However, it is good practice to mention any defects seen, such as leaking hydraulic fluids, perished pipes, corroded connections, and so on. There is one nasty habit that some hydraulic systems have: they look satisfactory on the outside and work adequately or even efficiently, but all the while hidden seals are failing. Only one has to break to make the whole system collapse. There is a theory that hydraulics hate idleness and give trouble after a long stagnant period, whereas if kept hard at work the same set of components gives little or no trouble. This is exactly what surveyors find with many things.

One final thought about motor yachts: most of them have high topsides, and if anyone falls overboard, getting them back on board may be extremely difficult. An extreme case of this occurred one summer in Greece, when a motor-cruiser went out on charter. The boat was far offshore, but the weather was perfect, so everyone on board decided to go for a swim. But they omitted to hang a ladder or rope over the side, and when it was time to get back on board no one could reach the deck-edge. The marks of desperately scrabbling fingernails were found on the fibreglass hull near the waterline...

. . . .

OUTBOARD BOATS

There are a great many small boats that are driven by outboard engines, and they vary from superbly built, well-equipped craft down to horrible boxes that stay afloat by a continuing miracle. The best and the worst in the boatbuilding world is seen in this range, but there are certain things most of these craft have in common.

Nearly all are at least moderately fast, so they are severely tested in rough seas. Most have well under half the total area between the gunwales decked over, so they lack 'box strength'. Most are built and sold under what might be called 'motor car' conditions, with emphasis being placed on good external finish that is not always matched by a strong underlying structure. Many of these boats are holiday toys, used for a few weeks or weekends each year and neglected in between. Though some of the owners are skilled, careful and conscientious sailors, a great many are more interested in fishing or other hobbies – hence their boats suffer. In short, the surveyor is likely to find defects when looking at this type of boat.

If the engine and loose gear can be removed and the hull turned upside down, then it is easier to do a full inspection of the bottom. Lying in the mud under any boat, gazing up at the underside of a hull that has no direct sunlight shining on it, is not the ideal way to spot thin, new, almost-invisible cracks. Bottom cracks, caused by pounding into the seas or running up the beach too fast, are found at the places where strong structural components terminate. The places to look hardest (though of course the whole bottom has to be examined) are where chines, rubbing bands and spray rails taper out. Also, where internal stringers and frames end, and on the bottom near internal strong points like bulkheads, floors and glassed-in lockers or buoyancy tanks. Other vulnerable areas are:

- Where the hull supports on the trailer are located.
- Where trailer roll-on wheels press upwards on the hull.
- Just forward of the transom.
- Forward and aft of the bulkhead, which forms the aft outboard well, provided this bulkhead extends right down inside the hull.
- On each side of a strong keel, where the hull bottom is weaker than the central backbone.
- At the bottom of the stem, where the round-down is chafed as the boat comes on to the beach.

Apart from all these areas, all edges are vulnerable to chipping, especially if the chine or transom edges are sharp. Here the resin may not have run into the mould properly, so there may be air holes under the gel coat. These collapse where there is no more than moderate pressure on them, leaving a hole that should be filled and faired.

A gentle pressure applied along these sharp edges, using the handle of a spike or screwdriver, may show up other bubbles that are just waiting for the tiniest accident to pop them.

Transom troubles

The transom is the equivalent of the engine bearers on an inboard boat, but lacks their advantages. Conventional bearers are in pairs, so they share the engine load. They are secured to the hull bottom along their full length, forming an inverted T-section of great potential strength. They are often bracketed together, with floors or knees to give mutual support. In any case, the engine binds the two bearers together, in effect acting like a strong linking system.

The transom has none of these benefits, and to make matters worse it carries the load of the outboard engine on top, which is the only unsupported edge. Though the top may be flanged over to give it some strength, this stiffener cannot be wide, otherwise the engine clamps will not fit over the transom top. What the transom needs, but does not always have, is a stout knee, or pair of knees, running well up the forward face, and along inside the hull. If there is a strong keel, or pair of longitudinal stiffeners, these should be joined to the transom by brackets. Even more important, there should be strong knees at the top corners of the transom. These quarter knees are fully effective if they extend well forward and well inboard, and taper out at their ends. Surveyors look for cracks at the ends of the knees, and at the 'throat' or middle of the curved forward line.

They also peer along the transom edges inside and out, and look under any doubling fitted to take the engine(s). This thickening may be of fibreglass, wood, metal, or a combination of these. It may be inside or outside the transom, and is often on both faces. Part of it may be 'sacrificial', so that when used and crushed by the engine clamps for many years it can be replaced. Sometimes it is made of metal and expected to withstand the great compression when the engine bracket gripping screws are squeezed up as tight as the crew can manage. In this situation the metal plates or doublers may be able to take the punishment, but the underlying structure may fail. In practice, the most usual place for failures to occur is at the ends of the quarter knees, and where the transom meets the topsides. Sometimes there are fractures in the middle of the top of the transom, caused when the engine 'bucks' or jolts as the boat jumps a wave.

Forward of the transom there is sometimes a watertight well. This has (or should have) a high bulkhead at the forward end to prevent water flooding inboard over the low transom, which may be cut down on the centreline to take the engine. These wells can be dangerous because some are badly designed, and others are altered. Some have slots or holes for the engine controls, so the watertight integrity is lost. Some are weak and cannot support a full load of water. Some have drain holes through the transom that have been badly made, so that some water drains into the hull instead of overboard.

It might be thought that too much is being made of the troubles on the transoms of outboard boats. One reason why surveyors find so much to write about in this area is that boats are fitted with too much horsepower. Many of these craft are built with name-plates secured to the transom or some other prominent place, and on these plaques there will be a note stating the biggest size of engine that should be fitted. This is fine when the boat is new, but in the subsequent years all sorts of things happen. The name-plate gets lost or obscured, so no one knows what the biggest engine on the transom should be. Or the owner gets overtaken at speed by a rival, so he decides to get a slightly bigger engine – and, of course, no one realises that even a moderate increase in the horsepower can result in a big percentage accentuation of all the stresses. More horsepower also means more engine weight, and hence more stressing of the transom.

Sometimes a new owner does not have an engine small enough, so he just uses what he has. He may even think that the figure for maximum horsepower applies to *each* engine, and fits two! Occasionally, the boat is fitted with an extra big engine just for an afternoon, to see how fast she can go. This is enough to do extensive damage, especially if there is a vicious sea.

Deck gear

These small boats are made in large numbers, as swiftly and simply as possible. Some deck fittings are screwed or lightly riveted down, whereas they should be bolted. Cleats and fairleads may be secured with just two 25 mm (1 in) 8 gauge self-tapping screws, which may be seen on the underside of the deck, where they penetrate right through. Mooring fittings that have a single integral bolt are not acceptable if there is no substantial doubler under the deck, with a wide washerplate under the nut. Stemhead fairleads that are styled to look as if they are doing 100 knots when on moorings, are no good if they have sharp edges and nothing to hold the mooring rope or bow warp securely in place.

There should also be facilities for towing the boat, and this means a strong bollard or cleat, as well as a capacious stemhead fitting. The latter needs holes each side, so that a lashing can be secured across the top, or there must be a keep-pin.

The windscreen on these boats is partially a breakwater. It has to be tight down on the deck, otherwise water may stream under it and gradually fill the hull. For the same reason, the windscreen should extend right out to the gunwales to prevent heavy spray deluging round the ends and into the boat. It is hard to drive one of these boats in severe conditions and use a hand pump at the same time, always assuming that there is an adequate pump properly located. As the seas get up, speed has to be reduced, so that in time the bow may be going right under. Waves on the foredeck become heavy, so the windscreen has to be strong enough to stand up to them. In practice, few owners take these crafts out in anything approaching a gale, but the surveyor may have to point out the limitations of the type and size of craft. Few of them are built for use in heavy weather.

Steering gear

It is usual to have a steering wheel at the aft end of the foredeck, except on small moderate-speed boats that may be handled by the helmsman right aft, where he can grasp the tiller on the engine. Joining the steering wheel to the engine there may be a pair of flexible wires round sheaves, led to the tiller on the engine. However, the work involved in setting up this type of traditional equipment, and the fact that the two wires have to come to the engine from opposite sides of the boat, has resulted in a widespread change to a single-cable system.

This consists of a plastic tube with an enclosed flexible central cable, forced back and forth by a worm and wheel unit joined to the steering wheel. The aft end has a standard clip that links on to the front of the engine. Many of the parts of this steering linkage are hidden, so cannot be inspected. If there is much play, signs of corrosion, cracks in the casing by the wheel, or visible wear, it is usually best to renew the whole unit. Repairs to this type of equipment are normally carried out by fitting a new part, because of the difficulties involved in welding the metals used, and because replacement is often cheaper.

Components tend to be of steel poorly protected from rust. Also, it is common to find brackets held by only two fastenings, so these have to be above suspicion. Sometimes the clamp or clip on to the engine controls dozens of units of horsepower, but has no vestige of robustness. There should at least be proper protection from corrosion, and the linkage should be locked at detachment points with wire or bound over with tape or, better still, have both.

Buoyancy and safety

In some regions there are regulations that lay down the minimum buoyancy that has to be fitted to these boats. This minimum almost always becomes the maximum, and is often just enough to float the boat with the gunwales awash. Even in a calm it is impossible to bail these boats dry, so the crew have little chance of saving themselves. If the boat is overloaded, or an outsize engine is fitted, 'standard' buoyancy is seldom enough. Every year outboard boats get swamped and float with just the bows showing above water, almost invisible and offering no handhold for the struggling crew.

Because some outboard engines weigh as much as the hull they are fitted on, there has to be a great volume of buoyancy right aft. It can seldom be on the centreline, so it has to be along each side, and perhaps under the sole. The weight of the fuel tank is also located near the transom. Few owners appreciate the need to get some weight amidships, so reserve fuel supplies are normally stowed right aft as well.

To achieve a modest safety level, there should be enough buoyancy to float the flooded hull with at least 150 mm (6 in) of freeboard all round in a flat calm sea. This may seem a high standard to set, but when the potential accidents are considered, it is clearly not too stringent.

One January evening in the fading light I had an unusual opportunity to assess safety in one of these fast runabouts in a Scottish estuary. We were travelling at speed when we met iceflows with razor edges; they clattered against the hull, creating a noise that drowned the outboard. Not all these boats have to work in these conditions, but they do have thin hull shells that are vulnerable to drifting logs and other floating hazards.

The required volume of flotation tanks or foam plastic blocks is not hard to fit inside the hull, because this type of boat only requires enough sitting space for the crew. There is no need for 'accommodation', as on a cruiser. If there is a shortage of room due to obtrusive buoyancy, this will discourage overcrowding on board – a frequent problem with this type of craft.

It is common to find virtually no safety gear on these boats. Some do not even have a locker where flares and smoke signals can be stowed. Very few have a dry secure container for a portable VHF set, flashlights and spare batteries. Many do not carry lifebuoys or even basic ground tackle. Considering that these boats have a high accident rate, the lack of gear is absurd. Only one in ten has a good bilge pump or a capacious baler properly secured with a safety line.

In spite of their small size, a surveyor looking at one of these boats will find much to write about.

OPEN BOATS AND YACHT TENDERS

A box with a thick lid well secured down is strong. Kick it and knock it about, and it will survive. Take the lid off, and the box loses so much strength that it cannot stand up to much abuse. It is much the same with boats; those with decking, which is really just a 'lid', are much stronger than undecked craft. So when inspecting any open boat, plenty of trouble must be expected. If, as so often happens, the boat is regularly dragged up the shore, or hauled aboard over the gunwale of a larger craft, it is inevitable that the hard usage will show. There will be bashes and cracks, broken parts and torn fastenings.

Small fibreglass shells suffer from cracking on the outside along the bilge; chipped and gouged keels; broken and loose gunwale pieces; dents and worse on the stem; cracking along the edges of the transom; and loose seats and floorboards where the fastenings have failed. If there were some sort of chafing strips along the bottom, they will have been worn through in the first four or six years, often leaving jagged holes where the fastenings were. If the bottom is entirely of fibreglass, sometimes the skin is found to be chafed right through.

The cracking along the bilge is usually where the boat has been rolled over to empty out water, and where she has grounded when coming ashore. This means the worst damage is usually amidships and near the transom. It will probably be in the form of star cracks, and the hull strength will be affected in these areas. If there are built-in fibreglass components such as buoyancy tanks, thwarts and maybe a centreboard case, it is common to find corners and edges, as well as flanges that are too tightly radiused. Cracks show in these areas, and when repairs are specified it is a good idea to call for considerable stiffening – otherwise the cracks will soon return.

Almost all these craft are built with thin skins, so when recommending repairs, it is important to specify plenty of glassfibre doubling on the inside, as well as the usual repairs on the outside. If the hull is badly damaged, but there are lots of fittings in good condition, it may be cheaper to buy a new shell and transfer the fittings from the old to the new hull. The only trouble about this plan is that it is labour-intensive, since the work of removing fittings can be more time-consuming than putting them on the new boat. Getting out seized or partly jammed fastenings is slow and frustrating.

A weak point on many of these craft is where a fastening goes through fibreglass. There should be large washers under the head and nut, to spread the local loads. Screws need large washers too, otherwise the glassfibre cracks round the heads. This trouble is seen, for instance, in wooden quarter-knees fitted to stiffen transoms. If an outboard engine has been used that is too powerful for the hull, there will be cracks, splits and general floppiness all round the transom. A good way to strengthen any weakened hull is to add a foredeck, and maybe an aft one as well. The latter can have a 'cut-out' for the outboard engine. Alternatively, it may be fixed below the top of the transom, so that the engine bracket can be clamped in place in the usual way.

One weakness shared by the majority of these boats is the lack of buoyancy. It is usual for builders to fill the space under the thwarts with some cheap foam plastic, and this gives enough flotation to keep the boat up if she becomes flooded. However, she will only have a little freeboard left, so she will hardly support the crew and their gear. If there is an outboard on her, it may drag the whole lot down to the sea-bed. The trouble with outboards is that they are high up, heavy and right aft. To keep them afloat an open boat needs lots of buoyancy at the stern. An aft seat that reaches well forward and is in the form of a water-tight locker is needed. It must extend high up and be totally sealed all round on to the hull. To be safe there should be the same right forward, and again amidships. In fact, the safe boats that one comes across seem rather crowded inside with flotation compartments.

Those open boats that have double bottoms normally have plenty of buoyancy and float high enough to be baled after flooding. The best kind have some sort of self-draining aft, which means that the water runs out as fast as it comes in – provided the drain is in good working order, with a flap that is free and not clogged with dirt. Just to add a sour note:

double-bottomed boats have a bad habit of getting water between the skins, and this is:

- Hard to detect – but try lifting the boat and, if she is unaccountably heavy, it almost certainly means she is waterlogged between the inner and outer skins.
- Hard to get out – but sometimes a few holes drilled in the bottom work as drains, provided the boat is tilted to make the water run towards the holes. These temporary drain-holes are sealed over when the boat has had ample time to dry out.
- Hard to detect *where* it is coming in – but look along the gunwales for cracks and slit-shaped openings in the joins along the sheer. Also, search for cracks in the bottom, inside and out. The cracks may be hidden behind rubbing strakes.

When examining these double-skin craft, one presses the inner and outer fibreglass here and there to see if it 'pants', or moves without undue effort. This suggests the internal foam plastic is not tight up against the fibreglass skin. The most likely weak area is forward on the bottom, where pounding hammers the hull and causes separation of the layers.

The thwarts must be tested for rigidity. If they are loose or flexible, they do not give that valuable support to the topsides that is part of their job. Wooden boats have pairs of knees at each end of thwarts, showing just how vital these benches are to the overall strength of the boat. These knees should have three fastenings in each leg, and be tight up, with no looseness or cracks. If a thwart is loose, the trouble will get steadily worse, and fastenings through the topsides may in time stick out. Rowing while sitting on a loose seat takes the enjoyment out of this pleasant form of exercise. The same applies to loose rowlock holders and floppy gunwales.

Apart from a lack of buoyancy, the other common faults with open boats are found at the painter. These ropes break or pull free and cause a great number of insurance claims. A painter should be new, free from chafe, and of adequate length. Just what is long enough depends on such matters as the range of tide where the boat is kept, and whether she is towed out at sea. In general, a painter should be 9m (30 ft) long and 8 mm ($\frac{5}{16}$ in) diameter for any boat below 4m (13 ft) in length. Bigger boats need even larger painters.

The rope needs an eye-plate rather than an eye-bolt at the stem, held by two (or, better still, four) bolts, complete with extensive backing pad. The inboard end should be spliced round a thimble, with shackle on to the eye-plate. On the best-equipped boats there is a stern painter to the same specification, but this is rarely seen. In practice, the recommended level of perfection is seldom achieved, partly because owners dislike long painters. They find the length inconvenient, and no one has told them that the clever thing is to have a long and short painter secured to the same eye-plate. Polypropylene floating ropes are needed to avoid snarl-ups round the outboard propeller.

Yacht tenders have to have the parent boat's name painted on, otherwise insurance companies can refuse to pay up when the boat is lost. My view is that there is so much stealing that the sensible course is to mark the boat with manic enthusiasm. A good plan is to have a stencil made with the boat's name, so that it can be quickly painted on port and starboard, at the bow, amidships and at the stern, on the bottom in six places, and inside just as much. Most thieves will find it too much trouble to eliminate so many names. For good measure, careful owners add a plate or plaque with their own name, address and phone number on it. Then when the dinghy goes adrift, there is a good chance that it will be returned.

Wooden dinghies and tenders have the same faults as fibreglass ones. Even though they are made of timber that floats, they still need lots of built-in buoyancy. It should be more extensive than under the three thwarts, otherwise the crew will not be able to bale it out except in a flat calm, when flooding never happens anyway. The aim should be to have so much flotation inside the hull that the crew can potter home with the boat full of water. They may be damp, cold, fed up, shivering and frightened, but at least they will be alive.

Wooden boats tend to be knocked around a lot, and left without repairs for months simply because they are so tough and able to take hard knocks. It is usual to find the keel and bilge rubbers worn thin, and the metal stem band badly chafed. If these metal strips, (which are also found on bilge chafing pieces) are not mended in good time, they break, bend backwards, tear out fastenings, and cause all sorts of secondary damage. This can include holes right through where a fastening has been jolted and wrenched sideways or pulled through. In the same way, the gunwale may have minor damage that is ignored. In time this will cause weakening at the stem and transom, extra loading on the top planks – which may work loose or fracture the frames, and so on.

It is probably true to say that any lapstrake dinghy more than eight years old will almost certainly have at least one cracked plank and three broken frames. In themselves, these faults are not serious, but the weakness tends to spread outwards, particularly where the cracks in the frames are in line. Frames often break behind bilge stringers where they cannot be seen. They fracture mostly where the turn of bilge is tightest, especially amidships and aft. If there are breaks on the port side, they are liable to be mirrored on the starboard side.

From all this it can be seen that small boats have to be turned upside down for a full inspection. This job is not always one that can be safely tackled singlehanded, because a waterlogged boat can weigh twice as much as a new one. On the bottom of small boats it is a good sign to see not only good rub rails to take the chafe, but also rails that have cut-outs to form hand-grips. Then when the boat capsizes, the crew have something to hold on to until help arrives. These grab-handles are also useful for turning the boat the right way up, when the crew decide to rescue themselves.

To sum up, open boats are easier to survey than decked ones, but they tend to have more damage. This is cheaper to repair, but if it is extensive it may be better economics to buy a new boat.

. . . .

INFLATABLES

Inflatables fall into two classes: liferafts and dinghies. The former are not examined by a surveyor, because they are in sealed containers that are only opened when the crew are abandoning ship, or when the liferaft is being given its annual inspection. This is done by a specialist company or, in some countries, by a government organisation.

A few manufacturers say that their products need looking at every other year, but the majority require an annual check. The safety authorities of most countries also insist that every liferaft is opened up and examined by specialists once a year. Part of this overhaul consists of marking the outside of the container with a note that all is well until the next inspection, the date of which is marked on the container. All the surveyor has to do is note the type and serial number of the liferaft(s), and also the date when the next inspection is due.

Inflatable dinghies are altogether different. They come from a dozen makers, and vary from the superb to dreadful. The horrible ones cost one-quarter the price of the reliable models. Of course, the best-made dinghy in time grows old, and it may not have been looked after. A well-made one in good condition has no trouble holding its air for a couple of weeks, though it will get hard in hot weather and soggy at night when the temperature drops a lot. Some expensive versions have pressure relief valves to release air if the boat gets too hot and may want to burst when the air inside expands too much.

A dinghy that cannot hold its pressure for a couple of days certainly needs attention. If the rubber-like skin has come off the fabric so that the weave is clearly visible, the condition of the whole boat is doubtful. The indications are that repairs cannot be carried out because ageing has gone too far. If the condition is local, it may be possible to apply a patch or two and get a little more use out of the boat. A random pattern of little cracks on the surface of the rubberised cloth material indicates ageing. This defect may look like the crazing seen on old hoses, and it is just as serious.

If the glue lines are peeling, it is often a simple enough task to repair the boat, but the fact that the adhesive is letting go is a bad sign. It suggests poor original construction, failing glue or advanced age. Small cuts, chafes and gashes are repaired by gluing on patches. This can be done by amateurs, and the number of stuck-on pieces is an indication of how much hard work the dinghy has done. Peeling patches can be a sign that the wrong glue was used, or that the gluing was done in damp or cold conditions, or by someone untrained for the job. With most faults on inflatables, the best plan is to send the boat back to the makers or one of their service depots.

Because a dinghy is hauled over beaches, the bottom of it suffers a lot of wear and tear. Even boats that are quite well protected on the underside get chafed when the crew are a little careless. It is usual to haul a dinghy up bows first, so the aft end normally shows the greatest signs of wear. On the inside, wear is found at places adjacent to hard materials, such as by the corners of wooden seats and bottom boards. Transom top and bottom corners are weak points, and if a large outboard has been used there may be cracks in the transom and failing edge joins. Crushing where the outboard engine clamps go is common, but seldom important as long as it only penetrates the outer doubling pads.

If the inflation valves are damaged, the boat will probably have to be scrapped if the boat is a cheap type. The better makes can have new valves let in, and bronze valves that seize can normally be freed. This is not a job to do crudely, as freeing oil will attack some fabrics. Each valve should have a safety cap on a short length of line. Because inflatable dinghies seem so stable, there is a tendency to think they seldom turn over. However, when being towed they tip easily in a strong wind, so everything should be tied in.

The painters are often quite thin and too short for normal use. I recommend three painters, one on the front ring and one each side, so that when it is being towed, the boat can be hauled right up almost completely out of the water with the bow secured each side high on the aft pulpit. This prevents the boat turning over and a quantity of water building up inside it. The side painters have to be tied to the fore end of the carrying handles. If an outboard is used, the painters should be of floating rope or they will get wrapped around the propeller.

A good inflatable has a manufacturer's serial number, and this is noted by the surveyor. This number is useful in establishing the age of the boat and whether it has been stolen. These boats are so easily carried, even in a small car, that a lot of them are stolen every year. To discourage this, the boat's name (and possibly the owner's too) should be on each side at bow and stern. Many insurance companies will not underwrite a vessel's dinghy that is not properly marked.

Cheap blow-up dinghies last a short time, sometimes only one summer. Good ones can go on and on, so that valuing them is hard. On average, the best modern type should last for eight years, but double that time is not unknown in temperate climates. It is neglect and rough handling, aided by strong sunshine, that is the main cause of their demise. When there is time and opportunity, there is no substitute for blowing the dinghy up to see how long it will stay inflated. Good ones lose no pressure in a fortnight, provided they are not subject to excess hot sunshine.

Various special oars are supplied with these boats. Being light in weight, and often designed to divide in the middle for compact storage, these oars are not always as hard-wearing as the boats themselves. A thin oar cannot survive much chafe. A dividable oar is dangerous when the join becomes loose. There is one type that has the rowlock screwed to the middle. This weakens the loom (the long main part of the oar) at the worst point, and is just the sort of detail that a good surveyor learns to notice.

There is a tendency to use some inflatables as liferafts in an emergency. Cylinders of gas are secured to special valves to inflate the dinghy swiftly. Alternatively, there may be a 12 volt air pump, perhaps with its own battery, to blow the boat up in a hurry. When inspecting one of these boats the surveyor has to keep an open mind; the arguments as to whether this type of craft is acceptable in place of a dedicated special liferaft continue to rage. One viewpoint argues that a boat used for rowing ashore every weekend cannot be expected to save lives in severe weather. The opposition claims that liferafts that never come out of their casings (except for inspection) are less likely to be in good order when needed in a hurry than a dinghy that is used often and inspected weekly.

In some countries, there are regulations about what needs to be carried as life-saving dinghies and gear, so a local surveyor has to have a good knowledge of these rules.

ARBITRATION AND REGULATIONS

· · · · · · · · · · · · · · · · · ·

ARBITRATION

There was once a small but popular boatyard that built successful cruisers. The managing director was well known, the boats were built to a good design and, on the whole, to a reasonable standard. There were all the ingredients for a prosperous business, and from small beginnings the yard did better with each passing year. One summer the yard fell out with an owner over the matter of the propeller on his boat. The two sides argued long and with increasing bitterness, so that soon both sides brought in lawyers. More and more faults, real and imagined, were found on the boat.

After the usual legal delays, the case went to court and a decision was reached, but there was an appeal. This was contested, so that time and legal costs mounted. Eventually the yard lost the case; but by now the lawyers' fees and expenses were enormous, so the boatyard went bankrupt and the owner never did get his yacht. Both parties ended up hard up and defeated – and all over a propeller that was worth less than the fees for a senior lawyer for one day. An arbitrator would have settled the matter in two weeks, the owner would not have missed any sailing, the yard would have gone on giving a useful service, and everyone employed there would have kept their jobs.

There are plenty of people who will say with a good deal of emphasis that the whole small craft industry is so full of technicalities that it is far better to keep out the legal profession entirely, at least when the settlement of disputes is concerned. Owners and builders, designers and sailmakers can detail plenty of case histories to prove this point. The attractions of arbitration are that it is quick, normally not complicated, and virtually always costs a very great deal less than resorting to the law. It is used in many different countries, it is easier for everyone concerned to understand, the full costs are normally known in advance, and the people in dispute do not

have to waste days in court. Arbitration can often settle in days what the legal industry cannot resolve in years. Anyone who has a dispute over a boat should arrange to have arbitration very early, and without resorting to lawyers at all. In other technical industries it is common for lawyers to be called in first. They then sometimes, but by no means always, recommend arbitration. This misses half the point of arbitration, because there is usually no need to have any legal expenses, especially if one or other of the disputing parties has the sense to suggest arbitration before tempers are lost.

Someone who suggests arbitration but finds the proposal is not accepted promptly should point out how enormous the cost savings are. The arbitrator's fees and expenses are split equally between the two opposing sides. Payment of all or part of the money is made before the arbitrator starts work. Once he has stated his fees, everyone knows that no further cash will be required, unless the arbitrator finds he simply must have the assistance of an accountant to go through the payments, quotes and estimates, or he needs the help of a shipwright to open up part of the craft. These expenses are trivial compared with a lawyer's fees, which are seldom fully known until after judgement has been reached.

One side may wish to be represented by a solicitor in putting the case to the arbitrator, and in this instance the other side must also be given the opportunity to obtain legal help. In parenthesis, it is worth remembering that in any yacht club there are likely to be a few people who follow the law to earn their daily bread. It is worth seeking the assistance of a person of this sort who owns a boat because he will have a head start on any other lawyer who knows nothing about the intricacies of small craft.

A surveyor who is approached to act as an arbitrator should warn both sides that his ruling is binding. It has the force of law and is backed by the current legislation of the country where the arbitration takes place. What the arbitrator finally decides is similar to a pronouncement by a judge, and in general can only be appealed against if the award is based on a mistake in law.

An arbitrator will normally see the boat involved in the dispute, unless she has been sunk, or is very far away and there is plenty of evidence that will give the arbitrator all the knowledge he needs. This evidence will be in the form of plans, photos, statements from shipwrights and foremen, and so on. Both sides have to supply all the relevant letters, accounts, invoices, time sheets and drawings. One reason why arbitration should be started promptly is because workmen change jobs, forget details, get divorced and experience other distractions, and all this reduces the amount of evidence available.

Before starting work, the arbitrator receives a request in writing from both sides for his services, and an agreement to abide by his decisions. Sometimes the two sides in the dispute cannot agree on a common arbitrator, in which case either:

- Each side appoints an arbitrator and they get together to appoint one person to come to the final technical decision, or
- Each side appoints an arbitrator and they call in a third party; then all three decide the case, where necessary making a ruling by a majority of 2 against 1. The disadvantage of this arrangement is that there are three arbitration fees to pay, and the expenses will be higher – but still far below the costs of a legal wrangle.

Anyone involved with boats and money can foresee that there may be a disagreement. For instance, when building a yacht or having repairs carried out, there are many 'grey' areas, which no amount of careful specifying can eliminate. Here is a situation where the contract (drawn up before work begins) should include a comprehensive clause stating that arbitration will be used instead of legal fighting. The actual arbitrator need not be specified. Sometimes it will be agreed before work begins that the arbitrator will be chosen by name, or by:

- The president or chairman of a local body such as the boatbuilders' trade organisation.
- The chairman or president of a national trade organisation. In Britain this is the British Marine Industries Federation of Meadlake Place, Thorpe Lea Road, Egham, Surrey TW20 8HE, England.

Tel 0784 473377. Fax 0784 439678. This federation has worldwide connections, so its help can extend beyond its national borders.
- The commodore of a yacht club.

It is probably best to avoid approaching any national or major organisation that is not closely linked with the boat industry, but deals solely with arbitration. These bodies do not always have boat specialists. They do have lots of technical people in a variety of industries who may think that small craft are like large ships, or like buildings, or like road vehicles which travel over the sea. Only those of us who have discovered the vast difference between big ships and small craft know how much damage such experts can cause when they venture out of their own speciality into our own highly specialised field.

Surveyors usually make good arbitrators because they spend so much time deep down in bilges, up masts, and half under engines. They are used to standing between opposing parties such as an owner and a broker, or an owner and a boatyard manager. A surveyor can quickly learn about the boat in dispute by going over her as if he were doing a survey. Where a surveyor cannot be used, it is best to employ someone who has 'oilskins hanging in the hall, and overalls hanging in the office'. A yard manager or senior foreman, or a designer who has specialised in the type of craft under discussion, may be available.

When the argument is about costs, information like the wage rates charged and the overheads or 'on-costs' must be divulged by the boatyard. Materials and services such as telephone charges are discovered by going to the suppliers, so that independent evidence is obtained. Anyone assessing a repair job has to take into consideration the conditions at the time. If the boat was out in the open, with a gale blowing and continuous driving rain, the job will take extra time. A rushed job to get the boat back into commission is likely to be less meticulous than a relaxed repair done in the off season. If the owner has asked for his yacht to be mended in haste and put back afloat in time for a race, the yard cannot be blamed if it charges overtime rates, or takes reasonable short cuts, or if the varnish-work does not last long because it was carried out in poor conditions.

An arbitration decision must go against one side or the other, so someone is going to end up worried, irritated, and with less money than before. Surveyors are used to this. They spend a lot of time telling owners that the boat they have cherished for years has not had sufficient maintenance and now needs a lot of money spent on it. They have to tell buyers that the boat that seems so perfect has horrible problems and needs thousands spent on her if she is to be safe. Surveyors seldom become completely detached, but their constant contact with the hard facts of boat life make them good arbitrators. They can tell they have done a good arbitration job when both sides moan and make disgruntled comments. Both sides in the dispute know in their hearts that they have saved themselves lots of money. They know too that a swift decision has been arrived at that is technically correct.

LOCAL AND NATIONAL REGULATIONS

Small craft have to conform to a variety of regulations. In some countries these rules are detailed and fill several tomes, but in other lands they are few or even non-existent – at present, at least. However, by next year there may be dozens of new rules, especially if the local politicians suspect that they can raise taxes from the boatowners.

From a surveyor's point of view, these rules and regulations can be a source of worry. Naturally he has to learn them, or at least have a good working knowledge of those in his own area. However, he can never rely on them. He cannot be sure that just because a vessel fully conforms to the most comprehensive regulations, she is safe or worth the price asked for her. On the contrary, in some countries the cost of keeping up with the regulations means that not enough money is spent on annual maintenance. There is evidence that this applies in France.

Many of these rules are 'political footballs' kicked around by local and national politicians who seldom know much about safety afloat. Many rules are produced as a reaction to an accident or series of incidents that hit the headlines. The rules will typically specify the type and number of lifebuoys (or pumps, fire extinguishers or flares) that must be carried on a given size and type of craft. This standard is set as the minimum, but in practice it immediately becomes the maximum that any owner will carry. Even though experience and common sense shows that a particular number of an item of gear can be inadequate and the type too small (or too weak or inflexible in its use), few people will exceed the level set down in the regulations. The rules may well state that there must be a bilge pump capable of shifting so much water per hour. However, it is often found that nothing is said about how or where the pump is to be fitted, whether the handle has to have a safety line, or whether the suction must have a strum box, and so on.

On the other hand, local rules do help some surveyors on certain occasions. If a boat is not even half equipped with the required gear, it does indicate either that the owner is ignorant, lazy, callous or short of money – or several of these things. This in turn tells a surveyor that he must expect to find trouble throughout the boat as a result of lack of maintenance and/or carelessness and/or idleness, and so on. After all, a survey report is simply a collection of clues gathered under difficult circumstances and put on paper, followed by conclusions drawn from scraps of information that are often incomplete. The way an owner reacts to local regulations often says a lot about how he looks after his craft.

It is important to keep up with the changing regulations. Some surveyors have printed forms that they take on to a boat being inspected. They tick off the number and type of bucket (with lanyards as required), the size and type of seacock, the type of gas piping and the date it was last renewed, and so on. A copy of this printed form is retained with the surveyor's records, and a copy sent with the main report.

What has to be remembered is that only a small batch of forms should be printed at one time, because this year's checklist will be inadequate for next year. This is why it is handy to have a word processor with the form held in its memory. The form can then be updated as fast as the authorities change their minds and alter the rules. This type of standardised survey form can be useful for other parts of the survey. It helps many beginners, also people who have a bad memory, or who cannot afford the best secretarial help. For instance, there can be a form for deck fittings. It will assume that the inspection begins at the bow and progresses aft, and will begin something like this:

DECK FITTINGS

BOW PULPIT Fitted/not fitted. *Material* ___
Condition: Good/moderate/ dangerous
Cracks: Yes/no
Height: Adequate/inadequate
Fastenings: Tight/loose/broken
Signs of deck leaks at feet: Yes/no
General comments _____

The next item will be the stemhead fitting, then the bow fairleads, mooring cleat or bollard, and so on. Making up a form is easy enough. One sits on the deck of a well-equipped vessel and looks over her, noting all the equipment and possible alternatives that can apply to each component. Using a batch of old survey reports and this book will also be a help. After a few months the form will be improved, and every few years, as fashion and design techniques change, the form will need modernising.

In theory, these forms save time, for the surveyor can zip along the deck ticking where appropriate, crossing off what does not apply, and so on. In practice, a good surveyor has so many shorthand squiggles and so much experience that he can probably do the job as quickly without this sort of help. The trouble with standard forms is that they have to deal with all possible contingencies, so they ask a vast number of questions, many of which do not apply to plenty of craft. Perhaps the best advice that can be given about them is that they should be tried out. They may help with engine inspections, spars, rigging, sails, safety gear, furniture, electronics, plumbing, and so on.

In the United States, surveyors need to know the Coast Guard regulations. These are bulky and comprehensive and, in practice, surveyors tend to specialise in certain types of small craft, so the regulations applying to these are learned as much by heart as possible. The other two standards that US surveyors have to be familiar with are those set by the National Fire Protection Association and the American Yacht and Boat Council. On the whole, the US mariner is lucky, in that he is 'policed' with more intelligence than in many other nations.

In Britain, the Inland Waterways rules apply to craft that ply on their canals and rivers, and in Europe each country has a selection of regulations. Attempts are being made to standardise them, but they are very different at present.

It is a general feature of these so-called safety rules that they are applied more and more, all over the world, yet the number and severity of accidents afloat does not decrease per 1,000 craft afloat, or by any other criterion. This is encouraging to surveyors, who are becoming more (not less) important to the small craft industry. Like so many things, a surveyor has to keep the local regulations in mind, but not let them affect his work, energy or judgement.

Index